Each volume of this series of companions to major philosophers contains specially commissioned essays by an international team of scholars, together with a substantial bibliography, and will serve as a reference work for students and nonspecialists. One aim of the series is to dispel the intimidation such readers often feel when faced with the work of a difficult and challenging thinker.

Hannah Arendt was one of the foremost political thinkers of the twentieth century, and her particular interests have made her one of the most frequently cited thinkers of our time. This volume examines the primary themes of her multi-faceted work, from her theory of totalitarianism and her controversial idea of the "banality of evil" to her classic studies of political action and her final reflections on judgment and the life of the mind. Each essay examines the political, philosophical, and historical concerns which shaped Arendt's thought, and which prompted her to become one of the most unapologetic champions of the political life in the history of Western thought.

New readers and nonspecialists will find this the most convenient and accessible guide to Arendt currently available. Advanced students and specialists will find a conspectus of recent developments in the interpretation of Arendt.

THE CAMBRIDGE
COMPANION TO

HANNAH ARENDT

OTHER VOLUMES IN THE SERIES OF CAMBRIDGE COMPANIONS

Aquinas
Edited by Norman Kretzmann and Eleonore Stump (published)

Aristotle
Edited by Jonathan Barnes (published)

Bacon
Edited by Markku Peltonen (published)

Berkeley
Edited by Kenneth Winkler

Descartes
Edited by John Cottingham (published)

Early Greek Philosophy
Edited by A. A. Long (published)

Feminism in Philosophy
Edited by Miranda Fricker and Jennifer Hornsby (published)

Fichte
Edited by Günter Zöller

Foucault
Edited by Gary Gutting (published)

Frege
Edited by Tom Ricketts

Freud
Edited by Jerome Neu (published)

Galileo
Edited by Peter Machamer (published)

German Idealism
Edited by Karl Ameriks (published)

Habermas
Edited by Stephen White (published)

Hegel
Edited Frederick Beiser (published)

Hobbes
Edited by Tom Sorell (published)

Hume
Edited by David Fate Norton (published)

Husserl
Edited by Barry Smith and David Woodruff Smith (published)

William James
Edited by Ruth Anna Putnam (published)

Kant
Edited by Paul Guyer (published)

Kierkegaard
Edited by Alastair Hannay (published)

Leibniz
Edited by Nicholas Jolley (published)

Locke
Edited by Vere Chappell (published)

Marx
Edited by Terrell Carver (published)

Mill
Edited by John Skorupski (published)

Nietzsche
Edited by Bernd Magnus and Kathleen Higgins (published)

Ockham
Edited by Paul Vincent Spade (published)

Peirce
Edited by Christopher Hookway

Plato
Edited by Richard Kraut (published)

Plotinus
Edited by Lloyd Gerson (published)

Sartre
Edited by Christina Howells (published)

Spinoza
Edited by Don Garrett (published)

Wittgenstein
Edited by Hans Sluga and David Stern (published)

THE CAMBRIDGE COMPANION TO

HANNAH ARENDT

EDITED BY

DANA VILLA

University of California, Santa Barbara

CAMBRIDGE
UNIVERSITY PRESS

PUBLISHED BY THE PRESS SYNDICATE OF THE UNIVERSITY OF CAMBRIDGE
The Pitt Building, Trumpington Street, Cambridge, United Kingdom

CAMBRIDGE UNIVERSITY PRESS
The Edinburgh Building, Cambridge CB2 2RU, UK
40 West 20th Street, New York, NY 10011–4211, USA
477 Williamstown Road, Port Melbourne, VIC 3207, Australia
Ruiz de Alarcón 13, 28014 Madrid, Spain
Dock House, The Waterfront, Cape Town 8001, South Africa

http://www.cambridge.org

First published 2000
Reprinted 2002, 2005

Printed in the United Kingdom at the University Press, Cambridge

Typeface Sabon MT 10/13pt *System* QuarkXPress™ [SE]

A catalogue record for this book is available from the British Library

Library of Congress Cataloguing in Publication data

The Cambridge companion to Hannah Arendt / edited by Dana Villa.
p. cm.
Includes bibliographical references and index.
ISBN 0 521 64198 5 (hardback) – ISBN 0 521 64571 9 (paperback)
1. Arendt, Hannah – Contributions in political science. I. Villa, Dana Richard.
JC251.A74 C22 2000
320.5′092 – dc21 00-021835

ISBN 0 521 64198 5 hardback
ISBN 0 521 64571 9 paperback

CONTENTS

CONTRIBUTORS

RONALD BEINER is Professor of Political Science at the University of Toronto. He is the author of *Political Judgment* (University of Chicago Press, 1984), *What's the Matter with Liberalism?* (University of California Press, 1992) and *Philosophy in a Time of Lost Spirit* (University of Toronto Press, 1998). He is also the editor of Hannah Arendt's *Lectures on Kant's Political Philosophy* (University of Chicago Press, 1982) and *Theorizing Citizenship* (State University of New York Press, 1995).

SEYLA BENHABIB is Professor of Government at Harvard University. She is the author of *Critique, Norm, Utopia: A Study of the Foundations of Critical Theory* (Columbia University Press, 1986), *Situating the Self: Gender, Community, and Postmodernism in Contemporary Ethics* (Routledge, 1992) and *The Reluctant Modernism of Hannah Arendt* (Sage Publications, 1996). She is also the editor of *Democracy and Difference* (Princeton University Press, 1998).

RICHARD J. BERNSTEIN is Vera List Professor of Philosophy at New School University. He is the author of many books, including *Praxis and Action* (University of Pennsylvania Press, 1971), *Beyond Objectivism and Relativism* (University of Pennsylvania Press, 1984), *The New Constellation: The Ethical-Political Horizon of Modernity/Postmodernity* (MIT Press, 1992) and *Hannah Arendt and the Jewish Question* (MIT Press, 1997).

HAUKE BRUNKHORST is Professor of Sociology at Flensburg University, Germany. He is the author of *Hannah Arendt* (Beck Verlag [Munich], 1999) and articles on democratic theory and rights.

MARGARET CANOVAN is Professor of Political Thought at Keele University. Her books include *The Political Thought of Hannah Arendt* (Dent, 1974) and *Hannah Arendt: A Reinterpretation of Her Political Thought* (Cambridge University Press, 1992).

MAURIZIO PASSERIN D'ENTRÈVES is Senior Lecturer in the Department of Government, University of Manchester. He is the author of *Modernity, Justice, and Community* (1990) and *The Political Philosophy of Hannah Arendt* (Routledge, 1994). He is also the co-editor of *Habermas and the Unfinished Project of Modernity* (MIT Press, 1996).

MARY G. DIETZ is Professor of Political Science and Associate Faculty, Center for Advanced Feminist Studies, at the University of Minnesota. She is the author of *Between the Human and the Divine: the Political Thought of Simone Weil* (Rowman and Littlefield) and the editor of *Thomas Hobbes and Political Theory* (University of Kansas Press), as well as articles on the history of political thought, feminist theory, citizenship, and the thought of Hannah Arendt.

FREDERICK DOLAN is Associate Professor in the Department of Rhetoric, University of California, Berkeley. He is the author of *Allegories of America* (Cornell University Press, 1994) and the co- editor of *The Rhetorical Republic* (University of Massachusetts Press, 1993).

J. PETER EUBEN is Professor of Politics at the University of California, Santa Cruz. He is the author of *The Tragedy of Political Theory* (Princeton University Press, 1990) and *Corrupting the Youth* (Princeton University Press, 1997). He is also the editor of *Greek Tragedy and Political Theory* (University of California Press, 1988) and co-editor of *Athenian Political Thought and the Reconstruction of American Democracy* (Cornell University Press, 1992).

GEORGE KATEB is Professor of Politics at Princeton University. His books include *Utopia and its Enemies* (Schocken Books, 1963), *Hannah Arendt: Politics, Conscience, Evil* (Rowman and Allanheld, 1984), *The Inner Ocean* (Cornell University Press, 1992), and *Emerson and Self-Reliance* (Sage Publications, 1995).

JEROME KOHN is Adjunct Professor of Philosophy at Cooper Union and Lecturer in the Humanities at New School University. He is the author of numerous articles on Arendt, and the editor of Hannah Arendt's *Essays in Understanding: 1930–1954* (Harcourt Brace Jovanovich, 1994) and co-editor of *Hannah Arendt – Twenty Years Later* (MIT Press, 1996).

JACQUES TAMINIAUX is Professor of Philosophy at Boston College and former Director of the Center for Phenomenological Studies at the University of Louvain-la-Neuve. His books include *Dialectic and Difference* (Humanities Press, 1985), *Heidegger and the Project of Fundamental Ontology* (State University of New York Press, 1991), and *The Thracian Maid and the*

Professional Thinker: Arendt and Heidegger (State University of New York Press, 1998).

DANA VILLA teaches political theory at the University of California, Santa Barbara. He is the author of *Arendt and Heidegger: the Fate of the Political* (Princeton University Press, 1996), *Politics, Philosophy, Terror: Essays on the Thought of Hannah Arendt* (Princeton University Press, 1999) and *Socratic Citizenship* (forthcoming). He is also the co-editor of *Liberal Modernism and Democratic Individuality* (Princeton University Press, 1996).

JEREMY WALDRON is Maurice and Hilda Friedman Professor of Law at Columbia University. He is the author of numerous books and articles on law, philosophy, and political theory, including *The Right to Private Property* (Oxford University Press, 1990), *Liberal Rights: Collected Papers 1981–1991*, *Law and Disagreement* (Oxford University Press, 1999), and *The Dignity of Legislation* (Cambridge University Press, 1999).

ALBRECHT WELLMER is Professor of Philosophy at the Free University, Berlin. His books include *The Persistence of Modernity* (MIT Press, 1991) and *Endgames* (MIT Press, 1998).

ABBREVIATIONS

BPF Hannah Arendt, *Between Past and Future* (New York: Penguin, 1968)

CR Hannah Arendt, *Crises of the Republic* (New York: Harcourt Brace Jovanovich, 1972)

EJ Hannah Arendt, *Eichmann in Jerusalem* (New York: Viking Press, 1965)

EU Hannah Arendt, *Essays in Understanding, 1930–54*, ed. Jerome Kohn (New York: Harcourt Brace & Co., 1994)

HC Hannah Arendt, *The Human Condition* (Chicago: University of Chicago Press, 1958)

JP Hannah Arendt, *The Jew as Pariah*, ed. Ron H. Feldman (New York: Grove Press, 1978)

LKPP Hannah Arendt, *Lectures on Kant's Political Philosophy*, ed. Ronald Beiner (Chicago: University of Chicago Press, 1982)

LM Hannah Arendt, *The Life of the Mind* (New York: Harcourt Brace Jovanovich, 1978)

MDT Hannah Arendt, *Men in Dark Times* (New York: Harcourt, Brace & World, 1968)

OR Hannah Arendt, *On Revolution*, 2nd edn. (New York: Viking Press, 1965)

OT Hannah Arendt, *The Origins of Totalitarianism* (New York: Harcourt, Brace & World, 1973)

CHRONOLOGY

1906	Born in Hannover, Germany, the only child of Martha and Paul Arendt, secular Jews.
1909	Father's illness forces him to give up his job with an electrical engineering firm; family moves to Königsberg, East Prussia (Germany) where the extended Arendt family had long lived.
1913	Father dies.
1914	First World War breaks out; fearing the Russian Army, Arendt's mother moves with her daughter to Berlin. Returns to Königsberg ten weeks later.
1918–19	Mother hosts social democratic discussion groups. Socialist revolutions break out in Berlin and Munich following Germany's defeat in the war.
1920	Mother remarries; Hannah excels at the Luiseschule, until she is expelled for "insubordination."
1922–23	Studies classics and Christian theology for several semesters at the University of Berlin as a special student; prepares for university entrance examination (the *Abitur*).
1924	Enters Marburg University, where she studies philosophy with Martin Heidegger.
1925	Becomes romantically involved with Heidegger.
1926	Breaks off relationship with Heidegger; moves to Heidelberg to study with his friend and fellow existentialist philosopher Karl Jaspers. She writes her dissertation (on the concept of love in St. Augustine) with him.
1926–28	Sees Heidegger (who publishes *Being and Time* in 1927) episodically. Meets Kurt Blumenfeld, a Zionist and critic of German–Jewish assimilation, at a lecture given in Heidelberg. He initiates her into Jewish politics.
1929	Meets Gunther Stern, a young Jewish philosopher. Becomes romantically involved.

	Arendt's dissertation, *Der Liebesbegriff bei Augustin*, published. Marries Stern later that year.
1930	Arendt and Stern move to Berlin; begins work on *Rahel Varnhagen: the Life of a Jewess.*
1931–32	Becomes increasingly involved in Zionist discussions and activities.
1933	The Reichstag fire in Berlin (February 4); Stern, fearing Nazi persecution as a leftist, flees to Paris. Arendt offers their apartment in Berlin as a safe house for fleeing enemies of Hitler's newly installed regime. At Blumenfeld's instigation, she surreptitiously collects anti-semitic propaganda in the Prussian State Library. Arrested, and – along with her mother – held and questioned by the police for over a week. Succeeds in duping interrogator and flees with her mother – first over the border to Czechoslovakia, then to Geneva and (finally) Paris, where she joins other Zionists in exile. Begins eighteen years as a "stateless person."
1934	Meets and befriends Walter Benjamin and Raymond Aron in Paris. Begins work with Agriculture et Artisanat, an organization which helped to train young émigrés to Palestine (the "Jewish homeland"). Later becomes director of another Jewish organization, Youth Aliyah, with a similar mission. Also begins work for the Baroness Germaine de Rothschild.
1936	Meets and becomes involved with Heinrich Blücher, a gentile and leftist German political refugee.
1937	Divorces Stern. Struggles to protect young Jewish future immigrants to Palestine from rising French anti-semitism.
1938	Youth Aliyah relocates to London; Arendt goes to work for the Jewish Agency in Paris. Arendt's mother flees Königsberg; moves in with Arendt and Blücher in Paris.
1940	War declared between France and Germany; Blücher detained as an "enemy alien" in an internment camp in Villemalard. Released after two months; he and Arendt marry in May. Arendt and her mother detained at a camp for "enemy alien" women in the south of France at Gurs. France soon defeated, and in the confusion Arendt and her mother escape to Montaubon, France.
1941	The Blüchers escape Vichy France to Lisbon, and board a ship to the US. They arrive in May, briefly living in Massachusetts, then moving to New York. Arendt begins writing for *Aufbau*, a German-language newspaper in New York.
1942	Arendt learns of the German concentration and extermination

camps for Jews through newspaper reports. Writes columns in support of the formation of a Jewish Army to fight alongside the Allies. Becomes increasingly critical of the Zionist movement's focus on events in Palestine rather than Europe.

1944 Directs research work for the Commission on European Jewish Cultural Reconstruction, cataloging valuable manuscripts and other Jewish cultural treasures in Axis-occupied countries. Begins writing what will become *The Origins of Totalitarianism.*

1946 Publishes "What is Existenz Philosophy?," which includes praise of Jaspers and a biting critique of Heidegger, who had affiliated himself with the Nazis. Begins work as an editor at Schocken Books, New York.

1948 Death of mother.

1949 Becomes Executive Director of Jewish Cultural Reconstruction. Travels for six months to Europe to direct recovery operation of 1.5 million volumes of Hebraica and Judaica. Reunited with Jaspers and his wife Gertrude. Has tense meeting with Heidegger and his wife.

1950 Becomes senior editor at Schocken Books.

1951 Publishes *The Origins of Totalitarianism* to immediate acclaim. Delivers "Ideology and Terror" – which becomes the concluding chapter of *OT* in subsequent editions – as a lecture at the University of Notre Dame. Obtains American citizenship.

1952 Wins Guggenheim Fellowship. Begins work on the never-completed "Totalitarian Elements in Marxism."

1953 Gives the Gauss Seminars at Princeton University on "Karl Marx and the Great Tradition," in which she presents material from a never completed book-length critique of Marx.

1954 Delivers "Philosophy and Politics" at Notre Dame and "The Concern With Politics in Recent European Philosophy" at the American Political Science Association meetings.

1955 Takes first full-time teaching position – a visiting professorship – at the University of California, Berkeley.

1956 Give Walgreen Foundation Lectures on the *vita activa* at the University of Chicago.

1958 Gives the Frankfurt Peace Prize address in honor of its winner, Karl Jaspers. Publishes *The Human Condition.* Also publishes *Rahel Varnhagen: The Life of a Jewess.*

1959 Publishes "Reflections on Little Rock" in *Dissent.* Controversy follows. Lectures at Princeton on the idea of revolution. Awarded the Lessing Prize by the city of Hamburg.

1961 Travels to Jerusalem to cover the trial of Nazi Adolf Eichmann for *The New Yorker*. Publishes *Between Past and Future*.

1963 Publishes a five-part article "A Reporter at Large: Eichmann in Jerusalem" in *The New Yorker*, stirring great controversy. Revised, it is published (in book form) as *Eichmann in Jerusalem: A Report on the Banality of Evil*. Also publishes *On Revolution*. Begins part-time teaching (through 1967) in the Committee on Social Thought at the University of Chicago.

1967 Begins teaching full-time at the New School for Social Research in New York.

1968 Initially supports student demonstartions at Columbia University, but becomes disenchanted. Publishes *Men in Dark Times*.

1969 Arendt's teacher and mentor Karl Jaspers dies in February; she delivers a eulogy at the public memorial service in March. Gives support to the movement against the war in Vietnam. Publishes "Reflections on Violence," a critique of Third World revolutionary ideology and the violent fringe of the American and European student movements.

1970 Heinrich Blücher dies. Arendt publishes "Civil Disobedience." Gives Kant seminar (on judgment) at the New School (posthumously published in 1982).

1971 Publishes "Thinking and Moral Considerations."

1972 Takes part in conference on her work at York University. Publishes *Crises of the Republic*.

1973 Gives first series Gifford Lectures on thinking, at Aberdeen University.

1974 Returns to Scotland to give second series of Gifford Lectures, on willing. Suffers near fatal heart attack in the middle of the first lecture.

1975 Wins Danish Sonning Prize for Contributions to European Civilization. Goes to Marbach, Germany, to put Jaspers' papers in order. Visits the aging Heidegger one last time. Revises "Thinking" and "Willing" lectures. Barely begins "Judging," the third and final part of *The Life of the Mind*. Dies of a heart attack while entertaining friends on December 4.

1978 Posthumous publication of *The Life of the Mind* (two volumes), edited by her friend Mary McCarthy.

DANA R. VILLA

Introduction: the development of Arendt's political thought

Widely recognized as one of the most original and influential political thinkers of the twentieth century, Hannah Arendt remains an elusive figure. She never wrote a systematic political philosophy in the mode of Thomas Hobbes or John Rawls, and the books she did write are extremely diverse in topic, covering totalitarianism, the place of political action in human life, the trial of Adolf Eichmann, the meaning of the modern revolutionary tradition, the nature of political freedom and authority, and the faculties which make up "the life of the mind." These works are not constructed upon a single argument, diligently unfolded, or upon a linear narrative. Rather, they are grounded upon a series of striking conceptual distinctions – between tyranny and totalitarianism; action, labor, and work; political revolution and struggles for liberation; thinking, willing, and judging – which Arendt elaborates and weaves into complex thematic strands. The interconnections between the strands are sometimes left to the reader. Thus, it is no surprise that newcomers to her work are often baffled by how the pieces fit together (not only from book to book, but often within a single volume). They cannot help wondering whether there is, in fact, a consistent perspective behind her varied reflections on the nature of political evil, the glories of political action, and the fragility of civilized society (the "human artifice") in the face of mounting natural, technological, and political pressure. The situation is not helped by the fact that many commentators on Arendt have tended to seize upon one strand of her *oeuvre*, elevating her reflections on political action, or her theory of totalitarianism, to a position of unquestioned preeminence.

This chapter attempts a brief overview of the development and place of Arendt's political thought, highlighting the fears which animated her thinking as well as situating her with regard to some of the major figures in the Western tradition of political philosophy. My concern throughout is to give the reader some sense of the "hidden continent of thought" (to use Margaret Canovan's felicitous image) that underlies the various stops on Arendt's itinerary as a political thinker, and to show how the pieces fit together – if not into a comprehensive and systematic whole, at least into a sustained and profound reflection on the nature of politics, the public realm, and the forces that constantly threaten to turn modern life into a new form of barbarism.

I *The Origins of Totalitarianism*

The Origins of Totalitarianism was written, simply, to begin what Arendt called "the interminable dialogue" with a new and horrific form of politics, one which could not be understood through recourse to historical precedents or the use of homogenizing social scientific categories. It was in this book that Arendt began to grapple with the problem of political evil – evil as policy – on an enormous and hitherto unimaginable scale. She was convinced, from very early on, that the Nazi and Stalinist regimes represented an entirely "novel form of government" unlike anything ever cataloged by the likes of Aristotle or Montesquieu; one built entirely on terror and ideological fiction and devoted to a destructive perpetual motion. Indeed, in Arendt's estimation it was a grave mistake to view totalitarian regimes as updated versions of the tyrannies of old, which had used terror merely as an invaluable instrument for getting and preserving power. Thus, when Arendt surveys totalitarian regimes (and "their central institutions," the concentration and extermination camps), she stresses how little strategic rationality governed their use of terror. Not enemies of the regime (these had already been eliminated during the totalitarians' rise to power), but totally innocent populations (Jews, gypsies, homosexuals, intellectuals, wealthy peasants) were killed once the regimes were in place. This extermination of entire categories of innocents took place in accordance with a supposed Law of Nature or History, which reduced all historical development to the fundamental underlying "reality" of a war between races or classes.

Terror, then, was not a *means* for totalitarian regimes but, in Arendt's view, their very *essence*. But this raises two important questions. First, how can a regime whose essence is terror come to power in the first place? What was the basis of its mass appeal? Secondly, how is it that European culture, the culture of the West, gave birth to these pathological experiments in what Arendt calls "total domination"?

For Arendt, the appeal of totalitarianism lay in its ideology. For millions of people shaken loose from their accustomed place in the social order by World War, the Great Depression, and revolution, the notion that a single idea could, through its "inherent logic," reveal "the mysteries of the whole historical process – the secrets of the past, the intricacies of the present, [and] the uncertainties of the future" was tremendously comforting.[1] Once the premise of the ideology was accepted – that is, once the idea that all history is the history of class struggle (Marxism) or a natural development resulting from the struggle between the races (Nazism) – every action of the regime could be logically "deduced" and justified in terms of the "law" of History or Nature. The idea of class struggle logically entailed the idea of "dying classes" who would soon be swept into the dustbin of history (and should be helped on their way), just as the Nazis' conception of racial/cultural struggle entailed the idea of "unfit races" – races whose built-in inferiority would lead them to extinction in the ruthless Darwinian struggle for survival and domination. The unembarrassed claim of totalitarian ideology in both its Marxist and its National Socialist forms was that the logic of its central animating idea mirrored the logic of the historical or natural process itself. Hence, totalitarian regimes could claim an authority which transcended all merely human laws and agreements (which the regimes treated with thinly disguised contempt), an authority derived directly from the "laws of motion" which governed the natural or historical process.[2]

The certitude that arises from the apparent possession of such a "key to history" helps us understand the nature of totalitarianism's appeal. But what about the second question? How is it that Europe, the home of the Enlightenment and the Rights of Man, gave birth to a form of politics as brutally murderous as totalitarianism?

Arendt's answer to this question is complex and multi-faceted; any summary of it will be simplified to the point of distortion. Nevertheless, we can note that Arendt viewed modern European history as, in large part, a series of pathologies, with totalitarianism as "the climactic pathology."[3] Nazi and Soviet totalitarianism were not aberrations born of peculiarly dysfunctional national characters or political histories; rather, they were phenomena made possible by a particular constellation of events and tendencies within modern European history and culture. Foremost among these was the imperialism of the late nineteenth century, with its focus on expansion for the sake of expansion and the limitless accumulation of wealth. This boundless pursuit of wealth and empire undermined the self-limiting structure of the nation-state and prefigured the totalitarian pursuit of global conquest. Moreover, it represented, in Arendt's eyes, the triumph of the *bourgeois* (who lusted after wealth and power at any price) over the *citoyen* (who was concerned with the public realm and the preservation of rights and freedoms). Dissolving the stable boundaries of the public world in order to expand further and gain more, imperialism set the stage for political movements which were concerned no longer with care of a stable and limited public world, but with conquest and the self-assertion of national (ethnic or racial) identity.

Imperialism also brought Europeans in contact with aboriginal populations around the world, which – seen through the prism of prejudice and racist pseudo-science – had the effect of concentrating the Europeans' sense of racial superiority. Racism, along with imperialism, was the *sine qua non* of totalitarianism. In order to understand the link, Arendt takes us inside the mind of the European racist encountering a "primitive," non-white culture for the first time. Her primary example, in this regard, is the Boer colonists of South Africa, who developed a powerful racist ideology out of their initial confrontation with a group of human beings whose subservience to nature (and apparent lack of civilization) made them seem little better than animals. For the Boers, "Race was the emergency explanation of human beings whom no European or civilized man could understand and whose humanity so frightened and humiliated the immigrants that they no longer cared to belong to the same human species."[4]

The murderous policy of the Boers towards African natives was amongst the more heinous atrocities of the imperialist epoch, but it was hardly unique in its racist presuppositions. Europe's imperialist expansion encouraged the creation of a moral world articulated primarily not in terms of law, institutions, and rights, but rather in terms of the distinction between one racial group and another. Combined with the rise of what Arendt calls "tribal nationalism" in central and Eastern Europe, imperialism more or less guaranteed that racial and ethnic categories of group identity (as opposed to the legal category of citizenship) would become the fundamental moral reality for huge numbers of Europeans, the lens through which they perceived the world and those unlike themselves. That such categories would soon be used by Europeans against other Europeans was yet another consequence of the moral epistemology secreted by the newly fashioned "identity politics" of Western imperialism and nationalism.

In Arendt's view, imperialism and racism were necessary, but not sufficient, elements in the constellation of events and tendencies that gave rise to totalitarianism. A further essential condition was the delegitimation of established political institutions in the eyes of millions of ordinary people across Europe. The primary blame for this delegitimation lay, according to Arendt, with the continental *bourgeoisie*, who shamelessly exploited public institutions for the pursuit of private (or class) economic interests. Shut out from and alienated by the politics of the rising nation-state during the eighteenth and early nineteenth centuries, the *bourgeoisie* found themselves politically emancipated and empowered by the imperialism of the latter half of the nineteenth century, free to manipulate public instrumentalities in their pursuit of greater wealth and power. The result was the complete attenuation of the idea of citizenship, and a pervasive cynicism toward public institutions. This cynicism found its clearest expression in what Arendt calls "the alliance between the mob and the elite," a politically important convergence of intellectuals with the gutter-born movements of the radical left and right. These groups were united by their shared contempt for parliamentary politics and the patent phoniness of bourgeois appeals to "the public interest."

For Arendt, then, totalitarianism did not arise out of the murky ideological and philosophical currents of the nineteenth (or any other) century. Rather, it was made possible by the decline of the nation-state, the creation of concrete practices of domination (justified by racism) by the European imperialists, and the fact that enormous numbers of people had been made to feel isolated and vulnerable by traumatic social and political events. These people – the "masses" as opposed to the "mob" or the "elite" – turned to totalitarian movements because of their increasing disconnection from their fellows, the world, and the responsibilities of citizenship. This disconnection inclined them to find comfort in totalitarian ideology, and a sense of purpose in the single-minded activism it demanded. All this despite the assault on human nature and dignity performed by the totalitarians in the name of creating a "new man."

II From totalitarianism to the tradition

Arendt's analysis of the nature and preconditions of totalitarianism led her to draw several strongly held conclusions about the dangers confronting modern life, and the things necessary to avoid or contain them. Most prominently, the dynamic destructiveness of totalitarian regimes led her to place the highest possible value upon the relatively permanent structure created by the laws and institutions of a stable public realm. Like Hobbes and in accordance with the modern tradition of political thought generally, Arendt thought of political society as artificial rather than natural; as something created and preserved by human beings against the ruinous forces of nature and their own destructive tendencies. There is, as a result, a significant conservative dimension to Arendt's thought, one which emphasizes both the fragility and "artificiality" of civilized life, and the corresponding imperative of preservation or "care for the world."[5] Her fears concerning the way this carefully built up world might be swamped by the forces of cultural barbarism, or worn away by the capitalist intensification of the rhythms of production and consumption, led her to anxiously survey modern life. Her cultural criticism therefore focuses on the forces or tendencies which undermine our feeling for, and commitment to, the "world" – that is, to the artificial structure, standing between man and nature, which makes civilized life, and the tangible expression of human freedom, possible.

The political hubris of totalitarianism was only one such tendency. In *The Human Condition* (1958) Arendt would cite the modern tendency to make the politics subservient to economics as yet another.[6] For once the political sphere came to be seen as merely the administrative and protective apparatus required by the economic realm (the "national household"), it lost its claim to any intrinsic dignity. It also lost its character as the primary arena in which human beings tended to their shared world, maintaining and preserving it against a sea of natural (or nature-like) destructive forces. That this is no abstract or merely theoretical fear is seen in the way the activities of production and consumption, once relegated to the private or "household" realm, have come to dominate the lives of ordinary citizens and the concerns of political leaders and policy-makers around the globe. Increasingly, the economic sphere subsumes all others.

This brings us to another persistent theme of Arendt's work, one which also grew out of her analysis of totalitarianism. In *The Origins of Totalitarianism*, Arendt repeatedly draws the reader's attention to the devastating costs of avoiding civic responsibility, of leaving the care of the public world – its rights, freedoms, and institutions – to others. In her view, the pervasiveness of an egocentric or "bourgeois" attitude toward public life contributed mightily to making totalitarianism possible. Where civic life has become a vacuum or a farce, the forces of cultural barbarism can be counted on to fill the void. Any minority which withdraws from civic life or accepts the political exile imposed upon it by the majority risks losing not only its civil rights, but everything else. Such was the fate of European Jewry, and much of *The Origins of Totalitarianism* and Arendt's subsequent work is devoted to underlining the dangers of what she termed "alienation from the world."

Finally, *The Origins of Totalitarianism* left Arendt with a puzzle which would shape the course of her subsequent explorations in political theory. The early work, born of her own experience as a refugee from Nazi terror, was written largely with the German case in mind. Yet Arendt intended her analysis to apply to Soviet totalitarianism as well. She was all too conscious, however, of the inadequacy of her treatment of Stalinism. Moreover, she was troubled by the fact that, while National Socialism was a "gutter-born" ideology which represented a radical break with the Western tradition of political thought, the genealogy of Soviet Marxism could be traced back to the towering work of Karl Marx, German Idealist philosophy, and the French *philosophes* of the Enlightenment. How was it that a body of thought with such a distinguished intellectual pedigree, one that gave expression to the most cherished humanitarian hopes of the European Left, could serve as the basis of a totalitarian ideology predicated on the denial of human freedom and dignity? Arendt began to suspect that the substance of Marx's thought could not be easily isolated from its Stalinist deformation. Thus, in 1951, upon finishing *The Origins of Totalitarianism,* she proposed a project to the Guggenheim Foundation on "The Totalitarian Elements in Marxism," in which she would pursue this link.[7]

Arendt never finished her Marx book. In her Guggenheim proposal, she noted that "to accuse Marxism of totalitarianism amounts to accusing the Western tradition itself of necessarily ending in the monstrosity of this novel form of government."[8] While linear, "inevitable" intellectual genealogies of a Hegelian sort were never her stock in trade, Arendt found that her research on Marx led her to a prolonged reconsideration of the Western tradition of political philosophy itself. If there were, indeed, "totalitarian elements in Marxism," they were to be found in Marx's central ideas and basic conceptual apparatus: in, for example, his notion of freedom as the product of historical necessity; in the idea that mankind "makes" history, at first unconsciously and (later) with will and intent; in his notion that violence is the "midwife" of history; in his conception of revolutionary political action, which, like the fabrication process, consists in the violent working over of raw material to create something new; and, finally, in his preference for collective subjects – like the "proletariat" or "mankind" – which act in accordance with supposed class or species interests.

The more she thought about Marx, the more Arendt came to the conclusion that he was no friend of human freedom at all, and that his fundamental ideas and categories had effaced the phenomenal basis of the most basic political experiences (such as debate amongst diverse equals). The real shock for Arendt, however, was that Marx was hardly unique in this respect. The more she plumbed the depths of the Western tradition of political thought, the more she became convinced that the "anti-politics" expressed in Marx's thought had roots which reached as far back as Plato and Aristotle. It was, in other words, at the very beginning of the Western tradition of political thought that a conceptual framework hostile to popular participation, human diversity (what Arendt dubs "plurality"), and the open-ended debate between equals had been laid down. This framework came to provide the basic conceptual architecture of Western political thought, with enormous consequences for how we think about the nature of political action, authority, freedom, judgment and (above all) the relation of thought to action.

With these concerns in mind, Arendt's work of the mid to late fifties attempted a fundamental reorientation of political theory. This reorientation has two moments. First, there is a critical or "deconstructive" reading of canonical thinkers from Plato to Marx, a reading which aims at revealing the sources of the tradition's hostility toward plurality, opinion, and the politics of debate and deliberation amongst equals. Secondly, there is Arendt's attempt to provide a phenomenological description of the basic components of the active life (the *vita activa*), the better to distinguish the human capacity for political speech and action from activities driven by natural necessity (such as labor aimed at subsistence) or the need to create, through work or fabrication, the durable things which constitute the physical, objective dimension of the "human artifice." These two moments are closely related, since Arendt thought that the Western tradition of political thought had progressively conflated the distinct components of the active life (labor, work, and action), thereby creating a network of concepts which fundamentally distorted political experience and our understanding of it. More disturbingly, these concepts tended to produce moral horror whenever they were applied programmatically to the realm of human affairs.

III Rethinking political action and the public realm

The Human Condition (1958) and the essays collected in *Between Past and Future* (1961) are the results of this project, and mark Arendt's emergence as a political thinker of truly staggering range and depth. It is safe to say that these books, together with *On Revolution* (1963), constitute her most enduring legacy in political theory. The reader approaching them for the first time will, however, find them somewhat confusing. Central themes, such as the nature of justice, are barely touched upon. Instead, Arendt's primary energy is devoted to distinguishing the fundamental experiences and preconditions of the political or public realm from other spheres of life (economic, social, personal, religious, etc.). In *The Human Condition* particularly, Arendt seems obsessed with demarcating the specificity of the political realm in contrast to all others.

Arendt was convinced by her analysis of totalitarianism that many in the modern world were eager to abdicate their civic freedom and responsibility, thereby relieving themselves of the "burden" of independent action and judgment. The rise of totalitarian movements was the most spectacular expression of this tendency, but it could also be found in liberal democratic societies (such as the United States) and in the increasingly bureaucratic welfare states of Europe. If the majority of people in a particular polity thought of freedom as essentially the freedom *from* politics (as in America) or politics as the centralized administration of the needs of life (as in the European welfare state), then the public realm and its distinctive freedom were bound to be in jeopardy.

Of course, the history of political theory could hardly be held responsible for the growth of apolitical privatism or the conversion of citizens into clients receiving benefits and entitlements from the state. Nevertheless, the tradition's tendency to interpret political phenomena in accordance with hierarchical models it had derived from the patriarchal family or the realm of production conspired, along with the rise of capitalism and other social developments, to undercut whatever limited autonomy politics might have had in modern life. Indeed, as economic concerns came to dominate the political sphere during the nineteenth and early twentieth centuries, it became increasingly difficult to maintain even the *idea* of a relatively autonomous public realm, one characterized by the debate and deliberation of public-spirited citizens.

Arendt confronts this difficulty head on in *The Human Condition* and *Between Past and Future*, challenging at every turn our received ideas of what politics is and should be. Her method is not to lay down a blueprint of "genuine" politics or to imperiously issue a set of rigid definitions (although critics have charged her with both faults). It is, rather, to excavate and reveal what has been doubly hidden by contemporary experience and inherited categories.[9] Hence Arendt's numerous references to the politics of ancient Greek city-states, especially democratic Athens. She appeals to the experience of fifth century BC *polis* politics not because she considers Athenian democracy to be the best political regime, or because she thinks that ancient Greek politics was somehow free of brutal violence and the systematic coercion of women, slaves, and others (it obviously wasn't). Rather, she turns to the Greeks, and to Athens in particular, for the simple reason that the first flowering of democracy was among the most vivid and intense. Athenian political life was a politics of talk and opinion, one which gave a central place to human plurality and the equality between citizens (for the Greeks, the adult male heads of households). The politics of democratic Athens, transformed into something of an "ideal type" by Arendt, represents basic political experiences prior to the distortion (or worse, oblivion) they suffered at the hands of a hostile philosophical tradition.

Foremost amongst these fundamental experiences was the sheer clarity of the distinction between the public and private realms, a distinction which the Athenian citizen experienced every time he left the household in order to take part in the assembly or talk in the agora. According to Arendt, the Greeks identified the household (or *oikos*) with matters concerning material or biological reproduction. It was the part of human life where necessity held sway, and where coercion – in the form of the male property owner's domination over his family and slaves – was both unavoidable and legitimate. The public realm (as represented by the assembly and the agora), on the other hand, was the realm of freedom. It was a legally and institutionally articulated space in which equal citizens met for deliberation, debate, and decision on matters of common concern. It was, moreover, the space in which one acquired a public self in addition to (and distinct from) the private self of the household.[10]

In making these claims, Arendt is hardly expressing approval for the way the Greeks structured their private realm.[11] Rather, she is underlining the difference between the political sphere (the sphere of a man-made civic equality and freedom) and the economic or household realm (the sphere of hierarchy, necessity, and coercion). We moderns have lost the clarity of this distinction, thanks mainly to what Arendt calls "the rise of the social" and the penetration of "household" (that is, economic and administrative) concerns into public life. But we have also lost it because philosophers beginning with Plato have created false analogies between the political and the household realms, the better to make an authoritarian or hierarchical politics seem more plausibly "natural" to those schooled in a democratic understanding of civic equality.[12] To put Arendt's thought in a nutshell: the more we think of the political realm as concerned with matters of subsistence and material reproduction, the more likely we are to accept hierarchy in the place of civic equality; the more likely we are to see *rule* by elites of one sort or another as the quintessential political activity. Arendt's point is that, strictly speaking, ruling has nothing to do with *genuine* politics, since it destroys the civic equality – the equality of rights and participation, the *isonomia* – that is the hallmark of *political* relations and a democratic public realm.[13]

The image of the public sphere that Arendt extracts from the Greeks is extremely seductive and (for her critics, at least) overly utopian. It is the image of a public space in which debate and deliberation draws out the many-sidedness of a given matter or issue, thanks to the different perspectives individual citizens bring to bear on the same "object."[14] Indeed, according to Arendt, the very reality of the public realm emerges only through the robust exchange of talk and opinion emanating from a multitude of diverse perspectives. Where such exchange is lacking – where fear or lack of interest keeps individuals from publicly articulating their opinion, their "what appears to me" – there can be no lively sense of a *public* reality.[15]

Politics so conceived is, of course, subject to all the limitations of human judgment and all the ambiguities (and ironies) of political action. Arendt never tired of pointing out how political action – the "sharing of words and deeds" – invariably tangles the political actor up in a network of other acting beings, with the result that any given deed creates unforeseen (and potentially boundless) consequences, while rarely achieving its intended goal. In the celebrated chapter on action in *The Human Condition*, she emphasizes the "frailty, boundlessness and unpredictability" of political action and the realm of human affairs generally. This emphasis on the contingency of political action may strengthen our sense that politics is an unpleasant burden, one taken up only by hyper-responsible (or sadly misled) individuals. Yet Arendt celebrates this very contingency, seeing it (in quasi-existentialist fashion) as an authentic expression of the "tangible freedom" the actor experiences whenever he or she initiates a new and unpredictable sequence of events in the public realm. It is through utterly unpredictable words and deeds that the individual actor not only discloses a unique public identity, but illuminates the moral and political world shared by citizens.[16]

Arendt's enthusiasm for initiatory action in the context of a robust, talkative human plurality can hardly be said to be shared by the Western tradition of political thought. As she points out, nothing is more common in this tradition than the condemnation of what she calls the "nonsovereign" character of plural political action:

> It is in accordance with the great tradition of Western thought to think along these lines: to accuse freedom of luring man into necessity, to condemn action, the spontaneous beginning of something new, because its results fall into a predetermined net of relationships, invariably dragging the agent with them, who seems to forfeit his freedom the very moment he makes use of it. The only salvation from this kind of freedom seems to lie in non-acting, in abstention from the whole realm of human affairs.[17]

Arendt is referring to the age-old philosophical and Christian recommendation that we withdraw from the world in order to pursue either timeless wisdom or personal salvation. But philosophy's response to the rough-and-tumble world of democratic politics was not merely to counsel a withdrawal into the solitude of thought. On the contrary, with ancient Greek philosophy there begins a comprehensive effort to re-define political action and freedom, so that these phenomena appear amenable to rational control and hierarchical direction. The first step in this re-conceptualization was the patterning of political action after those human activities in which a good deal of control or mastery is, in fact, possible. Arendt credits Plato with modeling action along the lines suggested by the fabrication process. By imagining the polity in the image of a fabricated object, Plato was able to plausibly assert that political wisdom had nothing to do with the exchange of opinion amongst plural equals but was, in fact, a form of *expert* knowledge, similar to that possessed by a sculptor or a physician. Hence, the moral "expert" should rule in the realm of human affairs, while those lacking such knowledge should simply obey.

While Plato's proposal depended, perhaps dubiously for us, on his theory of transcendent Ideas, subsequent versions of what Arendt calls the "traditional substitution of making for acting" did not. We find a remarkable agreement among Western political thinkers that political action is, at best, a *means* by which an extra-political end – whether it be salvation, the preservation of life, the protection of property, or the self-assertion of the *Volk* – is secured. Even Aristotle, to whom we owe the distinction between action (*praxis*) and making (*poiesis*), viewed politics as essentially the *means* by which an elite inculcates a certain idea of virtue in ordinary citizens and the young. Almost to a man, Western political philosophers have missed the *existential significance* of political action itself, the stunning capacity of debate and deliberation amongst diverse equals to generate meaning and endow human life with a significance it otherwise lacks.[18] It is this failure which Arendt takes as the cue for her own reflections on the nature and significance of politics and the public realm.[19] She aimed at nothing less than providing a philosophical appreciation of the *meaning* of political action in the total economy of human existence.

Performing this task requires that political theory recover certain key distinctions (and the experiences on which they were based) which have been lost or obscured by the tradition. It also requires rethinking such central political concepts as action, freedom, authority, judgment, and power, since each of these concepts had been defined in a largely instrumental (and hence anti-political) way by a tradition hostile to human plurality and its attendant uncertainties. *The Human Condition* and *Between Past and Future* are devoted to this project of rethinking, as is *On Revolution* and the lengthy essay *On Violence* (1970). *The Human Condition* mines ancient Greek poetry, drama, and philosophy in order to show how, in its original understanding, political action was viewed as the very opposite of violence, coercion or rule. It was, in Arendt's rendering, the "sharing of words and deeds" by diverse equals, whose "acting together" generated a power quite different from the forceful ability to "impose one's will" which we normally identify with political power. Political talk and persuasion between equals is valuable not only for what it achieves (for example, the founding or preservation of a polity), but for its own sake. As the performance of initiatory action in a public "space of appearances," political action manifests the actor's capacity for freedom, demonstrates his equality with his peers, and discloses his unique identity – his "public self" – in myriad, unforeseeable ways.

Arendt extends this rethinking of fundamental concepts in *On Revolution*, her most extensive consideration of *modern* political action and the nature of constitutional politics. Working against the regnant liberal and Marxist interpretations of the French and American revolutions, she argues that the significance of modern revolution is not the gallant but futile attempt to overcome poverty (the "social question" which, she believes, was responsible for the failure of the French Revolution), or the establishment of limited government (typically seen as the great achievement of the American

Revolution). Rather, what the modern revolutions demonstrated was how individuals, acting together with a common purpose, could create a new space of tangible freedom in the world, relying on nothing more than the power implicit in their own mutual promises and agreements.

This founding moment – the *constitutio libertatis* – was an event which occurred *after* the violent struggle for liberation from oppression, the struggle usually (and wrongly, in Arendt's view) identified with revolution. Revolution, properly conceived, was coextensive with the creation of a new set of republican political institutions. These institutions did more than limit the range of political power by creating a federal system of checks and balances (which rendered the idea of centralized sovereignty an anachronism). They also marked out a new space for public freedom, one which expanded, in principle, the opportunities for participation on the part of ordinary citizens. According to Arendt, the French Revolution did not succeed in constituting such a stable space for civic equality and freedom, since its primary energies were directed towards ameliorating the suffering of the masses of poor rather than instituting and protecting civil and political rights. The American Revolution, however, was able to effect the *constitutio libertatis*, thanks to the adoption of the Constitution and the agreement of all – founders and ordinary citizens alike – to abide by it.

On Revolution marks a significant moment in Arendt's political thought, a progression almost as great as her move from the analysis of a "novel form of government" (totalitarianism) to the consideration of the fundamental phenomena of politics. Her interpretation of the "revolutionary moment" graphically counters the impression given in *The Human Condition* that genuine political action is a thing of the distant (Greek or Roman) past. The memory of freedom, of "acting together, acting in concert," turns out to be much fresher than that. Moreover, the *kind* of "words and deeds" which qualify as genuinely political for Arendt takes on a decidedly modern cast. No longer does Achilles serve as the poetic symbol of the political actor par excellence, as someone who was able to create his own life story in the course of performing a single outstanding deed.[20] The *new* paradigmatic political actors are the American Founders, whose debates and deliberations concerning the drafting and adoption of the Constitution are presented by Arendt as every bit as exemplary as anything recounted in Homer or Thucydides.

This summary may make *On Revolution* sound like a grateful émigrée's uncritical celebration of the "Founding Fathers." But this is hardly the case. Appreciative as Arendt was of the Founders' achievement, she nevertheless regarded the American Revolution as, at best, a partial success.[21] Partial because the Founders had failed to create an institutional space which would enable the average citizen to become a "participator in government." The ingenious new "system of power" devised by the Constitution, while extremely effective in balancing power against power, reduced the significance of the kind of grass-roots political participation that had characterized life in the colonial townships and wards. It is for this reason that Arendt resurrects Thomas Jefferson's proposal for a "ward system" of local citizens' councils, linking it to the spontaneous creation of workers' and soldiers' councils which accompanied the revolutionary outbreaks of 1905 in Russia and 1918 in Germany. Her concern was to find ways of revivifying the love of "public happiness," a love which had animated the revolutionary "men of action" of the eighteenth century.

Yet while Arendt celebrates the "public happiness" that flows from being a "participator in government," she hardly thinks that political participation or engagement *as such* is necessarily praiseworthy. On the contrary: unless these activities are undertaken in the right spirit, out of a care for the *public* world and a respect for the activities of debate and deliberation, they may well become the vehicles for anti-political passions and concerns. Thus, the preponderant force of *On Revolution*'s critique of the French and Marxist revolutionary traditions is to make us doubt that radical social reform qualifies as an authentically *political* project, and to make us suspicious of the unalloyed passion to do good (a passion that has animated much of the radical politics of the nineteenth and twentieth centuries). One of Arendt's more unsettling suggestions is that a politics energized by the emotion of compassion or the strictures of an absolute morality is bound to be impatient with the deliberative project of talk and compromise, preferring instead direct, and often violent, action aimed at remedying society's ills. From this flows her even more unsettling suggestion that a morality appropriate to politics must arise from within the activity of politics itself, rather than be imposed on it from without.[22]

Arendt's celebration of "local" political action (done in the right spirit) notwithstanding, she cannot really be grouped with proponents of "radical" or "direct" democracy. Her experience of totalitarianism led her to place a very strong emphasis upon the importance of worldly institutions and legal frameworks. These provide an arena for, but also limits to, the energies of political action and participation. Only where the "worldly artifice" was shored up by the kinds of institutions created by the Founders could political freedom hope to survive. Thus, while Arendt sees the American "revolutionary spirit" as the "lost treasure" of a political culture which has generally preferred to equate freedom with the pursuit of private happiness, she hardly blames the Constitution for this. She knows all too well that "permanent revolution" is the most destructive and futile form of politics there is.

This emphasis on institutional frameworks as providing a "home" for worldly freedom suggests that Margaret Canovan is right in placing Arendt's political thought within the classical republican tradition of political thought.[23] This tradition (which begins, ambiguously, with Aristotle, and includes Cicero, Machiavelli, Harrington, Montesquieu, and Rousseau) placed a great deal of emphasis on active citizenship, civic virtue, the rule of law, and political equality. These were the essential ingredients for preserving a free republic from internal corruption and external threat. But whereas Machiavelli, Harrington, and Rousseau emphasize the kind of civic virtue and patriotism embodied in the "citizen soldier" willing to sacrifice his life for the preservation of republican liberty and civic equality, Arendt places far greater emphasis upon Aristotle's identification of citizenship with participation "in judgment and authority," and upon Montesquieu's insistence that the laws of a republic establish not just boundaries between public and private (and thus limits to action), but relations (*rapports*) between citizens as well.[24] This is not surprising, given Arendt's persistent stress on human plurality and the sharing of diverse opinions as the *sine qua non* of any politics worthy of the name. She has little use for the Rousseauean idea that the level of civic virtue in a polity can or should be measured by how closely it approached unanimity of opinion. Her experience of totalitarianism's attempt to create "one Man of gigantic dimensions" out of plural and unique individuals made her rightly skeptical of *any* attempt to inculcate a univocal sense of the public good in citizens.

On the other hand, Arendt did agree with Machiavelli (and the mainstream of the classical republican tradition generally) that the "islands of freedom" which human beings have been able to establish through joint action have been few and far between, and are surrounded by a sea of hostile political and social forces. The "public thing" (the *res publica*) is in constant danger of being overwhelmed, whether by external enemies of freedom, or by citizens' forgetfulness of the joys and responsibilities of *public* happiness. The latter possibility, Arendt regretfully concludes, was the fate of the American Revolution, as generations of Americans – deprived of an institutional space in which to experience "public happiness" and the joys of political debate, deliberation, and decision – came to define the "pursuit of happiness" in increasingly private (and materialistic) terms. For Arendt, the loss of the "revolutionary spirit" figures as a serious, perhaps even fatal, development for the health of the Republic.

IV Thinking and judgment

Arendt's encounter with the "thoughtless" Adolf Eichmann at his trial in Jerusalem left her mulling over the possibility that our faculty for thought –

for internal dialogue with ourselves – might be crucial to our ability to render moral and political judgments and preserve us from complicity with political evil.[25] In her 1971 essay "Thinking and Moral Considerations" she put the matter thus: "Might the problem of good and evil, our faculty for telling right from wrong, be connected with our faculty of thought? . . . Could the activity of thinking as such . . . be among the conditions that make men abstain from evil-doing or even actually 'condition' them against it?"[26]

The encounter with Eichmann led to Arendt to focus increasingly on the activities of thinking and judgment as they relate to politics. But it would be wrong to conclude that Arendt, having devoted great intellectual energy and passion to the question of political action, grasped the importance of these more reflective activities only late in life. As Richard Bernstein suggests, thinking and judgment can be seen as persistent themes of her political thought.[27] This concern animates her analysis of thought-deadening ideologies (in *The Origins of Totalitarianism*) and her reflections on the problem of understanding (and properly judging) a phenomenon as unprecedented and initially incomprehensible as totalitarianism (in *OT* and the 1953 essay "Understanding and Politics"). The concern with judgment is further developed in her consideration of the links between opinion, facts, deliberation and judgment in two essays from the sixties, "The Crisis in Culture" (1960) and "Truth and Politics" (1967). It receives its most extensive (but hardly definitive) articulation in her posthumously published *Lectures on Kant's Political Philosophy* (culled from a seminar given in 1970) and her two-volume *The Life of the Mind* (1976). The third volume of the latter work – on judgment – was left unwritten due to Arendt's untimely death at age sixty-nine in 1975.

Yet despite the presence of this concern from the very beginning of her theoretical work, there does appear to be a significant change in emphasis in Arendt's thought during the late sixties and early seventies. She seems to move away from the elucidation of the nature and meaning of political action to a consideration of the role thought, will, and judgment play – not only in our moral and political lives, but as independent faculties which make up "the life of the mind." Much has been made of this progression in the scholarly writing on Arendt. It seems that the pre-eminent theorist of the *vita activa* concluded her life by re-engaging the *vita contemplativa* and her "first love," philosophy – this time without casting aspersions on its "anti-political" character.[28] The fact that Arendt's consideration of the faculty of judgment shifts from the judgment of the engaged political actor (in the essays from the sixties) to that of the detached spectator (in the lectures on Kant from 1970) lends credence to this view. We move from an analysis of the modes of thinking and judgment appropriate to citizens engaged in debate and deliberation to an analysis of the redemptive power of the judgments rendered retrospectively by the poet or historian. The latter type of judgments help to "reconcile us with reality," even when – especially when – that reality is horrific and apparently beyond comprehension.[29]

I do not want to enter the debate about whether Arendt actually has two theories of judgment instead of one (as Ronald Beiner has suggested).[30] Nor do I think that it is plausible to suggest that Arendt came to abandon her stress on what Jerome Kohn calls "the priority of the political" in favor of a secular form of theodicy. It is better, I think, to view this phase of Arendt's work as an attempt to think through the tension between the life of the citizen and the life of the mind. In many respects, this tension occupied Arendt throughout her intellectual career, finding notable expression in her reflections on the hostility of philosophers and thinkers to the *bios politikos*, and in her moving depiction of Socrates as the first – and perhaps last – "philosopher-citizen."[31]

What happens to this tension between the life of action and the life of the mind in Arendt's later work? If she does not simply abandon action for thought, does she, perhaps, attempt to resolve or overcome the tension between these two activities? It has been suggested by some that the third volume of *The Life of the Mind*, on judgment, would have provided such a synthesis, a crowning final statement in which the claims of thinking and acting would each be given their due and reconciled in the activity of judgment. Judgment, according to Arendt, is the faculty which brings thinking – solitary, abstract, and concerned with "invisibles" – down to earth, manifesting it in "the world of appearances."[32] Hence her characterization of judgment as the "by-product" of thinking in "Thinking and Moral Considerations." While Arendt adamantly opposed Hegelian-Marxist ideas about the "unity of theory and practice," her later work nevertheless offers the tantalizing suggestion that judgment is indeed the mediating link between thought and action. It is therefore tempting to conclude that Arendt ultimately overcame the strong and uncompromising distinction between thinking and acting that provides the architecture for much of her earlier work.

Tempting, but, I think, wrongheaded. In her last book, Arendt continued to presume the distinction between thinking and acting, and went out of her way to preserve the tension between the life of the mind and the life of action. Her phenomenological descriptions of the activity of thinking in *The Life of the Mind* stress its solitary character, the fact that thinking demands a "withdrawal from the world." Thinking at its most profound – *philosophical* thinking – is, according to Arendt, always engaged in "an intramural warfare" with common sense (the "sixth sense" which fits us into a shared world of appearances with others).[33] It is an endless process, an open-ended quest for meaning, one which produces neither knowledge nor usable practical wisdom. Thus, all genuine thinkers cultivate an alienation from the world – they "take on the color of the dead" – the better to prolong their initial experience of wonder at existence, a state or *pathos* of the soul which (as Plato reminds us) lies at the origin of philosophy itself.[34]

Of course, Arendt hardly denies that there are other, non-philosophical modes of thought which are crucial both to the acting and the judging agent. "Representative" thinking – the capacity to think in the place of someone else – is specifically described as a political mode of thought, one which facilitates the rendering of valid judgments.[35] Similarly, the "dialogue of me with myself" that constitutes thought has the effect of introducing a kind of plurality into the self. This plurality lies at the root of conscience itself, enabling it to be something more than the simple internalization of social or creedal norms. We should, however, view these morally relevant modes of reflection as forms of "ordinary" thinking, which we have a right to expect from every mature individual. Hence Arendt's shock – and our own – when we encounter the "sheer thoughtlessness" of someone like Eichmann, whose "conscience" was defined almost entirely by his station and its duties, and who therefore lent himself enthusiastically to the commission of the most unimaginable crimes.[36]

Arendt's appreciation of the horrors enabled by ideological belief, combined with her experience of individuals who, like Eichmann, fail to think and (thus) to judge, led her to consistently praise the capacity for independent thought and judgment. She praised this capacity even when it threatened to dissolve the moral verities of a culture or put the judging individual at odds not only with the majority, but with the "moral taste" of his or her epoch.[37] It is not for nothing that she poses Socrates as the "model" thinker whose capacity to undermine custom and convention leads to an enhancement of moral judgment. For it is only by developing the capacity for "independent thinking for one self" (*Selbstdenken*) that the individual can hope to avoid moral catastrophe in those situations where "everyone else is carried away" by a wave of misguided conviction or enthusiasm. We see how Arendt balances her appeal (in *The Human Condition*) for a strengthened "community" sense with a strong appreciation of moral and intellectual independence, an appreciation of the moral importance of the "pariah's point of view."

In *The Life of the Mind*, however, Arendt is not concerned with engaged or political thought, but with what (for lack of a better term) might be called "extraordinary" or philosophical thinking. In fact, her last work is as adamant as *The Human Condition* in its insistence that *this* activity stands in the greatest possible tension not only with the life of the citizen, but with *worldly* existence in general. Thus, while she had the greatest possible respect for "extraordinary" thinkers from Plato to Heidegger, she continued to distrust them. The very nature of their activity led them to counsel, and to practice, withdrawal from the world. For Arendt, the stakes were too high, the potential for disaster too great, for her to praise the unworldliness of the philosophers.[38] Only Socrates, in her view, was able to practice both "ordinary" and "extraordinary" thinking without sacrificing the one to the other.

Does this suggest that there is a kind of stasis in Arendt's mature thought, a stubborn unwillingness to modify her own overly strict definitions and oppositions? There is little question that in some instances – for example, her distinction between the political and the social, or her distinction between the public and private – Arendt was too rigid for her own good. With respect to her distinction between the life of the mind and the life of the citizen, however, this is not the case. In making this opposition central to her reflections on politics and the tradition, Arendt is hardly saying that the life of the citizen is or ought to be "mindless." Her repeated appeals to debate, deliberation, judgment, and the perspectival formation of opinion obviously place a premium upon the moral-rational capacities of ordinary citizens. Her point, rather, was to remind us that there can be no easy synthesis of these two fundamentally opposed ways of life. Between the life of the citizen and the life of the philosopher there lies a unavoidably tragic choice.

Confronted by this choice, Hannah Arendt never waffled. She was a thinker, but a thinker who resolutely and consistently threw her weight on the side of the political life, the civic life animated by public-spiritedness, "care for the world," and independence of judgment. Haunted by the failure of many to resist the rise of totalitarianism and suspicious of a philosophical tradition whose quest for wisdom led it to devalue both politics and human plurality, she devoted her enormous intellectual talents to revealing the unsuspected meaning of a life devoted to the active preservation of worldly freedom.

NOTES

1 Arendt, *OT*, p. 469.
2 Ibid., p. 462. Cf. Hannah Arendt, "What is Authority?" in Arendt, *BPF*, p. 97.
3 See George Kateb, *Hannah Arendt: Politics, Conscience, Evil* (Totowa, NJ: Rowman and Allanheld, 1983), p. 66.
4 Arendt, *OT*, p. 185.
5 Margaret Canovan, "Hannah Arendt as a Conservative Thinker," in Larry May and Jerome Kohn, eds., *Hannah Arendt – Twenty Years Later* (Cambridge, MA: MIT Press, 1996), especially pp. 14–21.
6 See Arendt, *HC*, chapters 2 and 3.

7 The prospectus for this project may be found in the collection of Arendt's papers at the Library of Congress, MSS Box 17.
8 Arendt, "Project: Totalitarian Elements in Marxism," quoted in Canovan, *Hannah Arendt*, p. 64.
9 See, in this regard, Arendt's reflections on Walter Benjamin's "pearl fishing" in her essay on Benjamin in Arendt, *MDT*, pp. 201–206. Arendt notes the similarity of Benjamin's "method" to that of Heidegger's in his various readings of the history of philosophy. The family resemblance between all three thinkers' approaches to the past is marked.
10 Arendt, *HC*, pp. 28–37.
11 Although see Hauke Brunkhorst's chapter in this volume, pp. 178–198 below.
12 Arendt, *BPF*, pp. 104–114.
13 Ibid., p. 104.
14 Arendt, *HC*, pp. 57–58.
15 I should note that *opinion* is something of a term of art in Arendt. It does not refer to our knee-jerk, ideologically conditioned political views on a given issue; rather, an opinion is something that gets formed through thought, discussion, and debate. It expresses a perspective on a particular issue, not the idiosyncrasy of personal feelings or the predictable residue of a world-view. The fact that we think of opinion as subjective, as *mere* opinion, devoid of rationality, has to do with the philosophical devaluation of this faculty, most famously performed by Books VI and VII of Plato's *Republic*. In her theoretical work, Arendt devotes a good deal of energy to reminding us how the formation of an opinion involves a wide range of moral and intellectual capacities, and (thus) that opinion is one of the most sadly neglected of our rational faculties.
16 Ibid., pp. 193–194.
17 Ibid., p. 234. Cf. *HC*, p. 195.
18 See Arendt's discussion in *The Human Condition* of how public words and deeds – unlike other human activities – have an almost "natural" capacity to create stories (*HC*, pp. 181–188).
19 See Kateb, *Hannah Arendt*, pp. 2–3.
20 Arendt, *HC*, pp. 193–194.
21 See the chapters by Albrecht Wellmer and Jeremy Waldron in this volume, pp. 220–241 and pp. 201–219 below.
22 See her discussion of Jesus in *HC*, pp. 238–242, as well as her discussion of the dangers of absolute goodness (as illustrated by Melville's "Billy Budd") in *OR*, pp. 82–87. See also George Kateb's chapter in this volume, pp. 130–148 below.
23 Margaret Canovan, *Hannah Arendt: A Reinterpretation of Her Political Thought* (Cambridge: Cambridge University Press, 1992) p. 202.
24 See Aristotle, *The Politics*, Book III, chapter 3 (1275a22), and Montesquieu, *The Spirit of the Laws*, translated by Anne Cohler, Basia Miller, and Harold Stone (Cambridge: Cambridge University Press, 1989), Book III.
25 See the chapters by Benhabib, d'Entrèves, and Bernstein in this volume, pp. 65–85, 245–260 and 277–291 below.
26 Hannah Arendt, "Thinking and Moral Considerations: A Lecture," *Social Research*, 50th Anniversary Issue (Spring/Summer 1984): 8.
27 See his contribution to this volume, pp. 277–291 below.
28 See, for example, Ronald Beiner's "Interpretive Essay," in Arendt, *LKPP*.

29 See, especially, Arendt, *LKPP*, pp. 52–56.
30 See Beiner, "Interpretive Essay," in Arendt, *LKPP*, p. 93.
31 See Hannah Arendt, "Philosophy and Politics," *Social Research* 57/1 (Spring 1990) for her characterization of Socrates. See also Frederick Dolan's contribution to this volume, pp. 261–276 below.
32 See Richard Bernstein's essay, "Judging: the Actor and the Spectator," in Bernstein, *Philosophical Profiles* (Philadelphia: University of Pennsylvania Press, 1986).
33 Arendt, *TLM*, vol. 1, *Thinking*, pp. 80–88.
34 Plato, *Theaetetus*, 155d. See Arendt, *Thinking*, pp. 141–151.
35 See Arendt, "Truth and Politics," in Arendt, *BPF*, pp. 241–242.
36 Kateb, *Hannah Arendt*, p. 195.
37 See Arendt, "Thinking and Moral Considerations" and *LKPP*, especially pp. 27–40. Cf. Hannah Arendt, "On Humanity in Dark Times," in Arendt, *MDT*.
38 The case of Heidegger's affiliation with the Nazis is an object lesson in this regard.

PART I

Totalitarianism and nationalism

I

MARGARET CANOVAN

Arendt's theory of totalitarianism: a reassessment

Introduction

The Origins of Totalitarianism, first published in 1951, established Hannah Arendt's reputation as a political thinker and has a good claim to be regarded as the key to her work, for trains of thought reflecting on the catastrophic experiences it seeks to understand can be traced to the heart of her later and more overtly theoretical writings. Half a century after the book's appearance there has been a revival of interest in the idea of totalitarianism, but the concept itself[1] remains controversial. Far more than a technical term for use by political scientists and historians, it has always incorporated a diagnosis and explanation of modern political dangers, carrying with it warnings and prescriptions. This chapter will argue that "totalitarianism" as understood by Arendt meant something very different from the dominant sense of the term. The final section will attempt a reassessment of her theory.

Two concepts of totalitarianism

There are almost as many senses of "totalitarianism" as there are writers on the subject,[2] but a few broad similarities have tended to hide a fundamental difference between Arendt and most other theorists. Like the rest, she is concerned with a novel political phenomenon combining unprecedented coercion with an all-embracing secular ideology; like the rest she finds examples on both the left and the right of the mid-twentieth-century political spectrum. But these apparent similarities conceal more than they reveal, and much confusion has arisen from failure to realise that there is not just one "totalitarian model," but at least two which describe different phenomena, pose different problems of understanding, and carry different theoretical and political implications.

The better-known model (on which there are many variations) depicts a totally coherent socio-political system: a state built in the image of an ideology, presided over by a single party legitimized by the ideology, employing unlimited powers of coercion and indoctrination to prevent any deviation from orthodoxy. The construction of such a polity is associated by some theorists with the attempt to build Utopia; others interpret its perpetuation in a state of frozen immobility as a quasi-religious retreat from the anxieties of modernity. Despite the regular inclusion of Nazism under the "totalitarian" heading, the clearest examples have been found among communist regimes, and appropriate diagnoses and prescriptions have followed. Diagnostically, totalitarianism has been seen as an affliction caused by over-ambitious political ideas and radical actions. The remedy for this political fever is to avoid excitement: to lower our expectations from politics and ideas alike, falling back upon the invaluable if unglamorous blessings of liberal politics, skeptical philosophy and free market economics.[3]

Reassessment of Arendt's theory is impossible unless we first realize that hers is quite different from this dominant model. True, the equation of left and right is still there (though including only the regimes of Hitler and Stalin, not Fascist Italy, nor the Soviet Union before or after Stalin); the stress on coercion and ideology is still there (though we shall see that Arendt understands these vital ingredients in distinctive ways), but the differences are crucial, and have a great deal to do with Arendt's focus on Nazism and particularly on the Holocaust.[4] In fact the picture of totalitarianism that she presents forms a stark contrast to the more familiar model. Metaphorically, one might say that if the dominant picture suggests the rigidity, uniformity, transparency, and immobility of a frozen lake, Arendt's theory evokes a mountain torrent sweeping away everything in its path, or a hurricane leveling everything recognizably human. Instead of referring to a political system of a deliberately structured kind, "totalitarianism" in Arendt's sense means a chaotic, nonutilitarian, manically dynamic movement of destruction that assails all the features of human nature and the human world that make politics possible.

A view from Auschwitz

The Origins of Totalitarianism consists of three volumes in one, *Antisemitism, Imperialism,* and *Totalitarianism*, and the theory it contains is enormously complex and notoriously hard to get to grips with.[5] This section will pick out for examination some of the distinctive features of Arendt's model, while the next will look at the way she approached the problem of trying to account for this new phenomenon. We can perhaps find a point of entry in a theme that she stressed over and over again: the *novelty* of the political phenomena with which she was concerned. "Everything we know of totalitarianism demonstrates a horrible originality . . . its very actions constitute a break with all our traditions. . ."[6] In other words, totalitarianism illustrated the human capacity to *begin*, that power to think and to act in ways that are new, contingent, and unpredictable that looms so large in her mature political theory. But the paradox of totalitarian novelty was that it represented an assault on that very ability to act and think as a unique individual.

This new phenomenon seemed to Arendt to demonstrate the self-destructive implications of what she called "modern man's deep-rooted suspicion of everything he did not make himself."[7] Believing that "everything is possible"[8] totalitarian movements demand unlimited power, but what this turns out to mean is not at all the building of utopia (which would itself set limits to power and possibility) but unparalleled destruction. "Experiments" in total domination in the concentration camps that are the "laboratories" of the new regimes gradually make clear that the price of total power is the eradication of human plurality.[9] The characteristics that make us more than members of an animal species – our unique individuality and our capacity for spontaneous thought and action – make us unpredictable and therefore get in the way of attempts to harness us for collective motion. Only *one* can be omnipotent,[10] and the path to this goal, discovered separately by Hitler and by Stalin, lies through terror on the one hand and ideology on the other.

"Total terror" as practiced in the camps is, Arendt claims, "the essence of totalitarian government."[11] It does not simply kill people but first eradicates their individuality and capacity for action. Any remnant of spontaneity would stand in the way of complete domination. "Total power can be achieved and safeguarded only in a world of conditioned reflexes, of marionettes without the slightest trace of spontaneity. Precisely because man's resources are so great, he can be fully dominated only when he becomes a specimen of the animal-species man."[12] Unlike the violence and coercion used by ordinary tyrants it does not have a utilitarian purpose such as repressing opposition, and it reaches its climax only after genuine opposition has already been repressed; its only function is to further the project of total domination by crushing out all human individuality. "Common sense protests desperately that the masses are submissive and that all this gigantic apparatus of terror is therefore superfluous; if they were capable of telling the truth, the totalitarian rulers would reply: The apparatus seems superfluous to you only because it serves to make men superfluous."[13]

Ideology complements terror by eliminating the capacity for individual thought and experience among the executioners themselves, binding them into the unified movement of destruction. Ideologies – pseudo-scientific theories purporting to give insight into history – give their believers "the total explanation of the past, the total knowledge of the present, and the reliable prediction of the future."[14] By making reality as experienced seem insignificant compared with what *must* happen, they free ideological thought from the constraints of common sense and reality. But in Arendt's view the most dangerous opportunity they offer (seized by both Hitler and Stalin) is their stress on logical consistency. Both leaders prided themselves on the merciless reasoning with which they pursued the implications of race- or class-struggle to the murder of the last "objective enemy." In their hands the ideologies were emptied of all content except for the automatic process of deduction that one group or another should die. Ideological logicality replaced free thought, inducing people to strip themselves of individuality until they were part of a single impersonal *movement* of total domination.[15] For totalitarian ideologies do not support the status quo: they chart an endless struggle that is inexorable in its destructiveness.

Total power turns out, then, to mean inevitable destruction. The job of the totalitarian regime is simply to speed up the execution of death sentences pronounced by the law of nature or of history. Arendt points to the stress laid by both leaders on historical necessity: on acting out the economic laws of Marxist class-struggle or the biological laws of struggle for racial supremacy. Seeking to distinguish totalitarianism from the innumerable tyrannies that had preceded it, she laid particular emphasis upon this. The hallmark of tyranny had always been lawlessness: legitimate government was limited by laws, whereas tyranny meant the breach of those boundaries so that the tyrant could rage at his will across the country. But (as experienced by its adherents) totalitarianism was not lawless in that way, though its laws were not civil laws protecting rights, but the supposed "laws" of Nature or of History.

According to those inexorable laws, human existence consists of the life or death struggle between collectivities – races or classes – whose motion is the real meaning of history. For totalitarianism, "all laws have become laws of movement."[16] Neither stable institutions nor individual initiative can be allowed to get in the way of this frantic dynamism. "Total terror . . . is designed to translate into reality the law of movement of history or nature," and indeed to smooth its path, "to make it possible for the force of nature or of history to race freely through mankind, unhindered by any spontaneous human action." Human beings (even the rulers themselves) must serve these forces, "either riding atop their triumphant car or crushed under its wheels,"[17] and individuality is an inconvenience to be eliminated by "the iron band of terror, which destroys the plurality of men and makes out of man the One who unfailingly will act as though he himself were part of the course of history or nature."[18]

The picture of totalitarianism in power presented by Arendt is very far from the familiar image of an omnipotent state with unified and coherent institutions. On the contrary, it is a shapeless, hectic maelstrom of permanent revolution and endless expansion, quite unaffected by utilitarian concerns.[19] Its central institution is not the civil service or the army but the secret police, and even they have a function that defies comprehension in terms of ordinary common sense. Whereas in earlier tyrannies the job of the secret police was to ferret out covert opposition to the regime, their totalitarian successors are no longer concerned with anything that individuals may actually have done. "Suspects" are replaced by "objective enemies"[20] who need not be suspected of any subversive thought or action. In due course the killing machine may demand that the secret policeman himself should become a victim, and if the process of ideological indoctrination is working properly he will obligingly accuse himself of the required crimes.

To sum up, Arendt presents the baffling paradox of a new phenomenon which at one and the same time illustrates human inventiveness and is dedicated to its destruction. Testimony to the contingency of human action, which can bring forth utterly unexpected new things, the phenomenon represents a flight from contingency as individuals turn themselves and others into flotsam and jetsam on the supposedly inexorable current of history. Pursuit of total power leads to impotence: the faith that "everything is possible" only to the demonstration that "everything can be destroyed."[21] Reflecting on the traditional assumption that "human nature" sets limits to human power, she observes with bitter irony, "we have learned that the power of man is so great that he really can be what he wishes to be."[22] If men decide to reduce themselves and others to beasts, nature will not stop them.

Tracing the elements of totalitarianism

Starting from completely different backgrounds and circumstances, Nazism and Stalinism had arrived at this same terminus, demonstrating that what had happened under the two regimes could not be reduced to events within the particular histories of Germany and Russia.[23] The key factor making it possible was in Arendt's view the widespread experience of "superfluousness," which prepared the way for the concerted eradication of human individuality. "Political, social, and economic events everywhere are in a silent conspiracy with totalitarian instruments devised for making men superfluous."[24] Not only are uprooted people who have lost a stable human world easy victims for terror, but loss of the world also damages people's hold on reality. Such people are receptive to ideologies that may be insane but are at least consistent, and to movements that provide an alternative reality, a "fictitious world."[25] Furthermore, breakdown of the stable human world means loss of the institutional and psychological barriers that normally set limits to what is possible. But what were the sources of these general conditions and of the specific organizational methods used by totalitarian movements and regimes? To what extent could the advent of this hurricane of nihilism be explained?

Two thirds of Arendt's long book is devoted to these questions. Not that she was looking for "origins" in the sense of "causes" that made totalitarianism happen or that could in principle have allowed it to be predicted. She insisted that any such determinism was out of place in the realm of human affairs, which is the arena of novel actions and unpredictable events.[26] What she offered instead was "a historical account of the elements which crystallized into totalitarianism,"[27] and her choice of "elements" has often surprised her readers. Her first section is concerned with the question why the Jews in particular should have been singled out for destruction, a choice of priorities that underlines her stress on Nazism in general and the death camps in particular. But the heart of her argument lies in the second section, on "Imperialism," for (without ever suggesting that Nazism amounted to a German copy of British imperialism) she argued that imperialism had set the stage for totalitarianism and provided its perpetrators with useful preconditions and precedents.

Before we consider these it is worth noting a few places where she does *not* look for explanations. We have already seen her justification for leaving aside the particular histories of Germany and Russia, in which others have tried to find explanations for Nazism and Stalinism. More surprising is her neglect of the personal role played by Hitler and Stalin and their responsibility or otherwise for the catastrophic course of events. This is particularly striking in view of the stress she places on the key position of the leader in totalitarian movements and regimes,[28] and even more so in the light of her own admission that the Soviet Union was totalitarian only during Stalin's rule.[29] Unlike most theorists of totalitarianism, finally, she does not seek for its origins in intellectual sources. Even when, after publishing *Totalitarianism*, she set out to write a companion volume tracing the roots of Stalinism, and conceded that features of Marxist theory (and even of the whole Western tradition of political philosophy) had helped to make it possible, she still denied any direct causation.[30] Where the antecedents of Nazi racism were concerned she chronicled the theories of Gobineau and others, but observed that "there is an abyss between the men of brilliant and facile conceptions and men of brutal deeds and active bestiality which no intellectual explanation is able to bridge."[31] Elsewhere she wrote that "what is unprecedented in totalitarianism is not primarily its ideological content, but the *event* of totalitarian domination itself."[32]

Nevertheless, that event could to some extent be made comprehensible by looking at precedents for the modes of thinking, acting, and organizing developed by totalitarian movements, and at processes that had prepared the way for it by breaking down the political and social structures that would have stood in its way. In Arendt's view, both preconditions and precedents were to be found in the economic, military, and political upheaval known as "imperialism," which had in the late nineteenth century seen European conquest of great tracts of the world in the wake of capitalist expansion, and which had also disrupted European states,[33] economies, and societies. Much of the story she tells is a tale of disrupted structures and uprooted people, amounting to a massive loss of the human world of civilization. For to be civilized human beings (not just members of the natural human species) we need to inhabit a man-made world of stable structures. We need these to hedge us about with laws, to bestow rights upon us, to give us a standing in society from which we can form and voice opinions, to allow us access to the common sense that comes with a shared reality.

Arendt maintained that most of the recruits to totalitarian movements belonged to the "masses": uprooted, disoriented people who no longer had any clear sense of reality or self-interest because the world they had inhabited had been destroyed by the upheavals of unemployment, inflation, war, and revolution. But their condition was only one facet of a more widespread experience of "superfluousness." If these helpless, passive people were ideally suited to mass membership of totalitarian movements, the leaders and activists came from an older group of "superfluous" people whom Arendt calls "the mob": a criminal and violent underworld generated by the unsettling dynamism of economic growth.[34] Imperialism had exported unscrupulous adventurers like these across the globe and offered them "infinite possibilities for crimes committed in the spirit of play."[35] This nihilism and its practices, reimported into Europe by movements seeking to emulate imperialism, was one of the sources of totalitarian violence.

But why was it so easy for that violence to find victims on such a massive scale? What happened to the European tradition of protecting individual rights? Arendt finds part of the answer in a different experience of "superfluousness": statelessness. One of the first moves the Nazis took on the road to the "final solution of the Jewish question" was to deprive Jews of their citizenship. They joined the increasing number of those who had become stateless after the First World War. These were people who were not criminals but had no rights and were not wanted by any government. In a chapter on "the decline of the nation-state and the end of the rights of man," she describes how these events had exposed the fatal flaw of the classic European state. Supposedly a civilized legal order committed to defending the rights of all its inhabitants, it was (when the crunch came) a *national* state, and only those who could successfully claim membership of the nation had rights. Lacking the rights bestowed by citizenship, "natural" human beings were simply a nuisance, even in liberal states. "If the Nazis put a person in a concentration camp and he made a successful escape, say, to Holland, the Dutch would put him in an internment camp."[36] People who are "superfluous," who have no place in the world, are ideal victims for totalitarian terror.

One of Arendt's main themes is the fragility of civilization and the ease with which (even in the heart of Europe) it could be replaced by barbarism once that protective world was swept away on a torrent of relentless dynamism. She traces this obsessive motion back to the dynamics of the capitalist market, arguing like Marx that dynamism is the crucial characteristic of capitalism, stemming from the conversion of solid property into fluid wealth. Before the advent of capitalism property had been a force for social and political stability, but once converted into capital it became mobile and expansive, with no respect for established boundaries or institutions and no natural limits. In nineteenth-century imperialism the economic imperative to expand one's capital came out of the boardroom, burst the bounds of the nation-state and its institutions, and turned into "the limitless pursuit of power after power that could roam and lay waste the whole globe."[37] "Expansion is everything," said its representative figure, Cecil Rhodes. "I would annex the planets if I could."[38] Arendt does not suggest that capitalism or any of the other sources she points to *caused* totalitarianism, only that the latter's startling novelty becomes more comprehensible in the light of such precedents.

One of the most paradoxical features of totalitarian regimes was the spectacle of dynamic leaders turning the world upside down while proclaiming their belief in necessity. Looking for precedents for this strange combination of activism with dedication to the service of an inexorable process, Arendt finds them within the British Empire in the figures of the imperial bureaucrat and the secret agent. Both lent their initiative, ingenuity, and idealism to serving "the secret forces of history and necessity."[39] In order to obey the empire's "law of expansion"[40] they were prepared to break all ordinary laws, illustrating one of the ways in which imperialism subverted political institutions as well as undermining political responsibility. Dynamic movement, expansion for its own sake, submerged other considerations. But the most distinctive imperialist precedent for Nazism was the development of racism, which offered a way of gathering uprooted people into a community that needed no stable institutional structures to hold them together. Within racist movements, claim to membership in a superior community rested on what one genetically *is*, not on anything one has done. Once established, ways of thinking and behaving that successfully denied the humanity of large sections of humanity were ready to be adopted in the practice of totalitarian terror.

Why should the Jews in particular have been such prominent victims of totalitarianism in its Nazi form? Arendt strongly resisted the notion that they became victims simply by accident. Her argument is that in the Nazi case anti-semitism became the "amalgamator" around which the other elements of totalitarianism crystallized, because the Jews were uniquely entangled with those elements in their peculiar relations with state and society. One important strand in her argument is that the Jews themselves (like those servants of empire who went with the tide of events) had shown a want of political responsibility. Another is that they had appeared to be a rootless community based on race and secretly working for global power. Where earlier anti-semites saw the Jews in this light and feared them, the Nazis saw them as a rival master race, a model to be emulated and overtaken. To them, "the Jews who have kept their identity without territory and without state, appeared as the only people that seemingly was already organized as a racial body politic. Modern anti-semitism wanted not only to exterminate world Jewry but to imitate what it thought to be their organizational strength."[41]

The lessons of *Totalitarianism*

Looking again at Arendt's theory we can hardly fail to be struck by its *strangeness*: the phenomenon she pictures is not only terrifying but weird and senseless, much less comprehensible than that presented in the dominant model. Totalitarianism as usually understood may be alarming but it also seems a viable political system that may be a practical alternative to liberal democracy. By contrast, Arendt describes a phenomenon that is purely destructive and futile. Even in the first edition of her book, written while Stalin was still alive and the defeat of Nazism very recent, she argued that it might well be short-lived. Such a political hurricane cannot establish a stable system; it must keep up its momentum toward world conquest or fizzle out. Perhaps (she suggested) her own generation might see the end of it, as totalitarianism disappeared, "leaving no other trace in the history of mankind than exhausted peoples, economic and social chaos, political vacuum, and a spiritual *tabula rasa*."[42] Even so, it seemed to her a matter of vital significance, for both practical and theoretical reasons.

The practical reason was that it might recur.[43] "Totalitarianism became this century's curse only because it so terrifyingly took care of its problems,"[44] pointing toward a new and alarming set of predicaments. In the first place, all this senseless destruction was connected with the increasingly widespread experience of "superfluousness." Political upheaval, social rootlessness, unemployment, overpopulation: all were combining to produce increasing temptations to totalitarian solutions. But these new temptations and opportunities were appearing in a world where human power and human unwillingness to leave anything alone were greater than ever before, and where, moreover, human beings are now so interconnected that all our fates are bound up together. Responsibility for what happens across the entire world must be shouldered by human beings, acting without traditional authority to guide them. Arendt comments that "the greatness of this task is crushing and without precedent."[45]

The more theoretical reasons for trying to understand this new phenomenon were twofold. The first is simply the human imperative to "come to terms with and reconcile ourselves to reality" through understanding. "If we want to be at home on this earth, even at the price of being at home in this century, we must try to take part in the interminable dialogue with the essence of totalitarianism."[46] But the other reason is that these unprecedented and catastrophic events cast into relief important and neglected features of the human condition. Running through the book, entwined with Arendt's diagnosis of totalitarianism, are clusters of general reflections, many of them developed in her later work. One of these trains of thought concerns our relation to nature and to the human world of civilization. Reflecting on victims reduced in the camps to human beasts, on stateless people discovering the emptiness of "natural" rights, on imperialist explorations of the scope for barbarism at the edge of the human world, Arendt came to the conclusion that "man's 'nature' is only 'human' in so far as it opens up to man the possibility of becoming something highly unnatural, that is, a man."[47] To be able to appear and act in our human plurality we need the frame, the limits and the setting provided by the human world of civilization, and that world is very fragile.

The fragility of the human world and the danger of losing its setting and its limits links this theme to another cluster of reflections, this time on contingency and novelty, freedom and necessity. The advent of totalitarianism itself (as of imperialism and capitalism) was evidence of the human capacity for novelty: anyone observing human affairs would do well to expect the unexpected, and this is alarming as well as encouraging. For human initiatives set off processes that are hard to stop and that may threaten or undermine the stable human world. Because the future is open and human powers are incalculable, we may destroy the world and ourselves, altering the conditions of human life to the point where we turn ourselves into beasts. "Human nature" itself is contingent and fragile, for totalitarianism and its antecedents show that we can perversely choose to embrace necessity and make ourselves and others slaves of supposedly necessary processes. Arendt saw in modern conditions a vicious spiral, in which the human world is broken apart by disruptive processes inadvertently set in motion (notably by the growth of capitalism) and that breakdown itself facilitates more destructive processes, partly because there are no longer solid institutions to stand in the way of headlong change, and partly because uprooted people who have lost their world and the common sense that goes with it are only too happy to lose themselves in the momentum of a movement. Our only hope of escape from this danger must lie in the capacity for a new beginning that lies in every human birth.[48]

Totalitarianism as portrayed by Arendt was not a plague that had descended on humanity from some external source. It was self-inflicted, the outcome of human actions and the processes they set off, and part of the story she tells is a classical tale of hubris followed by nemesis, as the quest for total power leads to destruction. While totalitarian regimes were exceptional events, they were in her eyes the most extreme example of a phenomenon that was alarmingly common in the modern world, as men set off destructive processes, and then (instead of trying to check them) do their best to speed these processes along. The most obviously dangerous examples are in science and technology.[49] Optimistic humanists suppose that what is gained by these developments is an increase in collective human power. "Everything is possible," and we can remake the world to suit ourselves. But that is to mistake action for fabrication and fail to see the significance of human plurality, which means that there is no collective subject, no "humanity" to exercise such power. All that happens when a process of this sort is set off and helped on its way is that the human world and all those in it are put at risk. Much of *The Human Condition* is concerned with the most far-reaching of these processes; economic modernization, which pulverizes the human artifice and casts off ever more "superfluous" human beings as it proceeds.

All theories of totalitarianism are dialectical, diagnosing an evil and *ipso facto* positing a good, but in most cases the dialectical opposites are conceived as rival political systems: totalitarianism casts into relief the virtues of pluralist democracy. The dialectic of Arendt's theory is more radical. What her analysis throws into relief is the political condition itself. Reading her later work in the context of *Totalitarianism* underlines the point that her account of the human condition is as much concerned with its limits as with its possibilities, including the limits and dangers of action. The only answer to the contemporary predicament lay, in her view, in affirming and putting our faith in the aspect of the human condition that totalitarianism had denied: human plurality, the fact that "not a single man but Men inhabit the earth."[50] If human beings stop worshiping necessity and recognize their own limited powers to establish "lasting institutions"[51] by making and keeping promises, they can "give laws to the world"[52] and bestow on one another rights not given by nature. The lesson totalitarianism teaches is the vital importance of politics as the arena of initiatives and agreements among plural human beings and the space in which the unique individuality denied by totalitarianism can appear.

Totalitarianism in retrospect

No one can deny that Arendt's meditations on totalitarianism produced a rich harvest of political ideas, but how does her theory look in the light of half a century of controversy and historical research? Generalized comments on the defects of "the totalitarian model" tend to pass it by.[53] Nevertheless it is open to discussion at a number of levels. With hindsight we can distinguish three different aspects of Arendt's enterprise. She was in the first place concerned to identify and describe events that called for understanding because they were new, dreadful, and baffling. Secondly she offered an account of a general phenomenon, "totalitarianism," as a way of getting an intellectual grip on those events, and thirdly she pointed to sources and precedents that might make their advent more comprehensible.

The first aspect of her theory is simply her focus on events that pose a key problem for political understanding: the perpetration of ideologically justified mass murder under two opposed regimes. Contrary to common belief she does not pretend that Nazism and Stalinism were overwhelmingly similar.[54] What strikes her is precisely the fact that in spite of the many genuine differences between them, the two regimes committed similarly incomprehensible crimes, and as far as this point is concerned she seems to be on strong ground. In retrospect, the activities of both regimes seem as appalling and baffling now as they did in 1951, and the collapse of communism has indeed focused renewed attention on the parallels.

Interestingly, a number of recent descriptions given by historians are strikingly evocative of Arendt's account. The very strangeness of her picture of totalitarianism seems more adequate than most to the events with which she was concerned, especially in relation to Nazism. One of the leading scholars in the field tells us that "her emphasis on the radicalizing, dynamic, and structure-destroying inbuilt characteristics of Nazism has been amply borne out by later research."[55] Her account of colossal human expendability for the sake of senseless motion seems to get close to the experience of those caught up in the frantic momentum of the regimes. Hans Mommsen speaks of "cumulative radicalisation and progressive self-destruction as structural determinants of the Nazi dictatorship,"[56] and observes that "Nazi politics unleashed an unbridled political, economic and military dynamic with unprecedented destructive energy, while proving incapable of creating lasting political structures." For Michael Mann, Nazism and Stalinism alike offer two of the rare examples of "regimes of continuous revolution," characterized by extraordinary levels of terror and a "persistent rejection of institutional compromise."[57] Treated simply as a piece of historical description, then, Arendt's improbable picture of a political hurricane of frantic, irrational, nihilistic motion, shapeless and incapable of anything but destruction, seems to have some scholarly support, underlining her fundamental claim that what happened challenges our understanding of politics and of human potentialities.[58]

The second aspect, her attempt to get an intellectual grip on these events through her analysis of "totalitarianism" as a general phenomenon, is much more controversial. In the (post-*Origins*) essays that contain her most explicitly theoretical accounts[59] she made it clear that she was consciously following in the footsteps of Montesquieu, adding a generalized account of a new kind of regime to the typology of "republic," "monarchy," and "despotism" he had provided two hundred years earlier.[60] Montesquieu had distinguished the familiar forms of government by analyzing the "nature" of each and the guiding "principle" that set it in motion,[61] and Arendt believed that in doing so he had shown how these age-old forms of government were anchored in different aspects of the fundamental experience of human plurality from which politics arises.[62] Her claim is that totalitarianism must also be recognized as a distinct phenomenon with a determinate nature and mode of functioning, which is despite its novelty also based on a fundamental human experience – the quintessentially modern experience of worldless "loneliness." It is clear, in other words, that when she uses the general term "totalitarianism," it does not indicate an abstract Weberian ideal-type used simply to aid research into particular cases. Instead she is engaged in an explicit attempt to recognize and understand a new phenomenon that has appeared in the world, manifested in certain aspects and activities of the Nazi and Stalinist regimes.

Vivid and haunting as her account is, it creates its own problems. The most serious is that she appears at times to reify "totalitarianism" and treat it as a subject with intentions of its own, as when she says that "totalitarianism strives not toward despotic rule over men, but toward a system in which men are superfluous."[63] How are we to make sense of this? There are undeniable difficulties of interpretation here, and the account I shall offer is to some degree conjectural.[64] However, I think there may be a way of reading such passages that is consistent with Arendt's continual insistence on the contingency of events and on human responsibility for human actions. This reading treats her theoretical analysis of totalitarianism as an account of the logic of a situation in which modern human beings (especially but not exclusively those caught up in the regimes of Hitler and Stalin) are liable to find themselves. According to the logic of this situation, and given certain aims, experiences, and deficiencies, people will tend to find themselves falling into certain patterns of behavior without consciously intending this, but also without being nudged into line by the Cunning of Reason.[65] Arendt gives color to this interpretation when she points out how remarkable it was that the very different regimes of Hitler and Stalin should have converged on the practice of similarly senseless terror;[66] when she speaks of the camps as "laboratories" carrying out "experiments" in the possibilities of domination, and when she says that totalitarian leaders only gradually discovered just what was involved in the course on which they had embarked.[67] On this reading, totalitarianism represents not so much a conscious project as the set of grooves into which people are likely to find themselves sliding if they come to politics with certain sorts of aims, experiences, and deficiencies, all of them characteristic of modernity. Foremost among the *aims* is a quest for omnipotence fueled by the belief that everything is possible and by "modern man's deep-rooted suspicion of everything he did not make himself."[68] The central *experience* is loneliness – that experience of "uprootedness and superfluousness"[69] that makes people cling to movements and to ideological logicality as a substitute for the lost world of common sense and reality. The key *deficiency* is the loss of the world itself, the stable human world of civilization that anchors human beings in a common experience of reality and hedges a space of free action with necessary limits and laws.

Reading Arendt's theory in this way perhaps enables us to see Nazism and Stalinism neither as incarnations of an alien presence, vehicles through which the monster "totalitarianism" worked its mysterious will, nor as systems deliberately created by the demonic will of larger-than-life leaders, but as horrors bizarrely disproportionate to the human stature of their perpetrators, results of a great many people taking the line of least resistance and following the logic of their situation. In these particular cases (for contingent reasons to do with the aftermath of war and revolution) loss of the world and its restraints made it particularly easy to slip into the grooves of totalitarian practices, which converge on the elimination of human plurality. Having separately discovered the power that could be generated through the organization of uprooted masses, and concurrently hit upon the core of mindless logic at the heart of ideology, Hitler and Stalin (confirmed in their belief that everything is possible) found themselves presiding over regimes of terror that reduced human beings to beasts.

An interpretation along these lines also helps to answer critics of the third aspect of her enterprise, which concerns the sources and precedents (not causes) of totalitarianism. As many commentators have pointed out, its apparent weakness is the lack of symmetry between the sources of Nazism and of Stalinism. While she may be right to point out that the Nazis drew on precedents set by the European overseas empires,[70] where Stalinism is concerned such precedents fade into insignificance beside more specific factors ranging from Russian political traditions and Leninist ideology to Stalin's paranoia and the legacy of the Civil War.[71] But if Arendt was talking not about causes but about contingent responses to the logic of a modern situation, such objections have less relevance. Although her theory was initially formulated in response to the experience of Nazism, convergent Stalinist experience could on this view only add confirmation. In revolutionary Russia just as much as in Nazi Germany, the *aim* of omnipotence, the *experience* of uprootedness, and the *deficiency* of a world that had been shattered were amply present, allowing Stalin (like Hitler) to stumble into totalitarianism.

Half a century later, similar aims, experiences, and deficiencies have not gone away. Should we therefore treat Arendt's account of totalitarianism as a diagnosis of a continuing danger? Or did her proximity to the disasters of mid-twentieth-century Europe distort her perspective? Despite Mao's Cultural Revolution, Cambodia's Year Zero, and assorted horrors from Rwanda to Bosnia, the past half century has been less grim than Arendt anticipated, especially in Europe. Part of the reason for this (again, especially in Europe) was that some people did make good use of the political capacities for forgiving and promising, and for erecting "lasting institutions" on which she laid such stress. But another very important reason for the success of these endeavors was surely the long post-war economic boom, which made it much easier for people relieved from the pressure of necessity to rebuild the human world.[72] Reassessing Arendt's hostile characterization of capitalism in the light of these developments, we may observe that in giving rise to so much economic growth capitalism may have prevented political catastrophes rather than facilitated them. She might answer, though, that the process of economic modernization does not stand still, but (aided by millions of willing servants of necessity) continues on its apparently inexorable path, destroying traditional worlds and uprooting millions, generating "superfluous" people as well as bringing unprecedented riches to others. Despite the defeat of the imperialist politics and racist ideology that provided the setting for Nazism, and the Leninist project that gave Stalin his chance, the possibility of a global recession on a scale much greater than that in the 1930s makes it unwise to assume that nothing like the political disasters of those years could happen again.

Looking around us at a time when ideological politics is discredited, and when free market liberalism has thawed frozen political systems and set them in motion, we might suppose (following more orthodox theories of totalitarianism) that the omens for the twenty-first century are encouraging. But Arendt's theory gives us no such grounds for complacency. Brilliant and baffling in equal proportions, it cannot yet be safely laid to rest.

NOTES

Some passages in this chapter have appeared in an article, "Beyond Understanding? Arendt's Account of Totalitarianism," in the first issue of the *Hannah Arendt Newsletter* (Hannover, 1999).

1 Not of course invented by Arendt: there is a useful survey of the background to her use of it in J. C. Isaac, *Arendt, Camus, and Modern Rebellion* (New Haven and London: Yale University Press, 1992), pp. 39–45.

2 Some sense (though an incomplete one) of the range of variation emerges from the pieces collected in *Totalitarianism Reconsidered*, ed. E. A. Menze (Port Washington, NY: Kennikat Press, 1981).

3 For sources of this composite picture see e.g. K. Popper, *The Open Society and its Enemies*, 2 vols., (London: Routledge, 1945); J. L.Talmon, *The Origins of Totalitarian Democracy* (Harmondsworth: Penguin, 1952); R. Aron, *Democracy and Totalitarianism* (London: Weidenfeld and Nicolson, 1965); H. Buchheim, *Totalitarian Rule: Its Nature and Characteristics* (Middletown: Wesleyan University Press, 1968); C. J. Friedrich and Z. Brzezinski, *Totalitarian Dictatorship and Autocracy* (New York: Praeger, 1967). C. Lefort, *Democracy and Political Theory* (Cambridge: Polity, 1988) and *The Political Forms of Modern Society: Bureaucracy, Democracy, Totalitarianism* (Cambridge: Polity, 1986).

4 See R. J. Bernstein, *Hannah Arendt and the Jewish Question* (Cambridge: Polity, 1996), pp. 88–100.

5 For a more detailed attempt at summary see M. Canovan, *Hannah Arendt: A Reinterpretation of her Political Thought* (Cambridge: Cambridge University Press, 1992), pp. 17–62. See also P. Hansen, *Hannah Arendt: Politics, History and Citizenship* (Cambridge: Polity, 1993), chapter 4.

6 "Understanding and Politics (The Difficulties of Understanding)", in *EU*, pp. 307–327, at p. 309.

7 This quotation is from the "Concluding Remarks" to the first edition of *OT*, published in Britain under the title *The Burden of our Time* (London: Secker and Warburg, 1951), pp. 434–435. In later editions these were replaced by the essay "Ideology and Terror."

8 *OT* (London: Allen and Unwin, 1967), p. 459.

9 *OT*, pp. 436–438.

10 Writing to Karl Jaspers in 1951, Arendt traced the appearance in their time of a "radical evil" to delusions of omnipotence on the one hand and the destruction of human plurality on the other. Arendt to Karl Jaspers, March 4, 1951, *Hannah Arendt/Karl Jaspers: Briefwechsel 1926–1969*, ed. L. Kohler and H. Saner

(Munich: Piper, 1985), p. 202. Cf. Bernstein, *Hannah Arendt and the Jewish Question*, pp. 137–153.

11 *OT*, p. 466.
12 Ibid., p. 457. Cf. "Mankind and Terror," and "On the Nature of Totalitarianism," both in *EU*, pp. 304, 354.
13 *OT*, p. 457.
14 Ibid., pp. 469–470.
15 Ibid., pp. 472–473.
16 Ibid., p. 463.
17 "On the Nature of Totalitarianism," p. 341.
18 *OT*, pp. 464–466.
19 Ibid., pp. 389–419.
20 Ibid., p. 423.
21 Ibid., p. 459.
22 Ibid., p. 456.
23 "On the Nature of Totalitarianism," p. 347.
24 *OT*, pp. 459.
25 Ibid., pp. 352–353, 438.
26 "Understanding and Politics," pp. 319–320.
27 "A Reply to Eric Voegelin," in *EU*, p. 403.
28 *OT*, pp. 373–375, 404–409. In a footnote to her 1966 essay on Rosa Luxemburg she dismissed the two as "non-persons," unworthy of full-scale biographies. *MDT* (London: Jonathan Cape, 1970), pp. 33–34. See the reflections on Arendt's treatment of totalitarian leadership in Hansen, *Hannah Arendt*, pp. 145–147; J. Stanley, "Is Totalitarianism a New Phenomenon?," in L. P. and S. K. Hinchman, eds., *Hannah Arendt: Critical Essays* (Albany: State University of New York Press, 1994), pp. 7–40, esp. pp. 12–14.
29 *OT*, pp. ix, xviii–xxi.
30 Cf. Canovan, *Hannah Arendt*, pp. 85–86.
31 *OT*, p. 183.
32 "Reply to Eric Voegelin," p. 405.
33 Arendt's account of "the decay of the nation-state" under the impact of imperialism is too intricate for summary here, but see Canovan, *Hannah Arendt*, pp. 31–35.
34 *OT*, p. 150.
35 Ibid., p. 190.
36 Ibid., p. 288.
37 "Preface to Part Two: Imperialism" (dated 1967) in *OT*, paperback edition (London: Andre Deutsch, 1986), p. xviii.
38 *OT* (1967 edition), p. 124.
39 Ibid., p. 221.
40 Ibid., p. 216.
41 "Preface to Part One: Antisemitism" (dated 1967) in *OT*, paperback edition, pp. xv–xvi.
42 "Concluding Remarks," p. 430.
43 Cf. *EJ* (London: Faber and Faber, 1963), p. 250.
44 "Concluding Remarks," p. 430.
45 Ibid., p. 437.

46 "Understanding and Politics," pp. 308, 323.
47 *OT*, p. 455.
48 Ibid., p. 479.
49 *HC*, p. 148.
50 "Concluding Remarks," p. 439.
51 *OR* (London: Faber and Faber, 1963), p. 81. *OR* consists largely of reflections on this.
52 Cf. *OT*, p. 221.
53 See for example J. Hiden and J. Farquharson, *Explaining Hitler's Germany: Historians and the Third Reich*, 2nd edn., (London: Batsford, 1989), p. 169; R. W. Davies, in *The Stalin Phenomenon*, ed. A. Nove (London: Weidenfeld and Nicolson, 1993), p. 65.
54 Thereby making irrelevant critical comments that draw attention to their differences, including some in my 1974 book on Arendt.
55 I. Kershaw, *The Nazi Dictatorship: Problems and Perspectives of Interpretation*, 3rd edn. (London: Arnold, 1993), p. 21. Ian Kershaw is more critical of her treatment of Stalinism and of her claim that totalitarianism is linked to mass society.
56 This is the title of Mommsen's chapter in I. Kershaw and M. Lewin, eds., *Stalinism and Nazism: Dictatorships in Comparison* (Cambridge: Cambridge University Press, 1997), pp. 75–87. See also Martin Broszat, quoted in Kershaw, *Nazi Dictatorship*, pp. 112–113.
57 M. Mann, "The Contradictions of Continuous Revolution," in Kershaw and Lewin, *Stalinism and Nazism*, pp. 135–157, at pp. 136, 144.
58 Kershaw, *Nazi Dictatorship*, p. 3.
59 Arendt tells us that the essay on "Ideology and Terror" contains "certain insights of a strictly theoretical nature" that she had not possessed when she completed the book itself. (*OT*, p. viii). That essay emerged out of her reflections on the "totalitarian elements in Marxism" and their connection with the tradition of Western political thought (cf. Canovan, *Hannah Arendt*, chapter 3), and it incorporates subtle shifts of emphasis which complicate the problem of interpretation.
60 *OT*, p. 467; "On the Nature of Totalitarianism," pp. 329–338.
61 Arendt observes that unlike the types of regime Montesquieu analyzed, totalitarianism does not need a "principle" of action, since its "nature" is the frantic motion of terror. Ideology, which prepares its subjects equally for the role of executioner or victim as required, substitutes for a principle of action. *OT*, p. 468.
62 Cf. Canovan, *Hannah Arendt,* pp. 206–207.
63 *OT*, p. 457. Hanna Pitkin maintains that totalitarianism-as-subject represents the first appearance in Arendt's work of what she calls "the Blob," a kind of monstrous force that seems to take over human beings and use them as its instruments. H. F. Pitkin, *The Attack of the Blob: Hannah Arendt's Concept of the Social* (Chicago: University of Chicago Press, 1998), pp. 93–96.
64 For a more extensive discussion, see Canovan, "Beyond Understanding?"
65 Or by Pitkin's "Blob."
66 "On the Nature of Totalitarianism," p. 347.
67 *OT*, p. 436.
68 "Concluding Remarks," pp. 434–435.

69 *OT*, p. 475.
70 M. Mazower, *Dark Continent: Europe's Twentieth Century* (London: Allen Lane, 1998), p. 184; A. Bullock, *Hitler and Stalin: Parallel Lives* (London: Fontana, 1993), pp. 756–757. Compare Ian Kershaw's account of "working towards the Führer" with Arendt's account of imperial servants working with the flow of expansion. I. Kershaw, "'Working towards the Führer': Reflections on the Nature of the Hitler Dictatorship," in Kershaw and Lewin, *Stalinism and Nazism*, pp. 88–106.
71 A. Nove, "Stalin and Stalinism – Some Introductory Thoughts," in Nove, *The Stalin Phenomenon*, p. 9; I. Kershaw and M. Lewin, "Afterthoughts," in Kershaw and Lewin, *Stalinism and Nazism*, pp. 354–355.
72 Cf. *OR*, pp. 62–63, 90.

2

RONALD BEINER

Arendt and nationalism

> There really is such a thing as freedom here [in America]. . . . The republic is not a vapid illusion, and the fact that there is no national state and no truly national tradition creates an atmosphere of freedom . . .
>
> letter to Karl Jaspers, January 29, 1946

> "love of the Jews" would appear to me, since I am myself Jewish, as something rather suspect. I cannot love myself or anything which I know is part and parcel of my own person.
>
> letter to Gershom Scholem, July 24, 1963

Hannah Arendt is sometimes regarded as an important source of, or inspiration behind, contemporary communitarian political thought.[1] There is some measure of truth to this view, but to think of her political theory as distinctively communitarian is more than a little misleading. For what characterizes communitarianism as a philosophical challenge to liberalism is a highlighting of how the self is constituted by collective or group identity, and an argument that insufficient concern with thick shared identities marks a central deficiency of liberal-individualist conceptions of political community. If, however, a properly communitarian argument emphasizes the collective constitution of selfhood, and the political salience of the shared identity so constituted, one would expect communitarians to exhibit significant sympathy for the politics of nationalism – a form of politics that places shared identity and thick communal attachments at the very core of its understanding of political life.[2] Yet, as we shall see, Arendt's thought shows itself to be, in this respect, pronouncedly anti-communitarian. Thus an examination of Arendt's stance toward nationalism should help to clarify those aspects of her thought that are located at the furthest remove from specifically communitarian concerns. Though the Arendtian and communitarian critiques of liberalism do overlap in important ways, there is a fundamental respect in which Arendt's criticisms of liberalism are motivated by a very different set of theoretical concerns than those characteristic of the communitarian critique.[3]

The easiest entry-point into the Arendtian view of nationalism is to look at her stance toward contemporary Zionism.[4] Zionism is a classic species of nationalist politics because it makes a shared experience of Jewish national belonging the foundation of a claim to statehood, and it makes shared nationality the pivot of an entire political universe. Arendt's political writings of the mid to late 1940s on the problem of Jewish politics sound a consistent theme. In these writings, notably in four important articles analyzing developments in the Zionist movement in the crucial lead-up to the formation of the State of Israel, Arendt presents Zionist politics as having opted for an obsolete conception of political community, and thereby betrayed both the genuine aspirations of an oppressed people and its own better impulses.[5] Arendt seems to suggest that in the epoch in which it first arose, namely the nineteenth century, nationalism offered a coherent and quite attractive political doctrine: after referring to nationalism as "this once great and revolutionary principle of the national organization of peoples," she claims that it becomes a force of evil once political circumstances change such that the nationalist principle "could no longer either guarantee true sovereignty of the people within or establish a just relationship among different peoples beyond the national borders."[6] Therefore the first thing to understand about Zionism is its ideological character, where for her ideology is more or less synonymous with the distortion of political reality. The Zionism of those "who may be truly called political Zionists," as distinct from the basically non-political idealists who comprised the *kibbutz* movement, belongs, she writes, "to those nineteenth-century political movements that carried ideologies, *Weltanschauungen*, keys to history, in their portmanteaus . . . it shares with [socialism or nationalism] the sad fate of having outlived their political conditions only to stalk together like living ghosts amid the ruins of our times."[7]

Arendt's essential view of Zionism is that it is a "sectarian ideology," employing the "categories and methods of the nineteenth century," and that it needs urgently to reconsider "its whole obsolete set of doctrines."[8] Herzl, she suggests, was a political thinker shaped by the political realities of the nineteenth century, and therefore his political vision "could hardly express itself in any other form than that of the nation-state. In his period, indeed, the claim for national self-determination of peoples was almost self-evident justice as far as the oppressed peoples of Europe were concerned, and so there was nothing wrong or absurd in a demand made by Jews for the same kind of emancipation and freedom."[9] This being so, Herzl could not be blamed for having failed to foresee "that the whole structure of sovereign national states, great and small, would crumble within another fifty years."[10]

The main problem with the Zionist movement was the unfortunate fact of bad timing: Zionism "did not ask for a state at a time when it might have been granted by everybody, but did ask for one only when the whole concept of national sovereignty had become a mockery."[11] Again, Arendt insists that nationalism is "outdated" because what has been witnessed in our time is "the catastrophic decline of the national-state system": Europe has come to the unavoidable realization "that the national state is neither capable of protecting the existence of the nation nor able to guarantee the sovereignty of the people."[12] These passages were written before Zionism achieved its objective of securing its own nation-state, and more than four decades before the end of the Cold War gave dramatically new impetus to the nation-state principle. Arendt claims that the way in which Herzl formulated his demand for a Jewish state, namely by an appeal to national self-determination, shows just how time-bound his political thinking was.[13] In retrospect, it is hard not to conclude that Arendt was much more time-bound in her dismissal of the nation-state principle than Herzl was in his embrace of it.

Central to her analysis is the conception of a kind of Zionism, seized on by intellectual elites, that involved kowtowing to Great Powers and selling out to imperialist potentates in the hopes of securing a quick and easy shortcut to a European-style nation-state in Palestine.[14] She thinks that twentieth-century Zionists fell for "the delusion of nationhood," in the sense of a political ideal that was no longer meaningful, and that Zionist leaders put themselves at the service of imperialist interests in order to reassure themselves that the delusion was still an attainable goal.[15] To this she opposes what she thinks could have been a more authentically revolutionary movement of Jewish political emancipation (although she is vague about the content of this more revolutionary Zionist politics).[16] She writes that "all those national-revolutionary movements of small European peoples whose situation was equally one of social as of national oppression" embodied a healthy amalgam of socialism and nationalism; but in the case of Zionism, there was from the outset an unfortunate split "between the social-revolutionary forces which had sprung from the east European masses" and the Herzlian ambition for strictly *national* emancipation.[17]

The historically dominant Zionism was an elite contrivance that passed over "the genuine national revolutionary movement which sprang from the Jewish masses."[18] "The alternative to the road that Herzl marked out, and Weizmann followed through to the bitter end, would have been to organize the Jewish people in order to negotiate on the basis of a great revolutionary movement. This would have meant an alliance with all progressive forces in Europe"; what was actually unfolded in the Zionist movement of the first half of the twentieth century was the dismaying "spectacle of a national movement that, starting out with such an idealistic élan, sold out at the very first moment to the powers-that-be – that felt no solidarity with other oppressed peoples whose cause, though historically otherwise conditioned, was essentially the same – that endeavored even in the morning-dream of freedom and justice to compromise with the most evil forces of our time by taking advantage of imperialistic interests."[19] In short, "the true revolutionary possibilities of Zionism for Jewish life" came to be sacrificed by the machinations of the Zionist leadership.[20] All of this appears to suggest that, in Arendt's view, there was the possibility of a kind of Jewish nationalist politics that would be genuinely emancipatory, focused on a broader social-revolutionary agenda, but that these possibilities were sabotaged by the sell-out mentality of Zionist leaders: contingent political choices were made that channeled the movement into a course of political action defined by a more narrowly nationalist ideology. In a sense, and one not without paradox, it more or less follows from Arendt's argument that nationalism was the undoing of Zionism.[21]

Another constant theme of her Jewish political writings is the disastrousness of the ambition for a uni-national state, and not just the desirability of, but the imperative need for, Jewish–Arab federalism. This line of criticism clearly cuts more deeply at the very heart of a nationalist politics. The essential thrust of Arendt's critique of Zionism in these writings is that instead of preoccupying themselves with how their political project stood in relation to the Great Powers of the time, Zionists ought to have paid more attention to the problem of building relations of trust with their Arab neighbours. Indeed, the "good" Zionists (supported politically by Arendt) did just that. The problem is that the good Zionists (notably, the Ihud group led by Judah L. Magnes) were marginal to the main Zionist movement, and became steadily more marginal. As Palestinian Jewry moved closer to statehood, Arendt's unhappiness with the Zionist project increased rather than diminished. In the wake of the UN's 1947 endorsement of the partition of Palestine and formation of a Jewish state, she remained opposed to partition and opposed to creation of a Jewish state.[22] She deeply regretted the evaporation of a non-Zionist opposition within Jewish politics that would formulate alternative political visions.[23] "With the support of a Jewish state by the great powers, the non-Zionists believed themselves refuted by reality itself."[24]

Obviously, with the unfolding of events, there came a time when Arendt had to recognize that her own non-Zionism was refuted by reality, but in 1948 she was still a non-Zionist.[25] Part of the story here, of course, was simply fear about wagering all on a Jewish–Arab war that the Jews after all might have lost, with incalculable consequences for the identity and even continued existence of the Jewish people; the stakes were simply too high to risk another (post-Holocaust) catastrophe.[26] And even if the Jews were to win the war, the creation of a garrison state surrounded by a sea of Arab hostility would consume all Jewish energies, and therefore undo what was already most impressive in the accomplishments of the Jewish community in Palestine, such as the *kibbutz* movement.[27] It is in this sense that she writes: "at this moment and under present circumstances a Jewish state can only be erected at the price of the Jewish homeland."[28] However, it seems fair to categorize these as prudential considerations: weighing up risks, balancing gains against losses; one might say that alongside (or perhaps underlying) these judgments, Arendt has a more principled basis for resisting the idea of a Jewish nation-state. She is profoundly committed to Jewish–Arab federalism, and even as Jewish–Arab warfare escalated in Palestine, she refused to give up on the notion that a kind of political community could be constituted in Palestine founded on concrete experiences of Jewish–Arab friendship and cooperation. Arendt concludes her article "To Save the Jewish Homeland" with a statement of principles that lays out clearly enough her alternative (non-Zionist) vision of Palestine: "[t]he real goal of the Jews in Palestine is the building up of a Jewish homeland. This goal must never be sacrificed to the pseudo-sovereignty of a Jewish state"; "[t]he independence of Palestine can be achieved only on a solid basis of Jewish–Arab cooperation."[29] The ultimate goal is a "federated structure [resting on] Jewish–Arab community councils": "[l]ocal self-government and mixed Jewish–Arab municipal and rural councils, on a small scale and as numerous as possible."[30] Again, part of the argument is a prudential one: Palestine is so small a territory that partition would leave two political communities, neither of which would be really viable and capable of meaningful independence.[31] "National sovereignty which so long had been the very symbol of free national development has become the greatest danger to national survival for small nations."[32] However, the deeper argument is straightforwardly normative: the world needs to be shown that two very different peoples are capable of cooperating within the compass of a bi-national political community.[33]

As seems entirely fitting for works of political journalism, Arendt's arguments appear highly historicized and contextual. If uni-national statehood is a disaster for small nations contesting a crowded territory, does nationalism continue to be a legitimate principle for large nations commanding a more expansive territory? If nationalist leaders were less interested in cutting deals with the big powers of the day and were more concerned with democratic mobilization, would that redeem their nationalism? If nationalism shows itself to be a species of ideological delusion because it no longer fits the political realities of twentieth-century political life, does that mean that the argument against nationalism is a historically specific one rather than one at the level of universal principles? The core of Arendt's challenge to the nation-state concerns its alleged obsolescence.[34] But as a political thinker who herself put abundant theoretical energies into championing arguably obsolete forms of political community, it is far from clear why this historicist standard should be normatively decisive.[35]

It seems clear that Arendt wanted Jewish politics but not Jewish nationalism, wanted a Jewish homeland but not a Jewish nation-state. To what extent are these the theoretical judgments of a political philosopher as opposed to the "merely" political judgments of a political onlooker and somewhat engaged political actor? To be sure, Arendt felt only a weak identity as a political philosopher, and the badge of the political philosopher was one she was reluctant to wear.[36] Be that as it may, if we seek a more general theoretical ground for her anti-nationalism, we ought to turn to her analyses of national movements and the nation-state in the middle volume of her towering historical-theoretical work, *The Origins of Totalitarianism*. The work as a whole is directed at showing how modern ideologies disfigure political life, and Arendt is in no doubt that nationalism counts as a full-fledged ideology in her culpable sense.

Arendt's main discussion of nationalism occurs in the context of a narrative explaining how the late-nineteenth-century to early-twentieth-century pan-movements (Pan-German and Pan-Slav) contributed to the horrors of the totalitarian movements. Her basic idea is that there is an intrinsic and deep tension (if not a contradiction)[37] between "nation" and "state" in the synthetic idea of a nation-state, and when confronted with the evil dynamism of the pan-movements and then full-blown totalitarianism, this tension was intensified to the point where the nation-state itself as it were exploded. According to Arendt, the pan-movements used claims to national rights to self-determination as "a comfortable smoke screen" for national-imperial expansionism.[38] While these movements borrowed their means of self-legitimation from nationalist ideology by claiming "to unite all people of similar folk origin, independent of history and no matter where they happened to live," they in fact embodied a "contempt for the narrowness of the nation-state."[39] Once the existing state system proved itself unable to contain this imperialistic nationalism, the way was clear for totalitarian movements to finish off the job of demolishing the very idea of a nation-state that claims to offer protection for its national citizens and respects the right of other nation-states to do likewise. The nation-state (with its defining idea of nation-based citizenship) both contributed to, and was ultimately the helpless victim of, much more dangerous and predatory ideologies that simply trampled over the mere state. The simplest way in which to encapsulate

Arendt's analysis is to say that the pairing of the state with the nation sets in motion a dialectic whose eventual outcome is the destruction of the state as a moral-juridical shelter for its citizens. Nationalism is a pathology of citizenship that, having subordinated the state to the idea of the nation, generates a further pathology in a more expansionary notion of nationhood surpassing the boundaries (and therefore the moral limits) of the state: with this double pathology, the nation-state itself gets utterly subverted. Therefore, following through this evil dialectic requires us to rethink the whole idea of the nation-state (and ideally, to conceive other non-national forms of political association as a basis for citizenship).

Having offered a quick overview, let us now look more closely at how Arendt understands this tension between state and nation at the heart of the nation-state idea. Arendt begins with a contrast between what she calls "Western nationalism" and what she calls "tribal nationalism" – corresponding more or less to what is now standardly referred to as the distinction between civic nationalism and ethnic nationalism.[40]

> The nation-state, with its claim to popular representation and national sovereignty, as it had developed since the French revolution through the nineteenth century, was the result of a combination of two factors that were still separate in the eighteenth century and remained separate in Russia and Austria-Hungary: nationality and state. Nations entered the scene of history and were emancipated when peoples had acquired a consciousness of themselves as cultural and historical entities, and of their territory as a permanent home, where history had left its visible traces, whose cultivation was the product of the common labor of their ancestors and whose future would depend upon the course of a common civilization.[41]

The fact that the process of fusing state and nationality commences with the French Revolution's assertion of popular sovereignty explains why Arendt consistently refers to France as the "*nation par excellence*"[42] (that is, the paradigm of Western nationalism, not tribal nationalism). "Sociologically the nation-state was the body politic of the European emancipated peasant classes . . . Western nationalism . . . was the product of firmly rooted *and* emancipated peasant classes."[43] Conversely, "in the Eastern and Southern European regions the establishment of nation-states failed because they could not fall back upon firmly rooted peasant classes."[44] In these regions of Europe, the "peasant classes had not struck deep roots in the country and were not on the verge of emancipation . . . consequently, their national quality appeared to be much more a portable private matter, inherent in their very personality, than a matter of public concern and civilization . . . they had no country, no state, no historic achievement to show but could only point to themselves, and that meant, at best, to their language . . . at worst, to their

Slavic, or Germanic, or God-knows-what soul."[45] With the constant changing of frontiers and continuous migration of populations, "no conditions existed for the realization of the Western national trinity of people-territory-state."[46] Tribal nationalism, she concludes, "grew out of this atmosphere of rootlessness."[47] (And it was this sort of nationalism, in turn, that provided a breeding-ground for totalitarianism.)

Leaving aside this pathological variant of nationalism, Arendt sees still grave problems in the nation-state idea even in its best (that is, Western) version:

> [T]he state inherited as its supreme function the protection of all inhabitants in its territory no matter what their nationality, and was supposed to act as a supreme legal institution. The tragedy of the nation-state was that the people's rising national consciousness interfered with these functions. In the name of the will of the people the state was forced to recognize only 'nationals' as citizens, to grant full civil and political rights only to those who belonged to the national community by right of origin and fact of birth. This meant that the state was partly transformed from an instrument of law into an instrument of the nation.[48]

In short, the state was conquered by the nation – that is, the nation, in appropriating the state for national purposes, diverted the state from functions that are proper to it *qua* state. Arendt relates this development politically to the downfall of absolute monarchy and sociologically to the rise of classes: "The only remaining bond between the citizens of a nation-state without a monarch to symbolize their essential community, seemed to be national, that is, common origin . . . [and] in a century when every class and section in the population was dominated by class or group interest, the interest of the nation as a whole was supposedly guaranteed in a common origin, which sentimentally expressed itself in nationalism."[49] She also relates it to liberal individualism, and to a simultaneous centralization of state administration: "It seemed to be the will of the nation that the state protect it from the consequences of its social atomization . . . only a strongly centralized administration . . . could counterbalance the centrifugal forces constantly produced in a class-ridden society. Nationalism, then, became the precious cement for binding together a centralized state and an atomized society."[50]

What ensues is what Arendt characterizes as a "secret conflict between state and nation" that was coeval with "the very birth of the modern nation-state, when the French Revolution combined the declaration of the Rights of Man with the demand for national sovereignty":

> The same essential rights were at once claimed as the inalienable heritage of all human beings *and* as the specific heritage of specific nations, the same nation was at once declared to be subject to laws, which supposedly would

> flow from the Rights of Man, *and* sovereign, that is, bound by no universal law and acknowledging nothing superior to itself. The practical outcome of this contradiction was that from then on human rights were protected and enforced only as national rights and that the very institution of a state, whose supreme task was to protect and guarantee man his rights as man, as citizen and as national, lost its legal, rational appearance and could be interpreted by the romantics as the nebulous representative of a 'national soul' which through the very fact of its existence was supposed to be beyond or above the law. National sovereignty, accordingly, lost its original connotation of freedom of the people and was being surrounded by a pseudomystical aura of lawless arbitrariness.[51]

Nationalism, she concludes, "is essentially the expression of this perversion of the state into an instrument of the nation and the identification of the citizen with the member of the nation."[52]

Crucial to this whole analysis is the idea of "the conquest of the state by the nation,"[53] a notion that Arendt draws from J.-T. Delos, and in a highly sympathetic review of Delos's two-volume work *La Nation*, Arendt provides additional formulations of the state–nation tension.[54] She writes: "The fundamental political reality of our time is determined by two facts: on the one hand, it is based upon 'nations' and, on the other, it is permanently disturbed and thoroughly menaced by 'nationalism'"; therefore we need "to find a political principle which would prevent nations from developing nationalism and would thereby lay the fundamentals of an international community, capable of presenting and protecting the civilization of the modern world."[55] Nation and state represent opposing principles:

> a people becomes a nation when [it arrives at a historical consciousness of itself]; as such it is attached to the soil which is the product of past labor and where history has left its traces. It represents the 'milieu' into which man is born, a closed society to which one belongs by right of birth. The state on the other hand is an open society, ruling over a territory where its power protects and makes the law. As a legal institution, the state knows only citizens no matter of what nationality; its legal order is open to all who happen to live on its territory.[56]

Here, contrary to how Arendt elsewhere depicts the relation between the state and the nation, it is suggested that it is the "open" power-seeking of the state that encourages expansionary ambitions on the part of the nation, whereas the nation, as a "closed" community, is wedded to its own territory. Hence "[t]he old dream of the innate pacifism of the nations whose very liberation would guarantee an era of peace and welfare was not all humbug."[57] However, reversing direction, she immediately goes on to present the nation as the more sinister partner in this unhappy alliance:

> The conquest of the state through the nation started with the declaration of the sovereignty of the nation. This was the first step transforming the state into an instrument of the nation which finally has ended in those totalitarian forms of nationalism in which all laws and the legal institutions of the state as such are interpreted as a means for the welfare of the nation. It is therefore quite erroneous to see the evil of our times in a deification of the state. It is the nation which has usurped the traditional place of God and religion.[58]

So there seems to be a genuine vacillation here on the question of whether the state corrupts the nation or the nation corrupts the state. In any case, the fusion of state and nation is a fatal one, with the imperialistic ambitions of the state henceforth claimed (and with greater potential for evil) on behalf of the nation.

"There is little doubt that civilization will be lost if after destroying the first forms of totalitarianism we do not succeed in solving the basic problems of our political structures."[59] Arendt's reference to "first" forms of totalitarianism clearly implies that the process whereby nationalism turned into fascism, the nation-state turned into the totalitarian state, can be replicated unless the nationalist bacillus can be neutralized. How can this be done? The key here is once again to drive a wedge between state and nation: "The state, far from being identical with the nation, is the supreme protector of a law which guarantees man his rights as man, his rights as citizen and his rights as a national . . . Of these rights, only the rights of man and citizen are primary rights whereas the rights of nationals are derived and implied in them."[60] "While these distinctions between the citizen and the national, between the political order and the national one, would take the wind out of the sails of nationalism, by putting man as a national in his right place in public life, the larger political needs of our civilization . . . would be met with the idea of federation. Within federated structures, nationality would become a personal status rather than a territorial one."[61]

In her 1967 preface to volume II of *The Origins of Totalitarianism*, Arendt states that the volume on *Imperialism* "tells the story of the disintegration of the nation state."[62] What does it mean to assert that the nation-state as such has disintegrated? Arendt attempts to answer this question in an important chapter entitled "The Decline of the Nation-State and the End of the Rights of Man."[63] The most obvious problem with a system of nation-states in Europe following the First World War was that with all the minorities who could not possibly be accommodated by the nation-state principle, one had a vast number of "nationally frustrated peoples."[64] And since the nation-state model furnished by the French Revolution had promulgated the notion of the inseparability of human rights and national sovereignty, the tens of millions of nationless people in Europe were also in principle rightless, because the nation-state principle had left them without an effective political guarantor of their rights. An equally (or in fact much more) grave problem was the situation of those suffering wholesale population transfers, peoples who were "repatriated" without a national home where they could be properly patriated.[65] If national minorities were "half stateless," the masses of deported refugees and de-naturalized aliens were completely stateless with respect to the protection of fundamental rights.[66] The idea of human rights that was born with the French Revolution was intended to be universal. But the states that embraced these doctrines of human rights were decidedly not universal, and the evolution of the state into the nation-state gave a correspondingly national definition to the scope of the community whose human rights were to be enforced. Those who found themselves lacking their own nation-states (again, a considerable proportion of the population of Europe) also discovered that "universal" human rights had a very insecure application to them, to put it mildly. The Rights of Man signified an assertion of ultimate human sovereignty, but

> man had hardly appeared as a completely emancipated, completely isolated being who carried his dignity within himself without reference to some larger encompassing order, when he disappeared again into a member of a people. From the beginning the paradox involved in the declaration of inalienable human rights was that it reckoned with an 'abstract' human being who seemed to exist nowhere . . . The whole question of human rights, therefore, was quickly and inextricably blended with the question of national emancipation; only the emancipated sovereignty of the people, of one's own people, seemed to be able to insure them. As mankind, since the French Revolution, was conceived in the image of a family of nations, it gradually became self-evident that the people, and not the individual, was the image of man.[67]

> The Rights of Man, after all, had been defined as "inalienable" because they were supposed to be independent of all governments; but it turned out that the moment human beings lacked their own government . . . no authority was left to protect them and no institution was willing to guarantee them.[68]

This "identification of the rights of man with the rights of peoples"[69] did not escape the attention of those who it left undefended, namely the minorities and the stateless. They themselves became convinced "that loss of national rights was identical with loss of human rights, that the former inevitably entailed the latter. The more they were excluded from right in any form, the more they tended to look for a reintegration into a national, into their own national community."[70] The widespread condition of degraded rights for minorities and rightlessness for the stateless in the twentieth century (continuing right up to our own day) establishes beyond a possibility of dispute the legitimacy of those anxieties. Thus the lesson of the ghastly politics of our century seems to be that supposedly universal human rights are meaningless unless rooted in a national community that is committed to enforcing these rights for its co-nationals; the fundamental "right to have rights"[71] presupposes some particular state agency that will guarantee human rights only for those it considers to be properly its own members. "[L]oss of national rights in all instances [entailed] the loss of human rights."[72]

Here there seems a real paradox in Arendt's argument. She argues that the principal human right is the right to have rights, which means the right to have a (national) state that will assume responsibility for guarding and enforcing one's rights. Thus (despite the fact that Arendt presents herself as a strong critic of a nationality-based conception of the state, and is committed to the notion of its obsolescence), the logic of her argument would seem to dictate a return to the nation-state rather than its supersession.[73] To the extent that Arendt has an answer to this paradox, her answer seems to be that given our experience in the twentieth century, with its spectacle of the "disintegration" of the nation-state in the face of proto-totalitarian and totalitarian challenges, the only way the state can be made a safe repository of human rights for its citizens is by taking the nation out of the nation-state.[74] (Arendt clearly believed that the United States as a political community had achieved this condition of nationless statehood.)[75] The way to do this is by meshing the state in a web of federal relations, both below and beyond the state, therefore getting away from the state as a site of *sovereignty*. Insofar as nationalism as an ideology is bound to the claim to national sovereignty, this reconfiguration of the state depends upon liberating ourselves from the nationalist legacy.[76]

It seems that fundamentally what Arendt meant by the decline and "disintegration" of the nation-state is that states organized on a principle of national belonging had, by their treatment of national minorities and stateless refugees, so thoroughly discredited themselves in the twentieth century that human beings would be obliged to conjure up some quite different way of conceiving citizenship. But a moral critique of the conduct of various nation-states cannot lead to a conclusion concerning the historical prospects of this kind of state: a catalog of the sins committed by the twentieth-century nation-state does not by itself guarantee the historical supersession of this idea of the state, or cancel out the widespread desire of people, rightly or wrongly, to define their citizenship in terms of shared nationhood.[77]

To conclude, let me offer two reflections on Hannah Arendt's theoretical legacy in the light of that watershed year, 1989. On the one hand, 1989 redeemed Arendt's prescient claim in *On Revolution* that revolution "will stay with us into the foreseeable future . . . this century . . . most certainly will remain a century of revolutions."[78] On the other hand, the increased salience of nation-state politics after 1989 (each defeat of communism became a triumph for nationalism) underscores the inadequacy of her theoretical response to nationalist politics. Like generations of liberals and Marxists before her, Hannah Arendt was too quick to assume that the nation-state had already been tossed on the dust-heap of history.[79] Given her general immunity to historicist arguments, it seems surprising that we need to make the following point with respect to her thinking concerning nationalism: if nationalism strikes one as offering a deficient basis for modern politics, one must respond to its theoretical and political challenge with a normative counter-argument rather than with an historicist trust that the sun has finally set on the nation-state.

NOTES

1 For instance, see Bernard Yack, *The Problems of a Political Animal* (Berkeley: University of California Press, 1993), p. 13, where Arendt's misleading account of Aristotle is connected to contemporary communitarian concerns. See also Stephen Holmes, *The Anatomy of Antiliberalism* (Cambridge, MA: Harvard University Press, 1993), pp. xi–xii; and Thomas L. Pangle, *The Spirit of Modern Republicanism* (Chicago: University of Chicago Press, 1988), pp. 48–49.

2 Charles Taylor and Michael Walzer both offer arguments intended to encourage greater sympathy for nationalist politics: see, for instance, their chapters in *Theorizing Nationalism* (ed. R. Beiner [Albany: State University of New York Press, 1999], pp. 219–245 and 205–217 respectively), as well as Walzer, "Nation and Universe," *The Tanner Lectures on Human Values XI: 1990*, ed. Grethe B. Peterson (Salt Lake City: University of Utah Press, 1990), pp. 509–556. While Michael Sandel rarely discusses contemporary nationalism (see *Democracy's Discontent* [Cambridge, MA: Harvard University Press, 1996], pp. 338–350, for a highly abbreviated discussion), there is good reason to think that his view of nationalism would be similar to those of Taylor and Walzer. Alasdair MacIntyre, too, is reticent on the question of nationalism, but his view seems to be that national sentiment is good whereas the modern state, and therefore the nation-state, is bad. It goes without saying that it is hard to approve of nationalism if one disapproves of the nation-state. Hence MacIntyre's anti-statism cancels out any sympathy for nationalism he might otherwise display.

3 Bonnie Honig, in a roundtable exchange with George Kateb published in *Hannah Arendt and Leo Strauss*, ed. P. G. Kielmansegg, H. Mewes, amd E. Glaser-Schmidt (Cambridge: Cambridge University Press, 1995), p. 186, rightly draws attention to Arendt's anxieties about identity-based politics and her hostility towards a politics geared to group identities. Cf. Margaret Canovan, *Hannah Arendt: A Reinterpretation of Her Political Thought* (Cambridge: Cambridge University Press, 1992), pp. 243–249, where Canovan argues (again rightly) that what Arendt desired was an understanding of citizenship that was *not* communitarian.

4 For a very clear and helpful summary of Arendt's critical responses to Zionism, see Richard J. Bernstein, *Hannah Arendt and the Jewish Question* (Cambridge, MA: MIT Press, 1996), chapter 5.
5 These four articles are: "Zionism Reconsidered" (1945); "The Jewish State: Fifty Years After" (1946); "To Save the Jewish Homeland" (1948); and "Peace or Armistice in the Near East?" (written in 1948 but published in 1950). They are re-published in Arendt, *JP*.
6 Arendt, *JP*, p. 141.
7 Ibid., p. 140. Cf. Arendt, *OR* (New York: Viking Press, 1965), p. 1: "the nineteenth-century ideologies – such as nationalism and internationalism, capitalism and imperialism, socialism and communism . . . though still invoked by many as justifying causes, have lost contact with the major realities of our world."
8 Arendt, *JP*, p. 163.
9 Ibid., p. 173.
10 Ibid.
11 Ibid.
12 Ibid., p. 161.
13 Ibid., p. 173. In a letter to Karl Jaspers dated August 22, 1960, Arendt seems to reject the principle of national self-determination: "self-determination as a right of nations applies to constitutional form and domestic political arrangements and by no means needs to include the so-called right to national self-determination"; the context is a discussion of German reunification (*Hannah Arendt–Karl Jaspers: Correspondence, 1926–1969*, ed. L. Kohler and H. Saner, trans. R. Kimber and R. Kimber [New York: Harcourt Brace Jovanovich, 1992], p. 398).
14 Arendt, *JP*, pp. 132–133: "Nationalism is bad enough when it trusts in nothing but the rude force of the nation. A nationalism that necessarily and admittedly depends upon the force of a foreign nation is certainly worse. This is the threatened fate of Jewish nationalism."
15 Ibid., p. 162. Cf. ibid., pp. 182–183.
16 Cf. Bernstein, *Hannah Arendt and the Jewish Question*, p. 112. As an alternative to Herzlian Zionism, Arendt counterposes the Jewish nationalism of Bernard Lazare: see "Herzl and Lazare" (1942), in *JP*, pp. 125–130; also pp. 171, and 153, where she characterizes Lazare as a kind of Zionist who "trusted the Jewish people for the necessary political strength of will to achieve freedom instead of being transported to freedom" and who "dared to side with the revolutionary forces in Europe."
17 Arendt, *JP*, pp. 136–137.
18 Ibid., p. 142.
19 Ibid., pp. 152–153. She immediately adds that one "should in fairness consider how exceptionally difficult the conditions were for the Jews who, in contrast to other peoples, did not even possess the territory from which to start their fight for freedom." This concession considerably blunts what would otherwise seem an extremely harsh assessment of the Zionist movement.
20 Ibid., p. 149.
21 In "Peace or Armistice in the Near East?" Arendt suggests that there have been nationalist and non-nationalist versions of Zionism. The Herzlian tradition, which ultimately prevailed, offered classic nineteenth-century nationalist

ideology, and would settle for nothing less than "a full-fledged sovereign Jewish state." A counter-tradition, which Arendt associates with Ahad Ha'am and which, she argues, had its finest fruition in the *kibbutzim* and the founding of the Hebrew University, was more interested in Palestine as a Jewish cultural center; the latter tradition resisted "the crude slogans of a Balkanized nationalism," and rejected a vision of Palestine based on "ethnic homogeneity and national sovereignty" (ibid., p. 213).

22 Subsequent to the UN's partition vote, the United States backtracked and instead supported trusteeship for Palestine. Arendt agreed with the (revised) US policy: "trusteeship over the whole of Palestine would postpone and possibly prevent partition of the country" (ibid., p. 190). Trusteeship would also "have the advantage of preventing the establishment of sovereignty whose only sovereign right would be to commit suicide" (ibid.).

23 Ibid., pp. 184–185.

24 Ibid., p. 184.

25 Even *after* the creation of the State of Israel, Arendt continues to follow Magnes and the Ihud group in arguing for a bi-national Palestinian Confederation: ibid., p. 218.

26 Ibid., p. 185.

27 Ibid., pp. 187–188. Arendt writes that "loss of the kibbutzim [in the event of Jewish defeat] . . . would be one of the severest of blows to the hopes of all those, Jewish and non-Jewish, who have not and never will make their peace with present-day society and its standards. For this Jewish experiment in Palestine holds out hope of solutions that will be acceptable and applicable, not only in individual cases, but also for the large mass of men everywhere whose dignity and very humanity are in our time so seriously threatened by the pressures of modern life and its unsolved problems" (p. 186). Cf. p. 214.

28 Ibid., p. 188.

29 Ibid., p. 192.

30 Ibid., pp. 191, 192.

31 Ibid., pp. 190–191. According to Arendt, what prevented both sides from recognizing the advantages for each of interdependence was *ideology*: on the Jewish side, "a Central European ideology of nationalism and tribal thinking"; on the Arab side, an anti-Western ideology that romanticized under-development (pp. 208–209).

32 Ibid., p. 222.

33 Ibid., p. 186. Cf. the statement Arendt quotes from Judah Magnes: "What a boon to mankind it would be if the Jews and Arabs of Palestine were to strive together in friendship and partnership to make this Holy Land into a thriving peaceful Switzerland . . . A bi-national Palestine could become a beacon of peace in the world" (p. 212). In "Peace or Armistice in the Near East?" Arendt, following Magnes, goes on to argue that federal or confederal arrangements in Palestine should be the stepping-stone to a larger regional federation: "Nationalist insistence on absolute sovereignty in such small countries as Palestine, Syria, Lebanon, Iraq, Transjordan, Saudi Arabia and Egypt can lead only to the Balkanization of the whole region and its transformation into a battlefield for the conflicting interests of the great powers to the detriment of

all authentic national interests. In the long run, the only alternative to Balkanization is a regional federation" (p. 217).

34 Cf. K. R. Minogue, *Nationalism* (London: Methuen, 1969), p. 21. Minogue quotes Hans J. Morgenthau – "That the traditional nation-state is obsolescent in view of the technological and military conditions of the contemporary world is obvious" – and then asks, "But is it obvious that the nation-state is obsolescent?"

35 In other contexts, Arendt is rightly suspicious of the appeal to historical trends as a basis for political principles. The problem is acutely highlighted when Arendt celebrates Russia's "entirely new and successful approach to nationality conflicts, its new form of organizing different peoples on the basis of national equality," and urges that this be looked up to as a model for "every political and national movement in our times" (Arendt, *JP*, p. 149). One may indeed sympathize with the Soviet ideal of forging a multinational federation, but the idea that one can bank on history turning its back on the nation-state turns out to be hopeless – the nation-state has a habit of bouncing back!

36 See Hannah Arendt, *EU*, p. 2.

37 See Hannah Arendt, *Imperialism* [Part II of *OT*] (New York: Harcourt, Brace & World, 1968), bottom of p. 110, where she refers to the state-nation relationship as a contradiction.

38 Ibid., p. 106.

39 Ibid., pp. 103–104.

40 This distinction, as the basis for a normative rather than sociological argument, has recently come under a lot of fire from political philosophers: see, for instance, the chapters by Bernard Yack, Kai Nielsen, and Will Kymlicka in Beiner, ed., *Theorizing Nationalism*, pp. 103–118, 119–130, 131–140 respectively. For criticism directed at Arendt's version of the distinction, see Joan Cocks, "On Nationalism: Frantz Fanon, 1925–1961; Rosa Luxemburg, 1971–1919; and Hannah Arendt, 1906–1975," in Bonnie Honig, ed., *Feminist Interpretations of Hannah Arendt* (University Park, PA: Pennsylvania State University Press, 1995), p. 237.

41 Arendt, *Imperialism*, p. 109.

42 See, for instance, ibid., p. 156; Hannah Arendt, *Antisemitism* [Part I of *OT*] (New York: Harcourt, Brace & World, 1968), pp. 50, 79.

43 Arendt, *Imperialism*, pp. 109–110.

44 Ibid., p. 109.

45 Ibid., pp. 111–112.

46 Ibid., p. 112.

47 Ibid. She goes on: "Rootlessness was the true source of that 'enlarged tribal consciousness' which actually meant that members of these peoples had no definite home but felt at home wherever other members of their 'tribe' happened to live." Hence the pan-movements, and their successors, the totalitarian movements, had no inclination to respect existing state boundaries. The more Arendt thinks about the nation-state in juxtaposition to these tribal nationalisms, the more sympathetic she becomes to the bounded (Western) nation-state: see ibid., contrasting the pan-movements with "national emancipation" within the "bounds of a national community," "the true national liberation movements of small peoples." Nationalism as such is a perversion of the state, but the

authentic nation-state, "even in its perverted form, [by comparison with the tribal nationalism of the pan-movements] remained a legal institution, [so that] nationalism was controlled by some law, and . . . was limited by definite boundaries" (p. 111).

48 Ibid., p. 110.

49 Ibid.

50 Ibid., p. 111.

51 Ibid., pp. 110–111; cf. pp. 152, 155, 170–172. See Istvan Hont, "The Permanent Crisis of a Divided Mankind: 'Contemporary Crisis of the Nation State' in Historical Perspective," *Political Studies* 42 (1994): 206–217. Apropos Arendt's critique of nationalism, Hont suggests that Arendt is really driven by a cosmopolitan longing "to see the world as a brotherhood or family of republics" (p. 216); therefore the ultimate target of her critique is an idea of sovereignty that is inherent to the concept of the modern state (with or without the nation as the seat of sovereignty). Accordingly, despite the misleading way in which she appears to put the chief blame on the nation, "her objection to *national* sovereignty is really a complaint about the notion of modern sovereignty *tout court*" (p. 209). It is significant in this connection that in *OR* (see for instance p. 152), Arendt becomes very critical of sovereignty as such – and correspondingly, becomes much more critical of Jacobin republicanism, with its own claims to sovereignty (cf. Canovan, *Hannah Arendt*, p. 32, n. 70). In "Zionism Reconsidered," Arendt had referred to "the grand French idea of the sovereignty of the people," and complained that, owing to Zionism's "uncritical acceptance of German-inspired nationalism," this grand idea was "perverted into the nationalist claims to autarchical existence" (*JP*, p. 156). Clearly, by the time she writes *On Revolution*, Arendt is no longer so enamored of the French Revolution's idea of popular sovereignty, which she comes to associate with the nationalist idea of an integral national will (see *OR*, pp. 154–155). With respect to the latter claim, William E. Scheuerman argues that Arendt carries her repudiation of French revolutionary thought much too far: see "Revolutions and Constitutions: Hannah Arendt's Challenge to Carl Schmitt," in David Dyzenhaus, ed., *Law as Politics: Carl Schmitt's Critique of Liberalism* (Durham, NC: Duke University Press, 1998), pp. 252–280. A pivotal text, both for Arendt and for her critics, in interpreting the kind of nationalism inscribed in the French Revolution, is Emmanuel Joseph Sieyès, *What is the Third Estate?*, ed. S. E. Finer, trans. M. Blondel (London: Pall Mall Press, 1963).

52 Arendt, *Imperialism*, p. 111.

53 Ibid., p. 110.

54 Hannah Arendt, "The Nation," *The Review of Politics* 8/1 (January 1946): 138–141. In fact, Arendt draws heavily upon her Delos review in the theoretical account of the nation-state summarized above (*Imperialism*, pp. 109–111).

55 Arendt, "The Nation," p. 138.

56 Ibid., p. 139.

57 Ibid.

58 Ibid.

59 Ibid., p. 140.

60 Ibid., pp. 140–141.

61 Ibid., p. 141. In *Imperialism*, pp. 111–112, n. 32, Arendt associates this proposal

to personalize or de-politicize nationality with Karl Renner and Otto Bauer, two Austro-Marxists who had addressed the nationality question. See *Austro-Marxism*, ed. and trans. Tom Bottomore and Patrick Goode (Oxford: Clarendon Press, 1978), pp. 102–125.

62 Arendt, *Imperialism*, p. ix. Significantly, Habermas continues to use the same language: "the classic form of the nation-state is at present disintegrating" (Jürgen Habermas, "Citizenship and National Identity," in R. Beiner, ed., *Theorizing Citizenship* [Albany, NY: State University of New York Press, 1995], pp. 256–257).

63 For a very helpful summary of Arendt's account, see Canovan, *Hannah Arendt*, pp. 31–36.

64 Arendt, *Imperialism*, pp. 151–152; see p. 152, n. 8 for some suggestion of the numbers involved.

65 Ibid., pp. 156–170.

66 Ibid., p. 156. Arendt notes the grim irony, which is obviously of some relevance to her critical judgments concerning the Zionist project, that those who were Europe's worst victims of minority status, de-naturalization, and statelessness proceeded to establish their own nation-state, thereby casting hundreds of thousands of Arabs who fled Palestine into precisely the condition of statelessness and rightlessness that the Jews had finally escaped (p. 170).

67 Ibid., p. 171.

68 Ibid., pp. 171–172.

69 Ibid., p. 171.

70 Ibid., p. 172.

71 Ibid., p. 176.

72 Ibid., p. 179.

73 Arendt seems to concede as much when she makes the following important acknowledgment with respect to the recovery of human rights by the Jews through the establishment of a Jewish nation-state: "the restoration of human rights, as the recent example of the State of Israel proves, has been achieved so far only through the restoration or the establishment of national rights" (ibid.). This supports Cocks's judgment that Arendt sees the national question "as a riddle with no solution" ("On Nationalism," p. 238).

74 Cf. Arendt, *Imperialism*, p. 155: "the danger of this development [semi-citizenship and statelessness] had been inherent in the structure of the nation-state since the beginning." Also, Arendt, "The Nation," pp. 138–139: "almost all modern brands of nationalism are racist to some degree."

75 See Arendt, *JP*, p. 158: "the United States . . . is not a national state in the European sense of the word." For a contrary view, see Roger Scruton, "The First Person Plural," in Beiner, ed., *Theorizing Nationalism*, pp. 289–290.

76 Contrary to this argument, the fact is that nationalists today are less and less inclined to assert national sovereignty: witness the enthusiasm of Scottish nationalists for European federalism, or the keenness of Québécois nationalists to be included in sovereignty-undermining arrangements such as NAFTA. Arendt is right that "[m]odern power conditions . . . make national sovereignty a mockery except for giant states" (*Imperialism*, p. 149), and that national sovereignty "has become the greatest danger to national survival for small nations" (Arendt, *JP*, p. 222); but contemporary nationalists seem to have taken this point.

77 Cf. Canovan, *Hannah Arendt*, p. 246: Arendt was determined to believe that "the future lay with non-national political forms" (federations or empires), and, Canovan notes, persisted in this view even while "nationalism revived in Europe and spread around the world." Also, see ibid., p. 36, n. 80. Cf. Judith N. Shklar, *Political Thought and Political Thinkers*, ed. Stanley Hoffman (Chicago: University of Chicago Press, 1998), p. 367.

78 Arendt, *OR*, p. 8.

79 Hannah Arendt's husband, Heinrich Blücher, who, as we know from his published letters in the Arendt–Jaspers correspondence, was an even harsher critic of nationalism than Arendt was, shared the same view: "As Hölderlin once said, the time of kings is past; and now the time of nations is past" (*Correspondence 1926–1969*, ed. Kohler and Saner, p. 278).

PART II

Political evil and the Holocaust

3

SEYLA BENHABIB

Arendt's *Eichmann in Jerusalem*

Among all of Hannah Arendt's writings, *Eichmann in Jerusalem* generated by far the most acrimonious and tangled controversy, which has since cast a long shadow on her eventful but otherwise respectable and illustrious career as a public intellectual and academic.[1] The Eichmann "affair" raised a host of questions about Arendt not only as a political thinker but as an individual Jew. Gershom Scholem's cruel phrase that Arendt lacked "Ahabath Israel" (love of the Jewish people) captures this collective bitterness.[2]

Ironically this book is Hannah Arendt's most intensely Jewish work, in which she identifies herself morally and epistemologically with the Jewish people. It is as if some of the deepest paradoxes of retaining a Jewish identity under conditions of modernity came to the fore in Arendt's search for the moral, political, and jurisprudential bases on which the trial and sentencing of Adolf Eichmann could take place. Arendt had struggled to bring together the universal and the particular, her modernist cosmopolitanism and her belief in some form of collective Jewish self-determination all her life. Precisely because this work was so close to who she truly was, it distracted from her equanimity and exhibited at times an astonishing lack of perspective, balance of judgment, and judicious expression. Arendt's thinly disguised and almost racist comments on Chief Prosecutor Gideon Hausner's "ostjüdisch" background, her childish partisanship for the "German-educated" judges, her dismay about the "oriental mob" outside the doors of the courtroom in Jerusalem, all suggest a certain failure of nerve and lack of distance from the topic at hand.[3] Arendt was punished by the Jewish community precisely because she, like so many others who were also Holocaust survivors, had not found the right public language, the right discourse through which to narrate past sorrow, suffering, and loss.

A letter to Mary McCarthy of October 1963 hints at Arendt's state of mind when writing this work:

> You were the only reader to understand what otherwise I have never admitted – namely that I wrote this book in a curious state of euphoria. And that ever since

> I did it, I feel – after twenty years [since the war] – light-hearted, about the whole matter. Don't tell anybody; is it not proof positive that I have no "soul"?[4]

The use of the term "light-hearted," like the phrase "the banality of evil," is a terminological infelicity; she did not mean that she was joyful or carefree about the whole matter; she meant rather that her heart was lightened by having shed a burden. By voicing in public the shame, rage, and sadness she had carried in private for thirty years, she was finally unloading some of the burden history had imposed upon her. Arendt had written about totalitarianism, anti-semitism, the extermination camps, the Nazi death machinery before. What was unprecedented in the Eichmann affair was that for the first time a struggle broke out among the Jewish community and the survivors of the Holocaust over how and in what terms to appropriate the memory of the Holocaust and its victims.

In writing *Eichmann in Jerusalem* Arendt could not recapture the lyrical and almost elegiac beauty of the loss of home and world expressed in her early article "We Refugees."[5] The question of narrative voice which had so preoccupied her during the time in which she wrote *The Origins of Totalitarianism* abandoned her in this work.[6] The unwieldiness of the narratives she tried to hold together in *Eichmann in Jerusalem* as well as the existential closeness of the subject matter gave rise to a work that still leaves one at times breathless, and at others puzzled, baffled, and irritated.

On May 11, 1960, members of the Israeli Secret Service kidnapped the Nazi fugitive Adolf Eichmann in Argentina, spiriting him out of the country so he could stand trial in Israel for crimes he had committed in the course of the "Final Solution." Eichmann's main responsibility during the Holocaust had been the organization of the transport of millions of Jews from across Europe to the concentration and death camps – a function he had carried out with zeal and efficiency. After the war, he escaped to Argentina, where he lived an anonymous life, although his presence was known to authorities. After a fruitless quarrel over his extradition with the Argentine government, the Israelis dramatically took matters into their own hands. Once Eichmann was safely in Israel, they mounted a riveting (and very public) trial, one goal of which was to bring attention to what Israeli prime minister David Ben-Gurion called "the most tragic in our history, the most tragic facts in world history."

From the beginning, then, the Israelis saw the trial of Eichmann as serving a dual function. First, and most obviously, Eichmann was to be brought to justice for the crimes against humanity he had committed in helping to implement the Nazis' "Final Solution" to the "Jewish question." Second (and almost equally important from the Israeli point of view) was the education of public opinion, in Israel and the rest of the world, about the nature and extent of the Nazi extermination of European Jewry. The enormity of the crime was known, but – until the Eichmann trial – there had been relatively little public discussion of the legal, moral, and political dimensions of the genocide. The Nuremberg trials had set a precedent for the legal consideration of "crimes against humanity," but they had treated the administrative murder of millions of Jews as but one item in a long list of outrages committed during the war by a "criminal regime."

When Hannah Arendt heard that the Israelis intended to try Eichmann in Israel, she immediately proposed herself as a trial reporter to the editor of *The New Yorker*, William Shawn. He accepted, and Arendt found herself attending Eichmann's trial in Jerusalem (the main part of which lasted from April 11 to August 14, 1961). She was taken aback by what she later described as the sheer ordinariness of the man who had been party to such enormous crimes: Eichmann spoke in endless clichés, gave little evidence of being motivated by a fanatical hatred of the Jews, and was most proud of being a "law-abiding citizen." It was the shock of seeing Eichmann "in the flesh" that led Arendt to the thought that great wickedness was not a necessary condition for the performance of (or complicity in) great crimes. Evil could take a "banal" form, as it had in Eichmann.

However, an "ordinary" Eichmann did not fit the role the prosecution in the case (led by Gideon Hausner) had in mind. They presented a diabolical and fanatical Eichmann, inflating his actual crimes into a near comprehensive responsibility for the Holocaust. That Arendt had little patience for the prosecution's exaggeration of Eichmann's role and personal brutality (in her view, his unembellished activities as a zealous transport director more than warranted the death sentence) is amply attested to in the pages of *Eichmann in Jerusalem*, as is her disdain for what she viewed as Hausner's courtroom dramatics. The sarcasm Arendt directed at him and the prosecution in the case alienated many readers of the original *New Yorker* articles (published in early 1963), as did her suggestion that some members of the Jewish Councils (formed by the Nazis to help govern Jewish populations in Poland and elsewhere) had been unwitting collaborators, insofar as they had supplied the Nazis with lists of their fellow Jews, who were then evacuated for "special treatment" in the killing centers in the East.

On December 11, 1961, after a four-month recess, the three-judge panel hearing the case in Jerusalem reconvened to pronounce judgment. Adolf Eichmann was found guilty of committing "crimes against the Jewish people" with the intent to destroy the people. He was sentenced to death and hanged. Arendt's "trial report" appeared as a book in the spring of 1963. The controversy which has embroiled it preceded its publication,[7] and continues (in some quarters) to this day.

There are at least three sociohistorical narratives in *Eichmann in Jerusalem*, each of which could have been the topic of separate volumes: first is Arendt's reporting of the circumstances of Eichmann's arrest, detention, and trial by the Israeli authorities, including the behavior of Chief Prosecutor Gideon Hausner during the proceedings. Second is the account of the role of the Jewish Councils (*Judenräte*) – the special committees appointed by the Nazis with a decree of September 21, 1939 – in the administration of the Jewish populations of Poland, the Baltic countries (Lithuania, Latvia, and Estonia), and the occupied areas of the USSR (Belorussia and Ukraine), and of their role in cooperating with the Nazis in carrying out the Final Solution.[8] Third is her attempt to come to grips with the behavior of so-called "ordinary German citizens" during the Nazi regime and the Holocaust. Eichmann becomes for her a paradigm case for analyzing how neither particularly evil nor particularly intelligent people could get caught in the machinery of evil and commit the deeds they did.

It is the coming together of these narratives with her philosophical thesis concerning the "banality of evil" that baffled her readers. At one level it seemed as if Arendt was accusing her own people and their leaders of being complicitous in the Holocaust while exculpating Eichmann and other Germans through naming their deeds "banal."[9]

Recent historical research has shown that on a number of occasions Arendt's judgments were insufficiently documented and ill-founded. In his introduction to the 1986 German revised edition of *Eichmann in Jerusalem*, the historian Hans Mommsen notes that the book "can be faulted in several respects":

> It contains many statements which are obviously not sufficiently thought through. Some of its conclusions betray an inadequate knowledge of the material available in the early 1960s. Its treatment of the historical events involved, besides making some use of Gerald Reitlinger's older work, was based primarily on the account by Raul Hilberg of the extermination of the European Jews which had appeared in 1961. Although she was very critical of Hilberg's overall interpretation, his conclusions were very similar to her own on critical points. She also sometimes betrayed a journalistic approach in her evaluation of information whose authenticity could only be established by careful historical analysis and, to a great extent, by a further examination of the original sources.[10]

Mommsen lists several such issues: Arendt had minimized the resistance to Hitler and in the original edition had mentioned the anti-Hitler conspir-

acy of July 20, 1944 only incidentally;[11] she still held onto
view that German communists had entered the NSDAP (
massive numbers; she had underestimated the communist
Hitler.[12] Mommsen observes: "She did not adequately explai
reasons why a general will to resist the regime did not develop. As
pretation of the collaboration of many Jewish officials, she made t ce
of a willingness on the part of individuals to sacrifice their lives the yardstick of her judgement."[13]

Indeed, of all the thorny historical and moral issues touched upon by Hannah Arendt, her evaluation of the behavior of the Jewish Councils remains the most difficult. It was also her passing judgment on these events and the individuals involved in them which earned her the wrath, rejection, and condemnation of the established Jewish community.[14] To be sure, Arendt should have distinguished more carefully among the various stages of the "silent" cooperation between the Nazi regime and Jewish organizations and committees. Before 1936 there was some collaboration between the Gestapo and Zionist organizations which shared "a negative identity of aims" in that each, albeit in different ways, wanted the Jewish population to leave Germany and other European territories.[15] Until 1938 the Central Committee of German Citizens of Jewish Faith retained the hope of being able to find some *modus vivendi* with the regime. Arendt had initially used the term "der jüdische Führer" (the Jewish Führer) to describe the activities of Leo Baeck, the former Chief Rabbi of Berlin, a terminology that she dropped in later editions of the book.[16]

Arendt was concerned about the role of the Jewish Councils from the very beginning of the Eichmann controversy. She wrote to Karl Jaspers on December 23, 1960, before the beginning of the trial:

> I'm afraid that Eichmann will be able to prove, first of all, that no country wanted the Jews (just the kind of Zionist propaganda which Ben Gurion wants and that I consider a disaster) and will demonstrate, second, to what a huge degree the Jews helped organize their own destruction. That is, of course, the naked truth, but this truth, if it is not really explained, could stir up more anti-Semitism than ten kidnappings.[17]

A few years later Arendt was still convinced that the reason why the Jewish "establishment" (her term) was taking such an extraordinary interest and using such massive resources in attacking her was that "the Jewish leadership (Jewish Agency before the State of Israel was founded) has much more dirty laundry to hide than anyone had ever guessed – at any rate, I don't know very much about it. As far as I can see, ties between the Jewish leadership and the Jewish Councils may be involved."[18]

establishing the extent and nature of the cooperation with the Nazis on the part of various Jewish organizations, which were faced with extremely diverse territorial and demographic conditions, extending from the Jewish communities of Berlin to the Jewish Councils of the ghettos of Łódź, Vilna, and Bialystok, will be the task of future historians of the Holocaust. Arendt's position on the role of the Jewish Councils remains ambiguous: on the one hand, one can read her as if her sole concern was with the lack of Jewish resistance and uprising of the kind that subsequently took place in the Warsaw ghetto. Given her left-Zionist sympathies, which went back to her student days, this reaction was of course understandable. On the other hand, she was extremely critical of Chief Prosecutor Gideon Hausner in the Eichmann trial, who would ask witnesses precisely why they did not resist. Arendt herself considered this line of questioning "cruel and silly."[19]

What then were her own motives in raising questions about the role and responsibilities of the Jewish Councils? Was it so difficult to understand that Jewish communities and their leaders could not grasp the magnitude, as well as the unprecedentedness, of the crime which was being perpetrated against them? Was it so hard to grasp that they interpreted Nazi extermination policy as simply a more massive form of the traditional anti-semitism to which they had been subjected since time immemorial?[20] Was it so impossible to see that the Jewish Councils had tried to keep a semblance of order and everydayness in running the lives of their communities, but had somehow still entertained the hope that they could influence and maybe even postpone the worst from happening?[21] If it was "cruel and silly" to ask the Jews to have resisted under such circumstances, as Arendt accused Gideon Hausner's questions of being, then what was she after herself?

An interview recently discovered in her posthumous papers, and not yet available to the larger public, throws some interesting light on these questions. On September 19, 1963 Samuel Grafton, who had been commissioned to write an article for *Look* magazine about the reaction to *Eichmann in Jerusalem*, sent Arendt some questions. She agreed to answer them on the condition that she would be able to review the article. In response to Grafton's query about when the community leaders should have urged "Cooperate no longer, but fight!" Arendt observes:

> There never was a moment when "the community leaders [could] have said: 'Cooperate no longer, but fight!'" as you phrase it. Resistance, which existed but played a very small role, meant only: we don't want that kind of death, we want to die with honor. But the question of cooperation is indeed bothersome. There certainly was a moment when the Jewish leaders could have said: We shall no longer cooperate, we shall try to disappear. This moment might have come when they, already fully informed of what deportation meant, were

> asked to prepare the lists for the Nazis for deportation . . . I answered your questions with respect to this point, but I should like to point out that it was never my intention to bring this part of our "unmastered past" to the attention of the public. It so happened that the *Judenräte* came up at the trial and I had to report on that as I had to report on everything else. Within the context of my Report, this plays no prominent role . . . It has been blown up out of all reasonable proportions.[22]

The ironic use of the term "unmastered past" in this context, "unbewältigte Vergangenheit," which was coined to describe German attempts to come to terms with the Nazi past in the postwar period, again shows the gratuitous sarcasm with which Arendt could offend in this debate. Since there was not and could not be any symmetry between the position of the victims and that of the perpetrators around the questions of guilt and cooperation, to refer to both with the terminology of coming to grips with the past was insensitive. But Arendt is also on the defensive in her reply to Grafton's questions because the *Judenräte* had preoccupied her already before the Eichmann trial, at the time of Kasztner's death. Her letter to Karl Jaspers of December 23, 1960 clearly supports this reading. Kasztner, a prominent member of the Hungarian Jewish community who settled in Israel after the war, had been charged with providing Eichmann himself with a list of Jews not to be deported to the camps, including members of his own family. This accusation led to an emotion-laden slander trial in Israel in 1955. Kasztner was killed in Tel Aviv in March 1957.[23] It was widely believed, and certainly Arendt herself thought so, that he had worked for the Jewish Agency (the "establishment" Zionist organization, led by Chaim Weizmann, which was based in Palestine prior to the founding of the state of Israel in 1948). Given her preoccupation with the question of Jewish collaboration from the very start, it is hard to accept at face value her claims that these topics were merely of secondary interest to her.

Nevertheless, despite the contentiousness of many of her judgments, Arendt is to be credited for being among the first to encourage facing the facts of the Nazi regime and the Holocaust in all their naked horror.[24] She herself struggled with the questions of who speaks for the memory of the victims, if anyone at all, and in what terms one can do so.[25] Her attempt to retain a voice and vantage point outside the established organizations of the State of Israel and world Jewry got her into trouble. Where was she speaking from, and on whose behalf was she speaking? She was not an Israeli citizen, or a concentration camp survivor – although she had been in a detention camp in Gurr in the south of France. She had become an American resident in 1941 and had practically abandoned Jewish politics, with which she had been intensely involved since 1933, after the death of Judah Magnes in

1948.[26] When she wrote her pieces on the trial of Adolf Eichmann for the *New Yorker* magazine, many did not know of her previous intense involvement with Jewish and Zionist politics or her work with Jewish organizations.

Hannah Arendt had left Germany in 1933 because she was collecting material for her friend Kurt Blumenfeld on German professional organizations and business associations which were beginning to take punitive action against their Jewish members. Blumenfeld would in turn present this material at the 18th Zionist Congress in 1933.[27] She was arrested by the Gestapo and briefly detained, and subsequently left Germany. After coming to Paris she worked for an Aliyah organization which was settling children in Palestine. In New York she wrote on Jewish issues for the Yiddish periodical *Der Aufbau*. Noteworthy in this context is her call for a Jewish army to fight against the Nazis in cooperation with Allied forces.[28] After the establishment of the State of Israel, and particularly after the failure of Judah Magnes's efforts for the establishment of a binational, democratic federation in Palestine, and the hostility expressed toward this view among American Jewry, Arendt fell silent on the "Jewish question." Her Eichmann book sent her back to the memories of a past in which she had been not only a persecuted and stateless Jew, but a political militant and left-thinking Zionist who was very much part of the milieu of European socialist and communist sympathizers, fighters, and organizers. Her recently published correspondence with her husband, Heinrich Blücher, who was a member of the Spartakist Bund, gives one a full flavor of this "milieu." Here is a brief exchange on some aspects of the "Jewish question":

In a long disquisition of August 21, 1938 on the "Jewish question" Blücher writes to Arendt:

> Once the radio of the world has announced a couple of times that Mordechai Veiteles, conductor of the first train of the 2nd company of the first Jewish volunteer battalion, has fallen in Saragossa – then these Jewish names will have a very strong echo . . . And when we have all been emancipated by freedom, then it will be time to tell these Jews: look at this, together we have won the world. If you want to take your part of it to develop yourself in it further, then do so.[29]

Arendt answers tongue in cheek, referring to Blücher himself as the "Golem":

> The Golem is wrong when he argues that the Jews are a people, or a people which, like others, is in the process of realizing itself. In the East they are already a people without territory. And in the West, God knows what they are (including myself) . . . And if we want to be a people, some territory or other which the world revolution will one day give us will not do . . . Palestine is at

> the center of our national aspirations, not because the gentlemen from whom we are all said to be descended in one form or another lived there 2,000 years ago, but because for 2,000 years this most crazy people of all peoples has amused itself by preserving the past in the present, because for this people "the ruins of Jerusalem are buried in the heart of time." (Herder)[30]

By the time Hannah Arendt wrote *Eichmann in Jerusalem* these historical options had been played out. State Zionism and not utopian socialism won the day in Palestine, and a federation of European peoples, among whom the Jews could have had a place, was killed in the gas chambers of Auschwitz, Majdanek, and Bergen-Belsen. Part of the tragedy behind Arendt's report on the Eichmann trial is the passing away of the memory of this historical milieu, which in the 1920s and 1930s had brought into contact Bundists, who wanted to build a Jewish entity as part of a federated Soviet Socialist Peoples' Republics; national Zionists, who wanted a separate Jewish state in Palestine; labor Zionists, who thought the dream of socialism could only be realized in a Jewish state, after the "Jewish question" had been solved; and communist militants, Jewish and non-Jewish, who fought in the International Brigade in Spain; of these last some were subsequently murdered by Stalin, a few joined the Nazis, and a number found their way to Palestine. Although she was not a militant herself, Hannah Arendt was molded by the dreams and hopes of this political milieu, this "other Europe," which she then saw realized in the French Resistance to the Nazis after 1941. Many of her judgments about the behavior of established Jewish organizations during the Holocaust express the standpoint of a Jewish political militancy which, ironically, at times brought her into the company of the militant Zionist Revisionist leader Ze'ev Jabotinsky and his group within the Zionist movement.

Emerging out of this milieu, Hannah Arendt also had a much more differentiated and nuanced judgment of the behavior of individual Germans and Jews during the Nazi regime. For her, generalizations about German national character, German anti-semitism, and so on would have been impossible precisely because, as one who had lived through this period, she had a sense of individual choices, biographies, and commitments, all of which indicated that "it could have been otherwise." The case of Sergeant Anton Schmidt, who helped Jewish partisans by supplying them with forged papers and military trucks until he was arrested and executed by the Germans, movingly exemplified for Arendt this possibility, this "other Europe." With reference to Schmidt she writes:

> And in those two minutes, which were like a sudden burst of light in the midst of the impenetrable, unfathomable darkness, a single thought stood out

> clearly, irrefutably, beyond question – how utterly different everything would be today in this courtroom, in Israel, in Germany, in all of Europe, and perhaps in all countries of the world, if only more such stories could have been told.[31]

In the last pages of *The Origins of Totalitarianism* Hannah Arendt had written of the Holocaust and in particular of the extermination camps as the appearance of "radical evil" on earth. This term, which originates in Kant's *Religion within the Limits of Reason Alone*, was subsequently dropped by her.[32] Writing the Eichmann book was a "cura posterior" (posterior cure) for her.[33] Exactly why this was so is harder to explain, for Hannah Arendt did not give up her claim that with the establishment of concentration and death camps "some radical evil, previously unknown to us," had occurred. What had occurred defied all hitherto known standards and confronted us with the realization that "something seems to be involved in modern politics that actually should never be involved in politics as we used to understand it . . ."[34] Arendt insists at the end of *Eichmann in Jerusalem* that "every act that has once made its appearance and has been recorded in the history of mankind stays with mankind as a potentiality long after its actuality has become a thing of the past . . . that the unprecedented, once it has appeared, may become a precedent for the future, that all trials touching upon 'crimes against humanity' must be judged according to a standard that is today still an 'ideal.' "[35]

Arendt changed none of her views on these questions in *Eichmann in Jerusalem*, but the phraseology of the "banality of evil" and of "thoughtlessness" which she used to describe Eichmann's deeds was greatly misleading. Arendt forced the English language into a procrustean bed to convey her own complex, and perhaps even ultimately inconclusive, reflections on the issue of "personal responsibility under dictatorships." She did not mean that what Eichmann had helped to perpetrate was banal or that the extermination of the Jews, and of other peoples, by the Nazis was banal. It takes either a great deal of hermeneutic blindness and ill will or both to miss her meaning in the usage of this term, even if one may disagree with the assessment of Eichmann's psychology. The phrase the "banality of evil" was meant to refer to a *specific quality of mind and character* of the doer himself, but neither to the deeds nor to the principles behind those deeds.[36] Rereading *Eichmann in Jerusalem* one can feel Arendt's bafflement at Eichmann's persona and conduct before and during the trial. Writing in the "Postscript" that she would have welcomed a general discussion of the concept of the "banality of evil," she continues:

> Eichmann was not Iago and not Macbeth, and nothing would have been farther from his mind than to determine with Richard III "to prove a villain" . . . He

> *merely*, to put the matter colloquially, *never realized what he was doing*. It was precisely this lack of imagination which enabled him to sit for months on end facing a German Jew who was conducting the police interrogation . . . It was sheer thoughtlessness – something by no means identical with stupidity – that predisposed him to become one of the greatest criminals of that period . . . That such remoteness from reality and such thoughtlessness can wreak more havoc than all the evil instincts taken together which, perhaps, are inherent in man – that was, in fact, the lesson one could learn in Jerusalem.[37]

To solve, or more correctly to think through, the philosophical problem of moral judgment which this trial had raised in all its urgency, Arendt would turn in the years to come to Kant's moral and political philosophy.

These deep perplexities of moral philosophy about thinking, judging, and moral action were what really preoccupied Arendt in her attempt to analyze Eichmann's actions. Precisely because she herself had not resolved some of these perplexities, the wider public found it difficult to grasp what she was after. The phrase the "banality of evil" was secondary to Arendt's preoccupations with these moral issues and may not even have been her very own coinage. The following comments by Karl Jaspers in a letter to Arendt of December 13, 1963 are quite illuminating on this issue:

> Alcopley told me that Heinrich [Blücher] suggested the phrase "the banality of evil" and is cursing himself for it now because you've had to take the heat for what he thought of. Perhaps the report isn't true, or my recollection of it is garbled. I think it's a wonderful inspiration and right on the mark as the book's subtitle. The point is that *this* evil, not evil per se, is banal.[38]

Whatever the origins of this term, whether invented by Arendt or Blücher or, as some evidence suggests, even Jaspers himself, Arendt's views on evil were of quite a different nature than what was commonly associated with this term in Western thought. In using the phrase the "banality of evil" and in explaining the moral quality of Eichmann's deeds not in terms of the monstrous or demonic nature of the doer, Arendt became aware of going counter to the tradition, which saw evil in metaphysical terms as ultimate depravity, corruption, or sinfulness. The most striking quality of Eichmann, she claimed, was not stupidity, wickedness, or depravity but one she described as "thoughtlessness." This in turn led her to the question:

> Might the problem of good and evil, our faculty for telling right from wrong, be connected with our faculty of thought? . . . Could the activity of thinking as such, the habit of examining whatever happens to come to pass or attract attention, regardless of results and specific contents, could this activity be among the conditions that make men abstain from evil-doing or even actually "condition" them against it?[39]

She asked: "Is our ability to judge, to tell right from wrong, beautiful from ugly, dependent upon our faculty of thought? Do the inability to think and a disastrous failure of what we commonly call conscience coincide?"[40]

That these issues in moral philosophy lay behind her ill-chosen phrase and other terminological infelicities is also evidenced by her correspondence with Mary McCarthy. On August 10, 1945 McCarthy wrote to Arendt with a philosophical query. She had been pondering Raskolnikov's old problem in Dostoevsky's *Crime and Punishment*: "Why shouldn't I murder my grandmother if I want to? Give me one good reason."[41] Arendt responded with a professorial gesture which acknowledged the depth as well as the difficulty of McCarthy's question: "The philosophic answer would be the answer of Socrates: Since I have got to live with myself, am in fact the only person from whom I never shall be able to part, whose company I shall have to bear forever, I don't want to become a murderer; I don't want to spend my life in the company of a murderer."[42] McCarthy is unconvinced: "The modern person I posit would say to Socrates, with a shrug, 'Why not? What's wrong with a murderer?' And Socrates would be back where he started."[43]

The Eichmann affair showed the centrality of moral and political judgment for human life in many and varied ways: there was the retrospective judgment which every historian and narrator of past events had to exercise; there was the moral judgment of the contemporaries who stood in judgment over Eichmann and his actions; and there was also the lack of a faculty of judgment on Eichmann's own part. Even in her subsequent reflections on these questions Arendt could not integrate all these aspects of judging into a coherent account, and resolve the issues in moral philosophy which this trial had posed for her.[44]

Arendt's contribution to moral and legal thought in this century will certainly not be the category of the "banality of evil." Rather, I want to suggest, the category that is closest to the nerve of her political thought as a whole, and one which has gained significance with the end of the twentieth century, is that of "crimes against humanity."

After Eichmann's kidnapping in Argentina by the Israeli Secret Service on May 11, 1960, both Karl Jaspers and Hannah Arendt were anguished about the illegality of this act and about the moral and legal issues involved in his being tried by an Israeli court.[45] Arendt was convinced to the very end that the State of Israel had committed a "clear violation of international law in order to bring him to justice."[46] She also notes that what enabled Israel to get away with this in the international world community was Eichmann's *de facto* statelessness. Neither postwar Germany nor Argentina, where he had settled under false pretenses, was to claim him as their citizen.

Inasmuch as she questioned the justifiability of the circumstances surrounding Eichmann's capture, Arendt did not differ from Jaspers. Yet while the latter wanted Israel to hand over the jurisdiction of the trial to an International Court or body, she defended Israel's right to bring Eichmann to trial and to pass judgment upon him.[47] There were three kinds of objections raised to the trial: first was the objection voiced in the case of the Nuremberg trials as well, that Eichmann was tried under a retroactive law and appeared in the court of the victors. Arendt thought that the Israeli court's reply to this objection was justifiable: the Nuremberg trials were cited in the Jerusalem court as precedent, and the Nazi Collaboration (Punishment) Law of 1950 in Israel was based on this precedent. Her observations on the principle "nullum crimen, nulla poena sine lege" (no crime, no wrongdoing without the law) are interesting. She observes that the principle of retroactivity, that no one can be condemned for an act that was not against the law at the time it was committed, only "meaningfully applies to acts known to the legislator."[48] If a previously unknown crime makes its appearance in human history, such as the crime of genocide perpetrated during the Holocaust, justice in this instance demands a new and unprecedented law. The Eichmann trial did not violate the principle of retroactivity, for prior to the Nuremberg trials there had been no law established by a human legislator under which he could have been tried.[49] The Nuremberg trials established such a law through the Charter (the London agreement of 1945), and Israel invoked its own law against genocide of 1950, which was based in turn on the 1945 Nuremberg Charter. Arendt was not, therefore, particularly concerned with the argument that the justice meted out at the Nuremberg trials as well as in the case of Eichmann was the "justice of the victor" (*Siegerjustiz*), since she held to the view that the crimes perpetrated by the Nazi regime were of such an unprecedented nature that one needed new categories, new criteria for judging them. The Eichmann trial posed the dilemmas of judging "without banisters," i.e., without recourse to established precedents, for everyone involved, from the jurors to the journalists and to world public opinion.

To the second objection, that the court in Jerusalem was not competent to try Eichmann, Arendt gave a more equivocal answer, for this issue concerned the State of Israel's right to represent and speak in the name of all the victims of Adolf Eichmann. Arendt is firm that insofar as Eichmann had participated in the killing of Jews because they were Jews, and not because they were Poles, Lithuanians, Romanians, etc., a Jewish political entity could represent his victims. The basis on which Israel could do so, she maintained, could be made consistent with the Genocide Convention adopted by the United Nations General Assembly on December 9, 1948, which provided that "persons charged with genocide . . . shall be tried by a competent tribunal of the States in the territory of which the act was committed or by such an international penal tribunal as may have jurisdiction."[50]

Arendt's gloss on this rather technical question of defining territorial jurisdiction leads to some rather surprising conclusions:

> Israel could easily have claimed territorial jurisdiction if she had only explained that "territory," as the law understands it, is a political and legal concept, and not merely a geographical term. It relates not so much, and not primarily, to a piece of land as to the space between individuals in a group whose members are bound to, and at the same time separated and protected from, each other by all kinds of relationships, based on a common language, religion, a common history, customs, and laws. Such relationships become spatially manifest insofar as they themselves constitute the space wherein the different members of a group relate to and have intercourse with each other. No State of Israel would have ever come into being if the Jewish people had not created and maintained its own specific in-between space throughout the long centuries of dispersion, that is, prior to the seizure of its old [sic!] territory.[51]

This is indeed a curious claim. If a citizen of a particular country or the consular space of a certain country is attacked in foreign territory, the government of the country of the victim would have the territorial competence to judge the perpetrators and ask for their extradition. But is Hannah Arendt suggesting that the State of Israel has a claim to represent *all* Jews in the world, even those who are not Israeli citizens, on the grounds that this state itself could not have come into being "if the Jewish people had not created and maintained its own specific in-between space"? The main objection to this formulation would be that it would make membership in a state not an act of consent, choice, or other indication of positive will, but simply a result of one's ethnic or national heritage. This analysis collapses the categories of citizenship and nationality by almost suggesting that all ethnic Jews are potential Israeli citizens. This is a principle accepted by Israel's Law of Return; the obverse side of this Law is, of course, the denial of full citizenship rights to those Palestinian Israelis whose ethnic identity or nationality is not Jewish but who nonetheless live in the territories under the jurisdiction of the State of Israel. Arendt's reflections on the matter of Israel's territorial jurisdiction to judge Eichmann thus run contrary to her otherwise careful distinctions between citizenship rights and national identity.

This unresolved tension between the universal and the particular is nowhere more evident than in her articulation of the central category under which she thinks Eichmann should have been condemned, namely "crimes against humanity." This was the third set of jurisprudential issues which the trial had raised for her. Arendt criticized the sentence of the Israeli court for its juridical confusions. In particular, she was critical of its use of the category of "crimes against humanity," "to include genocide if practiced against non-Jewish peoples (such as the Gypsies or the Poles) and all other crimes, including murder, committed against either Jews or non-Jews, provided that these crimes were not committed with intent to destroy the people as a whole."[52] For Arendt, this way of stating the question was utterly wrongheaded and was based on a fundamental misunderstanding of the category itself. The unprecedented category of "crimes against humanity" was invented, she insisted, precisely to name a new kind of act: namely, the act of genocide which was perpetrated against a people simply because it existed on the face of this earth as *this specific kind* of people, as exemplifying one way of being among the many possible modes of "human diversity." Jews had been killed not because they were enemies of the regime, class traitors, spies against the Führer, but because *qua* Jews they were said to be certain kinds of beings who had no right to be on this earth. Genocide requires some form of race-thinking as its basis because it aims at the elimination of a people in virtue of the collective characteristics which it is constructed as possessing. All genocide is a form of "ethnic cleansing," as the war in former Yugoslavia – fifty years later – has taught us. Arendt observes:

> Had the court in Jerusalem understood that there were distinctions between discrimination, expulsion and genocide, it would immediately have become clear that the supreme crime it was confronted with, the physical extermination of the Jewish people, was a crime against humanity, perpetrated upon the body of the Jewish people, and that only the choice of victims, not the nature of the crime could be derived from the long history of Jew-hatred and anti-Semitism. Insofar as the victims were Jews, it was right and proper that a Jewish court should sit in judgment; but insofar as the crime was a crime against humanity, it needed an international tribunal to do justice to it.[53]

Hannah Arendt wanted finally to reconcile the universal and the particular, the ideal of humanity and the fact of human particularity and diversity. The concept of "crimes against humanity" immediately invokes the concept of the "right to have rights" discussed in *The Origins of Totalitarianism*.[54] In both cases an anthropological normative universal is being invoked. In virtue of our humanity alone, Arendt is arguing, we are beings entitled to be treated in certain ways, and when such treatment is not accorded to us, then both wrongs and crimes are committed against us. Of course, Arendt was thinking along Kantian lines that we are "moral persons," and that our humanity and our moral personality coexist. Yet these are not the terms which she will use; nor will she, like Kant, seek to ground the mutual obligation we owe one another in our capacity for acting in accordance with the principles of reason. Even her formula the "right to have rights" is frustratingly ambiguous: if we have a right to have rights, who could deprive us of it? If we do not already all have such a right, how can we acquire it? Furthermore, what is meant by "a right" in this formula: a legally recognized and guaranteed claim by the lawgiver, or a moral claim which we, *qua* members of a human group, address to our fellow human beings, to be recognized as their equals? Clearly it is the second, moral meaning of the term "rights" that Arendt has in mind. But she is not concerned to offer a justification here.[55] She was not a foundationalist thinker and she stayed away from strategies of normative justification. The Eichmann trial was a watershed of sorts because it brought to the fore the contradictions with which she had struggled with existentially and conceptually all her life.

There is a normative "melancholia" in Hannah Arendt's work. Her inconclusive reflections and ruminations on the fragility of human rights; her belief that we are not born equal but become equals through being recognized as members of a moral and political community; and her ironic acknowledgment that Eichmann, the former Nazi, was a "stateless" person like herself, the persecuted Jew, and that neither would be protected by an international legal and normative order – these episodes are some of the more salient instances when her melancholia about the twentieth century comes to the fore.

Arendt was skeptical that moral beliefs and principles would ever be able to restrain or control politics in the twentieth century and give it a direction compatible with human rights and dignity. There is therefore a resistance on her part toward justificatory political discourse, toward the attempt to establish the rationality and validity of our beliefs in universal human rights, human equality, the obligation to treat others with respect. Although her conception of politics and of the political is quite inconceivable, unintelligible even, without a strongly grounded normative position in universal human rights, equality, and respect, one does not find her engaging in any such exercises of normative justification in her writings.

Hannah Arendt's thinking is deeply grounded in a position which I shall call "anthropological universalism." *The Human Condition* treats human beings as members of the same natural species, to whom life on earth is given under certain conditions, namely those of natality, plurality, labor, work, and action.[56] This philosophical anthropology proceeds from a level of abstraction which treats all forms of cultural, social, and historical differentiation among humans as irrelevant when measured up against the "fundamentals" of their condition. There is an implicit ethical gesture in approaching the human condition from this level of abstraction, one that proceeds from our fundamental equality and commonality as members of the same species. This philosophical anthropology can be viewed as a form of coming to one's senses morally, i.e., as a form of "Besinnung," a form of taking a hold of one's senses by grasping what it is to be human. What are some of the elements of such coming to one's senses? In the first place, an awareness of our natality as well as mortality, a cure for the sin, in St. Augustine's terms, of thinking that we are the ground of our being. We are not: we are fundamentally dependent creatures, born promiscuously to others like ourselves and radically dependent upon the good will and solidarity of others to become who we are. Furthermore, we are embodied creatures whose material needs must be satisfied by a constant engagement and metabolism with nature. This process of material engagement with the world is also one of world-constitution and world-creation. Like the young Marx in the 1844 *Economic and Philosophic Manuscripts*, Hannah Arendt also stresses the world- and object-creating qualities of human activities through her distinction between labor and work. Furthermore, we are creatures immersed in a condition of plurality: we are sufficiently like other members of our species so that we can always in some sense or other communicate with them; yet, through speech and action, we individuate ourselves, we reveal how distinctive we are. Plurality is a condition of equality and difference, or a condition of equality-in-difference.

This anthropological universalism contains an ethics of radical intersubjectivity, which is based on the fundamental insight that all social life and moral relations to others begin with the decentering of primary narcissism. Whereas *mortality* is the condition that leads the self to withdraw from the world into a fundamental concern with a fate that can only be its own, *natality* is the condition through which we immerse ourselves into the world, at first through the good will and solidarity of those who nurture us and subsequently through our own deeds and words. Yet insight into the condition of natality, while it enables the de-centering of the subject by revealing our fundamental dependence on others, is not adequate to lead to an attitude of moral respect among equals. The condition of natality involves inequality and hierarchies of dependence. By contrast, Arendt describes mutual *respect* as "a kind of 'friendship' without intimacy and without closeness; it is a regard for the person from the distance which the space of the world puts between us."[57] It is the step leading from the constituents of a philosophical anthropology (natality, worldliness, plurality, and forms of human activity) to this attitude of respect for the other that is missing in Arendt's thought. Her anthropological universalism does not so much justify this attitude of respect as it presupposes it. For, in treating one another as members of the same species, we are in some sense already granting each other recognition as moral equals. Arendt does not examine the philosophical step which would lead from a description of the *equality of the human condition* to the *equality which comes from moral and political recognition*. In Kantian terms, Arendt answers the question of "quaestio juris" – by what reason or on what ground should I respect the other as my equal? – with a "quaestio facti," a factual-seeming description of the human condition. The path leading from the anthropological plurality of the human condition to the moral and political equality of human beings in a community of reciprocal recognition remains philosophically unthematized.

Eichmann in Jerusalem is a work that is volatile and difficult to decipher precisely because Adolf Eichmann's kidnapping, trial and sentencing became the prism through which some of the most touching and difficult issues of Arendt's life and work were refracted.

NOTES

1 Arendt, *EJ*, rev., enlarged edn. (New York: Penguin, 1992).
2 Gershom Scholem, "'Eichmann in Jerusalem': An Exchange of Letters between Gershom Scholem and Hannah Arendt," *Encounter* 22 (Jan. 1964): 51–56; reprinted in Hannah Arendt, *The Jew as Pariah: Jewish Identity and Politics in the Modern Age*, ed. Ron H. Feldman (New York: Grove Press, 1978), p. 241.
3 On Gideon Hausner, see *Hannah Arendt – Karl Jaspers: Correspondence, 1926–1969*, ed. Lotte Köhler and Hans Saner, trans. Robert and Rita Kimber (New York: Harcourt Brace Jovanovich, 1992), p. 434; on the "oriental mob," see ibid., p. 435; on the "German-educated judges," see *EJ*, p. 4.
4 *Between Friends: The Correspondence of Hannah Arendt and Mary McCarthy, 1949–1975*, ed. Carol Brightman (New York: Harcourt Brace Jovanovich, 1995), p. 168.
5 Hannah Arendt, "We Refugees," originally published in the *Menorah Journal*, reprinted in *The Jew as Pariah*, pp. 55–67.
6 See my discussion in *The Reluctant Modernism of Hannah Arendt* (Thousand Oaks, CA: Sage Publications), pp. 62ff., for an exploration of these issues.
7 See Elisabeth Young-Bruehl, *Hannah Arendt: For Love of the World* (New Haven: Yale University Press, 1982), pp. 347–349.
8 See the authoritative volume by Isaiah Trunk, *Judenrat: The Jewish Councils in Eastern Europe under Nazi Occupation* (New York and London: Macmillan, 1972); Raul Hilberg, *Perpetrators, Victims, Bystanders: The Jewish Catastrophe, 1933–1945* (New York: Harper Collins, 1992).
9 See Jacob Robinson, *And the Crooked Shall Be Made Straight: The Eichmann Trial, the Jewish Catastrophe, and Hannah Arendt's Narrative* (New York: Macmillan, 1965). Robinson makes clear in his preface that his task is to "correct" Arendt: "Miss Arendt does not convey reliable information. She has misread many of the documents and books referred to in her text and bibliography. She has not equipped herself with the necessary background for an under-

standing and analysis of the trial" (p. vii). See also the acrimonious exchanges between Hannah Arendt, Gershom Scholem, and Walter Laqueur collected in *JP*, pp. 240ff.

10 English translation published as "Hannah Arendt and the Eichmann Trial," in Hans Mommsen, *From Weimar to Auschwitz: Essays in German History*, trans. Philip O'Connor (Princeton: Princeton University Press, 1991), p. 255.

11 See her own comments on this issue in the "Note to the Reader" of the 1964 edition; reprinted in the 1992 Penguin edition used here.

12 Mommsen, "Hannah Arendt," p. 270.

13 Ibid.

14 Arendt was accused of every possible posture, extending from Jewish self-hatred to anti-Zionism, from insensitivity to tastelessness and of course arrogance. The reaction of the American Jewish community has been documented by Alan D. Krinsky's senior thesis, "The Controversy" (Boston University, 1990). I would like to thank Professor Hillel Levine for making this thesis available to me. For a documentation of the German controversy, see F. A. Krummacher, ed., *Die Kontroverse: Hannah Arendt, Eichmann und die Juden* (Munich, 1964).

15 Mommsen, "Hannah Arendt," p. 268.

16 On the circumstances surrounding this question, see Young-Bruehl, *Hannah Arendt*, pp. 363ff. The reference is missing in the revised edition, see *EJ*, p. 119.

17 Letter to Karl Jaspers, December 23, 1960, in *Hannah Arendt – Karl Jaspers Correspondence*, 417.

18 Letter to Jaspers, October 29, 1963, in ibid., p. 524.

19 *EJ*, p. 12.

20 Arendt herself suggests this question in the "Epilogue" to ibid., p. 267.

21 For a masterful analysis of the "rationality" which may have guided the behavior of the Jewish Councils, in particular in those situations where there was a Jewish work force occupied in various German factories, see Dan Diner, "Historical Understanding and Counterrationality: The *Judenrat* as Epistemological Vantage," in Saul Friedlander, ed., *Probing the Limits of Representation: Nazism and the "Final Solution"* (Cambridge, MA, 1992), pp. 128–143.

22 Hannah Arendt, "Answer to Grafton, Draft," in Arendt Archives as cited by Richard J. Bernstein, *Hannah Arendt and the Jewish Question* (Cambridge, MA: MIT Press, 1996), 209–210.

23 For the circumstances surrounding the accusations against Kasztner, his assassination and the public furor around this issue in Israel, see Tom Segev, *The Seventh Million: The Israelis and the Holocaust* (New York: Hill and Wang, 1993), pp. 255–259, 282–284, 305–309.

24 See Michael R. Marrus, *The Holocaust in History* (Toronto: Lester and Orpen Dennys, 1987), pp. 4–5: "Up to the time of the Eichmann trial in Jerusalem, in 1961, there was relatively little discussion of the massacre of European Jewry . . . Since then scholarship has proceeded apace . . . Hannah Arendt's *Eichmann in Jerusalem*, originally an assessment of the trial for *The New Yorker*, prompted a debate in the historical literature that echoes to our own time."

25 The volume edited by Saul Friedlander contains many interesting perspectives on these issues. See his introduction, as well as Yael S. Feldman, "Whose Story

Is It Anyway? Ideology and Psychology in the Representation of the Shoah in Israeli Literature," in *Probing the Limits of Representation*, pp. 223–240.

26 The significance of Jewish cultural and political issues for Arendt's political philosophy has been highlighted by Bernstein, *Hannah Arendt and the Jewish Question*. In *The Reluctant Modernism of Hannah Arendt*, I discuss Jewish politics and German *Existenz* philosophy, particularly the thought of Martin Heidegger, as the sources from which Arendt's thought springs.

27 See Young-Bruehl, *Hannah Arendt*, p. 105, and my discussion of Arendt's involvement in Jewish politics in those years in *The Reluctant Modernism of Hannah Arendt*, pp. 35ff.

28 At the time there was also a Committee for a Jewish Army based in New York created by the extremists of the Revisionist Party and their leader Vladimir Ze'ev Jabotinsky. When Arendt and Joseph Maier, her colleague from *Der Aufbau*, realized that the Committee was a Revisionist front, they formed a group of their own called "Die jungjüdische Gruppe." See ibid., 38ff.

29 *Hannah Arendt – Heinrich Blücher, Briefe. 1936–1968*, ed. Lotte Köhler (Munich: R. Piper Verlag, 1996), pp. 54– 55 (my translation).

30 Ibid., p. 58 (my translation).

31 *EJ*, p. 231.

32 Arendt, *OT* (1951; New York: Harcourt, Brace & World, 1979), p. 443. Immanuel Kant, *Religion within the Limits of Reason Alone*, trans. Theodore M. Greene and Hoyt H. Hudson (New York: Harper and Row, 1960), p. 32.

33 See Young-Bruehl, *Hannah Arendt*, pp. 367ff.

34 *OT*, p. 443.

35 *EJ*, p. 273.

36 See Arendt's comment on Eichmann's last words under the gallows: "'After a short while, gentlemen, *we shall all meet again*. Such is the fate of all men. Long live Germany, long live Argentina, long live Austria. *I shall not forget them*' ... It was as though in those last minutes he was summing up the lesson that his long course in human wickedness had taught us – the lesson of the fearsome word-and-thought-defying *banality of evil*." Ibid., p. 252 (original emphasis).

37 Ibid., pp. 287–288 (original emphasis). Arendt dealt with what she saw as a widespread attitude of profound and almost neurotic detachment from reality on the part of postwar Germans in a number of essays such as "Besuch in Deutschland," in *Hannah Arendt: Besuch in Deutschland* (Berlin: Rotbuch Verlag, 1993).

38 *Hannah Arendt – Karl Jaspers Correspondence*, 542.

39 Hannah Arendt, *LM*, vol. 1, *Thinking*, p. 5.

40 Hannah Arendt, "Thinking and Moral Considerations: A Lecture," *Social Research* 38/3 (Autumn 1971), reprinted in ibid., 50th Anniversary issue (Spring/Summer 1984): 8.

41 *Between Friends*, p. 19. See my review of their correspondence in *The Nation*, Mar. 27, 1995, 423–425.

42 *Between Friends*, p. 22.

43 Ibid., p. 27.

44 Benhabib, *The Reluctant Modernism of Hannah Arendt*, pp. 185ff.; Bernstein, *Hannah Arendt and the Jewish Question*, pp. 154–179.

45 See *Hannah Arendt – Karl Jaspers Correspondence*, p. 413ff.

46 *EJ*, p. 263.
47 *Hannah Arendt – Karl Jaspers Correspondence*, p. 414.
48 *EJ*, p. 254.
49 For a masterful analysis of the Nuremberg trials, see Judith N. Shklar, *Legalism: An Essay on Law, Morals and Politics* (Cambridge, MA: Harvard University Press, 1964).
50 Quoted in *EJ*, p. 262.
51 Ibid., p. 263.
52 Ibid., pp. 244–245.
53 Ibid., p. 269.
54 *OT*, pp. 290ff.
55 See Frank Michelman, "Parsing 'A Right to Have Rights,'" *Constellations: An International Journal of Critical and Democratic Theory* 3/2 (Oct. 1996): 200–209.
56 Arendt, *HC*, (Chicago: University of Chicago Press, 1973).
57 Ibid., p. 253.

4

MARY G. DIETZ

Arendt and the Holocaust

> all efforts to escape from the grimness of the present into nostalgia for a still intact past, or into the anticipated oblivion of a better future, are in vain.
>
> Hannah Arendt

Hannah Arendt spent much of her life and a great deal of her writing in an effort to comprehend the destructive forces of the twentieth century, some of which, as she never ceased to remind us, were fundamentally unprecedented and incomprehensible in any ordinary or conventional sense. Within the domain of the social sciences, Arendt argued, there are data which "respond to our commonly accepted research techniques and scientific concepts," and then there are data "which explode this whole framework of reference" and defy our categories of explanation concerning human social and individual behavior. In the face of such data, Arendt noted, "we can only guess in what forms human life is being lived when it is lived as though it took place on another planet."[1]

Arendt thought that the line between the comprehensible and the incomprehensible, between human life on earth and some other planet, between human evil and absolute evil, was crossed in the final stages of totalitarianism when Nazi anti-semitism transmogrified into the Holocaust, as anti-Jewish legislation, the herding of Jews into European ghettos, and the establishment of forced labor camps,[2] mutated into the creation of death factories for "the fabrication of corpses" undergirded by a methodical and mechanized program for the extermination and annihilation of human beings. Arendt insisted that, although the incomprehensible crime at issue was committed in its largest measure against the Jews of Europe, it was in no way limited to the Jews or the Jewish question.[3] The deeds of horror perpetrated by the Nazi regime and totalitarianism "wherever it ruled" threatened to destroy the very "essence of man"; thus the incomprehensible Holocaust had to be reckoned with as a crime against humanity.[4]

Over the past two decades, many scholars and writers have tried to confront the Holocaust through philosophical, sociological, psychological, symbolic, literary, and religious formulations. Indeed, the literature is by now so voluminous that there is a genre called "Holocaust studies" that locates it.[5] My aim in this chapter is to explore Arendt's political theory, and particularly her most famous text, *The Human Condition*, within the specific context of the Holocaust. I wish to suggest that approaching Arendt from this perspective not only underscores the originality of her theorizing totalitarianism, but also illuminates the depth and profundity of her contribution to our thinking through the most fiercely inhuman and horrific event of twentieth-century Europe.

Comprehending the Holocaust

What does it mean to comprehend what is historically incomprehensible? Spoken or unspoken, this question lies at the center of Arendt's thinking about the Holocaust and the fate of European Jewry in the twentieth century. Arendt argued that we must begin by resisting the urge to make shocking, outrageous, and unprecedented realities "comprehensible" in terms of reductive commonplaces.[6] "The greatest danger for a proper understanding of our recent history," she wrote, "is the only too comprehensible tendency of the historian to draw analogies. The point is that Hitler was not like Jenghiz Khan and not worse than some other great criminal but entirely different."[7] Thus, comprehension does not mean "explaining phenomena by such analogies . . . that the impact of reality and the shock of experience are no longer felt," but rather requires "examining and bearing consciously the burden which our century has placed on us – neither denying its existence nor submitting meekly to its weight." Arendt concluded that comprehension "means the unpremeditated, attentive facing up to, and resisting of, reality – whatever it may be."[8]

The difficult task of comprehending totalitarianism, and of simultaneously facing up to and resisting the absolute factual evil of the Holocaust, posed at least two problems of thinking for Arendt.[9] The first concerned historiography. In her reply to Eric Voegelin's review of *The Origins of Totalitarianism*, Arendt stated that the problem was "how to write historically about something – totalitarianism – which I did not want to conserve but on the contrary felt engaged to destroy."[10] Arendt wanted to avoid an impulse that she thought characterized the "extraordinarily poor" scholarship of many contemporary historians of anti-semitism. In recovering the history of a subject which they did not want to conserve, these historians "had to write in a destructive way" and, Arendt concluded, "to write history for purposes of destruction is somehow a contradiction in terms."[11] Making the Jews "the subject of conservation" was no solution in these matters. In Arendt's view, to look at the events only from the side of the victim resulted in apologetics, "which of course is no history at all."[12] Thus the problem that comprehending "the particular subject matter" of totalitarianism posed for Arendt was how to face the reality of certain "facts and events" objectively and on their own terms without at the same time robbing them of their hellishness or appearing to condone them.[13]

This first, historiographic, problem led Arendt to criticize the standard approaches of the social sciences as well as political theoretical frameworks along the lines of Voegelin's. In both modes of inquiry, she argued, there was a failure to recognize "phenomenal differences" of factuality and "to point out the *distinct quality* of what was actually happening" in particular events.[14] Thus certain "inarticulate, elementary, and axiomatic assumptions" that form the basis of social scientific presumptions regarding human behavior are absolutely unable to account for or perhaps even appreciate exceptions to the rule. Arendt noted, for example, that "utilitarian" presumptions about human behavior and institutions are utterly unable to understand the concentration camps, which were distinguished by the *absence* of utilitarian criteria, rendering them precisely the curious and seemingly "unreal" phenomena that they were.[15] Similarly, theoretical frameworks that attempt to locate totalitarianism along a historical continuum of "intellectual affinities and influences" fail to appreciate that which is unprecedented, thereby threatening to minimize truly radical breaking points within the human condition by making them appear as though they are merely aspects of "a previously known chain of causes and influences."[16]

The second problem that Arendt faced in comprehending the absolute evil of totalitarianism was on a different plane than historiography and in a different province than the historian's. On this plane, we move from what we know of the event to how to remember it; in Lawrence Langer's words, it "shifts the responsibility to our own imaginations and what we are prepared to admit there."[17] Arendt alluded to this problem in the very personal and dedicatory letter that she wrote to Karl Jaspers as the preface of her book *Sechs Essays*, published in Germany in 1948. Here too she was concerned with factuality, but of another kind than the factual reality that she wanted to identify and trace in the historical unprecedentedness of totalitarianism. Indeed, this reality had less to do with totalitarianism than it had to do with what Arendt called the "factual territory" that the Holocaust had created for the Germans and the Jews. To Jaspers she wrote:

> The factual territory onto which both peoples have been driven looks something like this: On the one side is the complicity of the German people, which the Nazis consciously planned and realized. On the other side is the blind hatred, created in the gas chambers, of the entire Jewish people. Unless both peoples decide to leave this factual territory, the individual Jew will no more be able to abandon his fanatical hatred than will the individual German be able to rid himself of the complicity imposed upon him by the Nazis.[18]

For the Jews, Arendt tells Jaspers, the decision to leave this factual territory "is difficult to make." The difficulty has nothing to do with the miserable but comprehensible saga of anti-semitism and Jew-hatred in modern Europe; for even in this hostile context, Arendt wrote, "the possibility of communication between peoples and individuals" was alive. "One could defend oneself as a Jew," she continued, "because one had been attacked as a Jew. National concepts and national membership still had a meaning; they were still elements of a reality within which one could live and move."[19]

Leaving the factual territory of German complicity and Jewish blind hatred instead involved dealing with the construction of concentration camps and "the fabrication of corpses." With Auschwitz, Arendt wrote, "the factual territory opened up an abyss into which everyone is drawn who attempts after the fact to stand on that territory."[20] After Auschwitz, the space one occupies if one "pulls back" from the abyss is "an empty space where there are no longer nations and peoples but only individuals for whom it is now not of much consequence what the majority of peoples, or even the majority of one's own people, happens to think at any given moment."[21] Thus we might understand the second problem of comprehending the incomprehensible that Arendt faced as the problem of how to repair "the empty space where there are no longer nations and peoples but only individuals," in a way that leaves the factual territory behind and national pasts surmounted, even despite the pervasiveness of what Arendt called "the image of hell."[22]

By now it is commonplace to hold that Hannah Arendt took up the problematic task of comprehending the factual reality of totalitarianism and absolute evil primarily in two works that, in Dagmar Barnouw's words, "may turn out to be [Arendt's] most important achievements": *The Origins of Totalitarianism* (1951) and *Eichmann in Jerusalem: A Report on the Banality of Evil* (1963).[23] Less well known is the fact that Arendt assumed the task of finding out and recording factual reality in many articles on Nazism, totalitarian terror, and extermination that she wrote between 1945 and 1955.[24] In *Origins* and *Eichmann* as well as the articles on Nazism, Arendt was primarily (and monumentally) concerned with what I have identified as the first problem of comprehending the reality of totalitarianism, and with telling the "the real story of the Nazi-constructed hell" – her task was about finding out, witnessing, recording, and reflecting (Arendt 1946, 200).[25] *The Human Condition* (1958), written between *Origins* and *Eichmann*, is a different matter.

Political theory as response to trauma

Like all great works of political theory, *The Human Condition* can bear, and indeed it has invited, a superplenitude of possible readings, some of them contradictory and some better than others. Yet while *The Human Condition* is often (and usually) read within the context of modernity and world alienation, its significance in relation to *Origins* and *Eichmann*, and hence to the specific historical and political reality of the Holocaust under Nazism, has not been sufficiently recognized or explored by Arendt scholars. Usually, *The Human Condition* has been read outside, or at least beyond, the context of totalitarianism – perhaps as the nostalgic evocation of a finer past linked to the ancient Greek *polis* (for which Arendt is often criticized), or as the prospective hope for a better future that forwards a theory of participatory, even deliberative, democratic citizenship, or (under the shadow of Heidegger) as a critique of mass society and technological civilization.[26] Despite the power of many of these interpretations, very few have approached Arendt's text in a way that specifies its relation to the task of comprehending what Barnouw terms "the space and time in which a figure like Eichmann had been possible."[27]

In what follows, I want to sail against the prevailing interpretive winds and present a reading of *The Human Condition* that not only places it within the context of totalitarianism and the Holocaust but also understands it as a profound response to the trauma inflicted upon humanity by the Nazi regime. I also maintain that *The Human Condition* is situated quite differently in relation to these events than are *The Origins of Totalitarianism* and *Eichmann in Jerusalem,* because it is primarily concerned with the second problem of comprehending reality, with surmounting what Arendt called "the facts [that] have changed and poisoned the very air we breathe . . . [that] inhabit our dreams at night and permeate our thoughts during the day . . . and [are] the basic experience and the basic misery of our times."[28] Shoshana Felman clarifies the distinction I am drawing between "finding out" and "surmounting" in the following way:

> To *seek* reality is both to set out to explore the injury inflicted by it – to turn back on, and to try to penetrate, the state of being *stricken, wounded* by reality [*wirklichkeitswund*] – and to attempt, at the same time, to reemerge from the paralysis of this state, to engage reality [*Wirklichkeit suchend*] as an advent, a movement, and as a vital, critical necessity of *moving on.*[29]

In reading *The Human Condition* as an attempt to undertake this second problem of comprehension, or what Felman calls the effort to "reemerge from paralysis," I will suggest that the act of political conceptualization that Arendt enacted there was a direct and personal effort to offer both Germans and Jews a way back from the abyss so that, as individuals, they might be guided out of trauma and brought together "from their dispersion."[30]

The Greek solution

As a way of situating *The Human Condition* as a response to the trauma of the Holocaust, I wish to begin with Section 474 of Friedrich Nietzsche's text *Human, All Too Human*.[31] Entitled "the evolution of the spirit feared by the state," the section concerns Thucydides, as well as the resistance and hostility with which the Greek *polis* met the evolution of culture. Nietzsche ended on a telling note that, as is often the case with his observations, carries dimensions of meaning and possibility beyond the immediate subject to hand. Nietzsche wrote:

> one should not invoke the glorificatory speech of Pericles: for it is no more than a grand, optimistic illusion as to the supposedly necessary connection between the *polis* and Athenian culture; immediately before night descends on Athens (the plague, the rupture of tradition), Thucydides makes it rise resplendent once again, like a transfiguring evening glow in whose light the evil day that preceded it could be forgotten.[32]

In this complex statement about a traumatic event that shattered the life of a people, Nietzsche cautioned against reading Thucydides' great invention, the Funeral Oration of Pericles, in a way that stirs a nostalgic yearning for a still intact past that might be recovered and restored in some futuristic moment yet-to-come. The Athenian *polis* that Thucydides invents through the imagistic symbol[33] of the Funeral Oration is "no more," Nietzsche asserted, than a grand, evocative illusion: it bears no connection to the factual reality of a city-state called Athens that was dominated by the statesman Pericles in 431 BCE. By throwing the historical status of the Funeral Oration into question, Nietzsche also refused a reading that confines its temporal status solely to a moment preceding the catastrophe (the plague, the rupture of tradition) that befell Athens. In one sense, the Funeral Oration is such an event: in the chronological sequence of Thucydides' narrative, it appears, as Nietzsche notes, "immediately before night descends upon Athens."

In another equally important sense, however, the imagistic symbol of Athens that Thucydides creates is offered in the aftermath of catastrophe and as a possession for all time. It is Thucydides' powerful riposte to the devastating prior event that "spites healing and does not seek cure."[34] Thus in the evocative image of Athens rising resplendent, Thucydides fashions a dream that crosses out of the horror and delirium of plague and war, exposure and vulnerability, destruction and death, allowing the vehemence of their cruelty to be undone. Nietzsche put this idea in terms of the provocative simile that finds Thucydides' transforming illumination of Athens to be "like a transfiguring evening glow in whose light the evil day that preceded it could be forgotten."[35]

With this remark, Nietzsche transfigured Thucydides the historian as bearer-of-witness into Thucydides the theorist-as-healer. In this transfiguration, the act of facing up to reality – of making the facticity of certain traumatic events palpable and real – is also an act of creating a luminous and healing illusion that allows for a convalescence from pain and suffering, guilt and recrimination, as well as a kind of moving on. In keeping with Nietzsche's rendering of the Funeral Oration as a grand optimistic illusion, I mean to suggest that Thucydides is engaged in a project of inventing an imaginary time and space, an imaginary Athens, that serves a significant purpose. It creates a contrary world that does not so much obliterate the established fact of evil (the plague, the rupture of tradition), as interfere with, counter, or block the human impulse to ruminate upon and incessantly rekindle the perpetual memory of hardship and evil, thereby fanning the flames of desire for retribution and revenge. The Funeral Oration deflects this injurious impulse by offering the intervening image or "counter-memory" of Athens as glorious, magnificent: "the school of Hellas," where "the singular spectacle of daring and deliberation" are each carried to their "highest point."[36] The fixation upon "what was" is modulated by the liberating power of this imaginary world; the obsession with retribution is thereby deferred. By inventing an alternative world swept clean of horror, suffering, and degradation, Thucydides' solution offers the Athenians a way toward thinking themselves anew, and thus provides a path toward forgetting the evil of the day before.

In much the same way that Nietzsche suggests that Thucydides was engaged in assisting in the convalescence of the Athenians, so I want to suggest that, in *The Human Condition,* Hannah Arendt was responding to the trauma of survival that faced the Europeans, and especially the Germans and the Jews, in the wake of the overwhelming deadliness of Nazism and the burning darkness of the extermination camps. In the aftermath of this ultimate evil, Arendt created a powerful, iridescent image that counters the "reality of persecution"[37] that had decimated the Jews and in its aftermath robbed the Germans of "all spontaneous speech and comprehension, so that now . . . they are speechless, incapable of articulating thoughts and adequately expressing their feelings." [38] Perhaps we should not be surprised to learn that the resplendent and healing image that Arendt fashions in *The Human Condition* – the image of the public realm as "the space of appearance" – draws its own light from the transfiguring glow of Thucydides' luminescent Periclean *polis*.[39] As Arendt observed, "Pericles' speech, though it certainly corresponded to and articulated the innermost convictions of the people of Athens, has always been read with the sad wisdom of hindsight by men who knew that his words were spoken at the beginning of the end."[40] In Arendt's view, the Funeral Oration is placed by Thucydides at a point in the narrative preceding the dark night of plague and the rupture of tradition. Arendt also holds to a version of Nietzsche's greater insight when she writes, "The words of Pericles, as Thucydides reports them, are perhaps unique in their supreme confidence that men can enact *and* save their greatness at the same time and, as it were, by one and the same gesture."[41]

So let us not invoke the glorificatory speech of those Arendtian Greeks in the public realm in order to decry (as so many of her critics have done) Arendt's "nostalgia" for a romantic past that could be a perfect future; for Arendt's public realm of the space of appearances is "no more" than a dream, a grand, optimistic illusion.[42] In what follows, I shall attend instead to the way this grand illusion functions when it is drawn into what Arendt once called the gap of time between past and future, into "this small track of non-time" which "each new generation, indeed every new human being as he inserts himself between an infinite past and an infinite future, must discover and ploddingly pave . . . anew."[43]

(Re)Interpreting *The Human Condition*

The Human Condition is not directly or explicitly about totalitarianism, Nazism or the extermination of the Jews. Nowhere in the course of this text does Arendt make any detailed or specific reference to these circumstances. Indeed, two other ominous events were the explicit impetus for this work: the launching of Sputnik, which Arendt called "second in importance to no other"; and the advent of "automation," which she saw as the harbinger of a "society of laborers without labor," liberated into nothingness.[44] Thus, to continue to stake out a reading that places *The Human Condition* in relation to the Holocaust, I will draw upon two interpretive insights that justify the significance of what is "unspoken" in a work of art or a political theory text.

The first insight is the literary critic Harry Berger's compelling notion of the "conspicuous exclusion" of themes that are "saturatingly present" in great texts or artworks – but only as silence or *felt absence*.[45] Following this insight, a text or artwork can be read as holding certain themes at bay, but manifestly so. As Berger writes: "Conspicuous exclusion makes us attend to what has been left out; the omitted item is not merely missing but *present-as-missing*. It is one thing for an artist merely to omit . . . or ignore something. But it is another for him to make a point of his omission, directing our attention to it."[46] Berger suggests, for example, that the healing tranquility at the center of the paintings of Johannes Vermeer have the horrors of the seventeenth-century wars of religion as their indirect, conspicuously unstated background. Thus, "a whole set of anecdotal, allegorical, and narrative values hovers about Vermeer's painting. But none of them is firmly developed, articulated, or nailed down."[47] Berger locates the "felt absence" of war in the roaring lions that are carved into the filials that Vermeer bathed in the window light, and also in the maps of the bloodily contested Netherlands that adorn the walls where young women read in serene and intimate rooms.[48] When Vermeer is viewed in this way, the achievement of his paintings becomes all the more remarkable. As Lawrence Weschler has recently remarked, "It's almost as if Vermeer can be seen to have been asserting or *inventing* the very idea of peace" amid the horrors of a tremendously turbulent juncture in the history of his continent and country.[49]

The second interpretive insight involves a brief but telling observation that Karl Jaspers made to Arendt in December 1960, upon having read *Vita Activa* (the German title). Allowing that he grasped "the overall picture" of the book much more easily and quickly in the German than in English, Jaspers noted:

> What appeals to me so strongly in this book is that the things you explicitly state you will *not* talk about (right at the beginning and repeatedly thereafter) exert such a palpable influence from the background. That makes the book in some strange way very transparent for me. There is nothing quite like it today. All your important and concrete discussions are carried by another dimension. Therefore, despite their great seriousness, they become "light" in all their reality. Your many pertinent insights and illuminations and the historical profundity of your explanations provide concreteness and solidity.[50]

Jaspers did not proceed to specify what he thought the other dimension of *The Human Condition* was, the things that exerted their palpable influence from the background of the text in an indirect, unspoken, yet illuminating way. But if we consider his remark in relation to Berger's notion of conspicuous exclusion, then we might imagine that adumbrated around the edges of Arendt's great achievement is a theme that is saturatingly present but only as *felt absence* – a theme that is withheld but at the same time palpable. Thus, just as Berger's insight invites us to see more in Vermeer's art than may immediately meet the eye, so Jaspers' remark opens the possibility that there is more in *The Human Condition* than the things explicitly stated or directly addressed.

We might take these insights, then, as cautionary comments against reading *The Human Condition* too close to the surface, or in a manner that misses the depth and profundity of certain "concrete discussions" because it fails to see a dimension of meaning that is, at once, demonstrable and undisclosed in that text. For example, in the "Prologue" to *The Human Condition*, Arendt indicates one thing that she will not discuss, and some "preoccupations and perplexities" to which her book "does not offer an answer."[51] The topic undiscussed is the background against which she says the book was written: the "modern world" born with the first atomic explosions. The preoccupations and perplexities left unanswered are initiated by the two "threatening" events of Sputnik and automation. All three of these phenomena (the birth of the modern world, space exploration, and automatism) conspire toward a deeper issue, however. They introduce the specter of a rupture between "knowledge" (in the sense of scientific and technical know-how) and "thought." The possibility of such a rupture, Arendt notes, threatens to turn humanity into "helpless slaves" and "thoughtless creatures," "at the mercy of every gadget which is technically possible, no matter how murderous it is."[52]

Arendt's reference to the murderousness of certain human scientific and technical inventions of the modern world was not, I think, written solely in the face of the lurid glow of nuclear apocalypse. When Arendt wrote explicitly in *The Origins of Totalitarianism* that "a victory of the concentration-camp system would mean the same inexorable doom for human beings as the use of the hydrogen bomb would mean the doom of the human race," she invoked another type of murderous technology that lingered, palpable but unspoken, in the background of *The Human Condition*.[53] This is the dimension of meaning that suffused Arendt's project, and also gave rise to the "light" that Jaspers found at the center of *The Human Condition*, both in the sense of illumination (where light is a metaphor perhaps for truth) and in the sense of a defiance of gravity (where light is a metaphor for the release from weight or pain).

What I want to contend, then, is that the depth and profundity of Arendt's concept of the public realm of politics as "the space of appearance" can be fully appreciated only in terms of the features of a phenomenon that is saturatingly present but conspicuously held at bay in *The Human Condition*. The phenomenon is the "hellish experiment" that Arendt thought opened the abyss to the Holocaust, to the most extreme form of totalitarian evil: the SS concentration camps, where the whole program of extermination and annihilation of the Jewish people was enacted, and the crime against humanity was carried out. This hellish experiment is what a great deal of *The Human Condition* is all about, and what Arendt's luminescent invention of "the space of appearance" is meant to counter. Of course, not directly; but this does not mean that we cannot see the horrors of a human-made Hell both subtly insinuated and ultimately overcome in Arendt's text.[54] In what form, then, is the saturating presence of the Holocaust palpable but unspoken in *The Human Condition*?

Labor and work *in extremis*

As many of Arendt's commentators have noted, in *The Human Condition*, the concepts of labor (*Arbeit*) and work (*Werk*) can bear, and indeed they invite, a superplenitude of possible meanings, some of them contradictory. At their most basic level they designate, along with action, the fundamental human activities within the *vita activa*; and each corresponds to one of the basic conditions under which, Arendt wrote, "life on earth has been given to man."[55] The human condition of labor is life itself; the human condition of work is worldliness; and the human condition of action is plurality.

Yet even at this very basic level we would be mistaken to suppose that the *vita activa* is simply a conglomerate of three fundamental units (labor–work–action) that are things-in-themselves or enduring phenomena with particular definitive features or side-effects. This is partly because Arendt theorized the activities of labor, work, and action as externally bound to and connected by each other in sometimes compatible and sometimes incompatible ways. Equally importantly, however, Arendt took the more radical step of internally differentiating these concepts so that each presupposes a multiplicity of interconnected elements that defy attribution in terms of a settled meaning or unified synoptic picture. The concept of labor or *animal laborans*, for example, is the sum of the following multifarious elements:

> the blessing of life as a whole, nature, animality, life processes, (human) biology, (human) body, (human) metabolism, fertility, birth, reproduction, childbirth, femaleness, cyclicality, circularity, seasons, necessity, basic life-needs (food, clothing, shelter), certain kinds of toil, repetition, everyday functions (eating, cleaning, mending, washing, cooking, resting, etc.), housework, the domestic sphere, abundance, consumerism, privatization, purposeless regularity, the society of jobholders, automation, technological determinism, routinization, relentless repetition, automatism, regularization, non-utilitarian processes, dehumanizing processes, devouring processes, painful exhaustion, waste, recyclability, destruction (of nature, body, fertility), and deathlessness.

The concept of work or *homo faber* is the sum of the following multifarious elements:

> the work of our hands, the man-made world, fabrication, (human) artifice, (human) creativity, production, usage, durability, objectivity, building, constructing, manufacturing, making, violation, maleness, linearity, reification, multiplication, tools and instruments, rules and measurement, ends and means, predictability, the exchange market, commercialism, capitalism, instrumental processes, utilitarian processes, objectifying processes, artificial processes, vulgar expediency, violence, predictability, deprivation of intrinsic worth, degradation, disposability, destruction (of nature, world), and lifelessness.

As I have arranged them here, the features that Arendt assigned to labor and work can be viewed as points along a single continuum that shade from the human condition "under which life on earth has been given to man" into a condition *in extremis* under which life on earth is taken away. Near the end of the continuum, labor manifests itself *in extremis* in the form of dehumanizing automatic processes and compulsive repetitions that displace human death; work manifests itself *in extremis* in the form of dehumanizing fabricating processes and instrumentalized objectifications that violate human life. Now, along this continuum we might find the automatic processes of *animal laborans* and the instrumental processes of *homo faber* in the nullity that is advanced capitalism in late modernity. This is indeed what many readers of *The Human Condition* do when they (quite reasonably) interpret this text as an Arendtian critique of late-modern, post-war, technological consumer society, and (variously) approach Arendt's concept of action as an attempt in the face of this nullity to revitalize a deliberative or democratic or agonistic or destabilizing politics.

Yet I think that if we stop here we will miss the monumental theme that Arendt is holding at bay, but conspicuously so, in *The Human Condition*, and perhaps overlook the palpable significance of Arendt's concrete discussion of action as well. For the two forms of extremity that she warned of – labor as routinized deathlessness, and work as the objectified violation of life – have hitherto coupled in human experience, although only once and with terrible and traumatic consequences that defy comprehension. This coupling occurred in the "hellish experiment" of the SS extermination camps where, existentially speaking, the obliteration of human life was effected before it was actually accomplished. "Extermination," Arendt wrote, "happens to human beings who for all practical purposes are already 'dead.'"[56] The "skillfully manufactured unreality" of the human beings sealed off inside these camps was, at once, an existential condition of being dead and yet not annihilated, alive and yet not living.[57] Death-yet-not-death, life-yet-not-life.

The already-deadness/still-aliveness of the inmates had to do with another existential feature of the extermination camps – an extreme isolation that was carried to a perfection hitherto unknown in human experience. In their complete dehumanizing isolation, Arendt observed, "the camps were separated from the surrounding world as if they and their inmates were no longer part of the world of the living."[58] It was as if the human beings there had dropped off the face of the earth, into a life "removed from earthly purposes," for their departure from the world was not announced; nor were they even pronounced dead. The status of the inmates to those in the world of the living was such that it was "as though they had never been born."[59] Arendt thought that the horror of life in the concentration camps could "never be fully embraced by the imagination for the very reason that [this horror stood] outside of life and death."[60]

This existential condition of extermination was furthered by the development of certain new technological processes under which mass murder was mechanized, the death rate of inmates was regulated, and torture was "strictly organized" and efficiently calculated in a way that perpetuated dying without inducing death – that is, until "depopulation" was ordered so as to make room for "new supplies." [61] "The concentration-camp inmate has no price," Arendt noted, "because he can always be replaced; nobody knows to whom he belongs, because he is never seen. From the point of view of normal society he is absolutely superfluous."[62] There was, then, a paradoxical non-utilitarian utility to these camps. On the one hand, they were utterly useless to the Nazi regime for either the purpose of winning the war or for the exploitation of labor; on the other, the undefined fear the camps inspired was more essential to the preservation of the regime's power "than any other of its institutions."[63] It is in this non-utilitarian utility that we find the coupling of labor and work. In this obscene coupling of labor and work *in extremis*, where the routinized fabrication of corpses commingled with the instrumental cyclicality of extermination, human beings came face to face not with life on earth, but with living death on some other planet. Thus Arendt noted in *The Human Condition*:

> We are perhaps the first generation which has become fully aware of the murderous consequences inherent in a line of thought that force one to admit that all means, provided they are efficient, are permissible and justified to pursue something defined as an end.[64]

In an even more mundane and terrible sense, labor and work were also operative in the extermination camps. The "work camp" was the identity that served to mask the real function of the death camps, and *Arbeit Macht*

Frei ("Labor Gives Freedom") was the brightly illuminated sign over the large gate to Auschwitz. Nevertheless, as Arendt noted, "The concentration camp as an institution was not established for the sake of any possible labor yield; the only permanent economic function of the camps has been the financing of their own supervisory apparatus . . . Any work that has been performed could have been done much better and more cheaply under different conditions."[65] (Notice Arendt's own commingling of the terms "labor" and "work" in these sentences.) Pierre Vidal-Naquet contributes importantly to this subject when he notes that "Concentration camp labor *also* served the ends of exhaustion and control . . . [and] also had the characteristic of being indefinitely replenishable."[66] Although some camps (Chelmno, Sobibor, Belzec, Treblinka) were directed solely toward extermination, Vidal-Naquet notes that "Maidanek and (above all) Auschwitz . . . were living proof that extermination could go on side by side with exploitation of forced labor . . . between exploitation and extermination there was a tension, never a break."

When in *The Human Condition* Hannah Arendt affirmed the existential superiority of action over labor and work, I do not think that she was extolling the posturing hero (much less vanity and vainglory) in some sort of existential confrontation with mortality and death. Indeed, Arendt remarks upon the peculiar modern inability to appreciate the earnest aspiration to an "earthly immortality" as anything more than "vanity." She also attributes the tendency to "look down upon all striving for immortality as [nothing more than] vanity and vainglory" to the "shock" of the philosophers' discovery of the eternal.[67] Her concept of action and her invocation of glory are decidedly more human, and far more courageous, than that. What they attempt to counter is not death as such; for what Arendt called "the two supreme events of appearance and disappearance" (birth and death) merely delimit (although supremely) the time interval within which the other events of nonbiological life – this mortal, human, life of action and speech – take place.[68] Instead, what I think Arendt was attempting to confront and counter by asserting – and, yes, inventing – the public realm as the "space of appearance" that she called "action" was the existential unreality of "death-yet-not-death, life-yet-not-life": the living death/deathly life that was the horrific specter of the Holocaust.

Reinhabiting the empty space: the recovery of action

"If art is to survive the Holocaust – to survive death as a master . . ." Shoshana Felman writes, "it will have to break, in art, this mastery, which insidiously pervades the whole of culture and the whole of the esthetic project."[69] We might say the same here not only of political theory, but of all works of "outstanding permanence" that, in Arendt's words, release "the world-open and communicative" human capacity for thought.[70] I now want to turn to Arendt's action concept of politics and the imagistic symbol of the space of appearance, in order to consider how they create a healing illusion and a disruptive countermemory, attempting to reach over the historical abyss created by Auschwitz, and break the mastery of the Holocaust.

Arendt's concept of action carries within it a multitude of dimensions and meanings. Yet unlike her concepts of labor and work, "action" does not threaten to destroy itself, or point toward the precariousness of extremity. In the voluminous secondary literature that has developed around Arendt's political theory, the concept of action is usually affiliated with the notion of a public space of freedom and equality that comes into being when citizens speak together and act in concert; hence many of Arendt's commentators take their purchase on Arendtian politics from a perspective that casts it as the active engagement of citizens in the public realm. [71] But if we look closely, we can see that the concept of action is also the sum of the following multifarious elements:

> the web of human relationships, the realm of human affairs, the space of appearance, being together in the presence of others, being seen and heard by others, the sharing of word and deeds, the spontaneous beginnings of something new, plurality, equality, sameness in utter diversity, self-revelation through speech, the disclosure of the agent in the act, the appearance of "who" someone is, the active revelation of unique personal identity, the distinctiveness of each human person, courage, boldness, esteem, dignity, endurance, the shining brightness once called glory, the human capacity for *power* generated by action in concert, the human capacity for *freedom* born of acting, the distinctly human condition of *living on earth and inhabiting the world*.

The tendency of Arendt's contemporary commentators to construe this concept primarily in terms of participatory citizen-politics (whether in the form of agonal contestation or deliberative communication, classical republicanism or radical democracy) tends to occlude something that I believe is profoundly articulated in Arendt's concept of action, and also vital to a reading of *The Human Condition* in the context of dark times. This is the phenomenon of self-revelation, or what Arendt also called "the disclosure of the agent in the act." We might say that self-revelation is precisely what crystallizes in the space of appearance where human beings gather, and that spontaneous acting and speaking are the capacities through which the unique human person discloses his or her individuality, him or her as "self," as *sui generis*. In a particularly telling passage in *The Human Condition*, Arendt underscored the significance of action as the revelation of the unique and distinct identity of the agent:

> In acting and speaking, men show who they are, reveal actively their unique personal identities and thus make their appearance in the human world . . . This disclosure of "who" in contradistinction to "what" somebody is – his qualities, gifts, talents, and shortcomings, which he may display or hide – is implicit in everything somebody says and does . . . Without the disclosure of the agent in the act, action loses its specific character and becomes one form of achievement among others.[72]

It is the "who-ness" of acting, the "agent-revealing capacity" of action and speech, that Arendt repeatedly emphasized in her concrete discussion of politics in *The Human Condition*.[73] The "space of appearance" is the realm within which "I appear to others as others appear to me," through the disclosure and the exposure of myself – my uniquely individual, irreducible, and distinctively human self – through word and deed.[74] Arendt found in the willingness to act and speak at all, to "[leave] one's private hiding place and [show] who one is," a kind of "courage and even boldness" that are usually assigned to the hero.[75] The existential significance that she granted to the space of appearance was such that, "[t]o be deprived of it means to be deprived of reality, which, humanly and politically speaking, is the same as appearance."[76]

From one angle, it is difficult to appreciate Arendt's image of self-revelation in a space of appearance as adequate to the task of capturing what politics requires or entails. As Arendt herself admitted about the Greek concept of action,[77] so I am tempted to say of Arendt's action concept of politics: it is highly individualistic (although certainly not subjectivist), and stresses the urge toward collective self-disclosure at the expense of many other factors in political action, including the dimension of strategic or instrumental purposefulness that Arendt so resolutely opposed as an aspect of the political.[78] From another angle, however, I believe that there is a better way to make sense of the unique and *sui generis* conception of self-revelation in the space of appearance that Arendt creates in *The Human Condition*. This has little to do with the expectations that one might wish to impose upon a theory of politics, and more to do with what I take to be Arendt's attempt to conjure a magnificent transfiguring illusion, a *via gloriosa*, and so rehabilitate what she called "the empty space" to which humanity had withdrawn after Auschwitz.

We can appreciate the power and luminescence of Arendt's space of appearance only if we draw it into the gap between past and future, and recognize what it invites us to overcome. The luminosity of this space, where the condition of being a unique, individual, human personality is fulfilled in the ordinary glory of speaking and doing, is the absolute counter to "the disintegration of personality" that was achieved in the extermination camps, where the end result was "the reduction of human beings to the lowest possible denominator of 'identical reactions.'"[79] As Primo Levi wrote, of Auschwitz: "we have learnt that our personality is fragile, that it is much more in danger than our life; and the old wise ones, instead of warning us 'remember that you must die' would have done much better to remind us of this greater danger that threatens us." These are "the evil tidings of what man's presumption made of man in Auschwitz."[80]

In Arendt's imagistic symbol of the space of appearance, with its great glorification of "the paradoxical plurality of unique beings" there is illuminated a way back from Auschwitz's empty space.[81] For with this grand, optimistic illusion, Arendt did nothing less than bestow upon us the human personality rising resplendent in a space where we gather together from our dispersion. This space breaks the mastery of all contexts where who I am, as an individual human person, is made the object of a "what," and other human persons are manufactured into specimens, "ghastly marionettes with human faces."[82] If we take seriously this possibility, then we might read Arendt's concept of *action* – and especially its formulation in the image of the space of appearance – as a powerful and compelling rebuke to the living death and deathly life that is the horrific effect of the extermination camps, and a compelling counter-memory to the persistent specter of the Holocaust. With this powerful imagistic symbol, the political theorist offers to humanity a relief from dark times, a "recreative escape," a chance to give one's self over to the radiance of light and the "shining brightness" of the represented world.

In this sense, the grand, optimistic illusion of the space of appearance offers a new beginning to the sufferers and survivors of a trauma that is still very much with us, and has left so many stranded still in the factual territory of complicity and hatred that Hannah Arendt identified. It offers a way to think anew what we are doing, so that the evil day, with its old meaning and its legacy of grievances, can be mastered and perhaps some day surmounted. Thus might "the empty space of individuals" be reinfused with plurality and life. Accordingly, Arendt's great invention in *The Human Condition* does not simply, as is often said these days, rethink identity and celebrate diversity; rather, it strives to subvert, counter, and overcome a factual territory that was as assiduously invented and dark as its obverse was suffused with light. That Arendt accomplished this subversion of evil in a manner that was utterly devoid of both gratuitous moralizing and self-righteous condemnation is itself a kind of miracle. But this miracle was fully in keeping with the one that she thought saves the world: the human capacity to bestow upon human affairs the two essential characteristics of human existence – faith and hope.

one way in *Origins* and another in *Eichmann*, especially concerning the problem of evil and mythologizing the horrible. My rather more limited point is that, whatever else differentiates them, *Origins* and *Eichmann* might be cast as efforts to "come to terms with" the factual reality of the Holocaust, whereas *The Human Condition* needs to be understood in a different way, as a project directed toward the restorative surmounting of the "factual territory" (i.e. German complicity and Jewish blind hatred) that Arendt thought that Auschwitz had left in its terrible wake.

26 See, for example Joseph M. Schwartz "Arendt's Politics: The Elusive Search for Substance," *Praxis International* 9 (1989): 25–47; Pitkin, *The Attack of the Blob*, pp. 112–114; Seyla Benhabib, *The Reluctant Modernism of Hannah Arendt* (Thousand Oaks, CA: Sage Publications, 1992), pp. 199–215; and Dana Villa, *Arendt and Heidegger: The Fate of the Political* (Princeton, Princeton University Press, 1996). Villa also provides an instructive (critical) overview of the various neo-Aristotelian (republican), Nietzschean (agonistic), and Habermasian (discursive) appropriations of Arendt's concept of political action in the literature.

27 Barnouw, *Visible Spaces*, p. 223. An important exception is Margaret Canovan, *Hannah Arendt: A Reinterpretation of Her Political Thought* (Cambridge: Cambridge University Press, 1992), who explicitly seeks to explore the connections between Arendt's writings on totalitarianism and *The Human Condition*. Canovan asserts that "virtually the entire agenda of Arendt's political thought was set by her reflections on the political catastrophes of the mid-century" (p. 7). She interprets the central concepts of *The Human Condition* (especially "labor" and "society") as "moulded by [an] interpretation of totalitarianism," and in response to its "analogues": "the belief that everything is possible, and . . . that everything is determined within an inevitable process" (p. 103). Similarly, Barnouw (*Visible Spaces*) argues that the need "to strain against necessity . . . fed by the experience of total war and holocaust" was the main source of Arendt's distinction between labor and work in *The Human Condition*. Both Canovan and Barnouw recognize Arendt's "middle work" not only as a project addressing mass technocracy in late modernity, but also as an effort, in Barnouw's words, to articulate "a culturally secured quality of life which would defeat the senselessness of past mass destruction of human life" (p. 195). Richard Bernstein, *Hannah Arendt and the Jewish Question* (Cambridge, MA: MIT Press, 1996) also observes (more briefly) that "most of the motifs of [Arendt's] understanding of politics" in *The Human Condition* "are worked out in her attempt to comprehend the events of twentieth-century totalitarianism." I wish to endorse all of these insights by way of taking them (and the meaning of "comprehension") in a rather different direction.

28 Arendt, "The Image of Hell," p. 200.

29 Shoshana Felman, "Education and Crisis, or the Vicissitudes of Teaching," in Cathy Caruth, ed., *Trauma: Explorations in Memory* (Baltimore: Johns Hopkins University Press), p. 34. The capacity for "moving on" is a process for which English has no single word but German has two (lengthy) ones: *Geschichtsaufarbeitung* and *Vergangenheitsbewältigung*. Both capture the idea of "treating," "working through," "coming to terms with," or even "overcoming" the past, as Felman implies in the reference to "moving on." I do not wish

to confuse this idea with the effort to find some way of distilling hope, or at least consolation, from the vast sea of despair and systematic murder that was the Holocaust. If there is any element of the "triumph of the spirit" to be found here, it is not within the Holocaust itself, but rather in relation to its aftermath, and the surmounting of its pernicious legacy of evil, guilt, hatred, and recrimination.

30 This moving image of reunification I draw from Jaspers' remark (quoted by Arendt in "Dedication to Karl Jaspers," p. 216): "We live as if we stood knocking at gates that are still closed to us. Today something may perhaps be taking place in the purely personal realm that cannot yet found a world order because it is only given to individuals, but which will perhaps someday found such an order when these individuals have been brought together from their dispersion."

31 Friedrich Nietzsche, *Human, All Too Human: A Book for Free Spirits*, trans. R. J. Hollingdale (Cambridge: Cambridge University Press, 1996), 174. This starting point is not, however, as unusual as it may at first appear. Arendt often referred to Nietzsche and was certainly influenced by his thinking. A most provocative footnote (n. 83) in *The Human Condition* also provides a linkage between Arendt and Nietzsche on the meaning of memory and forgetting (p. 245). Arendt refers to two "unique" insights of Nietzsche's that mark off human from animal life, and are "frequently overlooked" by scholars. They are found in the first two aphorisms of the second treatise in *On the Genealogy of Morals* (New York: Random House, 1969). Although Arendt does not proceed to identify these insights, the curious reader will discover that in them Nietzsche addresses (1) "forgetting," as the "positive faculty of repression," and "active forgetfulness" as the "preserver of psychic order, repose and etiquette" (pp. 57–58); and (2) the origination of "responsibility" in the emancipated individual's "right" to make promises (pp. 58–60).

32 Nietzsche, *Human, All Too Human*, 174.

33 The term "imagistic symbol" comes from Harry Berger, "Conspicuous Exclusion in Vermeer: An Essay in Renaissance Pastoral," *Second World and Green World: Studies in Renaissance Fiction-Making* (Berkeley: University of California Press, 1988), pp. 460–461.

34 Felman, "Education and Crisis," 21.

35 Nietzsche's German reads: *noch einmal wie eine verklarende Abendrothe aufleuchten, bei der man den schlimmen Tag vergessen soll, der ihr vorangieng.* The German word *vergessen* can mean, in addition to "to forget," "to leave (behind)"; "overlook," "omit"; or "neglect." Perhaps it is instructive that Nietzsche chose this word, for unlike other German expressions for forgetting (e.g. *nicht denken an*; *nicht bedenken*; *verlernen*) *vergessen* does not seem to imply actively or intentionally blocking something out or choosing not to remember it, but rather suggests a forgetting that simply happens or occurs. (I thank Dan Hope for clarifying this point for me.) The significance of memory, remembrance, not-forgetting, and memorialization is a significant theme in Holocaust studies, which tend primarily (and variously) to focus the problem as one of "coming to terms with the past." See, for example, Saul Friedlander, *When Memory Comes* (1979); Pierre Vidal-Nacquet, *The Assassins of Memory* (New York: Columbia University Press 1985); Charlotte Delbo, *Days and Memory* (1985); Lawrence Langer, *Holocaust Testimonies: The Ruins of*

Memory (New Haven: Yale University Press, 1991); James Young, *The Texture of Memory* (1993); and Geoffrey Hartman, *The Shapes of Memory* (1993).

36 Thucydides, *The Peloponnesian War*, trans. Crawley (New York: Modern Library, 1982), 110.

37 Arendt, *MDT*, p. 17.

38 Arendt, "Social Science Techniques," p. 253.

39 Arendt, *HC*, p. 207.

40 Ibid., p. 205.

41 Ibid.

42 Arendt's critics are by no means incorrect in emphasizing the significance she places upon the "prephilosophical Greek experience of action and speech," the Hellenic world of the Greek *polis*, and the glory of Periclean Athens, "which bestowed upon politics a dignity which even today has not altogether disappeared" (*HC*, pp. 207, 205). What I wish to suggest, however, is that although accurate as descriptions, the critics' renderings of Arendt's recourse to Hellas as evidence of utopianism, or an antiquated nostalgia for a forgotten past, or a masculinist fixation with heroic glory, prematurely and hastily convert description to (negative) evaluation, without adequately attending to Arendt's own disparagement of nostalgic yearnings or, more importantly, without considering the complicated way in which the images of the Greek *polis* may be operating in *The Human Condition* as part of an interplay with the aftermath of the Holocaust.

43 Arendt, *BPF*, p. 13.

44 Arendt, *HC*, pp. 1, 4.

45 Harry Berger's work on conspicuous exclusion in the art of Johannes Vermeer ("Conspicuous Exclusion in Vermeer"; and "Some Vanity of His Art: Conspicuous Exclusion and Pastoral in Vermeer," in *Second World and Green World*, pp. 441–461, 462–509) is appropriated by Lawrence Weschler in his essay, "Inventing Peace," on the Yugoslav War Crimes Tribunal in The Hague (*The New Yorker*, 1996, pp. 56–64). Drawing upon Berger, Weschler suggests that when Vermeer was painting those images, otherwise the very emblem of peacefulness and serenity, "*all Europe was Bosnia*" (p. 57). Thus war is present-as-missing, a felt absence, in Vermeer's art. Viewed within this political context, Vermeer "can be seen . . . to have been asserting or *inventing* the very idea of peace," Weschler suggests, in response to the "horrors of his age" which are ever-present as "felt absence" in his art (p. 59).

46 Berger, *Second World and Green World*, p. 442.

47 Ibid., p. 448.

48 Ibid., p. 456.

49 Weschler, "Inventing Peace," p. 56.

50 Karl Jaspers, Letter no. 270 (Dec 1, 1960), *Hannah Arendt – Karl Jaspers Correspondence*, p. 407. Jaspers' remark about the lightness and transparency that mark what is simultaneously the "great seriousness" of *The Human Condition* echoes another intriguing hermeneutic theme that Berger develops under the terms "heterocosmic thought and the second world," and finds in certain works of Renaissance art, especially Vermeer's (*Second World and Green World*, p. 458). Heterocosmic thought "withdraws from the given world to alternate frames of reference," Berger suggests, and presents an alternate "imaginary

world" in "an attitude of serious playing; *serio ludere* means playing seriously with full knowledge; however seriously you play, you are only playing" (p. 459). The attitude of reflexive awareness embedded in playing seriously makes the imaginary world "secure for the systole of withdrawal but not secure enough to discourage or prohibit the diastole of return" (p. 459). I want to build upon both Jaspers' comment and Berger's notion to suggest that Arendt's image of the "space of appearance" may be appreciated as precisely such a form of withdrawal and return, as heterocosmic theorizing.

51 Arendt, *HC*, pp. 4, 3.
52 Ibid., p. 3.
53 Arendt, *OT*, p. 443.
54 If we take into consideration Joanne Jacobson's remark that, "the most profound legacy of the Holocaust may be silence; language's promise of order and beauty seems insulting" ("Speech After Long Silence," *The Nation*, 11/11, p. 30), then the conspicuous exclusion – the palpable but unspoken presence – of this trauma in *The Human Condition* becomes an even more poignant and powerful aspect of Arendt's writing. The most compelling Holocaust texts, as Geoffrey Hartman observes and Jacobson reports, "are those whose authors have intentionally let the difficulties of representation drift close to the surface . . . their art makes us feel there is something that cannot be presented" (p. 31). In this sense, Jacobson is correct to insist that, no matter how compelling they may be, trauma on the scale of the Holocaust remains at odds with explicit narrative and symbol and image.
55 Arendt, *HC*, p. 7.
56 Arendt, "Social Science Techniques and the Study of Concentration Camps," p. 236.
57 Arendt, *OT*, p. 445.
58 Arendt, "Social Science Techniques,"p. 239.
59 Arendt, *OT*, pp. 444–445.
60 Ibid., p. 444.
61 Arendt, "Social Science Techniques," p. 238.
62 Arendt, *OT*, p. 444.
63 Arendt, Ibid., p. 456; "Social Science Techniques," p. 236.
64 Arendt, *HC*, p. 229.
65 Arendt, *OT*, p. 444.
66 Pierre Vidal-Naquet, *Assassins of Memory: Essays on the Denial of the Holocaust* (New York: Columbia University Press, 1992), p. 109.
67 Arendt, *HC*, pp. 56, 21.
68 Ibid., p. 97.
69 Felman, "Education and Crisis," p. 39.
70 Arendt, *HC*, p. 168.
71 See, for example, Benhabib, *The Reluctant Modernism of Hannah Arendt*, chapter 6; Maurice Passerin D'Entreves, *The Political Philosophy of Hannah Arendt* (London: Routledge, 1994), chapter 4; Shiraz Dossa, *The Public Realm and the Public Self: The Political Theory of Hannah Arendt* (Waterloo, Ontario: W. Laurier University Press, 1989); Phillip Hansen, *Hannah Arendt: Politics, History and Citizenship* (Stanford: Stanford University Press, 1993); Jeffrey Isaac, "Oases in the Desert: Hannah Arendt on Democratic Politics," *American*

Political Science Review 88 (1994): 156–168; James Knauer, "Re-thinking Arendt's 'Vita Activa': Towards a Theory of Democratic Praxis," *Praxis International* 5 (1985): 185–194; Bikhu Parekh, *Hannah Arendt and the Search for a New Political Philosophy* (London: Macmillan, 1981). I am not suggesting that there is a uniform line on the meaning of Arendtian politics, or that Arendt's commentators are not fully appreciative of what Canovan (*Hannah Arendt: A Reinterpretation of her Political Thought*, p. 131) calls "the very considerable complexities" in Arendt's concept of action.

72 Arendt, *HC*, p. 179–180.

73 Ibid., pp. 182, 181–186, 194, 198–199, 208, 211.

74 Ibid., p. 198.

75 Ibid., p. 186.

76 Ibid., p. 199.

77 "No doubt this concept of action is highly individualistic, as we would say today. It stresses the urge toward self-disclosure at the expense of all other factors and therefore remains relatively untouched by the predicament of unpredictability," ibid., p. 194.

78 I have elaborated on this critique, and presented a very different reading of *The Human Condition* in M. Dietz, "The Slow Boring of Hard Boards: Methodical Thinking and the Work of Politics," *American Political Science Review* 88/4 (1994): 873–886.

79 Arendt, *OT*, pp. 447–457. In this powerful discussion, Arendt argued that the disintegration of personality was accomplished in three stages in the extermination camps: first, the "juridical person" was destroyed at the moment of arbitrary arrest (p. 447); second, the "moral personality" was destroyed and "human solidarity" utterly corrupted through the techniques of enforced isolation and living "in absolute solitude" (p. 451); and finally, the destruction of "the differentiation of the individual, his unique identity" (p. 453), beginning with "the monstrous conditions in the transports to the camps," and ending with the permanence and institutionalization of torture and the relentless processes of extermination.

80 Primo Levi, *Survival in Auschwitz: The Nazi Assault on Humanity*, trans. S. Woolf (New York: Collier Books, 1961), p. 49.

81 Arendt, *HC*, p. 176.

82 Arendt, *OT*, p. 455.

PART III

Freedom and political action

5

JEROME KOHN

Freedom: the priority of the political

For Dore Ashton

Many of us must have experienced a sensation of relief while celebrating the advent of the new millennium. The relief consisted first in having survived, and then in saying adieu to a century that more than any other in the long history of mankind had been marked by *evil*. As if torn from a corpse, the ligatures of that evil – binding total war to totalitarianism; the totalitarian destruction of entire peoples to the invention of nuclear weapons; and the proliferation of nuclear weapons in a post-totalitarian world to the unprecedented capacity of mankind to annihilate itself – revealed the identifying scars of the century that had come to its calendric end. But New Year and even millennial celebrations tend to be followed by sober, frequently painful awakenings. Has our "morning after" found us in a *new world*? Has the mere passage of time from the twentieth to the twenty-first century healed the wounds of the former and enabled us to be reconciled to the latter? If we heed the Russian poet Akhmatova, who was not thinking of the calendar when she spoke of "the real twentieth century,"[1] are we not forced to ask ourselves: What, if anything, has ended? Hannah Arendt might counsel us to ask a somewhat different question: What, if anything, has *begun*?

It is only in the present dimension of time – that which lies between past and future, between what has already happened and what is yet to come – that freedom and the priority of the political for the human world fully emerge in Arendt's thought. For her the political is by no means the be-all and end-all of human experience. It is distinct from "what we can do and create in the singular: in isolation like the artist, in solitude like the philosopher, in the inherently worldless relationship between human beings as it exists in love and sometimes in friendship."[2] The point is rather that apart from free political activity, which is to say apart from action and judgment, both of which depend on human *plurality*, human experience as such is thrown into jeopardy. Arendt was not born with this insight, but discovered the meaning and the importance of the political by witnessing its negation in the multiform linkages of evil that were manifest in her lifetime. These linkages, however, did not form a necessary concatenation of events; they were contingent, as everything human is contingent: man is "the dwelling place of the contingent,"[3] for better and worse. It is due to their contingency, to the fact that they were not causally related but the results of the "crystallization" of "elements" of Western history (to use Arendt's familiar language), that the story of "the real twentieth century" remains open. We turn our backs on it at our own peril, for the "elements" themselves have accompanied us into the new century, where they remain as dangerous as they were in the one that has passed.

On the other hand, in a world liberated not once but twice from totalitarian terror, and with the cold war also over, some of the past's *specific* linkages of evil appear weaker, at least for the time being. It is not relief that the new millennium offers, but a new opportunity for us to transform the "elements," such as anti-semitism and racism, decaying nationalism and global expansionism, and what Arendt calls the "alliance" of capital and the dispossessed. A moral revolution – unlikely in any event –is not required, but what may suffice is the human capacity to actualize the most elusive temporal dimension – the present – as more than the memory of the past and more than the anticipation of the future, by acting together *politically* with peoples whose histories and traditions are not our own, but with whom we inhabit and share an ever-shrinking earth. Regardless of intentions, there is no guarantee of the outcome of such action. But there is the possibility of a new beginning, insofar as human beings are themselves beginnings, which is Arendt's deepest conviction, stated over and over throughout her works, more often than not in the words of St. Augustine: *Initium ergo ut esset, creatus est homo, ante quem nullus fuit* ("That there be a beginning, man was created, before whom nobody was").

I

It would be difficult to reflect on Hannah Arendt without also considering the question of human freedom. It is not only the coherence of the *idea* of a free being that would be called into question, however, but the past and the present *status* of such a being and, in a sense, the past *in* the present. For the historical events that Arendt relates, ancient and modern, and the stories she tells of real and sometimes fictional or legendary persons, all have present relevance; they are examples intended to *illuminate* the present – resonant fragments, something to think about, and sometimes warnings.[4] Insofar as Arendt writes about the past she does so "monumentally," that is, not as one whose chief concern is to establish the continuity of history but in order "to awaken the dead" (as her friend Walter Benjamin put it) by revealing *action*. Her engagement is not to destroy but to *dismantle* the past, to see history's victories naked and strip "progress" of its necessity. She is convinced that "the thread of tradition," through which the past was transmitted from generation to generation for centuries, today is "broken" and its "authority" gone for good.[5] But unlike the stories traditionally told by monumental historians, hers are not meant to be imitated in the sense of being repeated; she does not inspire or exhort us to specific deeds, any more than she attempts to determine specific policies or proffer solutions to specific problems. She never tries directly to influence what lies ahead, for cautionary tales, reflection, and deliberation notwithstanding, she knows that at any moment, and toward no safe harbor, spontaneous and unpredictable action steers the course of the world. Put this way the question of human freedom presents a challenge to traditional ways of considering it, for it would be an error to infer that Arendt simply assumes freedom as an inherent and essential property of human nature. On the contrary, in her view human nature is unknowable by human beings, and if it were known it would only perplex or baffle freedom as she conceives it. If, moreover, the gift of freedom is imparted through birth, on which Arendt insists,[6] for her that does not imply that it can be imputed to humans as natural beings.[7] Man is not born free, as Rousseau believed, but born *for freedom*. A first preliminary response to Arendt's challenge might be, therefore, that freedom, as the great and identifying gift of human existence, is manifest in the *activities* that distinguish human from other forms of life.

With this emphasis on activities, freedom may be said to guide Arendt's thought as surely as Virgil guided Dante's progression through hell and purgatory. But Dante no longer needed Virgil when he entered paradise,[8] for there the pilgrim, his own activity suspended, came to rest in the *possession* of a vision of eternal love, an all-knowing and all-powerful love determining the movement of the universe and the fate of every individual within it.[9] The times Dante lived in were harsh, but the particular events through which Arendt lived some six hundred years later differed in their impenetrable darkness. That darkness precluded spiritual reconciliation, preventing all but the most evanescent image, much less the possession, of "an absolute standard of justice" indwelling in a transcendent god. In the twentieth century it was under no definition of wickedness – not even Hitler's or Stalin's – that human beings were banished to the man-made hells of Auschwitz and the Gulag (*OT*, pp. 446–447).[10] More than anything else it was due to this vision-defying darkness that freedom became the touchstone of Arendt's own formidable power of judgment. Thus a second preliminary response to the challenge posed by the question of human freedom might be that judgment is not only a divine but a human act, and that freedom is the test of whatever comes before it, no matter how strange, uncompromising, and controversial its exercise turns out to be.

The question of the status of a human being endowed with the gift of freedom became crucial for Arendt when, as a young, classically educated German Jew, she collided head-on with a totalitarian movement in the early 1930s. In that collision she experienced a shock of reality: the reality of an organized mass of mankind, masquerading as a political party,[11] that was intent on marring both the social *milieu* into which she was born and the private, reflective realm in which she grew to maturity. That shock was severe, and at first less connected with political insight than with plain outrage at the reactions, stemming from dissatisfaction and resentment, of many of her compatriots with whom she believed she shared that realm, its culture and its spirit.[12] Ultimately the German language, *die Muttersprache*, Arendt's principal and enduring medium of reflection, became the sole memorial of what then was vanishing from the world. But for her the German language was not the everyday language that even earlier than the 1930s had lapsed into "mere talk" (*Gerede*) of "the they" (*das Man*). This debased language, far from preserving German civilization, publicized and trivialized it, and was itself integral to the encroaching darkness. Owing to what was for her the undeniable givenness of being Jewish, Arendt lacked the opportunity open to others, some of whom she knew intimately, of withdrawing from "this common everyday world" and from a "public realm" permeated with its language. Henceforth Arendt would look upon withdrawing from the world to a "land of thought" (*LMT*, p. 87), a purely philosophic, thought-filled "solitude," with a degree of disillusion and misgiving.[13] There can be little doubt that the experience of the loss of what was most familiar to her lay close to the root of what later became central to her understanding of the political: her sharp, firm, and unwavering distinction between the private and the public realms of human existence.

In other words, the significance of what was lost at that time should not be underestimated, nor the fact forgotten that that loss was not entirely negative, at least in its consequences for Arendt's political thought. For at first German culture and the German spirit had seemed to her to encompass "the so-called Jewish question," which by her own admission she had found "boring." Her biography of Rahel Varnhagen,[14] on which she was working at precisely this time, and despite the fact that she was writing it from "the perspective of a Zionist critique of assimilation," subtly attests to this. For *for Rahel*, whom she described as her "closest friend, though she had been dead for some one hundred years,"[15] Arendt did not believe in "an independent history of the Jewish people"; and while she showed little respect for the would-be parvenu, she clearly loved Rahel's own love of "'the true realities of life . . . love, trees, children, music,'" none of which "have a link with originally and specifically Jewish substance." But by 1952, after the cataclysm of World War II, Arendt felt that her biography of Rahel was "alien" and "very remote" from her; she felt that she had been "politically naive" when she wrote it.[16]

By then the priority that the political had come to have for Arendt was profoundly connected to the war, the devastation of her homeland, and her own experience of uprootedness during eighteen years of statelessness. Which is to say that that priority probably cannot be comprehended apart from Arendt's own experience of a form of world alienation, the alienation she later found generally diffused throughout the world since the onset of the modern age, and which, especially as seen in her multivalent treatment of the processes of expropriation, was "so crucial to the formation of the lonely mass man and so dangerous in the formation of the worldless mentality of modern ideological movements" (*HC*, pp. 251–257). Her experience, moreover, never ceased to inform her thought, although it did so in different ways. On the one hand, she vigorously denied sharing the spiritual homesickness that for her typified not only German Idealism but also Nietzsche and Heidegger, both of whom were otherwise sources of inspiration to her (*LMW*, pp. 157–158). But on the other hand, the faculty of judgment, with which she ultimately hoped to resolve the most fundamental problems of action arising from her political thought – the judgment she had long since practiced but only turned to examine and analyze at the end of her life – *depended* on a degree of separation, on being situated at a certain remove from the world and its events.[17]

Arendt was not "by nature" an actor, and considered the ability to look at political action "from the outside" an "advantage" in trying to understand it.[18] For her the most and perhaps the only reliable guardians of the facts and events of this world are not those who enact them but spectators, poets to be sure, and also historians and all those who report them, fit them into stories, and judge them. That human beings are born for freedom means that their actions are fit subjects for stories, which alone give full measure to their contingency, their spontaneity, and their unpredictability. In the course of what probably still is the most profound meditation on the nature of time, St. Augustine says that in the recitation of a psalm his mind "is distended between the memory of what I just said and the anticipation of what I am about to say, although I am now engaged in the present transition from what *was* coming to what *is* past." This is "equally what happens" when the story of "a man's whole life" is told, "whose parts are his own actions, or with the whole world, whose parts are the actions of all men," until "anticipation dwindles," and is ultimately "canceled and the whole transaction resides in memory."[19] Therein, if anywhere, lies reconciliation to the world. Addressing much the same matter, Arendt says that it is the *story* that achieves "permanence and persistence," whose narration has "its place in the world," where "it can live on – one story among many," adding that "[t]here is no meaning to these stories that is entirely separable from them" (*MDT*, p. 22).

In the years following her flight from Germany, her sojourn in France, and her emigration to America, Arendt wrote *The Origins of Totalitarianism*, the major work in which she analyzed those hidden "elements" of modern European history that "crystallized" in totalitarianism. It was she who stressed the fact that those "elements" would not themselves disappear with the disappearance of totalitarianism (*OT*, p. 460), thereby raising the question, suggested at the beginning of these remarks, of what a genuinely post-modern world or post-modern age – a *new* world or age – would entail (cf. *HC*, p. 6). The totalitarian regimes she dealt with, Hitler's Germany and the Soviet Union under Stalin, were for her "an authentic, albeit all-destructive new form of government" (*HC*, 216), novel *and* criminal, bent on demonstrating in fact rather than argument that human freedom is altogether illusory. She judged their destruction of freedom to be not only criminal but an evil without precedent in human history, not because totalitarianism was crueler than previous tyrannies (which it may have been), but because its nihilism, the possibility and necessity of its will to annihilate every aspect of human freedom, private as well as public, was unlimited. This previously undreamed of, seemingly paradoxical fusion of possibility with necessity, though contradicting common sense, was realized in the world through terror.

When fully developed, totalitarian terror chose its victims "completely at random" (*OT*, p. 432), thereby rendering the guilt and innocence of individuals, along with their "responsibility" – their ability to respond – utterly superfluous. Arendt does not judge such terror "subjectively," as if she could feel what those who endured it felt, but likens it and its essential institutions, slave-labor and death camps, to "a band of iron" pressing human beings "so tightly together that it is as though their plurality had disappeared into One Man of gigantic proportions." Individuality, the question of who one is (*HC*, p. 11), is unanswerable when the space opened by "the boundaries and channels of communication," separating individuals in thought and connecting them in speech, no longer exists; individuality is meaningless when anyone can be replaced by everyone. Totalitarianism's total denial of freedom is achieved when the conditions and the meaning of action, of individuals joining together to manifest principles such as "love of equality . . . or distinction or excellence"[20] and even the "fear-guided movements and suspicion-ridden actions" whose rationale remains all too apparent in the "desert" of ordinary tyrannies, are eliminated (*OT*, pp. 465–466).

Without peer in this respect, the dynamism of the story Arendt tells of unmitigated human disaster is a function of the newness of totalitarianism. The force of her condemnation of the "overpowering reality" of the "radical evil" of full-fledged terror, its enslavement of human masses to the higher-than-human goals set by ideologically determined, supposedly immutable laws of Nature and History, is likewise a function of its newness (*OT*, p. 459). And it appears that at least in *The Origins* Arendt's treatment of traditional constitutional structures, along with the theoretical underpinnings of different kinds of government, including tyranny, all of which totalitarianism deranged, is deliberately curtailed in order to avoid relativizing the phenomenon itself, to highlight its newness and the attraction it held for lonely, worldless masses of mankind. These masses, along with equally misled members of both the mob and the elite (cf. *OT*, pp. 326–340), found that the inexorable movement of totalitarianism, while denying freedom in the real world, held out the illusion of freedom in a fictitious world: freedom for the unfree, one might say, ending in terror for all.

One result of her magisterial study of totalitarianism was to recognize the capacity for freedom as the source of human *plurality*, itself the condition through which politics is possible and without which it is not (*HC*, p. 7). But even when it was not political, freedom still was the resource that enabled historical groups of human beings, such as Jews, to remain more or less intact and persevere, and human individuals, in one way or another and in the most varied circumstances, to affirm and express gratitude for their finite lives. What is as new as totalitarianism itself, however, is the recognition that the human capacity for freedom may make life supremely worth living. This is the transparent meaning of the conclusion of Arendt's study of the revolutions that mark modernity with their attempts, which may never yet have proved successful, to constitute and establish freedom in the world. There she cites words fashioned by Sophocles at the close of his life, words evoking "in pure precision" the original sense of freedom: that when it is politically experienced – experienced as *action* – freedom can "endow life with splendor."[21] This is only one but perhaps the most startling way in which the realm of politics, as conceived by Arendt, takes precedence over all other realms of human activity. A third response, still preliminary, to the challenge of human freedom might be that in freedom men and women appear as a plurality of unique beings, irreducible to repeatable concretions of qualities, but when deprived of freedom, though still alive, they differ in only one significant respect from the multiplicities of other animal species: loneliness, the despair of lost desire, of "not belonging to the world at all" (*OT*, p. 475); that to conceive freedom as an inalienable human right is, from a political point of view, to misconceive it; and that speech and deed actualize freedom in the world without reifying it.

The foregoing intimations of freedom and unfreedom in the thought of Hannah Arendt are provisional, and all of them require qualification. To qualify them thoroughly would require tracing the web of Arendt's thought through virtually everything she wrote, a task far exceeding the limitations of the present essay. Nevertheless, some amplification is in order.

II

The human activities that concern Arendt – in active life: laboring, working, and acting; in mental life: thinking, willing, and judging – all bear different relations to freedom. Willing, for instance, "as the spring of action" is "'the power of *spontaneously* beginning a series of successive things or states'." But willing itself is unable – its discovery by St. Paul was an experience of the will's "impotence" or inability – to grasp how it does that and to what effect (*LMW*, pp. 6–7 [quoting Kant], 64–73). "Only when the I-will and the I-can coincide does freedom come to pass" (*BPF*, p. 160), but St. Augustine, perhaps the most acutely sensitive of those who examined the faculty of the will, found that *Non hoc est velle quod posse* ("to will and be able are not the same") (*LMW*, p. 87; *BPF*, p. 159). Moreover, in a great mystical prayer that begins and ends "If you will grant what you ask, you can ask what you will,"[22] Augustine has left the company of men and is radically alone with his God. Arendt's story of the will's career in Western thought leads to what she calls "the abyss of freedom"; however much it may individuate us, however closely it is associated with the condition of natality in which action is "ontologically rooted," in itself willing only *dooms* human beings to freedom (*LMW*, p. 217; *HC*, p. 247).

In the realm of human affairs, of historical events that would not *come to pass* except for human beings, the importance of action may seem obvious. In *On Revolution* Arendt speaks of action's "elementary grammar . . . and its more complicated syntax, whose rules determine the rise and fall of human power." Its grammar is "that action is the only human faculty that demands a plurality of men," and according to its syntax "power is the only human attribute which applies solely to the worldly in-between space by which men are mutually related" (*OR*, pp. 173, 175). While these remarks indicate how men acting "in concert" generate power and direct the course of the world, and also suggest how the loci of power shift, political activity – acting and judging – requires thinking about something different from the will. The problem is that the relation of thinking itself to politics is fraught with difficulty.

Arendt turns to Athens because it was the birthplace not only of politics but also of Western philosophy (or *thinking*, as she would say), and both appear most clearly in their origin. In the story she tells about philosophy and politics,[23] it was the trial and condemnation of Socrates by the people of Athens that prompted Plato to argue that the philosopher alone was fit to rule in the cities of men. From that point on, according to Arendt, philosophy and politics "parted company." The freedom of the thinking activity lies in its withdrawal from the sheer factual contingency of human affairs to a "land of thought," and the thinker who "resides" there tends to view action in the light of his own experience. The condition of thinking is to be in agreement with oneself, for the activity of thinking is stymied if it falls into self-contradiction. Another way to put this is to say that action, when thought about, becomes subject to moral rules derived from the rule of non-contradiction, and here it does not much matter whether those rules are thought to bind human beings universally, or, as customs (*mores*) and habits (*hexeis*), to do so relatively. In either case, the freedom of opinion of pre-philosophical Greek political experience – "neither to rule nor to be ruled" (*HC*, p. 32) – is compromised. When Plato, for example, turned to politics it was to construct an ideally balanced republic, one in which a philosopher would rule over the conflicting opinions of citizens. The adjudication of ordinary citizens' opinions according to the standard of philosophic truth meant that the *plurality* of those opinions, agreement with one's peers being a condition of action, no longer mattered. It also meant that the condemnation of a philosopher, which had happened in the case of Socrates, would not be repeated. In this sense Socrates is a pivotal figure whose life and death mark a crucial turning from concern with action and judgment, from the doing of politics (*politeuesthai*), to a philosophy of politics.

For Arendt Socrates himself is a more elusive figure, not simply a Platonic philosopher who lacked political authority. He was an Athenian citizen who sometimes "withdrew" from *polis* life in order to think, but who, when done with thinking, "returned" to it. Of course there is a sense in which every thinker does that necessarily, except that Socrates not only took up his own position as an Athenian citizen but also demanded accounts of what his fellow citizens *believed*, of how the world appeared to them from their positions in it and, since his interlocutors were almost always young and well-born, the leaders-to-be of Athens, of what appeared to them to constitute the excellences (*aretai*) of citizenship. It was the perplexity (*aporia*) that Socrates' questioning engendered in those he spoke to that made an old and poor man famous *and* set him against the status quo, whatever it happened to be. For neither Athens nor any other polity, ancient or modern, aristocratic or democratic, can afford to think of itself as a homeland for bewildered magistrates, in which the generation of power would be virtually impossible. Plato's most telling criticism of political activity lies in the failure of Socrates, his teacher, to establish not only the "truth" but even agreement among the plurality of opinions his interlocutors held regarding their common world. Yet Socrates, who mixed as little as possible in the affairs of his city and reached no conclusions useful for its policies, is an exemplary figure for Arendt. He alone not only was convinced but was willing to die for his conviction that the self-examination of one's life – part and parcel of the reflexivity that characterizes thinking – was itself the greatest good that could befall any city.

Arendt's story of Plato and Socrates comes from the past but has relevance for the present. It shows that the relation of thinking to politics was essentially problematic from its inception. And in the "new and yet unknown age" in which we live today (*HC*, p. 6), an age that *cannot* jump over the long shadow cast by the "elements" of totalitarianism, the need for a different faculty to comprehend freedom is not only shown but exercised. Socrates was a man who judged that his self-appearance in and for his city was worth more than his life, and in Arendt's own judgment that is who Socrates is, a man who had the courage to confront his death, his disappearance from the world, as something entirely new, a sort of adventure. At the end of his trial (in the *Apology*) Socrates sees his world clearly for the last time as if it were the first; he is between past and future, equally experiencing the forces of the future pushing him back and of the past propelling him forward. In other words he experiences the pathos of action and judgment, the pathos of relinquishing the known for the unknown.

In *On Revolution* what Arendt says, and how she says it, about Socrates' "unquestioned belief in the truth of appearance" is noteworthy. It exemplifies approximately half of what she herself means by judgment's realization and manifestation of thinking "in the world of appearances" (*LMT*, p. 193). She writes there that to Socrates "'Be as you would like to appear to others'" means "'Appear to yourself as you wish to appear to others'." But then, "ploddingly" paving her own "path of thought" in the mental present, between "an infinite past and an infinite future" (*LMT*, pp. 210–211), she immediately cites Machiavelli in a historically and otherwise different, even opposed, context. For him "'Appear as you may wish to be'" means "'Never mind how you are, this is of no relevance in the world and in politics, where only appearances . . . count; if you can manage to appear to others as you would wish to be, that is all that can possibly be required by the judges of this world'" (*OR*, p. 97; cf. *LMT*, p. 37). Machiavelli, "the spiritual father of revolution" (*OR*, p. 30), also dares to envisage the entirely new, "things never seen . . . thoughts never thought . . . institutions never tried before" (*OR*, p. 262). But for him, a Christian and a preeminent political thinker who gave not a fig for philosophy, the risk he took did not concern the mystery of his disappearance from the world, but rather the eternal damnation of his soul. He was willing to take that risk for the sake of founding a new political order in Italy, his homeland. For Machiavelli it was not a question of loving the world more than God but "whether one was capable of loving the world more than one's own self" (*OR*, p. 290). The risk implies that God might after all approve such a love, regardless of its "morality," which according to the rules derived from thinking's standard was certainly deficient. The examples of Socrates and Machiavelli, and both of them together, show the primacy of the world of appearances, albeit in distinct ways. For Socrates, the purer thinker of the two, it was only in the world in which he appeared to others that he could judge the worth of his appearance to himself. For Machiavelli it was only action, and neither the "goodness" or "badness" of human conduct, that can "shine in glory" in that same world of appearances (*HC*, 77).

III

In *The Human Condition* Arendt undertook to rethink the hierarchy of modes of activity that originally characterized the active lives of human beings.[24] For her such beings *labor*, *work*, and are capable of *action* in ways that distinguish them from other animal species. Some animals do, in a sense, labor and even work – they hunt and forage to keep alive, they procreate, and they build nests and hives and dams – but the meaning of the hierarchical ordering of human activity is that within it the specific ways men labor and work become intelligible in their relation to the highest activity, that of action, an activity unique to humans.[25] This is not meant teleologically (certainly no "final cause" or explanation by "design" is implied), but in the sense that of these activities *qua* activities action alone depends on a *plurality* of beings, each of whom is unique (*HC*, p. 7). No one, not even Achilles, can act alone, and a crucial theme in *The Human Condition* is the consequent boundlessness of action, its inherent unpredictability, and the strict limitation of the actor's own knowledge of what he is doing (*HC*, pp. 233, 239). Action to be free must be free from "motives and intentions on the one hand and aims and consequences on the other" (*HC*, p. 205). If we knew what we were doing when we act we would not be free but enacting or unfolding a plan, as if the course of the world were set like that of a planet plotted on a celestial map, itself a human artifact and an emblem of the "victory" of *homo faber*. To put it succinctly, "[t]he calamities of action all arise from the human condition of plurality" (*HC*, p. 220), and this "is the price [human beings] pay for plurality . . . for the joy of inhabiting together with others a world whose reality is guaranteed for each by the presence of all" (*HC*, p. 244).

What must be emphasized here is that it is only in action, in *acting*, that the uniqueness of the actor appears in the world, and that this "distinct identity" does not appear to the actor himself; it is not he but rather those to whom he appears who recognize and judge it, and those others are also equally unique beings (*HC*, p. 193).[26] If such recognition smacks of tautology, it is not empty. For action – which to Arendt signifies deed and speech, either a deed and its account, a deed accounted for, or speech-as-deed (*HC*, pp. 25–26) – insofar as it is free is by definition undetermined.[27] What is recognized, therefore, is nothing morphological, neither a face or a body nor anything that a mirror might reflect. Perhaps it could be likened to a temporally extended, fully articulate gesture, one that cannot be copied or repeated, although it may be imitated poetically and also, when recollected as an example, relived as a principle of new action. What is recognized is a passing image of "the most elementary and authentic understanding of human freedom," of a beginning inserted in the continuum of time (*HC*, pp. 225, 19). It is an individual image of spontaneous initiation, of the actualization of the uniqueness and origin that every human being is.

Free action transcends the necessity of labor and the utility of work, and transforms those activities. Thus human labor is organized in a variety of ways, frequently unjust and hardly ever equal, so that some men, wily or lucky enough to escape the fate of Sisyphus, are relieved of the *dolor* of ceaseless, endless labor and thereby released from serving the necessity of the biological processes of their own lives. Human work, the goal or purpose of which always lies outside the activity itself, not only complements labor by making tools that are useful for easing it and rendering it more productive, but with them constructs an artificial world, an elaborate and changing cultural artifact as structurally complex and intricately contrived as the web of relationships that sensibly and legally binds those who live together within it. Such a non-natural, artificial world is a condition for leading a free or fully human life, be it of honor or of shame, or even of honor enhanced by shame (the classic example of which is King Oedipus); in every case it is a life that does not merely reply but actively responds to the exigencies of the world, that which lies between and is common to those who share it. In Greek experience that life is typically viewed as heroic and tragic, in the literal sense an extraordinary life. As Arendt understands it, that life cannot be fully achieved by laborers, workers, or even by great artists, by anyone who strives to attain ends, whatever they may be, to which their own activity is a means. Within the relative stability or balance of the human artifice a space for free action may be opened, a space relating men who desire to act, thereby revealing who they uniquely are as beings in and of the world. Which is to say that it is a space for the sole activity of active life which, non-reflective and existing in "sheer actuality," is undertaken for its own sake and comprehended as its own end.[28]

Arendt calls this space *public*, a common space of disclosure not only for those who act or actively move within it but for everyone who perceives it. The remarkable claim she makes has already been alluded to: that apart from this "space of appearance and without trusting in action and speech as a mode of being together, neither the reality of one's self, of one's own identity, nor the reality of the surrounding world can be established beyond doubt" (*HC*, p. 208). The "reality" of the world is its "being common," its being between, literally its *interest* (*inter esse*) for all those who, through their common sense, hold it in common. It is common sense, "the sixth and highest sense," which, by relating the "five strictly individual senses" and their data that otherwise would be "merely felt as irritations of our nerves or resistance sensations of our bodies," fits what appears to it "into the common world." Just as in her discussion of action the identity of the self, alternatively called the person, does not appear to itself, so now the condition of its "reality" is also plurality, *inter homines esse*, living "politically" with others. Again it is common sense or *sensus communis*, "'a sense *common to all*, i.e. of a faculty of judgment,'" a community and communicative sense, that by judging them relates the appearances of all human beings, whether they have actualized their uniqueness in action or not, to one another.[29] Human reality is appearance, then, in the twofold, complementary sense of the appearances that form the common world, the world into which those who desire to act will act, and of the "presence" to each other of the persons to whom that world is visible and audible, and who can judge it. Actions are the appearances that are *ekphanestaton*, most shining forth, most *appearing*, and they are the original source of that reality (*HC*, pp. 274, 208–209, 283, 50–52, 199, 225–226). Yet at a crucial moment in the life of the *polis*, Athens's greatest statesman, Pericles, said that Athenians "love beauty within the limits of political judgment, and . . . philosophize without the barbarian vice of effeminacy" (*BPF*, pp. 213–214), thereby differentiating political activity from both sheer thought and sheer "creativity," even in action.

To the pagan Greeks the glory generated in the space containing free action was godlike, but its immortality depended on human memory. One reason the art or skill of politics – of *politeuesthai*, of doing politics, of caring for and preserving the *polis* as the situs of memory – was invented in Greece was to "remedy" the futility of action,[30] which in this context is tantamount to the futility of human life. For no actor can foretell where his beginning will lead, since he acts with and into a plurality of other free actors, but also, being its own end, having its end within itself ("nothing acts unless [by acting] it makes patent its latent self"[31]), the glory of action in itself leaves nothing behind in the world, is nothing but the image of the actor acting it reveals to spectators. Arendt emphatically *contrasts* the "immortality" of everlasting fame, clearly dependent on the "endurance in time" of a plurality of generations, with the solitary experience of eternity, an experience that is perhaps only enjoyed when "the glory of the world is surely over" (Sir Thomas Browne). Insofar as "'to cease to be among men' (*inter homines esse desinere*)" is "to die," the solitude of world-*withdrawal*, in which eternity is experienced philosophically or religiously, is "a kind of death" (*HC*, p. 8, 20).[32]

What for Arendt is perhaps most exemplary about the Greeks, and at the same time has the greatest relevance for the present, is that it was not just the memory of past actions but the possibility of new deeds, the novelty latent in newcomers, that made the laws that bound and secured the *polis*, conditioning political life in general and *constraining* action in particular, meaningful and bearable (*HC*, pp. 194–198). It is by virtue of "the new beginning inherent in birth," the fact that unique human beings are born and appear in the world, that "natality" is a far more politically relevant category than "mortality" (*HC*, p. 9); nor is it beside the point that for the Greeks natality likewise characterized the "deathless but not birthless" lives of the Olympian gods (*LMT*, p. 131). Here it is essential to add that, as Arendt understands it, the public, shared space of disclosure was not pre-designed for freedom but first cleared and then kept open by free action, thus not only inextricably linking politics with freedom but rendering the former dependent on the latter (*HC*, pp. 198–200). It is not that Arendt means or ever says that freedom is the only concern of politics. On the contrary, she states explicitly that freedom "only seldom – in times of crisis or revolution – becomes the direct aim of political action." Her point is that if men were not free initiators, if they never had lived together in the manner of speech and action, experiencing not only its joys but also its disasters, there would be no *reason* for them to organize themselves politically, no reason for them to concern themselves with matters of "justice, or power, or equality" (*BPF*, p. 146).

These reflections have been intended as no more than a sketch of Arendt's understanding of the human world, which is specifically opposed to the inhuman non-world of totalitarianism: that the origin of the human world lies in man's active life (*vita activa*); that the activities of active life become intelligible in the culminating experience of free action; that such freedom is constitutive of human reality which is, in a sense different from that of "other living or inanimate things," "explicitly"a realm of appearances (*HC*, p. 199); and that political activity is inseparable from the activity of judging, of ordering those appearances for the sake of the *plurality* of persons to whom they appear.[33] No attempt has been made to expound the richness of Arendt's conception of action or to resolve the complexities of its relation to moral activity, especially when viewed in the light of her chapters on keeping promises and forgiving trespasses, both of which also depend on human plurality (*HC*, pp. 236–247).[34] My endeavor has been solely to trace the relation of action and political judgment to human freedom, which Hannah Arendt puts almost too compactly when she writes:

> action and politics, among all the capabilities of human life, are the only things of which we could not even conceive without at least assuming that freedom exists . . . Without [freedom] political life as such would be meaningless. The *raison d'être* of politics is freedom, and its field of experience is action . . . (*BPF* 146)

NOTES

1 I am indebted to Jonathan Schell for this quotation and for much else in these introductory remarks. There is no more attentive or eloquent chronicler of the unconcluded story of "the real twentieth century" than he.

2 The quotation is from the "Conclusion" of a course of lectures entitled "History of Political Theory" delivered by Arendt at the University of California (Berkeley) in 1955. This "Conclusion," housed in the Arendt archive at the Library of Congress, has been edited by the present writer and will appear in a volume of Arendt's unpublished and uncollected works forthcoming from Harcourt Brace & Company.

3 M. Merleau-Ponty, quoted in D. Ashton, *À Rebours: The Informal Rebellion* (Las Palmas: CAAM; Madrid: Museo Nacional Centro de Arte Reina Sofia, 1999), p. 28.

4 It has been well said that Arendt's "use of exemplarity was not . . . to expect a modern jackass to run like an ancient horse, but to caution modern horses not to act like jackasses." K. M. McClure, "The Odor of Judgment" in *Hannah Arendt and the Meaning of Politics*, ed. C. Calhoun and J. McGowan (Minneapolis: University of Minnesota Press, 1997), p. 54.

5 Arendt, *LM*, vol. 1, *Thinking*, p. 212; hereafter *LMT*.

6 Arendt, *OT*, p. 479. Cf. "The miracle that saves the world, the realm of human affairs, from its normal 'natural' ruin is . . . the birth of new men and the new beginning, the action they are capable of by virtue of being born" (*HC*, p. 247).

7 In *HC*, pp. 9–11 Arendt distinguishes between "the human condition" and "human nature." On pp. 175–177 of the same work she elaborates differences between human and natural beings. In general, nature is associated with necessity and therefore opposed to freedom.

8 Literally of course Virgil, a pagan, was not *allowed* to enter paradise, but that is another matter.

9 Cf. Arendt, *LM*, vol. II, *Willing*, pp. 122–123; hereafter *LMW*.
10 Cf. "The Image of Hell" and "Reply to Eric Voegelin," in Arendt, *EU*, pp. 198–200 and 404 respectively.
11 See *OT*, pp. 250–266 for the distinction between parties and movements.
12 "What Remains? The Language Remains," in *EU*, pp. 10–12.
13 Arendt, *MDT*, pp. viii–ix. She speaks from her own experience of the "uncanny precision" of Heidegger's analyses of "mere talk" and "the they" in *Being and Time*.
14 *Rahel Varnhagen: The Life of a Jewess* (New York: Harcourt Brace Jovanovich, 1974).
15 E. Young-Bruehl, *Hannah Arendt: For Love of the World* (New Haven: Yale University Press, 1982) 56.
16 See the elucidating exchange of letters in *Hannah Arendt – Karl Jaspers: Correspondence, 1926–1969*, ed. Lotte Kohler and Hans Saner (New York: Harcourt Brace Jovanovich, 1992), pp. 192–201.
17 In this same vein Dana Villa has argued convincingly that some of the most positive aspects of Arendt's political thought are not to be identified "with the *absence* of alienation." D. R. Villa, *Arendt and Heidegger: The Fate of the Political* (Princeton: Princeton University Press, 1996), p. 203.
18 From extempore remarks made by Arendt in Toronto, November 1972, in M. A. Hill, ed., *Hannah Arendt: The Recovery of the Public World* (New York: St. Martin's Press, 1979), p. 306.
19 *Confessiones* 11:38.
20 Arendt, *BPF*, p. 152.
21 Arendt, *OR*, p. 285.
22 *Confessiones* 10:40.
23 See H. Arendt, "Philosophy and Politics," *Social Research* 57/1 (Spring 1990): 73–103.
24 She did this among much else. Her overall purpose was to reconsider "the human condition from the vantage point of our newest experiences and our most recent fears" (*HC*, p. 5).
25 Arendt speaks of *animal laborans* and *homo faber*, but only *human* beings are capable of action. Thus action is the principal artery of what may be called her humanism. Moreover, while at least some animal species are *social* and every one of them "lives in a world of its own" (*LMT*, p. 20), none are *political*.
26 That this uniqueness (in Greek Arendt calls it the *daimon*, and what is in question is *eudaimonia*, its "well-being") "appears and is visible only to others" is the "misery . . . of mortals," the *curse* of action, and also stems from the fundamental "human condition of plurality, . . . the fact that men, not Man, live on the earth and inhabit the world" (*HC*, p. 7).
27 Speech-as-deed is explicitly distinguished from conveying "information or communication," and no doubt derives from Homer's *epea pteroenta*, the "wingèd words" that may or may not occur in deliberations. To say such speech is "persuasive" is to say too little, but it certainly is the precursor of persuasion as the medium of authentic political decisions.
28 One hopes that it is no longer necessary to add that Arendt draws upon ancient Greek texts – poetic and historical as well as philosophical – because the distinctions that were crucial to her are clearer there, in their distance from us, and not

because she wished to "revive" Athens. It was not *startings-over* but *new beginnings* that concerned her.

29 Arendt, *LKPP*, pp. 70–72. The quotation is from Kant, *Critique of Judgment*, § 40, and it is his emphasis. Arendt's interpretation of Kant's aesthetic reflective judgment does not, as has been alleged, represent a change in her understanding of *action*, but resolves a fundamental question about the possibility of *politics*. Already in the *Iliad* Thersites, no heroic actor (but in a sense the first anti-hero), is a *person* in a common world, and in the *Odyssey* there are women, Penelope and Nausicaa, who are *persons*. But strictly speaking the Homeric world contains only elements of political experience, and what Greek statesmen learned from the "educator of all Hellas" seems to have concerned action – the possibility of men acting heroically – almost exclusively (*HC*, p. 197).

30 Arendt is not concerned with supposed "historical causes" of the rise of the *polis*, but with "what the Greeks themselves [she refers to Pericles' Funeral Oration] thought of it," in other words with its *meaning*, for them and for us (*HC*, p. 197). Her concern with the meaning rather than the "causes" of the *polis* differentiates her not only from virtually all modern commentators, but also from Aristotle.

31 Arendt's translation of Dante's statement *Nihil . . . agit nisi tale existens quale patiens fieri debit* (*HC*, p. 175). See her comment on the difficulty of translating it (*HC*, p. 208 n. 41).

32 What is meant is not the termination of life, but that this experience is not part of and does not belong to *active* life in the world.

33 Arendt's concern with forms of government, in *On Revolution* and elsewhere, stems not from the recognition of human beings as persons but from personhood's historically diverse political embodiments.

34 Kant too, whose notion of moral self-determination, by definition independent of anyone other than oneself and liberated even from one's own natural inclinations, is not at all what Arendt means by free *action*, is fully aware of human plurality. Plurality in fact lies close to the heart of his moral philosophy: you must treat others as you would have them treat you, for your claim to be an end is grounded in the *idea of humanity*; you are an end only if every human being is an end, and not a means to anyone else's (including your own) end. Arendt's rejection of that philosophy is subject to misinterpretation, although it is of course true that for her the faculty of judgment and "*exemplary* validity" are politically more efficacious than practical reason in quickening action that reflects "mankind in general . . . independent of [the passage of] time" (*LKPP*, pp. 76–77).

6

GEORGE KATEB

Political action: its nature and advantages

In the years since her death in 1975, Hannah Arendt's large body of work has been ever more widely discussed. So far we can say that her readers have occupied themselves mainly with two contributions that Arendt made to political theory and the study of politics. One is her analysis of the political evil of the twentieth century, especially totalitarianism in its Stalinist and Nazi forms. The other is her analysis of the excellence of politics: its greatness and the place of individual excellence in it (*HC*, p. 49).

Totalitarianism pressed on her with such force that she had to respond and try to be theoretically adequate to those great horrors. But she began her life as a writer with a dissertation on the concept of love in St. Augustine. One imagines that uninterrupted by political evil, she could have gone on to write philosophically about the many faces that human experience and the human condition present to the determined philosophical observer. She perhaps would have turned her attention to politics eventually, as one more type of human experience, one more way in which human beings enter into relations or confront and deal with one another. I would say, therefore, that her analysis of political excellence grows without artificiality from her original interests. If anything, the horror of totalitarianism may have intensified her quest to find a reason to affirm existence, and to find it, curiously enough, in politics. Yet, whatever the impact of totalitarianism on the growth of her mind, the fact remains that for students of political theory, Arendt's effort to explore the nature of political excellence is the indispensable core of her work. In that effort she shows originality, a high creativity, together with the other virtues found in her work on totalitarianism and on such broad matters as modern culture. In this chapter, I wish to consider the reasons that Arendt gives for championing the excellence of politics. Her teaching is intricate, and one cannot always be sure that one has grasped her points properly. The abundance of differing interpretations of her analysis testifies to her richness but also to her difficulty.

In *The Human Condition*, her most powerful and extended treatment of the excellence of political action, Arendt says of Machiavelli that he was "the only post-classical political theorist" who made the "extraordinary effort to restore its old dignity to politics" (*HC*, p. 35). Arendt's project is to take up Machiavelli's burden again. What is the nature of politics? and What are its advantages that make it worthy of restored prestige? are her questions.

One way into these questions is to notice that Arendt is intent on determining the essence of what she often calls (especially in *On Revolution*) the authentically political. Her premise is that if the authentically political can be conceptualized properly, it will present itself as something so attractive, as well as so advantageous, that in the minds of her readers, and of others by a radiating influence, the dignity of politics will be on the way to being restored. The irony is that for Arendt the dignity of politics has nothing to do with using government as a weapon or instrument of social reform or even adaptation to social change.

Arendt's project of conceptualizing the authentically political bears a superficial resemblance to the comparable efforts of two somewhat earlier German writers, Max Weber and Carl Schmitt. All three are devoted to the dignity of politics; to restore it, in Arendt's case, after the experience of world war and totalitarian horrors; and to maintain it in a time of despondency, after German defeat and humiliation in the First World War, with the other two. In the project of ascertaining the authentically political, two contrasts can be posited. The first contrast is between the authentically political and what appears to be authentically political, but actually is not. The second is between the authentically political and other kinds or realms of human experience. We connect the two contrasts by saying that the authentically political is only a part of a much larger field of what is conventionally called politics, and further that the authentically political is superior to many, perhaps most, non-political activities.

As it turns out, the authentically political (or the truly or specifically political) means several things. In order to differentiate it from what is not authentically political, we must be able to say what properly inheres in or is properly present in the political realm. Hence we must theoretically exclude a good deal of what actually exists in it and what most other people – actors, theorists, and observers – mistakenly believe belongs to it. And in order to differentiate the authentically political from other modes of human experience, we must determine what advantages emerge only (or uniquely) in the political realm or are made possible only by it; or are achieved in a better manifestation than they are in other realms. Naturally, the properly political as well as the uniquely political and the politically enhanced must all be valuable, if the dignity of politics is to be restored and upheld.

Arendt's theory of the excellence of politics is a compound of elements. Some of them depend on her understanding of the politics of the ancient world and more recent history: she borrows ideas, or reworks them through interpretation or expansion, or imputes them as necessary to some larger sense. And she introduces new elements, some of which are suggested or intimated by such philosophers as Kant, Hegel, Marx, Nietzsche, and Heidegger, and some of which bear her own mark as an original political theorist. The compound in itself is a creative and distinctive achievement.

Let us turn first to Arendt's view of the nature of politics that is properly practiced, of authentic politics as distinct from the many inauthentic kinds. Arendt's understanding of authentic politics is dependent both on her interpretation of the political life of the ancient Greek cities, especially Athens, and on the sense she makes of events nearer to us in time and culture. These latter events include the American and French revolutions, and the episodes of particularly working-class rebellion that erupted in European affairs from 1848 up to the middle of the twentieth century. In her later political writings, Arendt added American civil disobedience in the 1960s to her list of authentic political occurrences. In turning these exemplary occasions into a theory of political action, Arendt recurrently provides a brief definition of the activity of authentic politics, and proceeds to fill out the definition by elaborating authentic politics – as distinct from the inauthentic kinds – in such dimensions as modes of action; personal motives, sentiments, and interests; personal passions and personal principles or commitments; collaborative purposes; and a moral code of action. In each dimension, Arendt tries to isolate the authentic. (Later, I will take up the advantages of authentic politics.)

What, then, is Arendt's definition of politics? Scattered throughout her work is the idea that politics is action and that action is speech in public about public affairs. For Max Weber (in "Politics as a Vocation"[1]) the authentically political activity is deciding for others, commanding them, wielding power over them, and affecting the course of events. Indeed, Weber's conceptualization is offered in the context of his theory of leadership. Politics is essentially what some do to others, rather than – as with Arendt – what all do together. She even holds that ruling is antithetical to authentic politics. In the case of Carl Schmitt (in *The Concept of the Political*)[2] the authentically or specifically political activity is a struggle against the enemy. The struggle is not between persons but between armed sovereign societies. The basic political relation, he says, is the dualism of friends and enemies; but there is next to nothing about a society's friends, and much about the inevitability – beyond that, the desirability – of having enemies. But for Arendt, violence is not political at all; much less is it the means that defines politics, as with Weber; and, equally important, she says, in one formulation, that great effects of political action come about "where people are *with* others and neither for nor against them – that is in sheer human togetherness" (*HC*, p. 180).

As Arendt's analysis of political action proceeds, its distance from more standard accounts grows. Authentic politics is political action. Although Arendt makes some effort in *The Human Condition* to distinguish action from speech because they are two separate faculties (*HC*, p. 25) it turns out that in the original Greek understanding "most political action, in so far as it remains outside the sphere of violence, is indeed transacted in words" (*HC*, p. 26). I take Arendt to be saying that individual feats of strength in war, in the manner of Homer's heroes, became secondary. The *polis* regularized political action, and that had to mean that political life was conducted in the medium of speech. But speech *is* action; it is more truly action than physical acts were or can ever be. The heart of Arendt's account of action in her writings is that authentic political action is speech – not necessarily formal speeches, but talk, exchanges of views – in the manner of persuasion and dissuasion. Political speech is deliberation or discussion as part of the process of deciding some issue pertaining to the public good.

When political action defined as public speech about public affairs takes place, what is its content? What did citizens of the *polis* and participants in revolutionary councils consider and discuss with one another? Arendt's suggestion is that the content of properly political action is politics itself. The deliberation and decisions have to do with the safety of the preconditions of deliberation and discussion, whether the project is to create a new form of government, or to maintain an existing form, that operates by speech.

Put simply, Arendt thinks that political action has to be something memorable. It exists to be memorable, to become the stuff of stories immediately after it is done, and the stuff of history in later generations. What is memorable, what transforms political action into memorable deeds cannot be, Arendt thinks, politics driven by concerns that are better handled by procedures that are administrative and hierarchical. That means that the content of political speech cannot be social or economic policies. For authentic politics to be possible, ordinary people must be able to make sense of their situation and give their sensible opinions. Extensive or technical knowledge cannot be directly relevant. What is more, there must be diversity of opinion if politics is to go on. Socioeconomic matters seem to be amenable to conclusively right answers; or, contrastingly, to the mere expression of preponderant will. Neither feature is authentically political. And when Arendt praises the insurgent working classes of Europe for their contribution to the annals of authentic politics through the spontaneous creation of revolutionary councils, she makes it clear that what she has in mind is not the contribution of such councils to the betterment of economic conditions, necessary as that was, but the ability of working men and women to think of something other than their interest. They discovered for themselves both the nature of directly democratic political participation and its advantages in experience rather than in economic gains (*HC*, pp. 215–216; also *OR*, pp. 258–266).

The content of authentic politics is therefore deliberation and dispute about what policies are needed to preserve and keep in good repair a political body, a form of government that has been designed to carry on its business by free deliberation, discussion, and dispute; or in an insurgent situation, about the creation of a government that institutionalizes the spontaneous deliberation and discussion that are now trying to bring it into being (*HC*, p. 8; "What is Freedom?", p. 153[3]). Constitutional questions, questions concerning the spirit of the laws or the interpretation of the laws or (especially in modern times) changes in the political ground rules – all these are the stuff of authentic politics.

To speak of the content of politics as politics, to speak of politics as speech concerned with the creation or perpetuation of the preconditions of such speech, is really to claim that the purpose of politics is politics, that politics (when authentic) exists for its own sake. That means in part that authentic politics cannot be contaminated by the necessary or the useful, but rather has an affinity to all beautiful things, to the realm of the aesthetic. Arendt characteristically accords as much dignity to great art as to authentic politics. Granted, the deeds of politics are not objective as works of art (including literary ones) are. Political speech can be worthy of memorialization, but as spoken it lives in the moment of its performance. At the same time, engaging in authentic politics is not like playing a game. Politics is deeply serious; it can be mortally serious, depending as it does on the actor's willingness to risk his life.

It is well at this point to notice that although Arendt is perhaps known best for her espousal of the politics of the *polis*, the impression which one could gain from her writings is that modern insurgent politics is a more faithful embodiment of her theory than the *polis* is. To be sure, her greatest philosophical achievement is *The Human Condition*, a book that places the *polis* at the center of its theory of political action. Yet even in that book, and later in *On Revolution*, a theme emerges; politics is all the more authentic when it is eruptive rather than when it is a regular and already institutionalized practice, no matter how much initiative such a practice accommodates. The reason is that eruptive politics is more clearly a politics of beginning and hence a manifestation of the peculiar human capacity to be free or spontaneous, to start something new and unexpected, to break with seemingly automatic or fated processes or continuities; in a word, to be creative. It is a burst of unfrightened, superabundant energy.

Arendt's talents are best engaged by what is extraordinary, not by the normal. She writes with the fullest power about imperialism, revolution, civil disobedience, and totalitarianism, while less urgent or dramatic phenomena mostly fail to set her mind in motion. The praise of authentic politics as, above all, making something new happen or starting a new political relationship or, most grandly, founding a new commonwealth and, with it, a new form of government dominates her political theory. Arendt defines natality as that element of the human condition that is of special relevance to politics: she holds that politics is most itself, most authentic, when political actors, liberating themselves from oppressive rule, suddenly find themselves immersed in a new kind of politics, the politics of deliberation and discussion, of persuasion and dispute. Going from no politics to authentic politics without transition is more splendid than going from one day to the next in a society that has grown used to authentic politics. Revolutionary councils turn out to be the supreme episodes of authentic politics. The newness of every human being shows itself in a political relationship that is itself not only new but also proceeds by a continuous and improvisatory creativity. She says that "the new beginning inherent in birth can make itself felt in the world only because the newcomer possesses the capacity of beginning something new, that is, of acting" (*HC*, p. 8). She adds that initiative is inherent in all human activities, not only in authentic political action. But the fact of natality is made most vivid and revelatory in politics.

Authentic politics can exist only if numbers of people are brought up to want to take part in political life and do so in "the right spirit," or finding themselves in a fluid situation because of insurgency discover for themselves the right spirit in which to take part. The phrase is mine, not Arendt's, and I use it to refer to various attitudes and virtues or traits of character that alone make authentic politics possible. Arendt is relentlessly devoted to disclosing what human qualities have been salient when the politics of preserving the political framework of the *polis* (on the one hand) and sustaining the insurgent form of council politics and trying to prolong it in more settled times (on the other hand) have existed. What must people be like if they are to participate with a whole heart in the deliberations and give and take on these issues, which for Arendt are the politically significant public ones?

Arendt gives a succinct answer to this question toward the end of *On Revolution*. She says that the requisite passions (by which she also means the virtues, in this context) are "courage, the pursuit of public happiness, the taste of public freedom, and ambition that strives for excellence regardless not only of social status and administrative office but even of achievement and congratulation" (*OR*, pp. 275–276). Missing from this list is the will to power, "the passion to rule or govern" which Arendt, contra Nietzsche and Weber, believes has played no role in authentic politics. Arendt goes on to say that though such qualities as courage and emulation are not rare, "they are certainly out of the ordinary under all circumstances" (*OR*, p. 276). The implication is that even in the *polis*, which was a whole way of life aimed at instilling and cultivating the requisite virtues of political life and then giving these virtues a serious and magnificent field for their display, not all citizens could be counted on. The crucial virtue is courage; among the Greeks, courage was "the political virtue par excellence"(*HC*, p. 36); and Arendt returns to it in a number of texts.

The essence of courage is the readiness of the political actor "to risk his life." In fact, "too great a love for life obstructed freedom" and "was a sure sign of slavishness" (*HC*, p. 36). When confronted with actual slavery, the slavish nature accepts it instead of resisting unto death or committing suicide. But in general Arendt does not demand heroism of the political actor. She says, "Courage is a big word, and I do not mean the daring of adventure which gladly risks life for the sake of being as thoroughly and intensely alive as one can be only in the face of danger and death." Rather, what is above all required, especially when violence is understood as not political at all, is a simpler courage. She says that "It requires courage even to leave the protective security of our four walls and enter the public realm, not because of particular dangers which may lie in wait for us, but because we have arrived in a realm where the concern for life has lost its validity" ("What is Freedom?", p. 156; also *HC*, p. 186).

In addition to courage, Arendt refers to such qualities as seeking one's happiness in the public realm, rather than in private; having a taste for public freedom, rather than defining freedom as the condition one is in when politics leaves us alone; and of a certain kind of ambition – the kind that strives for excellence, rather than the kind that tries to reach its goals by any means at all, no matter how base. These qualities are summed up in the word *virtù*, which Arendt takes, of course, from Machiavelli, and which she defines as "the excellence with which man answers the opportunities the world opens up before him in the guise of *fortuna*" ("What is Freedom?", p. 153). *Virtù* is like (but naturally not the same thing as) the virtuosity that skilled practitioners of the performing arts display. But the analogy is but "a feeble echo"; *virtù* in political action is incomparably greater (*HC*, p. 207).

It is noteworthy that Arendt follows Aristotle in holding that the virtues requisite for authentic politics are not mere tools or means. These virtues are immeasurably valuable in themselves, just as the authentic politics in which they are displayed is similarly valuable in itself. Neither is ranked higher than the other. There is a relation of mutual dependence: neither could exist without the other. Action elicits the virtues, but without the virtues action would not be authentic. Mutually dependent, they not only make each other possible, they exist for each other. She says that "This specifically human achievement lies altogether out of the category of means and ends... In other words, the means to achieve the end would already be the end; and this 'end,' conversely, cannot be considered a means in some other respect, because there is nothing higher to attain than this actuality itself" (*HC*, p. 207). Arendt's implication is that authentic politics results when actors, if only imperfectly, apprehend that their political virtues and their political actions are valuable in themselves, priceless and irreplaceable.

Arendt also speaks about the discipline that the political actor, possessed of the requisite virtues and attitudes, must impose on himself. In her discussion of what she calls "principles" and of the Roman idea of the mask, she undertakes to provide a sense of the commitment that an actor makes when his action is authentically political. The discipline is an attempted consistency in the positions he adopts on those occasions when the creation or maintenance of the form of government that gives or would give him his opportunity is at issue, or even at stake. (Not all authentic politics is emergency politics, even though it is all extraordinary.) At times Arendt suggests that such consistency will flow from the character of the political actor, from his particular identity, or even from his class position; but at other times, Arendt emphasizes its assumed or chosen quality. In all cases, a person's inward forces must be "transformed, deprivatized and deindividualized, as it were, into a shape to fit them for public appearance" (*HC*, p. 50).

Arendt says that action insofar as it is free – that is, insofar as it is action – "is neither under the guidance of the intellect nor under the dictate of the will . . . but springs from something altogether different which (following Montesquieu's famous analysis of forms of government) I shall call a principle" ("What is Freedom?", p. 152). The notion of principle, as Arendt uses it, is not altogether clear. The reference to Montesquieu's concept of principle is only moderately helpful: unlike hers, his concept points to pervasive and culturally induced attitudes rather than to individually appropriate or adopted roles.

I think that a principle, in Arendt's theory, is best understood as a commitment, whether chosen or assigned, that has a kind of logic to which one submits, but the submission feels like an expansion, not a constriction. In filling one's role, one fills out oneself, and, at the same time, partly shapes the role. There is nothing mechanical in the process. One does not rehearse one's lines; one's speech is creative, though certainly disciplined. One tries to make sure that everything one says is, however, in character. One does not play oneself; rather one enacts one's commitment and thereby shows who one is. One's own voice sounds through the mask, and only through it (*OR*, p. 106). Nevertheless, a living person's identity is "intangible," and registers only incompletely on one's fellow participants. Indeed, it can be conveyed more fully only through an "imitation" of oneself and one's political action in a theatrical drama where on the stage someone else plays oneself playing one's role. Correspondingly, the best language to describe authentic politics is theatrical; "the theater is the political art par excellence" (*HC*, pp. 187–188; also *OR*, pp. 106–107). All these considerations apply to a principle or to a mask that one as it were wears. Notice that the dictates of the role provide more than a mere motive: that last word is too narrow, too close-minded for Arendt's purposes. Nor is a role a matter of sheer will: that would be too willful. Nor is it a matter of intellect – that is, of cognition: an actor must be politically intelligent, but not a calculating machine. All categories but that of principle are more at home in the field of individual psychology than in the mentality of worldly political actors. The actor must "transcend" his individual psychology ("What is Freedom?", p. 151). In that transcendence lies a loss of empirical self that is freedom itself. Oddly or not, the empirical self is not the locus of one's identity, in Arendt's account.

Arendt offers an assortment of principles. All of them manifest political freedom, though not all contribute to creating or preserving it. She mentions "honor or glory, love of equality, which Montesquieu called virtue, or distinction or excellence . . . but also fear or distrust or hatred" ("What is Freedom?", p. 152). I interpret Arendt to be saying that though acting from the principle of fear or distrust or hatred manifests freedom, in the sense that one may speak creatively on public matters when submissive to any of these principles, one nevertheless contradicts oneself in acting from them. One helps to destroy the very relationships or procedures that provide the frame or setting for one's future speech, for the continuation of authentic politics, the politics of freedom. I suppose that is what she means when she says that the "opposite" of freedom appears in the world when (some) principles are manifested. But I cannot be sure that I have her meaning.

Additionally, we can say that even such dismaying principles as fear or distrust or hatred are needed to enrich and complete the drama of politics. They contribute to the failure of authentic politics; but the story of such failure is tremendously absorbing. Arendt writes with at least an equal power about failure – the specific failure of revolutions to remain faithful to their free, insurgent beginnings – as about the episodes of success. What can be more compelling than tragedy: failure and loss after great promise and eminence? For those who have had experience of the freedom of authentic politics, the political and the dramatic (or aesthetic) tend to merge, as much in failure as success, as much at the behest of freedom-destroying principles as at the behest of freedom-preserving or freedom-creating principles. At least that is the way it looks to the later theoretical observer.

Arendt's concept of acting from a principle gathers richness as her range of implication is detected. An important point that we should remember, however, is that she does not use the word to mean *moral* principle. That leads to the question as to the place of morality in Arendt's theory of authentic politics.

Arendt's views on morality in authentic politics have perplexed some of her readers. She seems to countenance indifference to morality, and even immorality. She contrasts what she calls "human behavior" and political action. Only the former is judgeable by "moral standards" (the quotation marks are hers) that take into account motives and intentions, and aims and consequences. But the only criterion of authentic politics, she says, is greatness, because it is the nature of action "to break through the commonly accepted and reach into the extraordinary" (*HC*, p. 205). She approvingly cites the funeral speech of Pericles, as presented by Thucydides, in which the glory of Athens is found in the everlasting remembrance of "their good and evil deeds," not their good deeds only (*HC*, p. 206). To be sure when Arendt writes about the insurgent politics of councils, she does not typically refer to glory. Their greatness is equal to or even higher than Greek greatness; their politics is at least equal in authenticity; but the individual and group passion to stand out and then to live forever in men's minds appears not to figure, or to figure very much.

Pericles was in no doubt that some Greek policies were unjust or tyrannical or evil, and Arendt herself is in no doubt that he is correct. Thus it seems clear that Arendt embraces moral inattentiveness as a necessary condition for the greatness of authentic politics. Authentic politics cannot be great, however, if it is too cruel: the reason is that too much cruelty or wickedness of any kind tarnishes glory. Ruthless short cuts violate the spirit of the activity; they are inelegant. Hence we could say that Arendt, like Machiavelli, tends to substitute aesthetics for morality as a restraint on political action. Nothing too awful can be great, but nothing great can be innocent. Her persistent meaning, whether overt or not, is that the principles she adduces as appropriate to politics are, most of them, not moral in nature. Only "love of equality," but equality only in a restricted political sense, approaches being moral ("What is Freedom?", p. 152). There is scant acknowledgment of economic justice, which, just by being economic, cannot be a political commitment. However, Arendt does include solidarity with the exploited as a politically appropriate principle. "But this solidarity, though it may be aroused by suffering, is not guided by it, and it comprehends the strong and the rich no less than the weak and the poor" (*OR*, pp. 88–89). Solidarity is sustained by an idea of "'the grandeur of man,' or 'the honor of the human race,' or the dignity of man" (*OR*, p. 88). These latter notions are perhaps more aesthetic than moral.

The charge that Arendt excludes morality from authentic politics is reinforced when we consider her analysis of the failure of the French Revolution. In a harrowing account, she attributes the destruction of incipient authentic politics – the face-to-face politics of municipalities, clubs, and other small political associations – to the effort to solve the urgent question of starvation. The revolutionaries were overcome by keenly observed and intensely felt compassion for misery, the misery of hordes of people. The compassion transformed itself, she says, into an abstract pity for humanity, and pity then, in turn, transformed itself into immitigable anger that brooked no opposition and established a despotism that was meant to be radically remedial. Arendt laments the demise of authentic politics at the hands of powerful moral passions and the derivative sentiments. Boundlessness enters the fragile political realm and ruins it. The necessities of sheer life overwhelm the experience of freedom. Thus, Arendt suggests that the great threat to authentic politics comes not from wickedness or even from apathy, but from the profoundly misguided attempt to act from intense moral distress.

Apart from scattered remarks about moral issues as they arise in the normal course of mostly inauthentic but altogether real politics (as we conventionally use that word), Arendt is silent. Concerning the absolute evil of the exterminationist totalitarianism of Hitler and Stalin, she does not think that the validity of moral condemnation has to be demonstrated. Totalitarian leaders and administrators were altogether beyond the reach of moral sentiment; they were not perplexed by moral uncertainty. Indeed, exterminationism is defined by "crimes which men can neither punish nor forgive." It cannot be traced to even the most "evil" motives, like "self-interest, greed, covetousness, resentment, lust for power, and cowardice." The initiators and managers of extermination comprised "this newest species of criminals," and they were "beyond the pale even of solidarity in human sinfulness" (*OT*, p. 459). Short of totalitarianism, Arendt spends little time bewailing or examining the effects of "evil" motives. Perhaps she can be reproached for this avoidance; perhaps she thought other philosophers did the job of ordinary moral scrutiny well enough.

Anyone wishing to exonerate Arendt from the charge of immoralism might go on to say that since her philosophical interest is in authentic politics, and since she excludes violence from it altogether, even if Pericles, one of her heroes does not, then the most problematic kinds of moral questions disappear. However this does not convincingly address the issue of the place of morality in authentic politics. In order to think this response adequate one would have to be utterly indifferent to the effects of deliberation and dispute, to the content of the decisions and the impact they have on people. It may be that looked at from the possible perspective of the political actor, all that matters is the very moment of speech, cut off from what preceded it and what may follow from it. The situation of speech may feel self-enclosed and autonomous, but it is not plausible that even when politics is done in the right spirit, political actors are oblivious to the effects of what they say and decide. It is very hard to avoid the sense that Arendt has produced a utopian picture of authentic politics, a picture cut off too drastically from the very reality of those infrequent episodes of actual authentic politics.

Arendt offers a moral view appropriate to authentic politics which, if unconventional, is perfectly in accord with her determined effort to draw a sharp line between authentic and inauthentic politics, and also to separate authentic politics from other realms of human experience. Her goal is not so much to show that authentic politics has actually been guided by her own view as to infer a moral view that authentic politics can be said to engender on its own and from its very nature. Her moral precepts are "the only ones that are not applied to action from the outside, from some supposedly higher faculty or from experiences outside action's own reach" (*HC*, p. 246). Just as every game has its own set of rules that creates, shapes, and confines the play, so authentic politics must have its own morality to inhibit and even inspire action. The only alternative to a morality that is internal to authentic politics is, oddly, not the doctrine of the lesser and necessary wrong, but "the 'moral' standards inherent in the Platonic notion of rule." These standards turn out to be based on "a relationship established between me and myself, so that the right and wrong of relationships with others are determined by attitudes toward oneself" (*HC*, pp. 237–238). But, Arendt insists, proper self-rule is no model for interaction with others.

Arendt's point against Plato, however, does not apply to the claims of ordinary morality. Then, too, Arendt sometimes says that the basic precept of morality is the Socratic adage that it is better for the person, for the person's inner harmony and ability to live with himself, to suffer wrong than to do it. Obviously, no politics, authentic or not, can accept that adage and still be politics. Politics is relentless self-preference of a worldly sort; a person or a group acts to prevail or, at least, endure. It would never occur to a committed actor to prefer for the good of his own soul that he not resist or try to overcome; he would never define doing wrong as resisting and overcoming. Ordinary morality, however, does not start with the Socratic adage; it does not make right conduct impossibly costly; it allows worldly self-preference, but only within strict limits. Its frequent situation is not a choice between doing or suffering wrong, but between doing or not doing wrong.

Arendt's proposal is apparently meant to be a sufficient guide to authentic politics. It is striking, however, that the morality that she says is inherent in action should be derived from the "frailty" or frailties of action, not from its excellence. It is as though morality, however understood, tends to be a tax on human endeavors rather than a crowning human achievement, or at least a set of constraints that dignifies what it constrains. In Arendt's theory political morality is an accommodation between action and restraint, with restraint accepted reluctantly, if perhaps magnanimously.

The frailty of political action shows itself in "the burden of irreversibility and unpredictability." She says that "He who acts never quite knows what he is doing, that he always becomes 'guilty' of consequences he never intended or foresaw, that no matter how disastrous and unexpected the consequences of his deed he can never undo it" (*HC*, p. 233). Thus, some of the features that make authentic politics great – especially the capacity to start something new and unprecedented – account for the need to evaluate greatness morally. Arendt is sufficiently troubled about the flow of unexpected consequences to admit that "Nowhere . . . does man appear to be less free than in those capacities whose very essence is freedom" (*HC*, p. 234). But then she recuperates her loss by suggesting that it is only an aspiration for an impossible individual sovereignty that could have ever led anyone to think that the effects of their action could be under their total control. It is a terrible error to mistake freedom for sovereignty. Human plurality precludes sovereignty. One may feel that, in making these points, she has perhaps changed the subject.

In any case, from these double-edged features of authentic politics, Arendt distills two moral qualities that are meant, precisely, to assuage "the burden of irreversibility and unpredictability." The faculty of forgiving redeems irreversibility and the faculty of making and keeping promises redeems unpredictability (*HC*, p. 236). She anticipates the objection that forgiveness is practically unheard of in politics, authentic or not. She knows that hoping for forgiveness in politics seems unrealistic because of its association with love, a passion that she steadfastly insists has no place in authentic politics. Forgiveness therefore does not figure very much in her political theory. In regard to promises, what she says in *The Human Condition* deals with, among other aspects, the salience of the social contract. She says that "the great variety of contract theories since the Romans attests to the fact that the power of making promises has occupied the center of political thought over the centuries" (*HC*, p. 244). Later, in *On Revolution* and "Civil Disobedience,"[4] Arendt returns to the idea of social contract in its varieties and explores it with subtlety and acuteness. In brief, forgiving and being forgiven would lighten the otherwise crushing sense of the ravages of action on oneself and on others; making and keeping promises establishes some stability in an otherwise unsettling and startling ocean of change.

The pages that Arendt devotes to the internal morality of politics really do not add up to a whole morality that is adequate to authentic politics, much less to all other politics. Forgiving and being forgiven cannot withstand the overwhelming force of consequences, not even when all the other aspects of authentic politics are in place. Concerning promises, the content of the social contract is decisive, not the idea of the contract in itself. One can give and keep one's word, expressly or even tacitly, for all sorts of purposes, including bad ones, even when political action is authentic. The claims of content go hand in hand with the claims of morality, which are not politically originated and which finally cannot be denied. Having said all this, however, I must add that in her treatment of the morality internal to authentic politics, Arendt has produced not a sufficient morality – one must go outside even authentic politics to keep it sane – but, instead, the outlines of a code for conduct. In this code we find some moral virtues that go together with the mostly nonmoral political virtues and attitudes we discussed earlier.

Taken as a code, it is inspiring. It extracts from Nietzsche – especially the first and second essays of *On the Genealogy of Morals*[5] – some of his most generous teachings on how the free person gives his word and then keeps it, despite all difficulties; cancels debts owed him and thus in going beyond the law, acts mercifully; accords justice rather than acting out of revenge or ressentiment; is suspicious of, even dismayed by, the will to punish; and may be said to love his enemies by shrugging off the slights and hurts inflicted on him. She quarrels with Nietzsche over the prominence he gives to the concept of the will to power, but admires his "extraordinary sensibility to moral phenomena" (*HC*, p. 245). She takes from him some invaluable insights into a code proper for free human beings as they undertake authentic political action. Indeed, the code is invaluable for honorable persons, whether or not they want to engage in political action, or have or lack the opportunity to engage in it. Alas, one must repeat that even this great code cannot by itself suffice to resolve all the questions of morality as they have inevitably appeared historically. In sum, Arendt's view of the place of morality in authentic politics remains unsatisfactory. It is, so to speak, the Achilles heel of authentic politics. A rather eccentric notion of how morality has traditionally been conceived – namely, as a Platonist relation between one and oneself and, relatedly, as Socratic care for the self – renders morality obviously irrelevant to most politics, authentic or not. Arendt says that "in wanting to be good, I actually am concerned with my own self. The moment I act politically I'm not concerned with me, but with the world."[6] This conception threatens to efface concern for others – who are not me and not the world – from morality. But such an upshot is absurd. It would be better to draw instruction from Arendt's theory of authentic politics until the moral question reasserts itself, as it must, and then rejoin common sense and ordinary morality, as did the practitioners of authentic politics, even if only like them, intermittently and without enthusiasm. We can learn from Arendt without endorsing every segment of her theory.

Authentic politics is rare and either episodic or short-lived. The story would not be finished, however, unless we paid a little attention to the advantages of authentic politics. These advantages, too, are part of the effort to restore the dignity of politics. And this part highlights advantages that are peculiar to authentic politics or that emerge from it in a better way or to a greater degree than from other realms of human experience. These advantages make up the intrinsic value of action to the actor, and also the philosopher.

It may be odd to speak of advantages when our emphasis in interpreting Arendt has been on the absence of the role of self-interest in actors. The crucial consideration is that the advantages to the actor cannot be sought, yet do come when unsought, provided, of course, that the political participation is done in the right spirit and for its own sake, and in the right modes of action. A good measure of self-forgetfulness is always needed for genuine action. There is less oddity in mentioning another category of advantages, namely, those to the philosopher who dwells on authentic politics. The philosopher as theorist, observer, even spectator, will take any advantage he or she can from action: the advantage is not personal, naturally, but rather is an advantage to philosophy, to reflection about the human condition. We must also notice that the advantages to the actor and to the philosopher of the human condition alike are not political in nature. The advantages of pure politics are not political. They must be formulated in non-political language. Politics done in the right spirit and for its own sake is immensely valuable for non-political reasons. Hating the tendency to instrumentalize politics, Arendt does not hesitate to make it yield some of its blessings quite outside itself. This is not to deny the existence of advantages that are recognizably political. For example, domestic oppression is abolished or alleviated under the aegis of authentic politics, whether in the *polis* or in a society briefly governed by councils. (Such liberation, however, is still not positive freedom.) But it may not be irresponsible to suggest that the greatest advantages that Arendt's theory of pure or authentic politics celebrates are experiential or existential; advantages that pertain to the enrichment of individuality and to the stature of the human race.

The advantages to the actor begin with the manner in which taking part in authentic politics confers an identity on him. The theme of identity is carried principally by *The Human Condition*. Arendt insists that a person can achieve an identity only through being seen and heard by his equals as they all deliberate the common fate. One's family or daily familiars or companions do not provide the occasion or the stimulus, Arendt thinks, that allow and even force oneself to show who one is. Who one is is, of course, "implicit in everything somebody says or does" (*HC*, p. 179). But full disclosure is possible – if it is possible at all – only in the circle of one's peers in public. One must be pieced together from the various perspectives on oneself that one's equals take. Only my equals can say who I am, and tell me. The public light is the only light strong enough for personal disclosure. And one must not search deliberately for one's identity or otherwise it will not come; self-disclosure is involuntary (*OR*, p. 285); and one must, Arendt holds, remain less known to oneself than to others. But one will be known; without the opportunity of authentic politics, one will pass into death without a full identity. Arendt links identity to immortality, immortal fame; but since many of those who have taken part in authentic politics are to us nameless, the attainment of immortality is out of reach for them. Yet a person can be satisfied with this much knowledge: he has become known in his own lifetime, even if he cannot ever know himself as he is known by others. He is somebody, and not just in his own self-misperceiving eyes.

Other advantages to the actor that figure in Arendt's analysis include the sheer exhilaration of action and, relatedly, the experience of being free. Again, these advantages, if they are to come, must come unsought. They are discovered after participation has begun for the purpose of, say, political liberation. "The charms of liberty," in John Jay's phrase, are discovered only in the action needed to gain it. Revolutionists and insurgents were surprised by joy: "they were not in the least prepared for these charms" (*OR*, p. 33). The exhilaration of authentic political action attaches itself, furthermore, to the experience of being free. Action is freedom. Of course, freedom is shown wherever human creativity is shown, whether in the crafts of fabrication or in works of art or in the exertions of thinking. But the freedom that is experienced in the pursuit of political newness is unlike the other manifestations. Leaving aside the activity of thinking, which Arendt occasionally holds to be the freest of all human endeavors (*OT*, p. 473), we see that Arendt believes that the experience of freedom is most pure when it arises politically: the political realm is "the only realm where man can be truly free" (*OR*, p. 114). In authentic politics, one may feel free of determination of almost any kind, free of anxiety over necessities, free of rigid rules, free of the limits set by standards of good taste. In authentic politics, spontaneousness best shows itself; spontaneousness is the most joyous freedom.

Identity, the exhilaration of action, the experience of freedom, are some of the intrinsic advantages of action to the actor, when action is authentically political. These advantages are, or come close to being, peculiar to authentic politics, politics done in the right spirit and for its own sake. And they are advantages that are located outside the political realm, beyond liberation from oppression and the usually doomed attempt to construct a constitution that will continuously accommodate authentic politics. The word advantages itself scarcely takes the measure of attained identity, unsurpassable exhilaration, and the experience of freedom.

So much of life is unsatisfactory and yet the remedies seem hopelessly unavailable. Arendt promises that authentic politics can provide a remedy. She speaks of the "instrumentalization of the whole world and the earth, this limitless devaluation of everything given, this process of growing meaninglessness where every end is transformed into a means" (*HC*, p. 157). As long as people lack something they value non-instrumentally in their everyday lives, they will endure meaninglessness, which brings on resentment and alienation. Arendt goes so far as to say that they will be deprived of reality, quite simply. Reality is "the same as appearance" in the public realm. Whatever is denied this appearance "comes and passes away like a dream, intimately and exclusively our own but without reality" (*HC*, p. 199). Of course, there is the life of the affections; there may be a consoling and reconciling faith. But Arendt wants her readers to want more than the life of the affections and though she is not irreligious, she certainly cannot spell out any grounds for belief. What does that leave? Surely not the economic life, the life of endless consumption, which converts all things into means out of an unappeasable desire for gratification. Authentic politics fills the gap at the heart of the human condition. The lucky ones who have had the experience of authentic politics may not sufficiently appreciate all that it does for them, and those who through inexperience are oblivious to its advantages must be told by the observer how significant their lack is and how their malaise may arise from such lack.

Finally let us turn to the advantages of authentic politics to the philosopher of the human condition. They go beyond the supply of raw material for stories that illuminate life memorably and thus delight or engross historians and imaginative writers. Perhaps there is no qualitative difference between the advantages that may be scarcely accessible to political actors and scarcely comprehensible to those who are both unphilosophical and unpolitical, and those arguments that have special appeal to Arendt the philosopher. In any case, we find a number of considerations that recur throughout Arendt's work that help to construct a case for the dignity of authentic politics. These considerations are unapologetically philosophical, and would occur and matter greatly only to philosophers and to poets and to some others who have the ambition to reflect on the human condition, not merely on one or another part of it.

Arendt's deepest philosophical passions are to affirm existence against reasonable or plausible causes for despair and resignation, and to affirm the human stature against those who reduce humanity to just another animal species locked in its nature, and locked as well in Nature. She thinks that authentic politics can serve, uniquely or at least saliently, as the basis for affirming existence and for affirming the human stature. The project of affirmation appears to be and doubtless is Kantian, to some extent; but there is a greater daring and a greater initial despair than Kant showed or had to show. Arendt may be closer to Nietzsche than to anyone else.

The two affirmations are intertwined. Human distinctiveness in relation to the rest of nature is the root of human stature, and it should intensify the wonder that may be felt at the philosophical thought that there is a world at all, rather than nothing. From wonder, affirmation should follow; from intensified wonder, greater affirmation. Humanity alone is capable of wonder and therefore can affirm existence; its own stature is in itself a cause of wonder. Yet it is also alone capable of destructive and self-destructive dejection and hatred of existence. The dejection and hatred may be fed not only by the prevalence of evil and natural suffering, or by the feeling of mortality, or by the experience of meaninglessness, but, just as bad, by all philosophical and scientific theories and systems that are reductionist of humanity, by making it as causally determined and (in principle) as predictable as the rest of nature. Humanity at its best redeems existence; but it may require an extraordinary philosophical effort to affirm humanity. Like the Greeks, we must feel the pathos, but also the grandeur, of having to find our place in a cosmos "where everything is immortal" except ourselves, and thus being alone in receiving the chance and the ability to earn immortality through our "capacity for the immortal deed" (*HC*, p. 19). "Action alone is the exclusive prerogative of man" (*HC*, p. 22). Knowledge of one's mortality drives the passion for immortality. Creatures are mere members of various (putatively) immortal species, but every human being is singular and irreplaceable, while also condemned to perish.

The key to affirming the human stature, celebrating the human distinctiveness, lies ultimately in freedom, of which only human beings are capable.

Freedom is supremely present in authentic politics, the politics of beginning something new and unexpected and hopeful. Without such politics, it would be more difficult to find evidence of freedom, though of course not impossible. But authentic politics displays freedom for all to see, if they have the eyes to see. The political activities of freedom release human beings from the hegemony of those fated pleasures yielded by nature. To be content with natural pleasures is to "live and die like animals" (*HC*, p. 19). Arendt is famous for having ranked political action well above labor and work in the scale of the *vita activa*. Labor for the sustenance of life remains immersed in natural processes. Work that fabricates the longer-lasting artifacts and implements may show creativity, but is still bound by specific purposes and indispensable rules. Both labor and work are but preconditions of freedom. Freedom itself is their raison d'être, as it is the raison d'être of politics ("What is Freedom?", p. 146). If we say, as we must, that art and science are also manifestations of freedom, Arendt certainly would not deny it; in fact, she insists on it. Yet her interest is to find evidence of freedom in activities that "traditionally, as well as according to current opinion, are within the range of every human being" (*HC*, p. 5). That leaves only authentic politics, where freedom, with all its philosophical advantages, can be manifested by ordinary humanity, and where the human distinctiveness is thus most pronounced, the human stature most surely evident, and the philosophical shock of wonder at existence is most easily joined to gratitude for the almost ineffable fact that there is a world at all.

NOTES

1 Max Weber, "Politics as a Vocation" (1919), trans. H. H. Gerth and C. Wright Mills in *From Max Weber: Essays in Sociology* (New York: Oxford University Press, 1946).
2 Carl Schmitt, *The Concept of the Political*, trans. J. Harvey Lomax (Chicago: University of Chicago Press, 1996).
3 "What is Freedom?" in Arendt, *BPF*.
4 "Civil Disobedience" (1970), in Arendt, *CR*.
5 Friedrich Nietzsche, *On the Genealogy of Morals* (1887), trans. Walter Kaufmann (New York: Vintage, 1969).
6 Melvyn A. Hill, ed., *Hannah Arendt: The Recovery of the Public World* (New York: St. Martin's, 1979), p. 311.

PART IV

Arendt and the ancients

7

J. PETER EUBEN

Arendt's Hellenism

Hannah Arendt is one of the few contemporary political and social theorists for whom ancient Greece retains its hold as a point of reference and inspiration. Of the very few who think with the Greeks she is distinctive in having recourse to the pre-philosophical articulation of *polis* life. Where other theorists understand and judge the *polis* in terms of a philosophical tradition largely hostile to it, she inverts that reading, condemning the tradition for effacing the originary and in some respects still quintessential expression of freedom and power present in the practices and literature of classical Greece, particularly democratic Athens. Thus, while she has much to say about Plato, it is mostly to chastise him for being anti-political. And though she says much more in praise of Aristotle, in the end she thinks he too misrepresents Greek political life.

There is something perverse about this inversion. For one thing, it rests on a sometimes flatfooted reading of *The Republic*, the text which provides the principal object of her most sweeping criticisms of the Platonic project. For all of Arendt's appreciation of the theatrical and performative dimensions of Athenian politics she is largely insensitive to the dramatic structure of *The Republic*. For another thing, she seems to romanticize a society, Athenian democracy, which is utterly remote from our own, and then compounds things by largely ignoring or excusing what seems most illiberal and/or undemocratic about it: substantial social and economic inequalities, slavery and patriarchy, imperialist adventures, exclusive citizenship laws, the absence of rights and the immoralism of greatness.

Finally, for all her glorification of Athenian politics Arendt is maddeningly elusive about what that politics was about. "What," Hanna Pitkin asks, "is it that they talked about together in that endless palaver in the agora?" "What does she [Arendt] imagine," Pitkin continues, "was the *content* of political speech and action and why is this question so difficult to answer from her text?"[1]

This seeming perversity has led even Arendt's sympathetic critics to seek ways of marginalizing or softening her Hellenism, and less sympathetic ones to dismiss her because of her Hellenism and dismiss ancient political thought because of Arendt.

In the pages that follow I want to look at the story Arendt tells about Ancient Greece and at why she tells it as she does. What does her Hellenism enable her to dramatize about modernity? What was it about Greece and Athens that she found so compelling and challenging, and how many of her enthusiasms should we share? I also want to rescue Arendt from her Hellenism and rescue Greece and Athens from Arendt. Arendt certainly got important things "wrong" about "the Greeks" and "the Athenians."

My construction of Arendt's Hellenism follows her instructions. "Let us," she writes in her essay "What Is Freedom," "go back once more to antiquity, i.e., to its prephilosophical traditions, certainly not for the sake of erudition and not even because of the continuity of our tradition, but merely because a freedom experienced in the process of acting and nothing else – though, of course, mankind never lost this experience altogether – has never again been articulated with the same classical clarity."[2] My choice from that tradition is tragedy, more particularly Sophocles' *Oedipus at Colonus*. Why tragedy?

First, though Arendt has no sustained consideration of any Greek tragedy, her discussion of politics and action are suffused by the language and imagery of theater. She talks of performance and audiences, of those who play a part and those spectators who see the entire play, and of spaces of appearance as stages upon which virtuosi speak and act in compelling and revealing ways. She even suggests that the specific revelatory quality of action and speech which manifests the agent and speaker is so tied to the flux of acting and speaking "that it can be represented and 'reified' only through a kind of repetition, the imitation of mimesis . . .which is appropriate only in the drama, whose very name (from the Greek *dran*, to act) indicates that playacting actually is an imitation of acting."[3] And she regards identities as forged by various performances in which men [sic] act politically.

Secondly, Arendt's thought, for all its "optimistic" emphasis on beginnings and natality, retains a tragic sensibility articulated in Sophoclean drama. This sensibility is central to her dramatization of modernity and helps constitute the kind of political thinker she represents herself as being. Thirdly, many of the central themes in Arendt's work – heroism and greatness, public and private, storytelling, judgment and impartiality, the importance of speech and action and the unpredictability of the latter with the attendant need for forgiveness and promises – are also the subjects of Greek tragedy as text and as performance. Penultimately, the study of tragedy, including the relationship between the action on stage and the role of theater in Athenian public life, can help dramatize strains in Arendt's work and the discrepant readings of her by her critics. Thus, the tensions between the agonistic and deliberative Arendt not only echoes the subjects of tragedy but is replicated in the tension between what happens in the theater and what happens outside it in the assembly, courts, juries, and agora. Finally, and perhaps most significantly, reading Arendt through the lens of tragedy helps dramatize aspects of her Hellenism and thought as a whole while that thought provides a ground by which to bring tragedy into dialogue with modernity and post-modernity.

I choose *Oedipus at Colonus* because the Wisdom of Silenus which she quotes from the play in the final paragragh of *On Revolution* inspires her most dramatic claim about the redemptive power of politics, itself perhaps her most provocative challenge to contemporary life and thought. Here is Arendt's rendering of "those famous and frightening lines": "Not to be born prevails over all meaning uttered in words; by far the second best for life, once it has appeared, is to go as swiftly as possible whence it came."[4]

This wisdom was forced out of Silenus by King Midas who, having hunted a long time for this companion (some sources say teacher) of Dionysus, finally captured him by getting him drunk. Though Silenus was at first sullen and uncommunicative, refusing Midas' request to tell him what he considered man's greatest good, Midas pressed him, expecting that Silenus would name the King's achievements of status and wealth. With what Nietzsche calls "shrill laughter," Silenus retaliates against Midas' coercion, with words as shattering as they were unexpected. Here is Nietzsche's version of Silenus' wisdom: "Ephemeral wretch, begotten by accident and toil, why do you force me to tell you what it would be your greatest boon not to hear? What would be best for you is quite beyond your reach; not to be born, not to be, to be nothing. But the second best is to die soon."

How is it possible to live with such wisdom? What could possibly redeem human life in the face of it? How are we to avoid hatred of the world, self-contempt, bitterness at existence or exhausting resentment after hearing it? If life is merely the beginning of death and the interim pain and excess, better to end it before it begins.

Nietzsche tells us that it was out of the need to avert their eyes from the full realization of such a paralyzing vision that the Greeks invented the Olympian gods "imposing a world of art between themselves and the world of suffering, casting a veil of beauty over the abyss." The gods are a conscious self-deception.

For (the early) Nietzsche it is tragedy that allows the Greeks to look at and look away from the abyss. Drama interposed itself between the blinding darkness of Silenus and the normal which veils it, allowing only an indirect light into the theater to remind the onlookers of the Dionysian sources of their energy and power. At the same time, the magnificence of tragedy's poetry and the greatness of its heroes transforms while incorporating darkness into a thing of beauty. For him drama redeems life against the wisdom of Silenus.

For Arendt, politics does, though it is a politics of art and theater. In her gloss on the Wisdom of Silenus, she says that Sophocles "let us know through the mouth of Theseus, the legendary founder of Athens and hence her spokesman, what it was that enabled ordinary men, young and old, to bear life's burden; it was the polis, the space of men's free deeds and living words, which could endow life with splendor – *ton bion lampron poieisthai*" (*OR*, p. 285).

I

If anyone's life proves Silenus wise it is Oedipus'. Given Laius' and Jocasta's disregard of the prophecy that the King would die at the hands of his son, Oedipus should never have been born, and if born, should have died before he killed the man at the crossroads who was his father and unknowingly received his mother as his wife. And who had endured more than Oedipus, each living day a reminder of his pain and transgressions?

The lines which immediately follow the statement of Silenus' wisdom constitute a lament by the chorus of old men for their lost youth. As they look back they see it as a time of confident strength where many friends and comrades sustained them in whatever afflictions or trials they encountered. In those days they had seen less evil and were less burdened by the sorrows that multiply cumulatively as the compass of life stretches beyond the bloom of youth. The longer one lives the more horror one experiences, horrors of war, civil strife, murder, and faction. The chorus goes on to liken old age to an implacable enemy and nature to an assaulting army against whom one is fated to lose. These images suggest that there is no refuge, no redemption, no hope; here and now Silenus is right.

To the degree that Silenus' wisdom is heard with particular acuity by the old, *Oedipus at Colonus* is a play about the revenge of the old against the young, the weak against the strong, and the past against the future, all of which provides dimension to Oedipus' incensed denunciation of his son Polyneices.[5] The son is hardly guiltless. But the depth of the father's passion for revenge goes beyond anything the latter deserves (and reminds us, if we need reminding, that the history of fathers and sons in this family is less than exemplary). The resentment ignores complexity and consequences in a way that recalls Silenus' revenge. In so far as Oedipus is held captive by his poverty and dependence, his turning against his son, whom he regards as the cause of his poverty and a potential captor and whom he refuses to help (causing the death of Laius' line and of Thebes), is analogous to Silenus' revenge against humankind.

But what about Theseus? His words, not Oedipus', are what Arendt quotes and relies upon.[6]

Theseus is the legendary unifier of Athens, which is why the play presents him as worshiping in the local deme as well as in the city proper and honoring Poseidon in both his aristocratic and his democratic representations. Theseus was also coming to represent the founding of Athenian democracy. The democracy dramatized in the play and embodied in Theseus is characterized by openness to persuasion, fearlessness, the sharing of authority and responsibility, decisiveness, a sense of justice involving mutual respect and reciprocity, a shared sense of human fallibility, the use of force without boastfulness to back up commitments given, a defense of the weak, and a capacious understanding of citizenship. We can imagine this city as a "space of men's free deeds and living words."

II

It was the *polis*, Arendt claims, that "enabled ordinary men, young and old, to bear life's burden." In this space of men's free deeds and living words life was endowed with meaning, significance, and beauty. In it men redeemed themselves, defying the paralyzing wisdom of Silenus.

If politics alone redeems us against this wisdom, then it is the most important activity of all since without it we would have no reason or will to live. "As long as the polis is there to inspire men to dare the extraordinary, all things are safe; if it perishes everything is lost" (*HC*, p. 206). It follows that maintaining the preconditions of *polis* life takes precedence over the specific content of that life. It also follows that the first task of a political people is to insure that the space for action and speech they enjoy is passed on to their posterity. It was the inability or unwillingness of the American founders to do this that led to what Arendt regards as the Revolution's failure.

But this still leaves us uncertain about what kind of politics it is that can redeem human life and what kind of redemption Arendt is endorsing. We know what (Arendt's) Plato thought the redemption of politics entailed, but we also know that she repudiates the philosophical "solution" to the frailty of human affairs.

Politics requires and presupposes the existence of a public realm, what Arendt calls "the space of appearance," where men speak and act before each other. The aim and consequence of their doing so is not, as we might expect, to accomplish some objective such as passing a piece of legislation, protecting their interests, increasing their wealth or assuring their security, but to be seen by others. She opens the chapter on "Action" in *The Human Condition* with the following quote from Dante:

> For in every action what is primarily intended by the doer . . . is the disclosure of his own image. Hence . . . every doer, in so far as he does, takes delight in doing; since everything that is desires its own being, and since in action the being of the doer is somehow intensified, delight necessarily follows . . . Thus, nothing acts unless [by acting] it makes patent its latent self. (*HC*, p. 175)

Acting in public gives us a sense of being alive and powerful. It provides an opportunity to communicate who we are, to manifest that style of action and traits of character that make us distinctive. And it is a way of inserting ourselves into history, announcing ourselves so that others must take note and notice of us.

In *Life of the Mind*, Arendt argues that this "urge toward self-display" is a quality of all living beings. All "make their appearance like actors on a stage" with other creatures to play with and spectators who recognize their existence. Though the stage is common to all it seems different to each species and, in the case of humans, to each individual. Thus what appears in the shared space of speech and action depends upon the perspective or standpoint of the spectator.[7]

Since the public realm is "permeated by a fiercely agonial spirit" (*HC*, p. 41), where everyone is constantly trying to distinguish themselves from others and to "show through unique deed or achievements he was the best of all," it is not clear how political life is possible let alone redemptive. How can citizens be competitive and cooperative at the same time? How is a "plurality of unique beings" possible and why is it desirable?

For Arendt, a *political* community as opposed to the ersatz politics of a Platonic city or a liberal state requires the contentiousness of strong-willed individuals who also appreciate how the world they share makes their individualism possible. "Human plurality," she writes, "the basic condition of speech, has the two-fold character of equality and distinction" (*HC*, p. 175). If men were not equal they could not understand each other, there could be no politics or community. But if they were not distinct, if they did not bring a distinctive perspective to bear on the world they continually reenact through speech and deed, there would be no need to speak and so no need for politics. The fact that everything that appears in public can be seen and heard by everybody, that others see what we see and hear what we hear assures us of the reality of our world and ourselves as actors in it (*HC*, p. 50). That reality is not vitiated by the fact that each of us sees it from a distinctive perspective, that truth is, as we now say, constituted discursively, since it is the nature of political truth and reason to be based on what appears to me and to us. It *is* vitiated by preoccupation with private life and by philosophical speculation.

To distinguish oneself presupposes the presence of others from whom one is distinct and against whose deeds and words one understands and measures one's own. Since each is engaged in a similar enterprise all are actors and audience, performers and spectators in turn. As this implies, there must be a certain agreement on shared understandings, judgments, and practices[8] if the agonistic politics is to have meaning. If men go too far and fail to recognize any limit in their drive for glory they will lose everything, including the *polis* and their chance for earthly immortality which drove them to act in the first place. Paradoxically, it is agonism itself which makes such mitigation possible because with it each is intensely alert to each and to the preconditions their striving for glory requires. This suggests how and why one could cooperate with one's competitor and depend upon those one seeks to outshine.

The *polis* exists to combat the frailty of human affairs, which it does by multiplying the occasions upon which men can win immortal fame and by being a form of organized remembrance. In the first instance it enables men to do permanently though "within certain restrictions" what was otherwise possible only infrequently: "make the extraordinary an occurrence of every day life" (*HC*, p. 197). In the second instance, the *polis* increases the chance that a deed deserving of fame will in fact be remembered. Elsewhere and less equivocally, Arendt says that the polis "assures" the mortal actor that his "passing existence and fleeting greatness will never lack the reality that comes from being seen, being heard and generally appearing before an audience of fellow men" (*HC*, pp. 197–198).

For the *polis* to turn back the Wisdom of Silenus and provide a stage for great actions, the public realm must "transcend" the life span of mortal men. Lacking such transcendence, "no politics, no common world, no public realm is possible" (*HC*, p. 55). It was for "the sake of this public realm and the chance it afforded to men to show who they inexchangeably were and out of love for the body politic that made immortality possible, that each was more or less willing to share the burdens of jurisdiction, defense and administration of public affairs" (*HC*, p. 41), to be political in our sense.

Politics, which is what gives meaning to human life, is a world of appearances. Politically speaking, what appears is the world, not some pale imitation of another world beyond it. The political does not lack firmer ground or more efficient organization, and it is not, as Plato's parable of the Cave seems to indicate, a shadowy place lacking splendor and beauty. It is, rather, a world rich with tone and texture. Worldly men are, in Nietzsche's phrase, "superficial out of profundity."

Since the political realm has its own integrity, problems that arise in it must be solved in its terms. The philosophical tradition regards this as unacceptable. Its siren's song lures men into renouncing action with its boundlessness, unpredictability, and irreversibility of outcome, and into rebelling against the outrageous fact that we are not in control of our actions, of "who" we are and so the stories told about us. The remedy is to substitute making for doing, politics as craft for politics as performance, and a metaphysics of truth for perspectivism. Then we will be able to see that behind the obvious multiplicity of the world's appearances, and behind the equally obvious plurality of man's faculties and abilities, there exists a single measure of validity and goodness. Grounded in a realm outside politics, immune to the instabilities and conflicts that leave men unable to understand and control what they do and how they live, it would clean up the messiness, the pretensions and the deficiencies of worldly existence. In this world there would be no place for Oedipus and so no place for *Oedipus at Colonus*, no place for tragedy as sensibility and institution.

From one point of view, "the" philosophical tradition offers itself as the answer to Silenus. But from another point of view, it is, and understands itself to be, complicit with him, as in Plato's recognition that, from a worldly point of view, philosophy is a kind of death. Arendt regards this anti-political vision of redemption as a snare and self-defeating. "The life span of men running toward death," she writes, "would inevitably carry everything human to ruin and destruction if it were not for the faculty of interrupting it and beginning something new, a faculty which is inherent in action like an ever-present reminder that men, though they must die, are not born in order to die but in order to begin" (*HC*, p. 246). Philosophers find the risk of the miraculous too unpredictable and either work against it or remove themselves sufficiently from the world of appearances so it cannot touch them.

By purging tragedy, philosophy generates an anti-political vision of redemption. It does so by positing a stark opposition between the utter chaos of the Dionysian and the perfect harmony, unity, and order of the Apollonian so that only the latter can redeem the former. In these terms plurality, perspectivism, agonism, worldly life, action, and of course politics itself can only be seen as dangerous and life-threatening. In these terms, performance, theater and drama are distractions since there can be no mediation between the Dionysian and the Apollonian.

Against this Arendt sides with politics and drama, the world of appearances and opinion, with truth as negotiation among competing viewpoints, and with a notion of redemption that retains tragedy as institution and sensibility.

III

Reading Arendt through the lens of tragedy illuminates her political thought, while her thought dramatizes aspects of tragedy in ways that bring it into dialogue with modernity. Of course, the lens illuminates the limitations and missed opportunities as well as the depth of her thought. Similarly, her political theory draws attention to aspects of tragedy she ignores and which make it both a more relevant and a problematic interlocutor in contemporary considerations of modernity.

Arendt talks about "the Greeks" despite her celebration of distinctness and about "the Athenians," even when, as in her discussion of Thucydides, there is a question of whether one can (any longer?) talk about "the" Athenians. Moreover, she seriously misrepresents "Greek" attitudes toward biological reproduction and turns warnings about conflating private and public life into polarities "the Greeks" themselves would not have recognized. Finally, she makes pronouncements about the pre-philosophical literature she invokes that ignore the multiple voices present, say, in *The Iliad* (which she reads as a straightforward endorsement of the heroic ethic), or indeed in *Oedipus at Colonus*.

Certainly the absence of qualifications and multivocality in a thinker who insists on plurality and distinctions should make us wary of the textual basis for her various claims about the Greeks. But is such absence also a reason to dismiss her Hellenism as a distraction from what she "really" wanted to or should have argued? Let me answer this first by suggesting parallels between Arendt's political thought and tragedy she did not articulate, and then turn to aspects of her Hellenism we do find in her work.

Though Arendt's idea of judgment owes much to Aristotle and Kant, it has Hellenic parallels in the performance conditions of tragedy. Theater provided a place and moment when citizen spectators could judge refracted versions of themselves on stage. In *Oedipus at Colonus* the chorus of Athenian citizens are judges in the disputes between Creon and Oedipus and Polyneices and Oedipus, just as their counterparts in the audience were jurors in the law courts. In addition, the dramatic festivals were themselves competitions in which ordinary citizens judged the plays and awarded prizes. If we consider all this, and if we regard each play as a point of view on issues, people, decisions, and cultural practices and think of how many plays each year and over a lifetime an Athenian citizen witnesses, we can imagine the development of something like the "enlarged mentality" Arendt distills from Kant's discussion of taste. The possibility of impartiality, of seeing the world from other points of view, of "going visiting," to use her phrase, in order to develop a capacity for independent judgment is an aspect of the theatrical experience.

This suggests that we can understand Arendt as I think she understood herself and as the tragedians certainly thought of themselves: as political educators of democratic citizens. "Theater," Carol Dougherty has written, "functions as a second agora, or public space, in which the community at large can discuss its political options . . ."[9] But these options are considered in a more comprehensive form than the urgency of decision present in the Assembly Council or Courts allow. Tragedy, like Arendt, sought to understand the conditions of action, but did not, any more than she does, prescribe particular acts. Tragedy and Arendt both seem less concerned with solving problems than with deepening our understanding of them, whether those "problems" have to do with empire, leadership, war, and democracy (as in Arendt's *Crises of the Republic*), or those larger cultural accommodations and exclusions (as in *her Human Condition*) which function as unproblematic conditions of collective life. In both instances each dramatizes the "unboundedness" and "unpredictability" of action. "In the tragic perspective," Jean-Pierre Vernant writes, "acting and being an agent has a double character. On the one side, it consists in taking counsel with oneself, weighing for and against and doing the best one can to foresee the order of means and ends. On the other hand, it is to make a bet on the unknown and incomprehensible and to take a risk on a terrain that remains impenetrable . . ."[10] "Because an actor always moves among and in relation to others," Hannah Arendt writes, "he is never merely a doer but always and at the same time a sufferer" (*HC*, p. 190).

Arendt shares this tragic sensibility with the Greek dramatists. It is a sensibility that appears in the narrative of modernity she tells in *The Human Condition*. The story of Oedipus, who was confident of his ability to solve any problem and of his powers of discernment, yet was nonetheless shadowed by some evil double so that he never quite knew what he was saying or doing, is paralleled by that of the scientific and technological pretensions that she regards as defining modernity. If we think of Oedipus's blindness not as a physical condition but as a metaphorical or even political one, then it makes perfect sense that some of Arendt's most profound reflections on modernity appear in a collection of essays entitled *Men in Dark Times*.

One can even think of Arendt as imitating the impartiality she admires in Homer, Herodotus, and Thucydides. True, she says the social ontology that made such impartiality possible, especially the assumption that greatness is instantly recognizable, is gone. The anti-political traditions that have shaped modernity have made greatness, like power, a dirty word. Yet she does believe that there is something like political greatness found in quite different historical occasions, such as the American revolution, the Russian Soviets, the French Resistance and, no doubt, had she lived long enough, Polish Solidarity. In this regard one could say that she, like

Herodotus, wished to preserve "from decay the remembrance of what men have done," prevent "the great and wonderful actions of Greeks and Barbarians from losing their due portion of glory" (I, 1).

One can also think of the tensions in Arendt's work through the lens of tragedy. Critics have noted a strain, even a contradiction, between an associative, communal, democratic, deliberative Arendt who admires the episodic revivals of political freedom, and an Arendt "captured" by the Greek model of greatness, heroism, agonism, and aestheticized politics. Mostly, they praise one Arendt or the other, wishing that she was not so committed, or arguing that she was not really so committed, to the one they find unpalatable.

This tension is dramatized by the tragedians. The question of what to do with what Bernard Knox calls "the heroic temper" in a democracy was, if not the text, then the subtext of many plays. The question of how one is to reconcile the agonism necessary for politics, including democratic politics, with the need for deliberation parallels the question of how one "fits" figures like Oedipus, who give life meaning precisely by their excess, into a community of political equals. The issues are not merely posed on stage, they are posed in the contrast between the dramatic and historical space of the play, between its content and context of performance.

The balance of proximity and distance from contemporary issues afforded by the theatrical experience provided a place and time for the Athenians to become spectators of themselves. Attaining a certain distance from the press of decisions and events provided an occasion for a reflectiveness impossible in other public settings. In saying this I do not want to underestimate the intensity of audience response, particularly if Nietzsche is right about tragedy removing the veil covering the Dionysian abyss. Nor am I suggesting that Greek tragedy is a morality play where the audience celebrates its superiority to the partial and distorted perceptions of those on stage. Pity yields to fear since anyone (and any city) could find themselves in the position of Oedipus, not because they will kill their fathers and marry their mothers, but because success and power leave us confident of our ability to solve problems "yet we can't see the problems we cannot solve." Certain that he understands the conditions of his life, Oedipus in *Oedipus Tyrannus* was "unable to recognize any dimension of his life's meaning other than the one he already knew." In this sense "he denied the possibility of tragedy until he was overwhelmed by it."[11] This is, I think, Arendt's view of the modern condition.

IV

Arendt is a dramatist of modernity who no more aims to return to ancient Athens than Sophocles aimed to return to the Athens of Theseus. But what, then, is the point of her Hellenism (especially her celebration of politics), and does her use of it explain, even if it does not justify, her reading of the Greeks?

Arendt's Hellenism is equal parts aspiration, remembrance, and recognition. We may still use words like action, power, politics, and freedom, but we do not understand their full meaning because we lack the experiences from which they spring, or cannot recognize those experiences for what they are when they do appear. If we could restore access to the *polis*, the full significance of those words and corresponding experiences would become clearer to us.[12] And we can gain such access because the "*polis*" is less a physical entity or specific historical configuration than an ever-present possibility, even under the inhospitable conditions of modernity. The *polis*, Arendt writes, is "not the city-state in its physical location; it is the organization of the people as it arises out of acting and speaking together . . . no matter where they happen to be" (*HC*, p. 98). It is, we might say, a myth or an invention like the Olympian gods.

If we want a sense of what a world without politics and with Silenus triumphant would be like we can look at Arendt's portrait of totalitarianism. For her, totalitarianism, which represents an extreme manifestation of developments present in modernity as a whole, fosters and responds to a radical loss of self, a cynical, bored indifference in the face of death or catastrophe, a penchant for historical abstractions as a guide to life, and a general contempt for the rules of common sense, along with a dogged adherence to traditions that have lost their point but not their hold.[13]

It is one of Arendt's most distinctive arguments that politics is an answer to totalitarianism; that, while totalitarianism is the domination of the state, it also represents the loss of politics. More positively, the fact that she ends a discussion of the French Resistance, which itself ends a book on the American Revolution, with the quote from Sophocles suggests that she believes that the experience of politics still has the capacity to redeem men from the Wisdom of Silenus. Indeed, one could read her work as one could read Homer and Thucydides: as telling a story about such experiences to sustain us in the absence of their presence.

This is hardly nostalgia. Arendt's project is, as she puts it in her most Hellenic work, *The Human Condition*, to consider that condition "from the vantage point of our newest experience and *our* most recent fears" in order "to think what *we* are doing" (my emphasis, *HC*, p. 5). In these terms her Hellenism is an attempt to think through the present without being presentistic.

Moderns have not only lost their capacity to understand the full meaning of words like politics and freedom, they have also lost their capacity to think politically. Arendt insists that she is not a philosopher but a political thinker, and the word "political" makes a difference not only in what she thinks about but what she takes thinking to mean. Indeed, one aspect of her political use of Hellenism is deconstructing the philosophical tradition's version of it, thus pluralizing the ways to see "the Greeks."

Arendt uses her Hellenism as a provocation. She seeks, in George Kateb's words, "to press the past into the service of establishing the strangeness of the present,"[14] to make the everyday to seem anomalous, thereby opening up the present for real thinking if not real political struggles. We have come to talk in clichés – language codes is what she calls them in *Eichmann in Jerusalem* – and no one can think in clichés. Her desire to deconstruct outworn notions and categories may explain her own protean identity, the difficulty critics have of pinning her person and her ideas down.

It is because Arendt is a political thinker and polemicist that words like "deliberative" misdescribe her project and why she is sometimes suspicious of rigorous standards of logical consistency. "Deliberation" is too pallid a word to describe the way she enacts in her own work the agonism she finds in the *polis*. As for the rigors of logic, Arendt praises Lessing because he "rejoiced" in what distressed philosophers – the fact that "truth when uttered is immediately transfigured into one opinion among many" – and went so far in his "partisanship" for the world to "sacrifice to it the axiom of non-contradiction, the claim to self-consistency . . ."[15] It was this that allowed him to be a writer who "anticipates dialogue with others," as I think Arendt herself does.

Penultimately, the Greeks were for Arendt what Greek tragedy was for the Athenians: a way of pushing the veil aside, of bringing contemporaries to look obliquely into the abyss, to hear the Wisdom of Silenus and recognize the resources to confront it.

But there is also, finally, a tempered romanticism about Arendt's Hellenism. She did believe that Ancient Greece contained "thought fragments" that could be pried loose from the depths of the past. In these terms (taken from Walter Benjamin), she is a pearl diver whose aim is not to resuscitate the past or renew extinct ages, but to introduce crystallizations of rare beauty and profundity into the lives we share with each other.

NOTES

1 Hanna Pitkin, "Justice: On Relating Public and Private," *Political Theory* 9/3 (August 1981): 327–352.
2 The essay is in *BPF*, p. 165.
3 Arendt, *HC*, p. 187.
4 Arendt, *OR*, p. 285.

5 Arendt also speaks about the dangers of the old dictating to the young and the past to the future. See "The Crisis in Education" in *BPF*, pp. 173–196.
6 For instance, it is not clear that when Theseus talks about endowing life with splendor he is talking about the city or *polis* in general rather than his life or what it is he shares with Oedipus (to whom the lines are directed). Nor is it clear that Theseus is the spokesman for the city as a whole or how exactly the line about endowing life with splendor relates to the Wisdom of Silenus, which comes some eighty lines later. In fact, I think it misleading to identify Arendt's claim about the redemptive possibilities of politics with the claim of the play. I owe this point to Richard Kraut.
7 Arendt, *LM*, vol. 1, *Thinking* (London: Secker and Warburg, 1978), pp. 21–23.
8 For a discussion of what these are and how they function, see Dana R. Villa, *Arendt and Heidegger: The Fate of the Political* (Princeton, NJ: Princeton University Press, 1996).
9 See Carol Dougherty, "Democratic Contradictions and the Synoptic Illusion of Euripedes' Ion," in Josiah Ober and Charles Hedrick, eds., *Demokratia: A Conversation on Democracies, Ancient and Modern* (Princeton, NJ: Princeton University Press, 1996), p. 262.
10 Jean-Pierre Vernant and Pierre Vidal-Naquet, *Tragedy and Myth in Ancient Greece* (New York: Zone Books, 1988).
11 The phrases are from Jonathan Lear's *Open Minded: Working Out the Logic of the Soul* (Cambridge, MA: Harvard University Press, 1998), p. 50.
12 This is a paraphrase of Hanna Fenichel Pitkin's characterization of Arendt's project in *The Attack of the Blob: Hannah Arendt's Concept of the Social* (Chicago: University of Chicago Press, 1998), p. 1 and passim.
13 Ibid., p. 88.
14 George Kateb, *Hannah Arendt: Politics, Conscience, Evil* (Totowa, NJ: Rowman and Allanheld, 1984), p. 149.
15 Arendt, *MDT*, p. 104. There are some striking similarities between this play about exile and Arendt's own life.

8

JACQUES TAMINIAUX

Athens and Rome

It is not unusual among the readers of Hannah Arendt to ascribe to her an exclusively performative conception of action and consequently to suspect a certain Graecomania in her meditations on the constitutive features of the political realm. Those readers would contend that, by reason of her distinction between genuine action and every mode of production of works or tangible results, Arendt limited the notion of action to the spontaneity of a pure performance which essentially consists in the glory of its ephemeral appearance. Consequently her political thought, so they argue, would have been excessively focused on the model of the Greek city. In short it would have been affected by a Graecomania of which those readers find evidence in her comments on the funeral oration attributed to Pericles by Thucydides. Indeed, referring to that oration in *The Human Condition*, Arendt claims that the Athenians ascribed a "twofold function" to the institution of their *polis*: (1) "to multiply the occasions to win 'immortal fame,' that is, to multiply the chances for everybody to distinguish himself, to show in deed and word who he was in his unique distinctness" (p. 197), and (2) "to offer a remedy for the futility of action and speech," thanks to "the organization of the *polis*, physically secured by the wall around the City and physiognomically guaranteed by its laws," an organization which was a kind of "organized remembrance" (pp. 197–198).[1]

I believe that neither the alleged spontaneism nor the alleged Graecomania hold up under examination. A careful scrutiny of Arendt's writings shows that her analysis of action is not at all confined to a celebration of pure performance for its own sake, and that the Athenian *polis* does not have in her political thought the status of a paradigm.

Let us first consider Arendt's analysis of action in *The Human Condition* which is a phenomenology of the *vita activa*. In this text the emphasis on performance obviously plays a decisive part, but such insistence does not amount to an unambiguous celebration. On the contrary, Arendt claims that the performative character of action is at once its blessing and its curse, a curse which necessitates a redemption. This ambiguity deserves closer attention.

The contrasting features of action and work

It is noteworthy that when Arendt insists on the performative character of action, she does so in order to distinguish it from work, a quite different mode of active life. While determining the constitutive traits of the activity of work or production, she uses positive words such as durability, objectivity, tangibility. By producing artifacts the activity of work manages to build a world endowed with permanence and solidity. By contrast, the products of labor are deprived of these characteristics because they are meant for consumption, hence for destruction; whereas the use of artifacts does not destroy them, even though a certain destruction in the form of wearing out is incidental to such usage. But solidity does not characterize only the products of work. It is already present at the very outset of the fabrication process which, as Plato and Aristotle observed, starts by beholding a model whose permanence is such that it is not threatened by the multiplication of similar end products. Instead the guiding model rules over all the stages of the process and makes it thoroughly predictable. Granted that a performance supposes the appearing of a performing individual, it is obvious that such appearing is in no way inherent in the activity of fabrication. Work is not the activity of an irreplaceable individual but of anyone who meets the overall qualifications and possesses the talent and know-how required for such and such type of production. Of course, such qualified workers are in a position of mastery regarding the means and ends of their activity, but what is at stake in the activity of work is not their individual uniqueness. What alone matters are the external products which prove their competence.

The activity called "action" is quite different. In this regard the first section of the chapter dealing with action, entitled "the disclosure of the agent in speech and action," is highly significant (§24, chapter 5). Indeed, action is the only mode of active life which reveals its agent. Such a revelation is conditioned by human plurality – the fact that all human beings are different – to the extent that the disclosure at stake is the manifestation of a unique individual to other individuals who themselves are each distinct. At the outset of her description of action Arendt carefully distinguishes it from the activity of production: "To act, in its most general sense, means to take an initiative, to begin . . ." But this beginning "is not the beginning of something but of somebody, who is a beginner himself" (p. 177).

Action, closely related to speech, is neither the beginning of something nor a means to an end. It becomes a means only when it loses the power of disclosing "who" the agent is, a disclosure which cannot take place without being inserted in a plurality of equal doers and speakers. "This happens," Arendt says, "whenever human togetherness is lost, that is, when people are only for or against other people" (p. 180).

In contrast to work which is thoroughly tangible, action, as "the manifestation of who the speaker and doer unexchangeably is, though it is plainly visible, retains a curious intangibility" (p. 181), an intangibility which pervades the human affairs "that go on between men directly, without the intermediary, stabilizing, and solidifying influence of things" (p. 182). Whereas the man-made world is a stable interval of things between human beings, the interval generated between them by their direct interaction and communication is in no way a physical in-between. Arendt calls it "the 'web' of human relationships," indicating by this metaphor its somewhat intangible quality (p. 183).

Generally speaking, the contrast between the tangibility of work and the intangibility of action is a dominant characteristic of Arendt's description of active life. Whereas the beginning of the fabrication process is the beholding of a consistent blueprint, the beginning of action, that is, the initiative of somebody in deeds and words, is from the outset entangled in an indefinable preexisting web whose innumerable threads are again and again rewoven by new partners. Hence the acting individual, instead of being like the master artisan, lives instead in the ambiguous situation of an actor who is a sufferer as well as an agent. Therefore, unlike the confident implementation of the blueprint by the worker, "action almost never achieves its purpose" (p. 184). In the final analysis it merely produces stories which may afterwards be reified in documents, monuments and works of art, but which, in their living happening, are of a different order precisely because of "the intangible identities of the agents" (p. 187), and because they were not made but enacted and therefore endured as well.

Accordingly human affairs are essentially fragile, whereas the man-made world of artifacts is essentially stable. Arendt's analysis multiplies the signs of that frailty in contrast to the solidity of work. One of them is the impossibility for action, because it is conditioned by plurality, to take place in isolation, whereas isolation is favorable to the worker. Another sign is the fact that action, because it supposes a web of relationships, cannot be the prerogative of a strong and superior individual, whereas *homo faber* rightly aims at just such a status. Still another sign is the fact that action is intrinsically boundless, because it continuously entails new relationships and reactions, whereas the activity of work is confined within clear limits between the blueprint and the end product. From this boundlessness derives the "inherent unpredictability" of action (p. 191), another outstanding characteristic which distinguishes it from work, an activity which at every step remains predictable. For all of those reasons, to the extent that action discloses unexchangeable agents, the light in which it lives is paradoxically hidden to them: "who" they are is fully revealed only at the end to the backward glance of the storyteller, which explains "the ancient saying that nobody can be called *eudaimon* before he is dead" (p. 192).

By stressing this just mentioned paradox, Arendt demonstrates that the emphasis she puts on the performance character of action does not amount to a one-sided celebration. To be sure, the emphasis is very strong, and it is in terms of "power," "greatness," "glory," "shining brightness," that she describes the space of appearance opened up by the sharing of words and deeds which defines action. But by so doing she merely retrieves in contemporary terms the analysis thanks to which Aristotle in *The Nicomachean Ethics*, and in the *Metaphysics* as well, was able to distinguish the activity called *praxis* from the activity called *poiesis*. For instance, when Arendt insists that the power or "potential character" of action "exists only in its actualization" (p. 200), she simply endorses the teaching of Aristotle about the intimate link between *dunamis* and *energeia* in the activity of *praxis*, in contrast to their dissociation in the activity of *poiesis*. The *dunamis* of work is not its *energeia*, since the former is a means which comes to an end in the latter, that is, in an end product, an *ergon* which falls out of the fabrication process. Likewise, when Arendt claims that the "specific meaning of each deed can lie only in the performance itself" (p. 206), she simply paraphrases the words of Aristotle in *The Nicomachean Ethics:* "doing and making are generically different, since making aims at an end distinct from the act of making, whereas in doing the end cannot be other than the act itself: doing well is itself the end" (1140b 3–6). Moreover there is nothing arbitrary about her simultaneous endorsement of both the teaching of Aristotle about *praxis* and the words of Pericles in the funeral oration, since Aristotle himself, in trying to illustrate what *phronesis*, the highest virtue of *praxis*, was all about, could find no better example than Pericles, one of the *phronimoi* who "possess a faculty of discerning what things are good for themselves and for human beings" (1140b 8–10).

But the point is to realize that when Arendt, in the context of her analysis of the frailty of human affairs, claims, once again in agreement with Aristotle, that "the old virtue of moderation, of keeping within bounds, is indeed one of the political virtues par excellence, just as the political temptation par excellence is indeed *hubris*" (p. 191), she is making clear that her emphasis on performance does not amount to a pure and simple celebration of it. The very fact that she uses negative words, such as boundlessness and unpredictability, to designate what she calls the "outstanding characters" of action is highly significant in this regard, as is her use of many other negative terms throughout her description, such as "futility," "irreversibility," "lack of sovereignty." The multiplication of these negative features in the picture of what *The Human Condition* considers to be the only properly human activity – since labor, defined by Arendt in agreement with Marx as the metabolism with nature, is an activity that human beings have in common with all living organisms, and since work, on the other hand, can be entrusted to machines – shows that Arendt's description, instead of celebrating performance for its own sake, stresses again and again the ambiguous and paradoxical nature of action. This paradox shines forth in the following lines: "the human capacity for freedom . . . by producing the web of human relationships, seems to entangle its producer to such an extent that he appears much more the victim and the sufferer than the author and doer of what he has done. Nowhere, in other words, neither in labor, subject to the necessity of life, nor in fabrication, dependent upon given material, does man appear to be less free than in those capacities whose very essence is freedom and in that realm which owes its existence to nobody and nothing but man" (pp. 233–234).

Thus the freedom inherent in action is both a blessing and a misfortune. Its unique capacity of initiative is always mixed with what Arendt calls "the disabilities of non-sovereignty" (p. 236).

The redemption of action

It is because of these disabilities that action demands a redemption. We believe that Arendt's treatment of the topic demonstrates that the reproach of Graecomania is unjustified.

But what does redemption mean here? And why does action need a redemption?

Let us first note that, according to Arendt, all the modalities of active life call for a redemption. Labor calls for a redemption because it traps within the eternal return of life the individual upon whom it is imposed by the necessities of survival. That redemption cannot come from the *animal laborans* who, by definition, is imprisoned in the devouring cycle of repeated needs, pains, and satisfactions. It can only come from a higher level. The misfortune of labor is redeemed by work, an activity which, by producing tools and useful artifacts, "not only eases the pain and trouble of laboring but also erects a world of durability" beyond the cycle of biological nature. In Arendt's terms, "the redemption of life, which is sustained by labor, is worldliness which is sustained by fabrication" (p. 236). But though it redeems labor, work itself calls for a redemption. Because work only pays attention to relations between means and ends, it is inclined to turn each end into a means for further ends, thereby devaluating all values and rendering the world meaningless. Here again redemption has to come from an activity of a higher level. In Arendt's words, "*homo faber* could be redeemed from his predicament of meaninglessness . . . only through the interrelated faculties of action and speech, which produce meaningful stories as naturally as fabrication produces use objects" (p. 236). However action itself calls for a redemption because of its specific disabilities which in sum consist in two basic predicaments: irreversibility and unpredictability. But the redemption at stake is quite peculiar compared to the previous ones. Instead of calling for the help of a higher activity, those two predicaments find their redemption in two potentialities of action itself.

The first potentiality is concerned with the past: "the possible redemption from the predicament of irreversibility – of being unable to undo what one has done though one did not, and could not, have known what he was doing – is the faculty of forgiving" (p. 237). The second potentiality is concerned with the future: "the remedy for unpredictability . . . in the faculty to make and hold promises" (p. 237).

According to Arendt, the proof that both potentialities belong to action itself is provided (1) by the fact that both guarantee the continuity of what is at stake in action, that is, the temporal identity of the self-disclosing agent; (2) by the fact that both potentialities are intimately linked to speech; (3) by the fact that both closely depend on plurality, since "forgiving and promising enacted in solitude or isolation remain without reality and can signify no more than a role played before one's self" (p. 237).

By insisting on the presence within action itself of these two remedies, Arendt distances herself from the traditional philosophical approaches to the predicaments of action. In general, those approaches consist either in turning away from human affairs and from the entire *vita activa* in order to adopt a contemplative way of life, or in recommending the substitution of the reliability of some sort of collective and unanimous fabrication for the uncertainties of interaction and speech between equal partners within plurality. Already developed by Plato, such views always toy with an ideal of the self-sufficiency of the sage, or of the sovereignty of the ruler, themes which are thoroughly incompatible with human plurality since they demand either a withdrawal from it or its repression.

The insufficiencies of the Greek experience of action

It is important to note that, according to Arendt, neither of the abovementioned modes of redemption were recognized by the Greeks as intrinsic potentialities of action. Arendt claims that Jesus of Nazareth is the one who discovered "the role of forgiveness in the realm of human affairs" (p. 238), but she insists that such a discovery, though obviously occurring in a religious context, is in no way confined to it. It sprang, she says, from an "authentic political experience" which remained unknown to the Greeks, but of which the Romans were able to gain some awareness. She writes accordingly: "The only rudimentary sign of an awareness that forgiveness may be the necessary corrective for the inevitable damages resulting from action may be seen in the Roman principle to spare the vanquished (*parcere subjectis*) – a wisdom entirely unknown to the Greeks – or in the right to commute the death sentence, probably also of Roman origin" (p. 239).

To be sure, in Jesus' teaching forgiveness is linked to love, which in essence escapes the space of appearance in which action takes place, and is therefore apolitical or even antipolitical. But this does not mean, according to Arendt, that there is no connection between forgiveness and action. On the contrary, the most plausible argument for the connection is the fact that forgiveness taken as "the undoing of what was done seems to show the same revelatory character as the deed itself. Forgiving and the relationship it establishes is always an eminently personal (though not necessarily individual or private) affair in which *what* was done is forgiven for the sake of *who* did it" (p. 241).

Neither was the power of promising recognized by the Greeks as an intrinsic potentiality of action. It can be traced back to "the Roman legal system, the inviolability of agreement and treaties (*pacta sunt servanda*)," although it is legitimate to see Abraham as its discoverer (p. 243). The faculty of making promises, which is at the root of all covenants, redeems action from its intrinsic unpredictability due to the unreliability of doers who cannot guarantee today who they will be tomorrow, and to "the impossibility of foretelling the consequences of an act within a community of equals where everybody has the same capacity to act" (p. 244). What Arendt calls "the force of mutual promise or contract" (p. 245) consists in keeping together those who interact. It succeeds in this not by planning their future – a legalistic temptation which would put in jeopardy their plurality and its constant renewal – but simply by establishing "islands of predictability" and erecting "guideposts of reliability" in what remains "an ocean of uncertainty" (p. 244). Arendt claims that the redemptive function of promise is necessary in order for faith and hope to be bestowed on human affairs. But on this point again, instead of celebrating the Greeks, she claims that they were at fault to the extent that they ignored altogether those two characteristics of human existence, "discarding the keeping of faith as a very uncommon and not too important virtue and counting hope among the evils of illusion in Pandora's box" (p. 247).

More generally, if it is the case, as Arendt claims, that legislative activity has a political meaning connected with the recognition of the redemptive function of promise in human affairs, then it turns out that her picture of the Greek views in matters of legislation cannot in any way be considered as appreciative. When she stresses that the *polis* relegated legislation to the low rank of the activity of work, it would be wrong to believe that she endorsed the Greek view and therefore conceived of legislation as inessential to the political realm. If that were the case, she could not claim, as a matter of course, in a passing remark, that the Romans were "perhaps the most political people we have known" (p. 7). She could not either, again in a passing remark, pay a tribute to "the extraordinary political sense of the Roman people who, unlike the Greeks, never sacrificed the private to the public, but on the contrary understood that these two realms could exist only in the form of a coexistence" (p. 59). Finally, she could not claim either, again in an abrupt remark, that the fundamental Greek experiences of action and politics were never extensive enough "to comprehend what later turned out to be the political genius of Rome: legislation and foundation" (p. 195).

Instead of praising the Greeks without reservation for their concept of action, Arendt explicitly states that, already in the prepolitical version of action expressed by Homer, "it stresses the urge toward self-disclosure at the expense of all other factors" (p. 194). It is indeed because it shared the legacy of that exclusive urge that the *polis* considered legislation as an activity which occupied the secondary rank of architecture. For the *polis* lawmaking meant the prepolitical and preliminary building of the limits of a space within which action could subsequently exert its disclosive function. Arendt makes clear that by confining legislation within the same category as architecture, the Greeks recognized that it is a factor of durability and permanence; but that they ignored, by the same token, that legislation can also belong to action itself and provide, on the basis of the power of promising, a remedy for its frailty. And this is precisely what the Romans did not overlook. It is significant in this regard that, whereas the Greek word for law, *nomos*, includes in its meaning the notion of a hedge or wall, the Roman word *lex*, as Arendt notices, "indicates a formal relationship between people rather than the wall which separates them from others" (p. 63, note 62). To be sure, the Greek political philosophers, Plato and Aristotle, elevated legislation to the highest political rank, but this does not mean at all, for Arendt, that they managed thereby to repair the ignorance of the relational character of legislation by the *polis*. On the contrary: not only did they themselves also take for granted, as did the *polis*, that legislation is a kind of fabrication, but they even augmented this misunderstanding about legislation since their intention in celebrating lawmaking was definitely not to enlarge the Greek experience of action, but, like Plato, to eliminate *praxis* and its conditioning plurality, or, like Aristotle, to depreciate its intrinsic frailty.

It is now obvious that Arendt's theory of action does not simply glorify pure performance, nor does it demonstrate Graecomania. At this juncture however, one might perhaps object to our analysis that in *The Human Condition* references to the Greek world are much more frequent and explicit than references to the Romans. It is indeed indubitable that Arendt elaborated her analysis of active life and her phenomenology of politics thanks to a meditation which was primarily focused on Greek sources, epic, tragic, historical, philosophical. But it would be wrong to base an accusation of Graecomania on that indubitable fact, since a careful scrutiny of her text not only reveals several strong reservations regarding the Greek concept of action, and the way the *polis* conceived of itself, but also reveals that those reservations turn to the advantage of Rome over Athens.[2]

The wider experience of action by the Romans

In *The Human Condition* the comparisons between Rome and Athens are rather elliptic and this is why they are easily overlooked. But recently published manuscripts which include an extensive comparison between Rome and Athens enable one to discard once and for all the reproach of Graecomania. The documents in question are drafts sketched by Arendt in preparation of a book-length introduction to politics that the German publisher Piper in 1955 proposed that she write. The book was never completed, but since the redaction of the drafts took place at the time when Arendt was also preparing her book on active life, they provide a helpful elucidation of the elliptic remarks of *The Human Condition* about Rome compared to Athens.[3]

The topic motivating the comparison made by these documents is the war of annihilation which was a looming threat at the time of the nuclear competition that characterized the initial stages of the cold war. Arendt's reflection on this topic induced her to meditate upon what she took to be "the archetype of the war of annihilation," that is, the Trojan war whose victors were considered in the ancient world to be the ancestors of the Greeks, and whose vanquished the ancestors of the Romans. Arendt contends that "by glorifying that war both the Greeks and the Romans defined with many similarities as well as many differences, for themselves and therefore for us as well to some extent, the true meaning of politics and its place in history" (p. 100).

Concerning the Greeks, Arendt recalls in these pages that Homer (whose epic poetry relates the Trojan war) was considered by them as their first teacher, the educator par excellence. She insists in this regard that Homer's narrative is above all a lesson of impartiality since it relates the deeds and words of Hector as well as those of Achilles, and treats with equal sympathy the Greek victors and the Trojan vanquished. Such an impartiality, also present in Herodotus, corresponds according to Arendt to the judgment of those who act, in contrast to what the moderns call the judgment of history which only knows the victors. She observes that the impartiality of the narrative somehow erases the annihilation. However, it remains confined within the limits of the poetic and historical memory. In other words, it merely amounts to a posthumous rescue of the vanquished. A properly political rescue of the defeated was never part of the Greek perspective, and Arendt believes that the eventual ruin of the Greek city-states was due to their incapacity to bring Homer's impartiality regarding the past to their political conception of foreign affairs.

This is not to say that impartiality was not an essential feature of the self-consciousness of the *polis*. It was indeed firmly pursued in the persuasive debates between citizens, and in their notion of the agora as the center of the city, not simply as a physical space in which they all met, but as "the only space in which all things could be evaluated by considering all their aspects" (p. 104). To that extent, the city inherited in a political manner the lesson of Homer, and Arendt does not hesitate to claim that the faculty of looking at all the aspects of an issue as well as the notion of *phronesis* as the criterion par excellence for the political aptitude of the citizen were "in the final analysis grounded in the Homeric impartiality" (p. 104). Likewise, Arendt attributes to the legacy of Homer the agonistic mentality of the *polis*, its taste for competition taken as the opportunity for everyone to show who he truly is, or to excel in his identity. Nonetheless she points out that all of these signs of a properly political retrieval of Homer are strictly confined to the inner circle of the relationship of the city with itself. Beyond that circle, it was a matter of course that only violence and the domination of the stronger, therefore annihilation of the weaker, could prevail.

Quite different was the self-conception of the Romans, notwithstanding the fact that they claimed to be the twin brothers of the Greeks. Indeed, they too appealed to the authority of the Homeric legend, since they claimed to be descendants of the Trojans through Aeneas who was a scion of the royal family of Troy, where, according to the *Iliad*, he was as much revered as Hector himself. Taking into account that kinship, Arendt calls attention to the legend of the foundation of Rome (such as it is related by Virgil in the *Aeneid*) and to several topics which for her demonstrate that the political genius of Rome consisted in remedying the deficiencies of the Greek political views.

She notices first of all that the Romans unlike the Greeks "consciously ascribed their own political existence to a defeat followed by a new foundation on a foreign ground" (p. 109). Consequently they were at the outset able to recognize politically the cause of the vanquished that the Greeks acknowledged only posthumously in the narratives of their poets and historians. More specifically, the Romans managed from the outset to incorporate that cause in what Arendt calls "the historical process itself," that is, in the ongoing movement of action, whereas for the Greeks it was only the object of a later remembrance.

Arendt finds no less remarkable the transformation by the Romans of the Greek notion of glory. Glory for the Greeks strictly meant the radiance of a great feat that discloses who somebody is. Significantly the Romans enlarge the notion in order to include a posterity. For example Aeneas, in his decisive duel with Turnus, a new Achilles, thinks of his son and his descendants, thereby demonstrating, in Arendt's words, that for the Romans "the guarantee for an earthly immortality" is no longer, as it was the case among the Greeks, merely the exploit of an individual but "the care for the continuity of one's lineage and its glory" (p. 110).

Accordingly the fire of a new hearth takes the place of the flames which had reduced the city of Troy to ashes. Such a substitution generates a balance between the private and the public domains which was missing in the Greek city, which used to sacrifice the private to the public. Moreover, the substitution obviously erases the annihilation.

But there is still a more important element in this metamorphosis of the Greek view. About the meaning of the metamorphosis Arendt writes the following: "In fact, the point was not only to light a new fire in order to reverse the outcome of the previous one, but to imagine a new outcome to a burning of such importance" (p. 113). The new outcome is the invention by the Romans of the alliance as "a kind of natural development at the end of all wars" (p. 113).

By putting the sharing of words and deeds at the core of its existence as a political community, the Greek city-state acknowledged that there cannot be a common world without a plurality of perspectives. But that acknowledgment was not broad enough to include the perspective of enemies or even of foreigners. And as a result the *polis* remained unable to understand that the annihilation of the vanquished "also concerns those who perpetrated the annihilation" (p. 113). What the Greek city did not see is this: if "politics in the strict sense of the word has less to do with human beings than with the world which is between them and which will survive them," then it follows as a consequence that "politics when it is destructive and brings about the ruin of the world becomes self-destructive as well" (p. 113). This is, on the contrary, what the Romans understood quite well and this is why they put covenants and alliances at the core of their political views. "What happened when the descendants of the Trojans arrived in the Italian ground is neither more nor less than the creation of politics at the point where it was reaching its limits" for the Greeks, that is, no longer "in relationships between citizens of one and the same City, but between foreign and dissimilar nations" at war yesterday and becoming allies tomorrow (p. 114).

According to Arendt, the Romans, by attaching a tremendous importance to alliances, demonstrated that their experience of the power of plurality – the condition of action – to create relationships was wider than the Greek experience. That wider experience is at the base of their concept of foundation as well; it explains why they traced back the foundation of Rome to a covenant between Aeneas arriving from Troy and the natives of Latium (cf. p. 119). It is from that larger experience that they also derived a properly political concept of legislation, since they understood law as the institution of a relationship between conflictual sides of a pluralistic interaction, in contrast to the Greek interpretation of lawmaking as a pre-political activity of fabrication which can be committed to the care of experts operating like craftsmen.

All of these analyses shed light upon the rather elliptic remarks of *The Human Condition* about the political genius of Rome. The analyses included in the drafts for the uncompleted book show clearly that Arendt had considerable admiration for the fact that in Rome, in contrast to the Greek city, both foundation and legislation came to be understood in terms of action within human plurality. In this regard, it is highly significant, for Arendt, that the earliest law of Rome, known as the law of the twelve tables, had been the outcome of "a covenant between two factions previously at war, the patricians and the plebeians, a covenant which was appealing to the consent of the entire nation, the *consensus omnium*" (p. 115). Consequently, says Arendt, "the *res publica* . . . born of the covenant was located in the intermediary space between the two factions which formerly were foes" (p. 116). She insists that "the law is then here something creating new relationships between men and which does not bind them in the sense of a natural law for which the natural conscience of all human beings naturally distinguishes right from wrong, nor in the sense of commandments imposed to all from without, but in the sense of an agreement between contracting individuals" (p. 116).

In the same context, Arendt clearly demonstrates that there is no trace of Graecomania in her views. "In order," she says, "to appreciate correctly the extraordinary political fecundity of the Roman concept of law," it is enough to compare it to the Greek concept of *nomos*, which, because it emanates from the activity of work, comprises an essential element of violence and domination such that those who are related to the *nomos* are related to it like the slave to the master. This means, in Arendt's words, that for the Greeks "law could not in any way constitute a bridge between nations, nor within the same nation, a bridge between a political community and another one" (p. 118).

NOTES

1 Arendt, *HC*.

2 I believe that in *The Human Condition*, Arendt's primordial concern with the Greek sources throughout her analysis of active life and her phenomenology of the political realm has much to do with the fact that the book was conceived by her as an attempt to elucidate and rehabilitate the political way of life (*bios politikos*) in contrast with the distorted image of it propagated by those among the Greeks who decided to opt for a purely contemplative way of life (*bios theoretikos*), that is, the philosophers regrouped by Arendt under the label "Socratic school." I also believe that, at the background of her attempt, an implicit debate with Heidegger played a decisive part, since Heidegger, of whom Arendt was a student in 1924–25, conceived of his own philosophy as a contemporary retrieval of Plato and Aristotle. Cf. Hannah Arendt, "Philosophy and Politics," *Social Research* 57/1 (Spring 1990); and, in the same issue, Margaret Canovan, "Socrates or Heidegger? Hannah Arendt's Reflections on Philosophy and Politics."

For a comprehensive discussion of the issues of political philosophy at stake in Arendt's confrontation with Heidegger, see Dana R. Villa, *Arendt and Heidegger: The Fate of the Political*, Princeton: Princeton University Press, 1996. For an analysis of the blind spots in the *bios theoretikos* as it is vindicated by Heidegger, cf. my book *The Thracian Maid and the Professional Thinker: Arendt and Heidegger*, translated and edited by M. Gendre (Albany: State University of New York Press 1997).

3 See the French translation of Hannah Arendt's drafts: *Qu'est-ce que la politique?*, by Sylvie Courtine-Denamy (Paris: Le Seuil, 1995).

9

HAUKE BRUNKHORST

Equality and elitism in Arendt

Hannah Arendt's idea of freedom can be said to have two main sources, the first being the Greek *polis* and the Roman *res publica*; the second St. Augustine and the Christian idea of a spontaneous new beginning (*creatio ex nihilo*). These two notions of freedom, which Arendt attempts to combine in her political theory, are not totally compatible. The first or *republican* idea of freedom is elitist in its content and presuppositions, whereas the second or Augustinian concept has an egalitarian core. This chapter examines both ideas, with specific attention to the tensions they generate in Arendt's work (section I). In the second (shorter and concluding) section, I show how Arendt's theory of political freedom is embedded in a narrative philosophy of history about the decline of man as a political animal, a narrative derived, for the most part, from the first (Graeco-Roman and elitist) concept of freedom. This concept of freedom also provides the normative basis for much of her critique of contemporary politics. We should, as a result, be somewhat skeptical about certain elements of this critique (Arendt's entirely negative view of politics as the quest for social justice, for example) even as we utilize her profounder insights about the nature of politics and freedom.

I The idea of freedom: a tale of two origins

In each of Arendt's major works, one or two central distinctions guide the entire argument, and provide the conceptual architecture for her descriptions of related phenomena. In *The Origins of Totalitarianism*, this structuring role is played by the distinction between the "people" and the "mob," a contrast whose roots lie in the distinction (drawn by Hegel and others) between "the state" and "civil society." In *The Human Condition*, the key distinction is the Aristotelian one between *fabrication* (*poiesis*) and *action* (*praxis*), which is joined to a related distinction between the household or economic realm (*oikos*) and the public or political realm (*polis*). In *On Revolution* the central contrast is between political *freedom* and social *emancipation* (or the liberation from poverty and oppression), while in the long essay "On Violence" it is between the *power* of associated citizens and the *violence* of the "strong man," despot, or revolutionary terrorist. Finally, in *The Life of the Mind*, *Eichmann in Jerusalem*, and the *Lectures on Kant's Political Philosophy*, the central distinctions are between "common sense" (*sensus communis*) and private sense (*sensus privatus*), imagination vs. deductive thinking, and independent judgment (or the ability to think without rules) vs. the thoughtless conformity of the "banal" individual. With these distinctions in mind, we are able to trace not only the evolution of Arendt's idea of freedom, but the shifting valences of egalitarianism and elitism in her thought.

In *OT*, Arendt uses the idea of "the mob" to analyze, first, the anti-semitic resentment mobilized during the infamous Dreyfus Affair in France in the 1890s; secondly, the links between European imperialism and racism; and thirdly the uniform movement of the fascist and Stalinist masses, whose appearance on the stage of history marks the lowest ebb of the European nation-state. Arendt sees the mob as first emerging as a political force under the hegemony of bourgeois society during the age of imperialism. The mob is made up of people who, as the result of the social upheavals wrought by nineteenth-century capitalism, no longer have a secure class position or any real connection to established political parties. She characterizes the constituents of the mob as "superfluous people" or "surplus population." "Mob politics" – born of the passions and frustrations of such marginalized individuals – refers to a pseudo- or anti-politics, one in which political speech and deliberation are reduced to the expression of sheer outrage and resentment. Such pseudo-politics replaces all matters of public concern with the dynamic and destructive motion of a politicized *ressentiment*.

For Arendt, the mob politics which provided the raw material for emergent totalitarian movements had no particular end beyond its own agitated motion: it therefore transgressed each and every political boundary or legal limit. To those caught up in it, this motion may well have seemed like freedom, but in fact it was not. The energy animating the mob's collective actions was actually entirely negative, drawn from agitation *against* aristocrats, plutocrats, Jews, foreigners, resident aliens, etc. The leaders of the mob did not appeal to any particular or concrete *interest* of their followers, but to their most generic, "biological" needs (for bread, ethnic survival, *lebensraum*, etc.). Hence, mob politics displayed absolutely no concern for building and maintaining the civil and legal structures of the republican nation-state, nor was it in any way attuned to the claims of impartial justice or political freedom. Only a "people" – by which Arendt means a body of public-spirited *citizens* who wield recognized and stubbornly defended political rights – has the potential (and the power) to build and maintain a republican nation-state. (Like Kant and Rousseau, Arendt views the notions of a "people," "nation," and "state" as somehow co-original: no single term of this triad can exist without the other two.) A "people" (or a definite social class, like the workers) may fight against elites for a leadership role in the nation-state, but the "mob" always submits to the leadership of the "strong man." A people is active, while the mob is passive or (better) reactive. "The mob," Arendt writes, "cannot make decisions"; it can only "acclaim" or "stone" the objects of its passions.

With the publication of *The Human Condition* in 1958, Arendt turned from the analysis of totalitarianism and its origins to a political form of philosophical anthropology. The central chapters of this work tease out the normative conceptions of humanity and political action which were tacitly assumed by her studies of total domination and dehumanization.

According to Arendt in *The Human Condition*, human beings are distinguished by two main cognitive/practical orientations in the world. The first such orientation she labels "work" or "fabrication," and it refers to a broad range of instrumental activities. Such activities concern what we might call (following the suggestion of the American philosopher John Searle) the man-to-world "direction of fit."[1] Instrumental action "fits to the world" if the agent's know-how and efforts achieve control over things or passive bodies (which might even include, through conditioning and manipulation, human psyches). For the most part, however, the result of instrumental action (or *poiesis*) is an artificial object that fits into a particular life-world. The products of work are used either within a particular form of life (for example, tables, skirts, books), or they limit it, in the shape of a perceptible border (for example, the wall surrounding a Greek city-state, or the door we close after entering our home or apartment). This "limiting" kind of product invites figurative elaboration, as when Arendt refers to laws as the "fences" that set the boundaries of the public-political realm.[2]

The second cognitive-practical orientation of man in the world characterizes communicative (or intersubjective) action. Communicative action (or simply "action," as Arendt puts it) concerns what might be called the person-to-person "direction of fit." An agent's communicative action "fits to" the meaningful action of others if the different views they express somehow come together to form a world of common goods or meanings. Arendt's fundamental example here is a group of citizens perceiving a common issue from different (and sometimes contradictory or incompatible) perspectives.[3] The outcome of the argumentative deliberation of such a plurality of agents is the full disclosure or illumination (in the Heideggerian/Greek sense of *aletheia*) of the matter in question. If the different opinions are presented, in all their variety, in public, then the "thing itself" appears, showing *all* the sides that it has for a *particular* political body.[4] Arendt's definition of political action as "acting in concert" (derived from Edmund Burke) must be understood as including these contradictions and dissonances: it is a risky and never fully controllable *performance* within a context of intersubjective deliberation and judgment.

Like Heidegger and Dewey before her, Arendt firmly rejected the traditional metaphysical distinctions between essence and existence, reality and appearance. As a result, she conceives *freedom* not as a mysterious inner capacity (the "free will" of the philosophers) but as the act of *being free* manifest in the performance of action within a context of equal yet diverse peers. Freedom truly exists – has the fullest phenomenal reality – only during action's performance.[5] Such action – the making of a speech before assembled citizens, or the creation, through mutual promise and agreement, of a new political body – can never be predicted. It is an unexpected *creatio ex nihilo*, one whose consequences we can neither fully predict nor control. The essential freedom of action is found in the fact that each action "cannot be expected from whatever may happen before." Referring to Jesus Christ, Arendt dubs this human capacity for unpredictable action a "miracle," in that it has the power to create new realities. Through this capacity, man is "able to perform what is infinitely improbable."[6] This is what makes the capacity for action worthy of astonishment and wonder. But is also the thing which makes action "the most dangerous of human faculties."

Arendt's celebration of the unpredictability of action sets her at odds with much of the Western philosophical tradition. Thinkers within this tradition emphasize how the agent must remain "in command" if his actions are to be truly free. They view action's unpredictability in a largely negative light, as a sign of sheer contingency and (as such) anathema to reason's search for causes and precedent. It is not surprising, then, that when Arendt turned to investigate the faculty of the will in *The Life of the Mind*, she rhetorically positioned herself as a critic of the philosophical tradition, asking "Could it be that freedom fits much less with the preconceptions of the professional thinkers than necessity?" The only philosopher she praises without qualification in *Willing* is the thirteenth-century theologian Duns Scotus, who defended the priority of the will's initiatory power over reason's demand for precedent and comprehensibility. This emphasis on spontaneity and unpredictability also led Arendt to break with the old European philosophical idea of the sovereign or "autonomous" subject. This dimension of Arendt's understanding of the "non-sovereign" quality of freedom has its roots, ultimately, in Biblical sources. However, before turning to the normative implications of this human capacity, I want to look at Arendt's republican idea of political freedom, an idea which stands at no small remove from the Augustinian (and Scotian) idea of action as a kind of *creatio ex nihilo*.

The political judgment of a plurality of diverse citizens expresses what could be called the political *aletheia* or *concrete truth* of the city or political association. The citizens' judgment is "true" only if it expresses all sides of an issue, and it is concrete only if it is the product of a *particular* assemblage of free and equal citizens. Following Kant, Arendt describes such judgment as a variety of "enlarged thought" (*erweiterte Denkungsart*). Thus, Arendt's idea of political action is internally related to a process of public deliberation and communication, in a manner parallel with Jürgen Habermas's well known idea of communicative action. However, unlike Habermas, Arendt thinks that the ground of common insight (or public *aletheia*) lies in the sometimes complementary, sometimes conflicting perspectives citizens have on things held in common, which *appear* in light of the public realm. For her, common insight and judgment stem not from the "coercion-free force of the better argument" (the quasi-rationalist norm governing the Habermasian conception of communicative action) but from an open-ended and robust process of debate and deliberation.

Communicative action in the Arendtian sense reveals man as an *inner-worldly* being – what Heidegger in *Being and Time* called "being-in-the-world" (*In-der-Welt-Sein*) or *Dasein* (existence). Action or speech among equals provides the constituent elements of public opinion, which is oriented toward a shared realm of public concern, and is animated by what Arendt, again following Kant, calls "common sense" (by which she means a "feeling for the world" or, simply, *worldliness*). Of all of man's active capacities, only action and speech have the power to transform what Arendt calls "the human artifice" into a *political* world or community. In ancient societies like Athens or Rome, this world was co-extensive with the *polis* or *res publica*; in later times, with the "kingdom" or nation-state.[7] The crucial point for Arendt is that political action and speech depend upon such a man-made world, one created through instrumental action. This artificial world separates humans from nature and natural necessity; it provides them with a potential arena for their political life.

This relation of dependence between the world of action and the world of artificial things may be illustrated by a simple example: we cannot have so-called "roundtables" on public issues if we have no actual tables, which are created through fabrication. Like the human artifice itself, a table "relates and separates" the actors around it, thereby making debate and deliberation possible. *Praxis* and *poiesis*, then, are intertwined in the political world without being reducible to one another. Man is a fabricator (*homo faber*), but he is *distinctively human* only insofar as he is a political actor, one who speaks, deliberates, and acts with others. Here Arendt follows in the classical tracks of Aristotle's *zoon politikon*.[8]

Now, according to classical political theory, a good or well-ordered society was a society built on a *stable hierarchy* between the (higher) realm of political (or communicative) action and the (lower) realm of work (or instrumental action). In the Greek *polis*, the former was localized in the public space of the assembly or agora, while the latter was confined to the private sphere of the household or *oikos* (what the Romans would call the *dominium* of the master). All social relations within the household were primarily relations of domination. In a well-ordered *oikos*, there was one (and only one) master of the house. Indeed, the master was the only free person in this patriarchal social microcosm. *Freedom* in this sphere meant that the master could do what he wanted or (to be more precise) what was in accordance with his nature. He was master of himself, of his own biological drives and passions, just as he was the master of his wife, children, slaves, animals, etc. The basic social relation in the household was thus one of command and obedience. If those who were supposed to submit to the master's rule were unwilling or disobedient, the master had to use *violence* to reassert his freedom and confirm his position atop the *dominium's* hierarchy.

Within this hierarchy, the lord of the household could, of course, have "higher-value" relationships with his wife and even (sometimes) with his more educated slaves.[9] Friendship could exist between the master and his wife, as well as between the master and his slaves or (as we know from Homer's *Odyssey*) the master and his dog. Yet friendship with women, slaves, dogs, or even young boys could never reach the highest, "most perfect" level of a completely reciprocal relationship between free and equal men.[10] Genuine friendship was strictly related to an ontological and social hierarchy, in which patriarchal domination based on physical violence came first. In the ancient world, the fundamental relation of master and slave constituted the "man-to-world" direction of fit (to use Searle's notion again). While Arendt hardly shares Aristotle's view that slavery is natural, in *The Human Condition* she raises no objection to his distinction between the political or civic inclusion available to heads of households, and the kind of social exclusion that all non-citizens must bear.[11]

In endorsing the Aristotelian idea that freedom is a function of the recognition equal peers give to one another, Arendt disputes Hegel's suggestion (in "Lordship and Bondage" section of *The Phenomenology of Spirit*) that there is an irreducible struggle for mutual recognition that ultimately involves *every* human being, including the slave. From the Aristotelian perspective, if a slave does not do as his master wants, the master simply uses force in the same way as he would use it to train a horse or a dog, or to fix a tool which is functioning improperly. In describing the *polis*, Arendt follows Aristotle in presenting the problem of slavery as, basically, a *technical* rather than a *moral* one. It is a question of inventing a technology or device which will provide a substitute for the necessary labor of the slave. The man-to-man "direction of fit" underlying Hegel's theory of mutual recognition thus, seemingly, has no bearing on the relations between free men (on the one hand) and women and slaves (on the other). From the Greek and Arendtian perspective, the identity of the free man in no way depends upon the yes or no, the consent or dissent, of the slave. Moreover, the slave has no chance of eventually overcoming his submission (and lack of recognition) by means of his own labor, since labor is nothing more than a brute repetitive process determined by biological necessity, one required for the reproduction of life and utterly without redemptive powers.

Labor – in contrast to work or fabrication – is "fertile" in an almost literal sense of the word.[12] Whereas the worker produces things in order to add them to a common world, the laborer is forced to remain "alone with his body, facing the naked necessity to keep himself alive."[13] For Arendt, labor is necessarily "alienated." She firmly rejects the Hegelian or Marxist idea that it could be a means to the realization of the laborer's powers and capacities. In this and other respects, Arendt remains completely in line with the elitist assumptions of ancient Greek philosophy and practice. For the Greeks, there could be no struggle for recognition between master and slave because these two types of human beings belonged to irreducibly different ontological spheres. Hence, "overcoming" the master/slave relationship in the name of human equality could never be the goal of *political* action, since *politics* occurred only amongst those who were already civic equals.

According to Arendt, whatever freedom we find in the sphere of the household is deficient or corrupt in some way. The same holds true for the large-scale "household" community one finds in tyrannies (where the despot takes the place of the household head) and in the contemporary "national household," where economic concerns dominate political matters and usurp the deliberative space of citizens. The "power" of the tyrant, like that of the master of the *oikos* or the Roman *pater familias*, is founded on *violence* rather than on any potential power of the people (a power which is realized only in public speech and action). Insofar as we can even speak of *freedom* in the household (the "realm of necessity"), we seem to be speaking of something entirely negative in character. The pre-political freedom of the *patres* was manifest in their *avoidance* of the need to submit to the will of others; of hard and demeaning physical labor; and of the inescapable biological needs that afflict women, children, and other "lower" types.

Such freedom may be negative, but it is negative in a sense far removed from what we moderns (following Hobbes or Constant) usually mean when we speak of "negative freedom." For Hobbes and the liberal tradition, we are free if there are no political or legal constraints that restrict or block the paths we desire to take. If I want to live a completely passive life, assuming social roles without responsibility or strenuous moral demands, I am free to withdraw into the private realm and do so. I may be poor; I may be homeless; I may even be morally unworthy – but I am still free in the sense of not having to live up to some positive and demanding set of social or political expectations. Not so in ancient political societies of the sort Arendt considers. Here, "negative freedom" or liberty does not mean that I am free to do what I want in the privacy of my own home (what Arendt refers to as the "darkness of the private realm"). On the contrary, the freedom of the ancient household head was negative in the sense that he was liberated from the necessity of personally reproducing the means for his own subsistence. This ancient form of negative liberty demands the presence of such positive preconditions as wealth, birth, and property. The ancients referred to it as a condition of self-control or self-mastery. Through this liberation and discipline, the free, property-owning male had the opportunity to "transcend his own [private] life," entering the public realm where he had, in effect, gained another (public) self. Positive political freedom thus had its ground in the master's self-mastery and the virtuous rule over the social hierarchy of the household it enabled.

For Arendt, the public realm was the realm of *true* freedom. She assumes that, for the inhabitants of the Greek *polis,* freedom was "located exclusively" in the "political sphere."[14] She also assumes (wrongly, in my view) that genuine, uncorrupt freedom could not exist "inside the sphere of the household."[15] Arendt believes that whatever pre-political freedom the *pater familias* enjoyed was entirely derivative in character. He was free, she argues, only insofar as he was free to "leave his house" and "to move toward the political space." The freedom born of self-mastery, realized in the male's rule of the household, had no *intrinsic* value.

This, it seems to me, is a very one-sided view, one which greatly exaggerates the role of political freedom in ancient societies. As Arendt would be the first to admit, it clearly does not account for Stoic philosophy and its followers. But even Aristotle distinguished between *ethics* and *politics*, and refused to reduce the "good life" to a life lived in public (the life of the *citizen*).[16] Similarly, Plato's *Republic* constructs a hierarchy of different levels of freedom, including non- political (for example, economic and commercial) spheres of life. Thus, while the *ultimate* end of freedom in the Greek and Roman worlds may well have been political, the "pre-political" life of the household head retained some independent value. Self-mastery, as well as domination of others, was considered to be an important, true, and proper aspect of human freedom by the ancients.[17]

Arendt's vision is blurred on this matter because she projects the German Idealist distinction between the realm of freedom and the realm of necessity back onto the ancient distinction between the *polis* and the *oikos*.[18] If we want to avoid this distortion, we would do well to distinguish between two levels of *positive* freedom open to the household head in ancient societies. On the first level, in the *oikos* itself, positive freedom existed in the master's capacity to govern himself and others, but it was incomplete. As Arendt correctly points out, to fully realize his freedom and capacity for self-government, the head of the household must enter the common or public world. Only if he attained to this *second*, public level of positive freedom did he stand a chance of realizing the *whole* of the "beautiful freedom of the Greeks" (Hegel) in the course of his individual life.

This Greek and Roman hierarchy of two levels of positive freedom (the self-mastery of household heads and the self-governance of citizens) expresses the reigning ideology of the ruling class in a slaveholding society. In ancient societies, it was assumed that a stable and lasting *order of freedom* was feasible only in a city-state. Perfect freedom was therefore *political* freedom. When the *patres* came together in the agora or assembly, free man met free man. There, in the public space reserved for political speech, it was possible to realize the freedom of a plurality of free individuals simultaneously. Contrary to self-mastery or the domination of others in the *oikos*, political relations between free men were *relations without domination*. The classical order of freedom was thus an order of equality among citizens, who were bound only by civic virtue and different, overlapping networks of reciprocal friendship (*philia* and *philia politike*). The political world, then, was a world of equality and freedom, but in nothing like the Christian sense of the equality of all men before God, or the Habermasian sense of the coercion-free communication found in the "ideal speech situation."

In ancient city-states this freedom amongst equals was bound to full citizenship and, as such, strictly circumscribed by the walls of the city. It presupposed *inequality* in the household and in the world surrounding the *polis*. Strictly speaking, this privileged space of freedom was neither aristocratic nor democratic, since it was not "-cratic" at all ("-cratic" deriving from the Greek *kratein*, which means rulership or domination). Arendt always describes this space as an order of public communication in which coercion or violence is absent. Another Greek word gives a better sense of such an order. It is *isonomia*, and it denotes an ethical order (or *nomos*) among equals (*iso-*).[19] If free men come together and act within such an order, a distinct kind of *power* arises, one free of the taint of violence and domination.[20]

"Power" for Arendt is a category that refers to the whole citizen body. It is not a commodity: it cannot be distributed, and it has no owner. Power is present when citizens assemble and act in public, and it vanishes when they become utterly absorbed by their private affairs.[21] Power unites a body of citizens and preserves the public realm; it becomes violent only when it strikes back against the enemies of the city, the enemies *outside* (but occasionally within) the walls of the city. Here the arts of violence (including war and slavery) are necessary means to maintain the public realm, the "space for the appearance of freedom." But – as Arendt *fails* to emphasize – power also becomes violence in any interaction between male citizens and those who are not (or no longer) full members of the political community. The latter category includes women, slaves, children, criminals, traitors, displaced and unworthy persons, aliens, idiots, and (of course) enemies.

In *On Revolution*, published five years after *The Human Condition*, Arendt makes a remarkable shift from the model of the Greek *polis* to that of Roman republican institutions. However, her basic idea of freedom remains much the same. The distinction between the spheres of *polis* and *oikos* – now *dominium* and *res publica* – has twin echoes within the Roman political order. First, the Roman people (or *populus)* is the whole body of citizens, both *patres* (the notables or "fathers" who represent the ancestors) and *plebs* (commoners). By its very nature, the plebeian class represented a permanent risk for the political order of freedom: it seemed driven by an almost biological force, one rooted in the "darkness of the household." Appearing in public, it could, apparently, transform itself into a violent and rebellious mob at any moment. However, the foundation of the Roman Republic integrated the *plebs* into a political body – the *populus* – which thenceforth became the institutionalized source of all power (*potestas*).

The second echo of the *dominium/res publica* distinction is found in the way the authority of the act of foundation came to be embodied in the Roman senate. With this institutional innovation, the *power* of the people (*potestas in populo*) was distinguished from the *authority* in the senate (*auctoritas in senatu*). The function of the senate was to stabilize the republican order by means of an institutional power that could limit popular power and prevent it from degenerating into mob violence.[22] The resulting institutional setting was much closer to the constitutional arrangements of modern societies than that suggested by the simple distinction between *oikos* and *polis*. The Roman example thus provides Arendt with a more suitable architecture for her analysis of the American founding in *On Revolution*. One might well remain skeptical, however, as to whether this set of elements is really complex enough, and whether the ancient understanding of political freedom is categorially adequate to the modern experience of political freedom. On the surface, at least, Arendt's argument in *On Revolution* presumes that it is. This accounts for her official, "neo-Roman" reading of modern political revolution in the eighteenth century (as "foundation" followed by "augmentation"). However, Arendt presents a different reading of political freedom just below the surface of this "official" story, one that is not covered by the ancient conception of republican freedom; one that centers, instead, on the universal human capacity for initiation.

The essential innovation of Arendt's political anthropology in *The Human Condition* was her idea of *natality*. "Natality" is the existential condition of possibility of freedom, and it gives a new and striking twist to Arendt's reconstruction of the classical republican idea of freedom. This idea has links to Heidegger's notions of *thrownness* (*Geworfenheit*) and *thrown projection* (*geworfener Entwurf*, implying a project into which we are "thrown").[23] As with these Heideggerian notions, natality signifies the new beginning inherent in human life and human action, as well as the contingency (of time and place) in which life and action unfold. Ontologically speaking, natality implies both activity and passivity: we can never choose the time, the place, or the circumstances of our birth and life; nevertheless, we must make our own decisions and lead our own lives. To do this, we must interpret the particular world in which we find ourselves (whether it be the world of the Greek *polis*, the early American republic, or an advanced industrial democracy); otherwise, we will not be able to act at all.

All action thus occurs within an historical situation into which we are involuntarily thrown. As Arendt puts it in *The Life of the Mind*, everything we do happens *relative* to this situation. Being *there*, in this particular historical situation, we make our own plans, which in turn intersect a world made up of a plurality of other people's projects and possibilities. Yet ultimately, what we do and who we are depends on ourselves, despite the situational aspect of our lives. This, for Arendt (as well as Heidegger and Sartre), is the *absolute* aspect of freedom. Hence, she describes freedom as a "relatively absolute spontaneity." Despite this similarity with the Heideggerian idea of a "thrown project," Arendt gives the idea of natality a distinctively communicative (and thus political) spin.

For Arendt, the freedom manifest in action does not appear on the day of our birth; rather, it begins at the moment when, for the first time in our lives, we find ourselves confronted by the choice of saying yes or no, of consenting or dissenting to a state of affairs. Arendt refers to this moment as our "second birth." It is followed (potentially, at least) by a series of similar rebirths, which attend every moment of active consent or dissent, affirmation or negation. The instant we say no to the solicitation of (or demand for) our consent, we begin to take responsibility for the "brute fact" of our birth. Indeed, this "second birth" introduces us to the ontological difference between what Heidegger (in *Being and Time*) calls a natural *factum brutum* and the existential facticity (*Faktizität*) or givenness of our existence, a difference between what we can and cannot assume responsibility for.

For Arendt, the emergence of this difference (and the kind of existential responsibility it implies) is internally related to a communicative context in which "yes" and "no" statements occur, rather than to the resolute solitude of an individual, mortal *Dasein*, manfully affirming its finitude. Because of this communicative quality, natality lies at the root of the *political* power of associated individuals who make a *new beginning*; who found a *new* political community through collective dissent followed by mutual promise and agreement, which opens up a new political reality (such as American democracy). To perform political action, then, means to take initiatory action in a communicative context where the foundation or preservation of a political association is at stake. Above all, it means acting and speaking where "words are not empty and deeds are not brutal, where words are not used to veil intentions but to disclose realities, and deeds are not used to violate and destroy, but to establish and create new realities."

The striking point here is how much Arendt's interpretation of the *constitutio libertatis* – of the new political beginning enabled by the fact of natality – diverges from the idea of freedom she derives from the ancients. Whereas her ideal of classical republican freedom is, as I have shown above, irreducibly elitist, her concept of the creative power that constitutes a "new space for liberty" is egalitarian. Arendt's notion of the disclosive power that marks such a founding differs not only from the Greek and Roman self-understanding, but from Heidegger's more romantic conception of "world disclosure," in which "new worlds" are opened through the creative, poetic violence of demigod-like artists and statesmen. By focusing on the role collective agreements (for example, the Mayflower Compact or the Constitution) can play in "opening new worlds," Arendt takes a decisive step away from the model of the legislator-artist that informs the tradition, orienting us towards the intersubjective *praxis* of a plurality of revolutionary actors.

The concept of freedom Arendt derives from natality and the communicative power behind the *constitutio libertatis* also diverges sharply from the Burkean idea of freedom that animates her criticism of natural (or abstractly universal) human rights in *The Origins of Totalitarianism*.[24] One of Arendt's objections to the "Rights of Man" heralded by the Enlightenment and the French Revolution is that it ignores the difference between (European) civilization and the (African or Australian) "naked savage."[25] Yet this objection betrays a confused and partial understanding of the implications of her own notion of human "natality." Human beings do not stand in need of an ethos of urban or "civilized" life in order to take initiative or to break through the repetition that characterizes the everyday dimension of our lives. They need only be able to say "yes" or "no" and to mean it. No civic ethos – neither *arete* or *virtus* – is presupposed by the "no" which led the Puritans to leave England in 1620 and to start a "New England" on the other side of the Atlantic. The anthropological root of all modern, egalitarian freedom lies in the ability of every human being (even the "naked savage") to make a new beginning through statements of dissent which interrupt – "out of the blue," as it were – the seeming continuity of a social life based on habit and repetition.

Arendt's idea of natality, thus understood, marks a sharp break with the Greek or Roman idea of political freedom as the exclusive freedom enjoyed by select peers. This is, perhaps, not so surprising when we consider that Arendt derives her idea of natality not from Herodotus or Aristotle, or from Livy or Cato, but from Augustine's doctrine that man was created to bring the possibility (*potentia*) of a new beginning into the world. The egalitarian potential for initiatory action turns out to be the origin of the peculiarly nonviolent power wielded by ordinary citizens (the "people") in civil society.

Arendt's 1928 doctoral thesis was on the concept of love in Augustine, and, beginning with the 1958 appendix to *The Origins of Totalitarianism*, she returned to his thought, citing repeatedly the sentence "*Initium ut esset homo creatus est*" – "that a beginning be made man was created."[26] In *The Origins of Totalitarianism*, Arendt added the following sentence to Augustine, the last of the book: "This beginning is guaranteed by each new birth." With this dramatic insistence upon the initiatory capacity inherent in man (the same "abstract" or universal man we find in the United Nations' 1948 "Declaration of Human Rights"), the inner tensions animating Arendt's idea of freedom come out into the open.[27] The republican freedom of equal *citizens* (the classical conception of freedom) turns out to be rooted in the creative and emancipatory power of equal *human beings* (the Christian, universalist conception). However, these two strands of freedom can not be said to coincide in Arendt's political theory, *except* in her understanding of the extraordinary event of foundation that marks the conclusion of successful modern political revolutions. Here they *do* coincide, albeit for the briefest of historical moments. In the history that follows this extraordinary moment, liberation and freedom, the equality of men and the equality of citizens, soon break apart. Arendt makes this the basis for her critique of modern society, a critique which signals the renewed predominance of the ancient republican conception of freedom in her thought. Hence, the last chapter of *On Revolution* invokes the virtues of a political "aristocracy" of self-chosen citizens against the materialism of the vulgar masses, who piggishly prefer the material comforts of "private happiness" to the more austere joys of "public freedom."

In general, it can be said that Arendt tries to keep the egalitarian (Augustinian or Judeo-Christian) roots of her understanding of freedom more or less concealed. Contrary to what is implied by her concepts of natality, initiatory action, and revolutionary foundation, she insists that the historical origin of *modern republican freedom* is mainly to be found in the pagan world. She is, of course, correct in claiming that the concepts of political freedom and republican citizenship are, as such, foreign to the text of the Bible. But it is a long way from *this* claim to her Nietzschean equation of Christianity with *otherworldliness*. In this regard, Arendt, like Nietzsche, cites the church father Tertullian: "Nothing is more foreign to us Christians than public affairs."[28]

Such statements allow Arendt to maintain that the roots of the Western democratic understanding of freedom are far removed from the Christian understanding. As she put it in the 1953 essay "Religion and Politics": "The free world, however, means by freedom not: 'Render unto Caesar what is Caesar's and unto God what is God's,' but the right of all to handle those affairs that once were Caesar's. The very fact that we, as far as our public life is concerned, care more about freedom than about anything else proves that we do not live publicly in a religious world."[29] The all-important nexus of background beliefs is now provided by civic republicanism and the idea of government "of the people, by the people, and for the people" invoked by Lincoln in the Gettysburg Address. The origin of the idea of self-governing, free, and equal citizens seems to her to have no resonance or relation whatever with Christian ideas of equality and freedom. Neither "Christian equality nor Christian freedom could ever have led by themselves to the concept of 'government of the people, by the people, for the people,' or to any other modern definition of political freedom."[30]

This, it must be said, is not a very convincing story. It veils the egalitarian dimension of political freedom which Arendt highlights with her concept of natality and her theory of modern revolution. One result of this lop-sided genealogy is a slanted reading of some famous American political texts. For example, in her interpretation of Lincoln's Gettysburg Address (in *OR*), Arendt turns a blind eye to an essential dimension of his speech. At the very beginning, Lincoln reminds his audience of the proposition on which the American nation was founded – that "all men are created equal." These words are directly related to the emancipation of black slaves as human beings, not (primarily) as citizens.[31] Lincoln's reference to the concept of equality in the Declaration of Independence is closer to Arendt's second, "Augustinian" concept of freedom than it is to the "beautiful freedom of the Greeks." The same (modernized and secularized) Christian moral universalism is also apparent when Lincoln describes democracy as an "unfinished" global project which should never "perish from the earth."[32] Neither Athenian nor Roman citizens would find this a very moving, or a very convincing, idea. For both Pericles and Cato, freedom ended at the wall of their own *particular* city. In fact, for the Romans, Rome was *the* City (*urbs*), and the surrounding world (*orbis*) of their empire was a Roman *dominium* without a single free city.[33]

Arendt's strong, but clearly one-sided, emphasis on the pagan origins of modern political freedom also leads her to undervalue the project of ameliorating the condition of the economically expropriated and socially repressed. Addressing what, for her, is the doomed attempt of many modern revolutions to "solve" the "social question" of poverty and oppression, Arendt draws a fundamental opposition between the political freedom of an elite and the more egalitarian goals of social emancipation. From this point of view, the dilemma confronting all modern revolutions is how to avoid entangling *liberation* and *liberty*, *social emancipation* and *political freedom*, with one another. Arendt acknowledges that, in order to get rid of oppressors or end servitude and slavery, the elemental violence of the humiliated and insulted "wretched of the earth" is often required. But, according to her, the "longing for liberation" from distress and the burdens of poverty is negative and pre-political. It does not express the admirable "will to freedom" and political participation that we find in those who are already free of such burdens (such as the men of the American Revolution).

For Arendt, the longing of the poor and oppressed for liberation is an understandable reaction to the often unbearable burdens of labor and natural necessity. Yet the dream of escaping this burden promotes an ideal of freedom which is self-undermining, one which lacks the limits built into freedom understood as the capacity for a certain kind of action within an institutionally articulated space. With this emphasis upon the contrastive essence of human freedom, Arendt returns to the German Idealist opposition of freedom and necessity. She insists, *contra* Marx, that we cannot, and ought not to, attempt to transcend these poles of human life. Indeed, seen from the perspective of civic republicanism, the desire to be liberated once and for all from the burdens of necessity represents a "conspiracy of poverty and necessity" against the value of limited (and artificial) *political* freedom. The latter is, to use Arendt's metaphor, a small island amidst a sea of natural or automatic processes. The will to overcome poverty by mass violence or political means is therefore viewed by Arendt as a violent "negation of the negation," one which entirely neglects the positive, constructive power needed to create a new, lasting and more just, political order. Such attempts only succeed in overwhelming the fragile "islands of freedom" with the much more powerful forces of natural necessity. In this respect, Arendt agrees with Bacon: "the rebellions of the belly are the worst."

With her Augustinian theory of the revolutionary founding of new political realities, Arendt apparently overcomes the fundamental opposition between the elitist political freedom of the ancients ("free citizens") and the freedom to initiate inherent in all human beings (including slaves and "naked savages"). But the tension between these two concepts of freedom returns in the critique of social emancipation (or liberation from material want) she gives in *On Revolution*. For Arendt, *all* such projects – from the utopian Marxist reconstruction of entire societies to the far more modest goals of social democracy – are anti-political and subversive of freedom. Arendt rests this point about the anti-political consequences of social emancipation upon an even grander philosophical narrative about the historical decline of man as a *political* animal over the course of 2,000 years. This decline, it turns out, begins not with "the rise of the social" in the modern age; rather, it is co-original with the foundation of Western philosophy and metaphysics. In my concluding section, I want to consider the role this metanarrative plays in Arendt's thought, and how it affects her unstable mix of elitism and egalitarianism.

II Arendt's philosophy of history and her diagnosis of our times

The shadows of Nietzsche and Heidegger loom over Arendt's story of the decline and decay of the "beautiful freedom" of the Greeks and Romans. According to her, the triumph of the Christian world-view meant that the memory of the freedom enjoyed by the ancient city-states was repressed. Unlike their Greek and Roman counterparts, the Christian ideas of equality and freedom were alienated, unworldly, and (as the quote from Tertullian above reveals) deeply anti-political. Thus, while the institutional structure of the Catholic church may have had deep roots in Roman law and politics, this did nothing to alter the basic fact that, for Christians, the transcendental freedom *from* politics (and from *this* world) always retained a basic priority.[34] In a very non-Augustinian moment, Arendt writes, "The Christian hope for eternal life after death set the seal on the demotion of the *vita activa*." The idea of an otherworldly realm of redemption closed the categorial and experiential gap which ancient citizens negotiated each day when they left the household realm to "step over, and climb up to the political sphere." This mixing together of what had been two distinct spheres of human life is seen in Thomas Aquinas's Latin translation of Aristotle's *zoon politikon* into the *animal sociale*. This, Arendt notes, is hardly a harmless slip of the pen.[35] It encouraged medieval Christendom to mistake the public realm of the king for the despotic regime of the *pater familias*. By equating *politicus* and *socialis*, Aquinas blurs what for Arendt is the all-important distinction between the a public, political actor and the head of the household.

This blurring sets the pattern followed by modernity as well. In the modern age, social, technical, and economic questions – the kind best dealt with by experts – increasingly usurp the space devoted to *political* questions (which are matters of common concern shared by citizens). Arendt's outline of the primary steps leading to this baneful result may be summarized as follows. First, the Aristotelian *koinonia politike* (political community) becomes a *societas civilis sive politice*. Then, in the sixteenth and seventeenth centuries, the political association is increasingly absorbed by the market and by the economic structure of society. The civic ideas of common sense, public freedom, and public happiness decay even further thanks to the Protestant marriage of Christianity to science and industry (Weber's "Protestant ethic"). Finally, the French Revolution opens all the doors to the *oikos* and its demands, with the result that the poor and downtrodden, previously hidden away, come streaming into the public realm, looking for revenge and fulfillment of their most basic material needs. As Heinrich Heine's ironic poem about the destructive powers of poverty and social revolt put it:

> There are two kinds of rat:
> One hungry and one fat.
> The fat one stays content at home,
> But hungry ones go out and roam.
>
> These wild and savage rats
> Fear neither hell nor cats;
> They have no property or money too,
> So they want to divide the world anew.[36]

The stable world of European monarchies and republics breaks down under the force of the assault by this "revolutionary torrent." Made up of the "numberless multitude" of the hungry and oppressed, it now smashes its way into the "bright light of the public sphere." This violent introduction of the sheer force of biological need into the public sphere guarantees that genuinely political speech and authentically public concerns will fade before the unyielding materialism of the poor:

> Of soup-bowl logic, breaded arguments,
> Of reasoning based on roast beef or fish,
> With sausage citations to garnish the dish.
>
> A codfish, silently sauteed in butter,
> Delights that radical gang of the gutter,
> Much more than the speeches of Mirabeau,
> And all orations since Cicero.[37]

For Arendt, this revolt, coupled with the rise of what Hegel and later social scientists would call "civil society," signals the downfall of an authentic public realm. For her, the modern state is little more than a national or collective household, one in which neither social needs nor human intimacy respect their former boundaries. What used to be a shared sense of the public good is now transformed into a fully privatized morality. The abstract rights of "a being freed from all bonds [and] completely isolated" take the place of the concrete political rights of the republican citizen. But, as Arendt writes in *On Revolution,* "The absolute as it is expressed in the concept of human rights can only have disastrous consequences if it attempts to achieve validity within the political domain."[38] The end result of these two tendencies is found in the twentieth-century social welfare state (which makes the consumer/laborer king), and in our idea of a universal, utterly de-contextualized human equality (which helps facilitate the transformation of republican *isonomia* into what Arendt calls the bureaucratic "rule of nobody").[39]

According to Arendt's quasi-Nietzschean perspective, the beginning of this story is found in Christianity's transfiguration of pain and suffering, which were elevated from the sphere of shame into signs of holiness. The men of the French Revolution appropriated this theme of "slave morality," and – confronted by the misery of the poor and hungry masses – praised suffering as a "source and warranting of virtue." Compassion therefore became the highest virtue. This same "slavishness" (to stay with Nietzsche) can be seen, Arendt implies, in the core values of the welfare state and mass democracy. Once we draw the full consequences for political freedom and self-governance implied by this particular "transvaluation of values," we see that "all men are equal" *actually* mean that all men are slaves, laboring consumers who are ruled by anonymous others.

The breathtaking inclusiveness of this stance may tempt us to characterize Arendt's diagnosis of our times as a variation upon Heidegger's thesis about the "forgetfulness of Being," which supposedly descends upon the West shortly with the passing of the pre-Socratic philosophers. With Arendt, however, "forgetfulness of Being" has become "forgetfulness of the political" and the taste for *public* freedom.[40] She calls this situation "worldlessness." Only in those rare moments of revolutionary political action does some of the old glory return, and the "bright light of the public realm" shine forth once again. But the very triumph implicit in such new foundations of liberty carries with it the risk of corruption and decay. This, at least, is the message of Arendt's analyses of the French and American Revolutions in *On Revolution*. For even where the revolutions succeed in clearing a "new space for freedom," they ultimately succumb to the gravitational pull of material interests and the call for "social emancipation." In the modern age, such needs always seem to overwhelm the newly created space of freedom in the end. Thus, the newly revived sense of the political fades with the passing of the revolutionary spirit.

As this brief sketch indicates, Arendt returns to the elitism of an aristocratic republicanism in her diagnosis of the fundamental ills of modern society. This is, perhaps, most apparent in her conclusion to *On Revolution*, where she proposes that we distinguish between an active, political minority (with all the rights of political participation, including the right to vote) and the broad, passive majority of consumers/citizens, who have (in effect) abdicated these rights.[41] For Arendt, making this distinction official seems one way out of the "dangerous, destructive" tendency of mass democracy to "widen the gap between rulers and ruled." Yet this solution – a "self-chosen" political aristocracy which wields greater power by dint of its greater political virtue – is as utopian as the sociological background of her view of contemporary society is reactionary.

Fortunately for us, Arendt's political theory includes the very tools necessary to counter this drift toward political elitism. Against consumer society; against old and new forms of despotism; against all varieties of political elitism (including classical republicanism), we can insist, with the "Augustinian" Arendt, on the egalitarian power to make a new beginning, a power that is co-original with every human being's ability to say no, to refuse, and to start again. The lasting legacy of Arendt's political thought is found in her incomplete (and often inconsistent) attempt to combine this egalitarian idea of the human capacity for initiatory action with the older civic republican idea of freedom as self-government. Even in a hyper-complex world, such an *egalitarian* republicanism may be the only hope we have if we still desire to be masters of our fate. For without a republican grounding born in the "living power of the people," contemporary society too risks a lapse into barbarism.

NOTES

1 See J. R. Searle, *Intentionality* (Cambridge: Cambridge University Press, 1983), pp. 7ff. I borrow the formula "direction of fit" from Searle, but use it here in a more inclusive way, not simply for speech-acts, but for action in general.
2 Arendt, *HC*, pp. 122ff.
3 Ibid., pp. 50–58.
4 Ibid. See also Hannah Arendt, "Einführung in die Politik," "Einleitung: Hat Politik überhaupt noch einen Sinn? A: Der Vernichtungskrieg," manuscript, Library of Congress, Washington DC, box 67.
5 See Dana R. Villa, *Arendt and Heidegger: The Fate of the Political* (Princeton: Princeton University Press, 1996), chapter 2 for a discussion of this point.
6 Arendt, *HC*, p. 178. Arendt calls Jesus the "discoverer" of the full unpredictability of human action. See *BPF*, pp. 167–168.
7 Of course, for Arendt the ideal or essential forms of the political association are ancient. She tends to view both the European "kingdom" (which mixed Christianity and politics) and the modern nation-state as deviations or less-than-perfect realizations of the public realm originally invented by the *polis* and the ancient republic.
8 Aristotle, *Politics*, 1253a.
9 Ibid., 1253b1–1255b40; 1259a–1260b20. Cf. Aristotle, *Nicomachean Ethics*, 1134b, 1160b–1161b.
10 For the hierarchical quality of relations between men and young boys in ancient Greece, see Michel Foucault, *The History of Sexuality*, vol. II, *The Use of Pleasure*, chapter 4.
11 See, for example, Arendt's observation in *HC*, p. 176, about the human character of the life of the slave-holder compared to the virtually non-human character of those forever barred from appearance in the public realm. In *OR* she goes so far as to propose a newly exclusive conception of republican citizenship. See my discussion below.
12 Arendt, *HC*, pp. 101–109. For a critical discussion, see Margaret Canovan, *Hannah Arendt: A Reinterpretation of her Political Thought* (Cambridge: Cambridge University Press, 1992), pp. 122ff.
13 *HC*., p. 212.
14 Ibid., p. 31.
15 Ibid., pp. 32–33.
16 Cf. Arendt's discussion, *HC*, pp. 36–37.
17 On this point, the otherwise quite different works of Michel Foucault and Martha Nussbaum coincide. See Foucault, *The History of Sexuality*, vols. II and III, and Nussbaum, *The Fragility of Goodness* (Cambridge: Cambridge University Press, 1986).
18 Arendt, *HC*, pp. 28–35. If Arendt associates the "enormous natural force of necessity" with the space of the household, she silently presupposes a modern concept of nature in making this judgment, while leaving it aside when it comes to the space of the *polis*. With regard to the latter, she connects freedom with the Aristotelian definition of man's *telos* or nature: to be a political animal and to live the "good (just or virtuous) life." Her fundamental opposition between the political and the household emerges from this self-induced categorial confusion.

19 See Arendt, *OR*, pp. 30–31.
20 See Arendt, "On Violence," in *CR*, p. 143.
21 Arendt, *HC*, p. 204.
22 Arendt, *OR*, pp. 200–201.
23 Martin Heidegger, *Being and Time*, sections 38–41.
24 Arendt, *OT*, pp. 290–302.
25 Ibid., p. 302. See also her description of the shock experienced by the Boers in their confrontation with the natives of South Africa, pp 191–197. The phrase "naked savage" is itself a reference to Burke's critique of the French Revolution and its idea of human rights. Arendt tries to take a middle road between Burke's localized conception of the "rights of free-born Englishmen" and Lockean or Rousseauean "natural" rights by focusing on what she calls "the right to have rights," or the right to be a member of a political community. For critiques of this strategy, see H. Brunkhorst, "Are Human Rights Self-Contradictory? Critical Remarks on a Hypothesis by Hannah Arendt"; and Frank Michelman, "Parsing a Right to Have Rights," both in *Constellations* 3/2 (Oct. 1996).
26 *OT*, p. 479. Other references to the same sentence may be found in *LM* (vol. II, p. 217), *HC* (p. 177), *OR* (p. 211), and *BPF* (p. 167).
27 This is a primary theme of my book, *Hannah Arendt* (Munich: Beck, 1999).
28 Tertullian, *Apologeticum*, 38.
29 Arendt, "Religion and Politics," in *EU*, p. 373.
30 Ibid.
31 Abraham Lincoln, "Address Delivered at the Dedication of the Cemetery at Gettysburg," November 19, 1863 in A. Lincoln, *His Speeches and Writings* (New York: 1969), p. 734.
32 Ibid.
33 The Catholic Church continues to follow in the old Roman tracks, as we can see from the Pope's Easter Blessing, which addresses *urbi et orbi*.
34 Arendt, "Religion and Politics," p. 373.
35 Arendt, *HC*, p. 23.
36 Heinrich Heine, "The Roving Rats" (*Die Wanderratten*), tr. Hal Draper, *The Complete Poems of Heinrich Heine* (Frankfurt: Suhrkamp, 1982), p. 783.
37 Ibid.
38 Arendt, *OR*, p. 149.
39 Arendt, *HC*, p. 40.
40 This is the theme that links *The Human Condition* and *On Revolution*. For the link/disjunction with Heidegger, see Villa, *Arendt and Heidegger*, chapters 4 and 5.
41 Arendt, *OR*, pp. 275–279.

PART V

Revolution and constitution

10

JEREMY WALDRON

Arendt's constitutional politics

I

In what sense (if any) is man a *political* animal? Hannah Arendt is commonly thought to have made more of the Aristotelian characterization[1] than anyone else in twentieth-century philosophy. I do not mean that she is a good expositor of Aristotle: in fact she is often criticized on that front.[2] I mean that she took the content of Aristotle's claim very seriously, particularly the question of what exactly in man's nature is political and what is not.

Historically, Arendt argued, humans have found their greatest fulfillment in politics. For people like Thomas Jefferson and John Adams, "life in Congress, the joys of discourse, of legislation, of transacting business, of persuading and being persuaded, were . . . no less conclusively a foretaste of eternal bliss than the delights of contemplation had been for medieval piety."[3] In politics, such men found something which managed to redeem human life from the cyclical futility of birth, reproduction, and death. Without that something, their existence would be as uniform and pointless as the life of any animal; or its point would be the biological process itself, the endless repetition of generation after generation. In politics, by contrast, our humanity gives us the chance to transcend the merely natural and to undertake unique initiatives that flare up in the public realm and linger indefinitely in memory and history.

It follows (from this contrast between life-process and politics) that the sense in which we are political animals must be quite a special sense for Arendt. In common speech, we call someone a political animal if he is hungry for power, and if he has the knack of manipulating people and institutions to get out of them exactly what he wants. (If it is a question of funding or promotion, he knows who to talk to, and he gets to them first.) Or, in a slightly different vein, we call someone a political animal if he has a talent for *politicizing* everything. (Things that other people would deal with informally – who pays for dinner, who takes out the garbage – he makes an issue of, and forces the rest of us into a huge debate about the fair allocation of responsibilities.) In a third sense, to say that someone is a political animal is to marvel at the way he "struts his stuff" on the political stage; it is to be dazzled by his speeches or his maneuvers as pure performance – as drama or ballet, perhaps – quite apart from their aims or their efficacy. I am not sure whether any of these types would qualify as a political animal on Arendt's account. Certainly for her they are not paragons or exemplars of the breed. In Arendt's view, a political animal is not someone who politicizes everything or who can manipulate institutions to his personal advantage. Nor is her political animal a mere virtuoso, though, as we shall see, her reasons for misgiving about the "performer" image are ambiguous and complicated.

The central case of an Arendtian *zoon politikon* is a person who engages seriously and responsibly in public business under the auspices of public institutions. He has the judgment to discern which issues are political and which are merely social or personal. He can see that what matter in politics are interests and purposes that are shared by all as agents in a community. He has the patience to listen to others and to respond to their intelligence in a way that treats them as equals. Above all, he has respect for the structures and procedures that frame the political enterprise and that make possible deliberation and action with others. He takes the framework seriously, and he resists the temptation to dazzle his audience or further his own aims by subverting the formalities it imposes.

This last point – about the importance of structure, formality, and procedure – has not been emphasized nearly enough in recent discussions of Arendt's political thought. Commentators notice what is sometimes referred to as Arendt's *agonistic* conception of politics – politics as a stage for action and distinction, a place where heroic deeds break through the barriers of the mundane, and live on in memory as something extraordinary and exhilarating.[4] They portray her as yearning for the public realm of antiquity, perhaps even archaic antiquity – a *polis* "permeated by a fiercely competitive spirit, where everybody had constantly to distinguish himself from all others, to show through unique deeds or achievements that he was the best of all."[5] The whole point of that style of "politics" is an unruly self-disclosure that challenges traditional forms. Alternatively, commentators notice that in her darker moments, Arendt put almost all her faith in what one might call irregular or extra-political action – the spontaneous councils of citizens that spring up at moments of crisis or revolt – and that she doubted whether even the most promising constitutions could contain the human impulse to freedom.[6] Put these two aspects of her work together, and it appears that Arendt's interest in constitutional structure has little to do with what she valued most about politics. Though no-one can deny her interest in "founding moments," it often seems as if these moments are valued primarily for themselves – the 1787 Convention or the Declaration of Independence as archetypes of political action[7] – rather than as the establishment of a framework for subsequent action. That impression is reinforced by what they take to be the dominant tone of Arendt's most "constitutionalist" work, *On Revolution*, a tone of regret that in the American constitution "there was no space reserved, nor room left for the exercise of precisely those qualities which had been instrumental in building it."[8]

I do not want to underestimate the tensions and ambiguities in Arendt's work. Her writing varies in mood, emphasis, and occasion much more than that of most political theorists. Even so, the theme of politics as something that requires not just virtuosity but constitution is so insistent in her work that if we neglect it, we risk trivializing Arendt's real-world concerns about alienation from institutions, first in Europe between the wars,[9] and secondly in modern America.[10] I think, too, that we should not overlook an important genealogical strain in her theory. To the extent that she presents a consistent view, it is not one in which agonistic self-disclosure and the "irregular" politics of councils and civil disobedience are *alternatives* to responsible modes of constitutional politics. Instead they are presented by Arendt as, in the one case, an archaic precursor to politics in the most fully structured sense, and, in the other, a despairing echo of constitutional politics – "strange and sad" – accompanying its lamentable decline.

II

That politics needs *housing*, and that building such housing can be equated with the framing of a *constitution* – this is an image that recurs throughout Arendt's writings. Sometimes the metaphor is less of bricks and mortar than of the furniture that enables us to sit facing one another in politics, in just the right way. Other times, Arendt invokes the imagery of construction outside the house: fences and boundary walls, which make politics possible by securing a space for the public realm.[11] Always the emphasis is on artificial structures, which are more rigid and durable than the actions they accommodate, and which exist as features of a world that men have made for themselves.

Arendt stressed this objective aspect of housing, even at some risk to her overall sense of the political nature of constitution-framing. For if constitutions were understood literally as fabrications – in the way she suggests the Greeks understood them – then constitution-framing would be making, not acting, and the framer would be

> like the builder of the city wall, someone who had to . . . finish his work before political activity could begin. He therefore was treated like any other craftsman or architect and could be called from abroad and commissioned without having to be a citizen, whereas the right to . . . engage in the numerous activities that went on inside the *polis*, was entirely restricted to citizens.[12]

That would be misleading for communities whose constitution-building was part of their own politics and no less political than any of the actions it was supposed to house and regulate. The image of fabrication tends also to suggest the singularity of the framer – one man making something out of other men[13] – rather than constitution-building as an activity that arises among men acting and speaking together.[14]

A different image, but more apt to capture these aspects of immanence and plurality, is that of political *grammar* or *syntax*.[15] Rules of grammar are not constructed up front; they are not distinct from usage; and certainly they are not established by individual grammarians. They present themselves instead as something implicit in on-going activity, regulating usage nonetheless and making possible certain forms of life that would be unthinkable without them.[16]

However, grammar does not quite capture an aspect of constitutional structure that Arendt wants to emphasize with her worldly images of housing and furniture. This is the aspect of "the *in-between*" – political structure as something that both separates people from one another and relates them to one another. Like a table or a seating plan, a constitution separates and relates us by putting us in different seats in one another's presence.[17] Now the world of objects does that generally for human life. For politics, however, the in-between is not physical but normative: it consists of rules not barriers, practices and commitments not impediments. Citizens are "bound to, and at the same time separated and protected from, each other by all kinds of relationships, based on a common language, religion, a common history, customs, and laws."[18]

True, Arendt did speak of the significance attached to constitutions as written documents, a significance that testified, she said, "to their elementary objective, worldly character."[19] In America, for example, it was important that the Constitution be

> an endurable objective thing, which, to be sure, one could approach from many different angles and upon which one could impose many different interpretations, which one could change or amend with circumstances, but which nevertheless was never a subjective state of mind, like the will. It has remained a tangible worldly entity of greater durability than elections or public-opinion polls.[20]

But paper constitutions by themselves are nothing: she cites the French Constitution of 1791 and the numerous, discredited documents – "[t]he constitutions of the experts" – imposed in Europe after the First World War.[21] A constitution, said John Adams (in a passage Arendt quoted with approval), "is a standard, a pillar, and a bond when it is understood, approved and beloved. But without this intelligence and attachment, it might as well be a kite or balloon, flying in the air."[22]

III

The abstract idea of the in-between and the imagery of housing, grammar, and furniture are all very well. In literal terms, what is a constitution supposed to do, on Arendt's account? Why is politics impossible without this housing? Why are non-institutional versions of politics so hopeless or so dangerous? What sort of structure, what sort of nexus of relation-and-separation do we actually need?

There are features of the housing and furniture metaphors which we can take simply at face value. They convey the importance of things like the proper design of legislative chambers, or (varying the context slightly) the shape of the table at the Paris peace talks during the Vietnam War. Other aspects are question-begging as they stand. Is it really true, for example, that politics is impossible without boundaries? The men of the eighteenth century "needed a constitution to lay down the boundaries of the new political realm."[23] What sort of boundaries did Arendt have in mind?

She mentions a number of connected issues. In her discussion of jurisdiction in the Eichmann trial, she observes that "the earth is inhabited by many peoples and these peoples are ruled by many different laws."[24] The point of this separation into peoples is partly a matter of preserving identity (though Arendt is ambivalent about the politics of national identity),[25] and partly a matter of the conditions under which a free politics is possible. The state, she said, is not suited for unlimited growth, "because the genuine consent at its base cannot be stretched indefinitely."[26] As Rousseau recognized,[27] there are limits on the scale on which people can deal with one another. Politics depends on freedom and equality, and equality itself, she writes, is "applicable only with limitations and even within spatial limits."[28] I will later examine her view that equality is something constructed not given. At this stage it is worth noting, however, that even if we accept her constructivist account, the argument for the separation of states succeeds only if an *un*bounded equality would necessarily have to rest on some naturalistic theory. Arendt assumes that it would – that is, she assumes that the equality implicit in international charters of human rights presupposes some account of human nature, and she shows the perils of such views in *The Origins of Totalitarianism*.[29] But she does not show that a *constructive* universalism is impossible (indeed her skepticism about the human rights project seems quite dated now). The only hints of argument to that effect seem to rest on a rather unpleasantly Schmittian view about equality: A and B can regard each other as equals only in their enmity to C.[30]

A second sort of boundary Arendt emphasizes has to do with the scope of politics. It is important, she says, to maintain fences between public and private, and boundaries which separate the world of politics from the life-world of labor and subsistence. She says we must sustain a sense of moderation that understands the futility of extending rules and commitments to every aspect of human life.[31] More astute commentators than I have tried and failed to elaborate a defensible version of Arendt's insistence that life-process issues must be forbidden the public realm.[32] I will say nothing about that in this essay, except that the reconstruction of Arendtian political theory, which is undoubtedly necessary in this regard, will surely leave us still with *some* restrictions on scope of the political realm for a constitution to patrol – even if it is just the old "wall of separation" between church and state.

Thirdly, Arendt talks of the importance of the fences between individual men,[33] the rules that separate as well as relate them to one another. "Positive laws in constitutional government are designed to erect boundaries and establish channels of communication between men whose community is continually endangered by the new men born into it."[34] Arendt does not flinch from the fact that one of the motives that brings men into community is "their obvious fear of one another."[35] To be sure, this is not all there is to human relatedness,[36] but Arendt sees that its mitigation by mutual assurance is the condition of anything more affirmative.

This brings us, then, to the internal aspect of constitutional structure. When *we* (liberals) think of the work that constitutions do, we tend to think of guarantees that are given to individuals, so far as their liberty and security are concerned. In much of her writing, Arendt plays down this aspect, as part of her project of de-emphasizing negative liberty and focusing more on the freedom that consists in participation in public affairs.[37] Even when she talks about respect for privacy and property, it is associated as much with the protection of the political realm from life-process issues as it is with the individual (or familial) needs that the private realm represents.[38] Still, civil liberties are not absent from her picture. Though they are not "the actual content of freedom," they are recognized as its *sine qua non,* and they fade into active political freedom in a way that makes any rigid demarcation unhelpful.[39]

This is one area where it is particularly important to integrate Arendt's concerns in *The Origins of Totalitarianism* into her more abstract philosophy of politics. "Freedom from . . ." various restraints and threats looks uninspiring by contrast with the active participatory freedom of the public realm. But Arendt's study of totalitarianism leaves us with a vivid sense of what in the real world we need security against if freedom is to flourish. True, the terror, torture, madness, and murder described in that work go far beyond anything that constitutional structures could reasonably be expected to protect us against. And Arendt herself draws a distinction between terror and tyranny,[40] which, when coupled with a characterization of tyranny as "merely" a lack of negative freedom, might persuade us that its prevention is beneath the notice of a theory of this kind. Still, tyranny is the precursor of terror (just as liberation is the necessary condition for true freedom),[41] and the fear that is associated with it in the modern world – fear of beatings, torture, and "disappearance" – is for the people who suffer it remarkably similar to the dissolving panic that Arendt describes in the total environment of the German concentration camps. Of course, we also suffer forms of tyranny that are well short of that.[42] But, to our shame, we have found it necessary even in modern democratic politics to offer one another assurances against more brutal forms of oppression as well. Moreover it is not enough for these assurances to be issued in theoretical proclamations. That was Arendt's criticism of the inefficacy of "the Rights of Man."[43] They need to be built into the civic structures of particular states, and enforced as part of the functioning of ordinary law.

Once security is guaranteed, the task is not to limit power but to constitute it, to build the conditions in which political freedom can flourish in an affirmative sense.[44] What sort of housing, what sort of structure are we looking for here?

It might be thought that the politics of deed, distinction, and display needs very little in the way of constitutive structure. Indeed, structure in the public realm may make men too "well-behaved," diminishing the prospects for the expression of *virtù* or ability.[45] What the political animal most needs, on this conception, is for his greatness to be noticed and his deeds to be remembered. I have already expressed my reservations about this take on Arendtian politics. Notice, however, that even at the level of deed and memory there can be nothing political without structure.

Politics orients itself towards action-in-concert and, as Arendt puts it, "action, though it may be started . . . by single individuals for very different motives, can be accomplished only by some joint effort, in which the motivation of single individuals . . . no longer counts."[46] For concerted action to be possible, men must give their word and play their part, furnishing one another with assurances that the cooperation of each in his assigned role will not be rendered futile by the unreliability of others. "This whole adventure," said the Mayflower compactors, "growes upon the joint confidence we have in each others fidelity and resolution herein, so as no man of us would have adventured it without assurance of the rest."[47] If it is to be anything other than "an extraordinary and infrequent enterprise,"[48] the structuring of action requires permanent arrays of ready-made roles (the structure of *an army* is not a bad paradigm) so that provision for action-in-concert does not have to be invented anew every time an idea is projected.[49] That may sound a little too Weberian for those whose view of Arendt is dominated by her worries about bureaucracy;[50] but those worries, important as they are, must not be construed in a way that condemns all regularized forms of co-operation in the institutional life of actual political communities.

Something similar is true for remembrance as well. Let us say that people do enter public life in order to evince some special excellence. This is something they cannot do unless there are others around to compete with and impress.[51] It might be thought that we do not need much more structure for this than a stage and an audience. Consider, though, what Arendt actually says:

> [N]o remembrance remains secure unless it is condensed . . . into a framework of conceptual notions . . . [T]he stories which grow out of what men do . . . sink back into the futility inherent in the living word and the living deed unless they are talked about over and over again. What saves the affairs of mortal men from their inherent futility is nothing but this incessant talk about them, which in its turn remains futile unless certain concepts, certain guideposts for future remembrance, and even for sheer reference, arise out of it.[52]

This condensation for reference and memory presupposes a "web of relationships and enacted stories" in which the living deed can take its place as something remembered.[53] George Kateb associates that requirement with the integrity of a community stable enough to evolve traditions of storing and revisiting memories.[54] But one can associate it also with more formal structures. When Arendt discussed the difficulties facing the totalitarian substitution of lies for truthful memory in the modern world, she cited the existence of archives, serials, and anthologies – the mundane apparatus of bibliographical structure – which ensure that it is no easy matter to blot out the achievements of (say) a Trotsky or a Zinoviev from human remembrance.[55]

Focusing on actor, audience, and archive gives us a grip on the requirements for a rather primitive Periclean politics of personal display. But it tells us very little about what is necessary for politics as *inter*-action, the politics that involves debate, deliberation, and the making of decisions. According to Arendt, a well-ordered republic is "constituted by an exchange of opinion between equals."[56] This involves several types of structural arrangement – to begin with, it involves structures that enable us to treat one another as equals, and structures that enable each person's opinion to be exchanged with the opinions of others, in a way that is capable of yielding a decision.

The first of these Arendt sometimes labeled *isonomy*[57] – the capacity of positive laws to make people equal in the political realm, even if they are in other respects different and unequal. By nature we are (depending where you look) either the same in our animality or utterly different in background and character; but by political convention we *hold* ourselves to be one another's equals.[58] In recognition of our engagement in the joint enterprise of polity,[59] the law creates for each of us an artificial *persona* that can take its place on the public stage, presenting us not exactly as the beings we naturally are, but as equals for political purposes.[60] Arendt's rejection of all theories of a natural basis for human equality is no doubt the reason that her observations about slavery and other forms of subjugation are expressed with sadness but not surprise:[61] on the one hand, nothing *forces* a community to extend isonomy to all humans within its orbit; and on the other hand, a theory of natural equality runs the risk of holding that our *natural* similarities and dissimilarities are the ones that matter, whether they turn out finally to support the notion of equality or not.[62]

What we actually *do* as equals in politics, according to Arendt, is not merely try to impress one another as *dramatis personae*, but talk to one another with a view to action-in-concert. People come to politics with diverse interests, and as common issues are raised they tend to develop diverse opinions.[63] Now, the formation of an opinion is not a straightforward thing, for Arendt. It is not just "happening to hold a view." Instead, it involves a serious effort to see an issue from the point of view of all those affected by it:

> I form an opinion by considering a given issue from different viewpoints, by making present to my mind the standpoints of those who are absent . . . [T]his is a question neither of empathy, as though I tried to be or feel like someone else, nor of counting noses and joining a majority but of being and thinking in my own identity where I am not. The more people's standpoints I have present in my mind while I am pondering a given issue . . . the stronger will be my capacity for representative thinking, and the more valid my final conclusions, my opinion.[64]

That last comment about *validity* might suggest that a valid opinion is, ultimately, the same for everyone. I do not think that Arendt means that. She envisages opinion-formation by a given individual, A, in the context of A's putting himself into the shoes of B and C, even while B and C are forming their opinions in the same sort of way, and there is no reason why his attempt to put himself in their shoes should end up the same as their attempt to put themselves in his.[65] Since "no one is capable of forming his own opinion without the benefit of a multitude of opinions held by others,"[66] diversity and disagreement are going to be present in this process from start to finish.

If politics is to resolve anything, these various opinions must come to together and yield decision through what Arendt calls "the drawn-out wearisome processes of persuasion, negotiation, and compromise."[67] That cannot happen unless there is a framework on which each person's contribution takes its place and is related to that of each of the others. Now, Arendt's remarks at this stage are not as concrete as one would like, but two sorts of structure seem particularly important. The first are the basic rules of political procedure – something like Robert's Rules of Order. By that I mean conventions determining such things as: how agendas are set; how debates are initiated and concluded; who has the right to speak, how often, and for how long; who may interrupt, who may exact an answer to a question, who has a right of reply; how a common sense of relevance is maintained; how deliberation is related to a community's powers of resolution and action. These matters – which I have discussed in detail elsewhere[68] – might seem beneath the notice of a political theory as exotic and exciting as Arendt's. But they are exactly what distinguish structured politics from the sort of undifferentiated welling-up of mass opinion in an extra-parliamentary context that so worried her. Morever, it is in rules like these that we can locate the equality that Arendt associates with citizenship. The right to be heard, the right that there be a system in which one's contributions are registered, are exactly what isonomy in politics amounts to.[69] To be sure, Arendt also emphasizes the spontaneity with which assemblies spring up whenever they are given the chance to do so. But it's intriguing how everyone seems to know on these occasions that if you constitute a public gathering, no matter how local the basis, no matter how spontaneous the impulse, there are procedures to be followed, chairs elected, motions moved, amendments considered, speakers for and against, points of order, questions put, votes taken, and minutes recorded. All this is "second nature" in our political culture – as much a part of our political being as the faculty of speech itself.

The other aspect of structure, about which Arendt says very little, is of course the matter of voting. Her comments on voting tend to be mostly disparaging – along the lines of "[t]he booth in which we deposit our ballots is unquestionably too small, for this booth has room for only one."[70] But if one leaves aside her concerns about self-interested voting (which she associates with negative safeguards against government and, at worst, with blackmail),[71] the disparagement is not of voting as such, but of forms of electoral politics which fail to provide people "with more opportunity to make their voices heard in public than election day."[72] Though occasionally she can be heard suggesting that face-to-face politics around a table might yield consensus and thus obviate the need for decision-procedures,[73] nothing like that is remotely compatible with her emphasis on diversity of opinion. In fact, she is not at all uncomfortable with the idea of majority decision –

> a technical device, likely to be adopted almost automatically in all types of deliberative councils and assemblies, whether these are the whole electorate or a town-hall meeting . . . In other words, the principle of majority is inherent in the very process of decision-making and thus is present in all forms of government.[74]

– provided first that it is pursuant to a genuine exchange of opinions, and secondly that it does not degenerate into what she calls majority-*rule* – "where the majority, after the decision has been taken, proceeds to liquidate politically, and in extreme cases, physically, the opposing minority."[75] (Once again we see here the importance of constitutional guarantees in securing such a distinction.)

Beyond these, Arendt mentions three other structures of a well-organized polity: representation, parties, and federalism. Though political freedom means the right to be a participant in government, "[o]bviously direct democracy will not do, if only because 'the room will not hold all.'"[76] We need federal structures to connect (in a large- or medium-sized polity) the smaller political units in which alone direct participation is possible. Arendt never imagined that everyone in a society would seek the joy of political action: she was interested in structures that would empower "those few from all walks of life who have a taste for public freedom and cannot be 'happy' without it."[77] For this self-selected few, the connections between the "elementary republics" in which they act directly are arguably as important as the internal constitutions of those republics themselves. Such relations work in many ways; Arendt is particularly intrigued by structures of *deputization*, whereby action on a larger scale becomes possible through the exchange of opinions among deputies, each of whom stands for an opinion formed in roughly the same way among participants at a more "grass-roots" level of politics.[78]

Sometimes Arendt writes as though we need representation in politics to sift opinions, "passing them through the sieve of an intelligence which will separate the arbitrary and the merely idiosyncratic, and thus purify them into public views."[79] In *The Origins of Totalitarianism* this idea occurs in the context of her concern about the fragmentation of political parties, and their supersession by mass movements, and the growth of public irresponsibility, procedural impatience, and general contempt for parliamentary institutions.[80] In these circumstances, there is a "chaos of unrepresented and unpurified opinions."

That chaos may crystallize "into a variety of conflicting mass sentiments under pressure of emergency," waiting for a strong man to mold them into a unanimous public opinion, which in Arendt's view spells death to all opinions.[81] To diminish these dangers she looked to two-party systems (like that of Great Britain) where effective participation in politics required both cooperation with others in "broad-church" arrangements and a degree of shared responsibility for the public world, born of the constant possibility that one might have to take office at the next election.[82]

IV

The structures we have been discussing are partly a matter of culture (like the ethos of a two-party system) and partly a matter of law (like rules governing the way votes are counted, and constitutional provisions protecting dissidents from coercion). Either way, we have reason to be concerned about their durability, for these structures have to hold their own against all sorts of onslaughts, from self-interest and self-righteous impatience to various forms of communal hysteria.

For Arendt, the solution to the problem of political instability is prefigured in the idea of a promise. There is something crucial for politics in the human capacity to bind oneself in the presence of others and publicly commit oneself, against the unknown exigencies of future circumstances, to play one's part in a scheme agreed in advance.[83] The paradigm of promise-based politics is the Mayflower compact – the affecting assumption by a group of men and women on the edge of a wilderness, that they had the power "to combine themselves into a 'civil Body Politick' which, held together solely by the strength of mutual promise 'in the Presence of God and one another,' supposedly was powerful enough to 'enact, constitute, and frame' all necessary laws and instruments of government."[84] Like a promise, a constitution might appear to limit our freedom; but at the same time it creates something special – the power of a political community – whose importance consists precisely in mitigating the incalculability that human freedom gives rise to.

What counts in promising of course is not the making of a promise but the keeping of it; and for the construction of a political community, what matters is not the admirable state of the furnishings when politics begins, but the on-going willingness of citizens to submit to them as regulative structures. The authority of a constitution is not a product of the strength or violence of its framers, or even of their virtue or the perfection of what they have crafted. It consists rather in a willingness on the part of all concerned to treat *this* event (the founding) and *this* body of law (the constitution), rather than any of the other acts and proposals that might crop up from time to time, as the starting point and point of reference for all subsequent politics. And they must do this not because of anything special or noticeable about this event or body of law, but simply because they acknowledge that there must *be* such a point of reference, that it is bound to be in some sense arbitrary, and that they are determined nevertheless to act from henceforth as though *this one* will do. In that regard, respect for a constitution matches the contingent resolution of promise-keeping. I might have made any one of a number of promises, and some of them might have been excellent; but *this* is the one that I happened to make, and so *this* is the one I am bound by.[85]

In case that conveys an excessive sense of immutability so far as political structure is concerned, it is worth adding that Arendt associated authority as much with improvement (*augere* – to augment and increase) as with conservation.[86] The order and predictability that we need in political affairs may change with changes in circumstances. A constitution is necessarily a work in progress. Still, the point about the authority of the particular arbitrary beginning remains important. Respect for an established constitution does not mean treating it as sacrosanct and beyond change; but it means treating *it* as the object of change and augmentation, rather than simply purporting to *begin again* every time we suppose ourselves to have accumulated more wisdom than our ancestors.

Promising is a important clue to constitutional durability; but in one respect it is misleading. In the liberal tradition of government by consent, there is an assumption that each new person can contract anew, and that no one need be bound by the promises of a previous generation. But that is incompatible with Arendt's conviction that constitutions must be able to outlast their mortal framers.[87] Law rests on consent certainly, in the sense that it constitutes and therefore cannot presuppose the power that would be necessary to compel obedience. But the rules that make up the public world must also *pre-exist* each individual's taking his place in that world, and make a claim on him that is prior to anything he might agree to:

> The point of these rules is not that I submit to them voluntarily or recognize theoretically their validity, but that in practice I cannot enter the game unless I conform; my motive for acceptance is my wish to play, and since men exist only in the plural, my wish to play is identical with my wish to live. Every man is born into a community with pre-existing laws which he "obeys" first of all because there is no other way for him to enter the great game of the world.[88]

V

Sometimes when one reads Arendt – and more often when one reads her commentators – the impression one gets is of an obscure and esoteric philosopher, concerned with large and mysterious issues like *Dasein* and *the agonal*, who has little to say to the ordinary student of politics. The Arendtian world, it seems, is a world for the initiated, a world of theoretical abstractions largely uncontaminated by mundane things like civil liberties, voting rights, Robert's Rules of Order, and the two-party system. I have not said all there is to say about Arendt's interest in constitutional structure.[89] But I hope I have redressed the balance a little, by showing, first, how engaged her work is with quite familiar issues about institutions, and secondly, how important structure is, even in her most abstract characterizations of human freedom. If we say Arendt was unconcerned with the formalities of political order, we can make little sense of her preoccupation with foundations, her omnivorous interest in constitution-building, her grasp of the need for patience and discipline in politics, and the orientation of almost all her work to the hard task of sustaining a realm where human freedom can become powerful and not spend itself in the futility she associates with the immediate, the unstructured, and the natural.

I have not forgotten Arendt's political despair, her belief that the American framers failed to provide within their constitution structures that could safeguard the spirit exhibited in their own revolutionary actions.[90] Nor have I forgotten her apprehension about the modern "transformation of government into administration, or of republics into bureaucracies, and the disastrous shrinkage of the public realm."[91] But when she says "it was the Constitution itself, this greatest achievement of the American people, which eventually cheated them of their proudest possession,"[92] that is not a rejection of constitutions or constitutionalism or constitutional structure as such: it is a lamentation of the failure of the framers and current inhabitants of *a particular constitution* to find a way of structuring for perpetuity the sort of freedom they were exercising. The lament is unintelligible without an understanding of the importance of structure.

In a recently translated biography, the German historian Christian Meier has written this about Julius Caesar:

> Caesar was insensitive to political institutions and the complex ways in which they operate . . . Since his year as consul, if not before, Caesar had been unable to see Rome's institutions as autonomous entities . . . He could see them only as instruments in the interplay of forces. His cold gaze passed through everything that Roman society still believed in, lived by, valued and defended. He had no feeling for the power of institutions to guarantee law and security, but only for what he found useful or troublesome about them . . . Thus what struck him most about the Senate was the fact that it was controlled by his opponents. It hardly seems to have occurred to him that it was responsible for the commonwealth . . . In Caesar's eyes no one existed but himself and his opponents.

> It was all an interpersonal game. He classified people as supporters, opponents or neutrals. The scene was cleared of any suprapersonal elements. Or if any were left, they were merely props behind which one could take cover or with which one could fight. Politics amounted to no more than a fight for his rights.[93]

And by "his rights," Meier meant not Caesar's interests or his wealth, but due recognition for his greatness.

Is this the paragon of a political animal? Is this the sort of thing Arendt laments that we have lost? On some readings of her work, one would have to say that it is. For here, in Caesar's case, we have the heroic "wish to excel."[94] Here we have "the self's agonal passion for distinction,"[95] the "unruly" but (*nota bene*) highly successful pursuit of immortality, breaking through the commonly accepted and reaching into the extraordinary. Caesar might have destroyed the institutions of the republic and created in their place nothing but the splendor of his own deed. But that, surely, is the mark of political *virtù*, "where the accomplishment lies in the performance itself."[96]

In fact, despite some of her rhetoric,[97] I suspect Hannah Arendt's judgment of Caesar would have been the same as Christian Meier's[98] – that there is something reckless, even pathological about a mode of political action in which the walls and structures intended to house actions of that kind become suddenly invisible, transparent, even contemptible to the actor. In a somewhat different context she observes:

> The weirdness of this situation resembles a spiritualist seance where a number of people gathered round a table might suddenly, through some magic trick, see the table vanish from their midst, so that two persons sitting opposite each other were no longer separated but also would be entirely unrelated to each other by anything tangible.[99]

Such drastically unmediated proximity – "Now there is just you, and me, and the issue of my greatness" – is alarmingly like the press of bodies against each other that Arendt associates with the destruction of the possibility of thought in mass society. Though thought may be solitary, it must still be articulate.[100] One cannot *think* (not even in a dialogue with oneself) unless there are structures that allow respect for and exchange of opinions with others (which one then might mimic in one's solitude). The ultimate prospect, then, at the end of any road through the public realm that is indifferent to structure, is what Arendt referred to in *The Life of the Mind* as "the possible interconnectedness of non-thought and evil."[101] To saddle her with that indifference, for the sake of a glamorous politics of self-expression, is to neglect the cautionary point of almost everything she wrote about the modern world.

NOTES

1 Aristotle, *The Politics* (Cambridge: Cambridge University Press, 1988), 3 (1253a): "[M]an is by nature a political animal."
2 For doubts about Arendt's reading of Aristotle, see Bernard Yack, *The Problems of a Political Animal* (Berkeley: University of California Press, 1993), pp. 9–13.
3 Arendt, *OR* (Harmondsworth: Penguin Books, 1973), p. 131.
4 See Bonnie Honig, *Political Theory and the Displacement of Politics* (Ithaca: Cornell University Press, 1993), pp. 76ff.
5 Arendt, *HC*, p. 41.
6 See George Kateb, *Hannah Arendt: Politics, Conscience, Evil* (Totowa, NJ: Rowman and Allenheld, 1984), pp. 20ff., drawing on Hannah Arendt, "Civil Disobedience," in *CR*, esp. pp. 96–102 and Arendt, *OR*, chapter 5.
7 Honig, *Political Theory*, pp. 96–109.
8 *OR*, p. 232.
9 See, e.g., Arendt, *OT*, pp. 115–116 and 251ff. I accept Margaret Canovan's suggestion in *Hannah Arendt: A Reinterpretation of her Political Thought* (Cambridge: Cambridge University Press, 1992), p. 63, that *OT* should be given more prominence in discussions of Arendt's philosophy.
10 See Arendt, "Civil Disobedience," p. 89.
11 Arendt, *HC*, p. 194.
12 Ibid., p. 194. (Cf. Rousseau's law-giver in *The Social Contract*, Book II, chapter 7.) See also Arendt on the craftsman-like work of Plato's philosopher-king in *HC*, p. 226–227.
13 See *OR*, p. 208 and *HC*, p. 188.
14 *HC*, p. 198. See also Hannah Arendt, "What is Freedom?" in *BPF*, pp. 153–154.
15 *OR*, p. 175.
16 See also Stephen Holmes, *Passions and Constraint: On the Theory of Liberal Democracy* (Chicago: University of Chicago Press, 1995), p. 163.
17 Cf. *HC*, p. 52.
18 Arendt, *EJ*, pp. 262–263.
19 *OR*, p. 164.
20 Ibid., p. 157. And she emphasized more generally the importance of positive law as a tangible social reality, compared with the merely notional existence of the *ius naturale*: see *OT*, p. 464.
21 *OR*, pp. 125–126 and 145–146
22 Cited in *OR*, p. 146.
23 *OR*, p. 126. See also *HC*, p. 191, where Arendt talks of "the various limitations and boundaries we find in every body politic."
24 *EJ*, p. 264. See also her discussion of the plight of the stateless in a comprehensive system of states in *OT*, pp. 293–294
25 The identity she has in mind "relates not so much . . . to a piece of land as to the space between individuals in a group whose members are bound to, and at the same time separated and protected from, each other by all kinds of relationships, based on a common language, religion, a common history, customs, and laws. Such relationships become spatially manifest insofar as they themselves constitute the space wherein the different members of a group relate to and have intercourse with each other." (*EJ*, pp. 262–263). See also *HC*, p. 19 where Arendt talks of "the

territorial boundaries which protect and make possible the physical identity of a people." For her hesitations about national identity, see *OT*, pp. 230–231.

26 *OT*, p. 126.

27 Rousseau, *The Social Contract*, Book II, chapter 8–9.

28 *OR*, p. 275.

29 See *OT*, pp. 297–302.

30 In *HC*, p. 32, Arendt suggested that equality "presupposed . . . the existence of unequals." See also Kateb, *Hannah Arendt*, pp. 152–153.

31 See *HC*, pp. 2, 28–37, and 244.

32 For an intriguing discussion, see Hanna Fenichel Pitkin, *The Attack of the Blob: Hannah Arendt's Concept of the Social* (Chicago: The University of Chicago Press, 1998).

33 *OT*, pp. 465–457.

34 Ibid.

35 See the account of the Mayflower Compact in *OR*, p. 167.

36 Compare the remarks on Hobbesian philosophy in *OT*, pp. 139–147.

37 *OR*, pp. 141–154 and 218.

38 Ibid., pp. 59ff. But see Arendt, "Thoughts on Politics and Revolution," in *CR*, pp. 212–214, for the significance of legal obstacles to "expropriation," and *HC*, pp. 70–73, for an account of the importance to individuals of the "darker ground" of privacy.

39 *OR*, p. 33. Compare Arendt's more ambivalent comment in "On Violence," in *CR*, p. 178: "The dissenters and resisters in the East demand free speech and thought as the preliminary conditions for political action; the rebels in the West live under conditions where these preliminaries no longer open the channels . . . for the meaningful exercise of freedom."

40 See *OT*, p. 460.

41 Ibid., p. 465.

42 See the discussion of Arendt on the debilitating hysteria of the McCarthy period, in Pitkin, *Attack of the Blob*, pp. 102–104

43 *OT*, pp. 290–302. I don't mean that Arendt rejects the international dimension altogether: see, for example, her remarks on *consensus juris* in *OT*, p. 462, and on Adolf Eichmann as *hostis generis humani* in *EJ*, pp. 260ff.

44 *OR*, pp. 148 and 154.

45 Cf. Honig, *Political Theory*, p. 76.

46 *OR*, p. 174.

47 Ibid., p. 173.

48 See *HC*, p. 197.

49 Ibid., p. 189.

50 See *EJ*, p. 289. See also Arendt, "On Violence," p. 137.

51 Arendt, *HC*, p. 95.

52 *OR*, p. 220.

53 *HC*, pp. 95 and 183; see also Seyla Benhabib, *The Reluctant Modernism of Hannah Arendt* (Thousand Oaks, CA: Sage Publications, 1996), 112–113.

54 Kateb, *Hannah Arendt*, 158; see also Dana Villa, "Hannah Arendt: Modernity, Alienation and Critique," in Craig Calhoun and John McGowan, eds., *Hannah Arendt and the Meaning of Politics* (Minneapolis: University of Minnesota Press, 1997), pp. 186–187.

55 Arendt, "Truth and Politics," in *BPF*, pp. 256–257.
56 *OR*, p. 93.
57 Ibid., pp. 30–31.
58 See the reflections on the wording of the Declaration of Independence in "Truth and Politics," pp. 246–247.
59 *OR*, p. 278: "Their title rested on nothing but the confidence of their equals, and this equality was not natural but political, it was nothing they had been born with; it was the equality of those who had committed themselves to, and now were engaged in, a joint enterprise."
60 Ibid., pp. 106–108.
61 Ibid., p. 71.
62 See the discussion of connections between "human nature" theories and "race" theories in *OT*, pp. 234–235.
63 Arendt accepts the view of James Madison: "When men exercise their reason coolly and freely on a variety of distinct questions, they inevitably fall into different opinions on some of them. When they are governed by a common passion, their opinions, if they are so to be called, will be the same." See *OR*, p. 225.
64 Arendt, "Truth and Politics," p. 241.
65 Arendt's most thoughtful discussions of this process is in *LKPP*, pp. 70ff. See also the discussion in Jeremy Waldron, "Kant's Legal Positivism," *Harvard Law Review* 109 (1996), at pp. 1559–1560.
66 *OR*, p. 225.
67 *OR*, pp. 86–87.
68 See Jeremy Waldron, *Law and Disagreement* (Oxford: Clarendon Press, 1999), pp. 73–82.
69 See also her discussion of statelessness in *OT*, p. 296, as "the deprivation of a place in the world which makes opinions significant and actions effective."
70 Arendt, "Thoughts on Politics and Revolution," in *CR*, p. 232.
71 See *OR*, pp. 143 and 269. See also Kateb, *Hannah Arendt*, p. 118.
72 *OR*, p. 253.
73 See, e.g., Arendt, "Thoughts on Politics and Revolution," p. 253.
74 *OR*, p. 164.
75 Ibid.
76 Ibid., p. 236 (quoting John Selden).
77 Ibid., p. 279. Cf. Arendt's comments on "elitism" at *OR* 275–280.
78 Ibid., p. 278.
79 Ibid., p. 227. There she also observes that "limitation to a small and chosen body of citizens was to serve as the great purifier of both interests and opinion, to guard 'against the confusion of a multitude.'" It is not clear whether this is Arendt's own view or that of the American framers she is discussing.
80 See *OT*, pp. 115 and 250–266.
81 *OR*, p. 228.
82 See Canovan, *Hannah Arendt*, p. 35.
83 Arendt draws on Nietzsche's argument in *The Genealogy of Morals* (Cambridge: Cambridge University Press, 1994): "To breed an animal which is able to make promises – is that not precisely the paradoxical task which nature has set herself with regard to humankind."

84 *OR*, p. 167. She continues (p. 173): "No theory, theological or political or philosophical, but their own decision to leave the Old World behind and to venture forth into an enterprise entirely of their own led into a sequence of acts and occurrences in which they would have perished, had they not turned their minds to the matter long and intensely enough to discover, almost by inadvertence, the elementary grammar of political action . . ."
85 Ibid., p. 206: "It is in the very nature of a beginning to carry with itself a measure of complete arbitrariness."
86 Ibid., p. 201ff. Cf. Jefferson's proposal to provide in the Constitution itself "for its revision at stated periods," cited on p. 234.
87 Hence Arendt's insistence, ibid., p. 182: "Neither compact nor promise . . . are sufficient to assure perpetuity, that is, to bestow upon the affairs of men that measure of stability without which they would be unable to build a world for their posterity, destined and designed to outlast their own mortal lives." See also *HC*, p. 55: "If the world is to contain a public space, it cannot be erected for one generation and planned for them only; it must transcend the life-span of mortal man."
88 Arendt, "On Violence," p. 193 (appendix xi). See also Arendt, *LM*, vol. II, *Willing*, p. 201.
89 I could have mentioned also her views on open government (*OR*, p. 253), institutional transparency (*OT*, p. 403), the rule of law (*OT*, pp. 243–244), procedural guarantees (*EJ*, p. 260), bicameralism (*OR*, p. 226) and judicial review of legislation (*OR*, pp. 200 and 226–231).
90 *OR*, pp. 232ff.
91 See Arendt, "On Violence," p. 178.
92 *OR*, p. 239.
93 Christian Meier, *Caesar*, trans. David McLintock (New York: Basic Books, 1995), pp. 358–359.
94 Kateb, *Hannah Arendt*, p. 31.
95 Honig, *Political Theory*, p. 80.
96 Arendt, "What is Freedom?" p. 153.
97 Especially, *HC*, pp. 205–206.
98 Meier's own judgment is complicated by his understanding that other participants in Roman politics failed to grasp that the institutions needed to be "seen" in a way that permitted the question of their restructuring to be raised: see Meier, *Caesar*, pp. 360–363.
99 *HC*, p. 53 (regarding the contempt for institutions in modern mass society).
100 Cf. the discussion in Kateb, *Hannah Arendt*, pp. 36–38.
101 Arendt, *LM*, vol. I, *Thinking*, p. 179.

11

ALBRECHT WELLMER

Arendt on revolution

In *On Revolution* Hannah Arendt tried to settle accounts with both the liberal-democratic and Marxist traditions; that is, with the two dominant traditions of modern political thought which, in one way or another, can be traced back to the Enlightenment.[1] Her basic thesis is that both liberal democrats and Marxists have misunderstood the drama of modern revolutions because they have not understood that what was actually revolutionary about these revolutions was their attempt to create a *constitutio libertatis* – a repeatedly frustrated attempt to establish a political space of public freedom in which people, as free and equal citizens, would take their common concerns into their own hands. Both the liberals and the Marxists harbored a conception of the political according to which the final goal of politics was something *beyond* politics – whether this be the unconstrained pursuit of private happiness, the realization of social justice, or the free association of producers in a classless society. Arendt's critique of Marxist politics has already become a *locus classicus* and requires no further justification. Her critique of the liberal and social democracies of the modern industrial societies seems more provocative from the point of view of the present. I want to raise the question of whether her provocation remains a genuine one.

Arendt develops the basic categories in terms of which she re-narrates the history of modern revolutions on the model of the American Revolution – in her view the only half-way successful revolution in modern times. Only in the American Revolution was the ultimate goal of all revolutionary peoples – the constitution of a space of public freedom – fulfilled in a large modern state, thanks mainly to fortunate circumstances, a long tradition of local self-government, and the political ingenuity and insight of the founding fathers. Moreover – and this is key for Arendt – in the American Revolution a space of freedom was established not only in the "negative" sense of a constitutional guarantee of equal basic *rights* for citizens, but also in the "positive," strictly political sense of a federal system of institutions in which the self-government of the citizens – from the level of local self-government to the level of the national polity – became a reality, one anchored in the habits of citizens and experienced ever anew in everyday praxis.

It was also on the basis of the American model that Arendt developed her idea of the council system as the political alternative to the traditional liberal-democratic and Marxist conceptions of the state. In the great revolutions following the American Revolution, in particular the French and Russian revolutions, Arendt claims that the idea of a council system was always rediscovered spontaneously by the revolutionary people, only to be repressed – according to the same brutal logic – by a revolutionary elite that had come to power, or by a conservative establishment that had regained it. Only the American Revolution led to the establishment of a federal system of self-government, in which something of the tradition of local self-administration was preserved, as well as the memory of the "public happiness" experienced by free and equal citizens acting together. Such "public happiness" had been experienced in the townships and wards before the Revolution, and on the national level during the founding of the American republic.

Of course, as Arendt observes, shortly after the American Revolution tendencies toward the establishment of a state based on partisan political parties grew increasingly strong; these would ultimately provide the basis for modern mass democracy. For Arendt, the distinguishing characteristic of the latter type of political system is the fact that its citizens are free only in the "negative" sense. They have lost their political freedom – the freedom of self-government based on common action and shared deliberation – to their delegates, to large political parties, to representative bodies, to a powerful bureaucracy and (lastly) to organized interest groups. According to Arendt, the Marxist dictatorships born of revolutionary socialism to a certain extent only drew the consequences of a development already occurring within the liberal-democratic party system: they merely completed its political infantilization of citizens and depoliticization of the political. Arendt perceives the latter as an inherent trait of modern mass democracy and, as such, a mortal danger for freedom in the modern world.

What is interesting in Arendt's theory is not her idea of a "depoliticized" mass democracy (not a particularly original diagnosis), but the way she underpins this idea by means of a bold conceptual strategy, one which is intended to question fundamentally the political self-understanding of modern liberal democracies; to question, as it were, the depth grammar of modern political discourse.

Political freedom, Arendt argues, was the secret center of gravity in all modern revolutions; but it was a *secret* center, since the idea itself was hardly ever adequately articulated in modern political theory and discourse. The result was that the most important revolutionary events of the modern age were usually perceived and reflected on by theorists, by "common sense," and even by the participants themselves in a confused and distorted way. Arendt's re-interpretation of the history of modern revolutions and her critique of the liberal tradition are therefore radical in a *philosophical* sense of the word. What she demands of her readers is a break with the central categories by means of which modern democratic societies have understood themselves politically. By setting these categories in motion and arranging them anew, Arendt tries to articulate an idea of political freedom which, in her view, was latently at work in all modern revolutions, but which was always at odds with the mainstream of political thought. Arendt's basic objection to the modern tradition of political thought is that it was forgetful of politics and the experience of political action among equal yet diverse peers; it therefore was incapable of articulating a robust idea of political freedom.

Arendt's political thought can best be described as the site of a dramatic encounter between Aristotle, Kant, and Heidegger, all of whom she brings face to face with the catastrophes of our time. Arendt's recourse to Aristotle, for instance, amounts, on the one hand, to a radical critique of Heidegger's politics (or antipolitics), while, on the other, it rests on a deeply Heideggerian rethinking of Aristotelian categories. In a way, she writes the political philosophy which, in her view, Heidegger, as a post-Kantian thinker, *should* have written (rather than flirting with the Nazis, as he did). The profound originality of Arendt's political thought cannot be grasped unless we see how she uses Aristotelian, Kantian, and Heideggerian categories to create a new constellation, revealing herself in the process as a deeply *modern* thinker rather than the nostalgic one she is often thought to be.

Traces of a Heideggerian rethinking of Aristotelian categories become obvious when Arendt describes the *constitutio libertatis* as the opening up of a common world; as a break with the continuum of history; as a radically new beginning. The constitution of a space of public freedom appears as a contingent performative deed executed by persons who decide to act together as equals. So viewed, this space necessarily appears as limited and local, as "fenced-in," to use Arendt's words.[2] It is, in essence, a finite space, the shining forth (as it were) of a light in which, for brief historical moments, the creaturely life of human beings "gleams" and opens itself onto a public world: a public world in which the actors can appear in their irreducible individuality and, in acting together, can begin something new; and in which the common world (the habitat of our ordinary private and social life) is endowed with a meaning and significance it normally lacks. At the end of *On Revolution*, Arendt recalls Sophocles' Theseus, through whose mouth the playwright tells us "what it was that enabled ordinary men, young and old, to bear life's burden: it was the *polis*, the space of men's free deeds and living words, which could endow life with splendor – *ton bion lampron poieisthai*."[3]

Arendt's thesis that political freedom can only exist in a limited space seems to mark a radical break with the liberal-democratic tradition and with its universalism of human and civil rights. And so it does; what has to be understood, however, is what this break really means. Arendt does not dispute the universalism of human rights in a moral – that is, pre-political – sense; and she even acknowledges the internal link – characteristic of Kant and the liberal tradition – between the universalism of human rights and a modern conception of civil rights. She takes it to be a human (that is, moral) right to have civil or citizens' rights. However, in contrast to the liberal tradition, Arendt considers such rights not as the *substance*, but only as a necessary *precondition* of political freedom. According to her, it is a *fateful error* to confuse the constitutionally based guarantee of basic civil rights with the constitution of political freedom.

Thus, while freedom may still be considered as something universal in the context of the modern constitutional state's *negative* freedoms (namely, as a *rule* of law which can claim to be generally binding[4]), the same does not hold for the *positive*, that is, *political* freedom we find in a republican form of government (the freedom to be "participators in government"). This latter kind of freedom Arendt more or less directly opposes to the universalist grammar of modern liberal political discourse. Yet there are numerous passages in *On Revolution* where traces of a universalist understanding of the idea of political freedom appear in Arendt's thought. These traces indicate that the revolutionary universalism of the French and Russian Revolutions had left its mark after all. Thus, Arendt's theoretical stance departs from standard republican or "communitarian" arguments in that it grounds positive political freedom in a universal human *possibility*.

One especially telling trace of Arendt's latent universalism is found at the conclusion of *On Revolution*, where she refers to a continuity leading from the American Revolution, by way of the Revolution in France of 1789 and the Commune of 1871 and the initial establishment of *soviets* in Russia in 1917, to the attempts to form councils in the Hungarian Revolution of 1956, and then remarks that "[a]s in the case of the early covenants, 'cosociations,' and confederations in the colonial history of North America, we see here how the federal principle, the principle of league and alliance among separate units, *arises out of the elementary conditions of action itself*."[5] What Arendt is saying here is that the ideal of political freedom, in a practical if not a theoretical sense, is inherent in the "elementary conditions of action itself." This is Arendt's own version of a revolutionary universalism, though it remains unclear (at least at first glance) how this universalism relates to liberalism's conception of human and civil rights.

What, then, does Arendt's break with the liberal-democratic framework really amount to? She herself often articulates it in terms of an opposition between "direct" and "representative" democracy, that is, between a system of councils and a parliamentary party system. However, while critically illuminating, this opposition is highly misleading. If taken literally, it would represent a naiveté on her part (the naiveté of political anarchism). The political institutions of complex modern societies can hardly be constructed anew on the simple model of a system of councils. I therefore take her idea of the council system to be a metaphor for a network of autonomous or partially autonomous institutions, organizations, and associations, in each of which something like the self-government of free and equal participants takes place – in each case in different ways, with different aims, and with different means for recruiting new members: a network whose units might be both horizontally and vertically connected, related to or dependent upon one another.

Complex structures of this kind can represent both the institutions of a federal political system (from the local to the national level) and the associations, organizations, and institutions of a democratic "civil society," in contrast to more "formal" political institutions. I think that with her concept of the council system Arendt must actually have meant *both*: the political institutions of a federal political system *and* a network of autonomous or partially autonomous associations and organizations along the lines of civil society. The joint action of free and equal individuals is, in principle, just as possible in the self-administration of the universities or the self-organization of citizens' initiatives as it is in the formal institutions of the federal system. Arendt's basic point, then, is that the taste for freedom and the experience of freedom can only come from diverse forms of active participation in common concerns. The idea of political freedom, therefore, has to be spelled out in terms of a network of institutions and associations, formal and informal; moreover, it must be articulated in such a way that it becomes a lived experience for those involved, "common issues" being (as it were) physically tangible to participants, who are then able to negotiate them in an autonomous manner. Viewed in this way, it seems obvious that political freedom means something different and something more than the constitutionally based guarantee of basic civil rights. Such rights are, as Arendt observes, a *precondition* of freedom, but not political freedom itself.

Here it is important to note that Arendt's idea of political freedom is framed in accordance with a conception of the modern age in which the appeal to tradition no longer resonates. She preserves a characteristic distance towards her favorite examples (the Athenian *polis*, but also the early years of the American republic), a distance characteristic of post-metaphysical thought. Her criticisms of it aside, what links her to liberalism is an awareness of the irrevocable break in the power of tradition as the transition to modernity is made; a break above all in the sense that tradition could no longer serve as the source of legitimacy and authority. Arendt described this break as the shattering of the "Roman" trinity of authority, religion, and tradition, which had been the foundation of the political up until the beginning of modern times.[6] In affirming this break, she is closer to liberalism than to contemporary communitarians. Accordingly, her critique of liberalism does not simply rest on a nostalgic appeal to either the Greek *polis* or the virtues of civic republicanism. Rather, it rests on a deconstruction of the whole "metaphysical" tradition of political thought starting with Plato and Aristotle. Her re-reading and critique of the Western tradition of political philosophy is therefore radical in Heidegger's sense, even as it attempts to set his deconstruction of metaphysics on its feet, and to turn it around politically.

What this means, in effect, is that Arendt traces the shortcomings of liberal thought – its forgetfulness of the political in favor of the "social," the "private," and an instrumental conception of action – back to a tendency deep within Western thought, one already manifest in Plato and Aristotle. This is the tendency to distort the essential character of action (*praxis*) and the political. Thus, even Aristotle, to whom Arendt owes the distinction between action and production, *praxis* and *poiesis*, had, in her view, ultimately subjected the realm of politics to standards deriving from the private or social realms.[7] In contrast to both liberalism and the tradition, Arendt wants to define and defend the *autonomy* of the political, and in two senses of the word. First, unlike the private and the social realms, the political sphere is autonomous in the sense that political action is or can be meaningful in itself, and does not rely on the presence of a purpose beyond politics (for example, the preservation of life, morality, or the pursuit of private happiness by individuals). Secondly, the political sphere is autonomous in the sense that it has no normative foundation provided, as it were, in advance, from some sphere beyond itself.

It is easy to see that, by asserting that the political sphere is autonomous in these senses, Arendt is attacking the liberal tradition, and from two directions at once. Ultimately, her criticism is directed at the central role played by human and civil rights within the liberal framework. Such rights provide a normative and indeed trans-political basis for liberal thought, justifying an understanding of politics according to which its purpose or *telos* lies in the securing of individuals' basic rights and in the promotion of their well-being. Of course, it is not the case that Arendt wants to deploy her concept of the political *against* the moral foundation (or the transitive purpose) of the liberal framework (in this, she differs from another thinker of "autonomous" politics, Carl Schmitt). Rather, her basic point is that the categories of liberal thought, derived from such a foundation, are simply not up to the task of supplying a concept of the political which adequately captures the basic experiences and phenomenological features of this realm.

For Arendt, "politics" is the joint action of free and equal citizens, acting together in a space of *public* appearances and *public* liberty. Only in such a space does the persuasive power contained in the speech and judgment of citizens trump the "scientific certainty" (and technical competence) of experts; only in such a space does the specifically human capacity to act, to begin something new, achieve its fullest reality; only in such a space does the basic fact of human *plurality*, which is constitutive of human life itself, become fully manifest and a force for the creation (and preservation) of a common world. Finally, only in such a space can political *power* be generated, since this arises from the "worldly in-between space" that initiatory action opens up between political actors. "The grammar of action: that action is the only human faculty that demands a plurality of men, and the syntax of power: that power is the only human attribute which applies solely to the worldly in-between space by which men are mutually related, combine in the act of foundation by virtue of the making and keeping of promises."[8] According to Arendt, it is through the constitution of such a space of public freedom that human life gains a meaning beyond the contingency and fragility of its creaturely existence; that it is delivered from the darkness of the merely private or social sphere and drawn into the light of a common world.

The difficulties raised by Arendt's concept of the political reside in its latent ambiguity. One can understand her conception as being part of a radical critique of modernity, such as we find in Heidegger. Viewed in this light, the Arendtian critique of the modern "forgetfulness of politics" would then hinge on an invocation of experiences and possibilities which remain thoroughly submerged in contemporary liberal democracies; experiences which have resurfaced only fleetingly during revolutionary or quasi-revolutionary moments in the second half of the twentieth century (such as the Hungarian Revolution of 1956, the civil rights movement in the United States, or various student movements from the 1960s). Yet the price of such a "Heideggerian" interpretation of Arendt – as one can see from Dana Villa's otherwise impressive book – would be (to put the matter paradoxically) a depoliticization of the Arendtian concept of the political.[9] This concept would no longer have any *recognizable* connection to the political experiences and possibilities inherent in the everyday life of complex democratic societies: politics would become the "other" of the political as we know it.

There are certainly textual grounds for such an interpretation in Arendt's work. Yet her political philosophy clearly aims at something other than a "totalizing critique" of the modern age, as is shown by her many affirmative references to the American Revolution's *constitutio libertatis*. This suggests a different sort of interpretation, one which attempts to integrate the Arendtian concept of the political into contemporary democratic theory (for example, the recent work of Jürgen Habermas).[10] This alternative type of interpretation is not without its dangers, however, since it threatens to squeeze Arendt's criticisms of liberal democracy into the parameters set by a discourse theory of democracy. Although, in what follows, I too will take the path of this second kind of interpretation, and attempt to re-interpret Arendt's idea of the political in terms amenable to contemporary democratic theory, I will also try to highlight the truly original features of her concepts of revolution and politics, as well as her criticism of the basic framework of liberal democracy, all the while resisting any hasty assimilation of these concepts to Habermas's discourse theory.

Let me begin by schematically contrasting the relation between universalism and particularism as it figures in Arendt's thought (on the one hand), and in the liberal tradition (on the other). I have already indicated that Arendt accepts the Kantian universalism of human and civil rights, even as she severs (so to speak) the links between human and civil rights in the liberal tradition, and civil rights and the idea of political freedom in the democratic tradition. Arendt interprets the idea of human rights in a purely moral (that is to say, a pre-political) way, and treats the idea of civil rights as pertaining merely to the legal framework of the polity, the "rule of law" (or *Rechtsstaat*). As noted above, these moves are connected with a "particularism" that characterizes her concept of the political. In Arendt, however, this particularism is linked, somewhat paradoxically, to an anthropological universalism. The lesser importance she grants to human and civil rights signifies (against the strongest representatives of political liberalism) that there is a decisive limitation on the political *meaning* of such rights. This refers us, once again, to her assumption that, on the conceptual level at least, there is a hiatus between the idea of civil rights and that of political freedom.

Against this conceptual move, both John Rawls and Jürgen Habermas have claimed (with good reason) that liberal and democratic rights have to be thought of as linked to one another in the following way: private and public autonomy refer to one another conceptually; they complement each other and cannot, in the end, even be conceived of separately. Yet difficulties arise. It is clear, for example, that Rawls's concept of "public autonomy" does not refer to the same thing as Arendt's "public freedom." Nevertheless, it seems to me to be beyond doubt that at least Habermas brings to light some of the democratic potential of Kantian (moral) universalism, a potential which Arendt largely overlooks and which points to an internal connection between human rights, civil rights, and modern political freedom. I shall come back to this problem.

First, however, I want to look at a problem of particularism inherent in the tradition of liberal democracy itself. It is precisely when one understands the Kantian universalism of human and civil rights in a strong Habermasian sense (that is, in the terms of a theory of democracy) that it becomes clear that there is already a tension between particularism and universalism in the liberal linkage of human and civil rights. This tension is of a different order from the one which I alluded to in Arendt. Rightly understood, however, it has consequences for her republican conception as well as for how we understand liberal democracy. The tension I have in mind results from the fact that the Kantian universalist transformation of natural human rights into positive civil rights simultaneously renders these human rights particular. Civil rights can only be the rights of those who belong; hence, it is no accident that the realization of human rights *as* civil rights in the course of the French Revolution was, at the same time, the European nation-state's hour of birth. That real conflict arises from this tension between the irreducible particularism of *civil* rights and the universalism of *human* rights is shown today wherever the particular interests of democratic societies come into conflict with these same societies' rhetoric of human rights. Yet the notion of human rights provides the foundation for the Western democracies' concept of legitimacy. Now, I would like to assert, without being able to support the claim here,[11] that the Kantian depth grammar of liberal-democratic discourse admits of only *one* solution to this tension between universalism and particularism which penetrates to the foundations of modern democracies: namely, the establishment of a liberal and democratic world society, in which the human and civil rights of *all* citizens are protected in accordance with the idea of social justice.[12]

Human rights, civil rights, justice: these are the primary concepts which rule the grammar of liberal-democratic political discourse. The universalism of this grammar is, in many respects, also that of Marx. The Marxist conviction that the revolution could only succeed as a world revolution represents (as it were) merely the materialist counterpart to the Kantian idea of a world society. Arendt was therefore not entirely wrong to draw liberal democracy and Marxism so close to one another, to present them as two complementary versions of a single historical perspective, so to speak.

Unlike Arendt, who focuses on the negative aspects of this convergence, I want to highlight the continuing significance of the historical challenge implicit in it. This challenge consists in the fact that the respective universalisms of liberalism and Marxism not only refer to one another; they also sketch the horizon of the modern age considered as a *political* problem. This problem can be formulated in terms of the collision of the material universalism of the economy (and technology) with the morally unsurpassable idea of human rights. The *material* universalism of the economy and the *normative* universalism of human rights can, it seems to me, only be brought into accord within the structure of a liberal and democratic world society (which, obviously, is something quite different than a world *state*).

The tension between particularism and universalism in Arendt's idea of revolution is of a different kind from the one which I have just discussed. Arendt's concern is not with justice but with (political) freedom. Hence, her brand of universalism is neither the normative universalism of human rights nor the inherent universalism of the modern economy. Rather, it is the universalism of a human *possibility*: the possibility of creating, in the midst of contingent historical circumstances, a space of public freedom; a space in which no law of progress and no eschatology holds sway; a space which no extra-political normative foundation secures or justifies. The *possibility* of political freedom is universal, insofar as it is inherent in the "elementary conditions of action"; whereas every *actual* constitution of a space of public freedom is necessarily the constitution of a limited, "fenced-in" space of freedom, the result of the contingent "revolutionary" action of a particular group of people acting in concert.

Here it is important to see that Arendt's rhetoric of the "opening up of a world" through the constitution of a space of political freedom is no mere *façon de parler*. Institutions of freedom must be *invented* (and their preservation in some sense amounts to their continuous re-invention); the establishment of such institutions can be more or less successful or fail, and their invention, where successful, will bring about a new grammar for political discourse, new experiences and attitudes – while conversely they remain dependent on such experiences and attitudes, on judgment and political virtue. Thus, the establishment of free institutions – the opening of a new space for freedom – cannot be equated with the creation (and institutional actualization) of individual or civil rights, since it requires that these rights be recognized and exercised according to a standard which is, in an important sense, external to them.

This, it seems to me, is Arendt's main argument: the criterion of "public freedom," which distinguishes direct from merely representative democracy, cannot be derived from the principle of equal rights in a democracy. This fact marks the irreducibility of Arendt's concept of political freedom, which includes the moment or idea of "beginning anew" as well as a strong sense of the "fragility" which attends all political action, and which constantly threatens freedom's continued existence. Because political freedom can be realized only through *particular* institutions or forms of organization, and because there is no normative principle which imposes the constitution of political freedom as a *duty* upon human beings, such freedom exists only within a limited, "fenced-in" space. This is the particularism of political freedom. A contingent, performative moment – which Arendt tries to conceptualize in terms of "beginning anew" and the idea of "mutual promises and agreements" – is an essential element of this freedom; as are inclination, experience, judgment, and fortunate circumstances. Unlike the demand for equal rights for all, none of these elements can be rendered universal by means of a normative principle.

The extent to which and the forms in which public freedom can become a reality in the modern world therefore depend on historical contingencies as well as on cultural traditions; on material circumstances as well as the commitment, imagination, and courage of the particular individuals involved. Moreover, once established, the institutions of public freedom always have to preserve and assert themselves against the profit motive of capital, the claims to power of political elites, and the authoritarian logic of the bureaucratic system. Yet despite this emphasis on the crucial role played by contingent actions and conditions, Arendt insists with equal vehemence that the possibility to realize political freedom as well as the desire to do so are inherent in the "elementary conditions of action." This makes political freedom into a project of *all* human beings, one possible in all times and places and hence, as it were, "natural." This clarification allows us to see that no contradiction is involved when Arendt attempts to combine conceptually the essentially "local" and particular character of the space of public freedom with the universal possibility that the revolutionary desire for freedom might seize "perhaps all the earth's peoples."

Yet it remains unclear how Arendt's (as it were) retracted and nearly "empirical" revolutionary universalism relates to the universalism of either the liberal or the Marxist tradition. I asserted that these last two kinds of universalism – the universalism of human rights and of economic and technological transformation – define an unsurpassable horizon for us and are in no way called into question by Arendt's arguments. As a factual matter, the universalism of the economy and technology cannot be eliminated from the world; nor is there any plausible alternative to the normative universalism inherent in the liberal-democratic framework of rights. The establishment of a liberal and democratic world society, in which everyone's human rights would have become an institutional reality, is the single alternative to the barbarism of new world wars. Hence, it represents a long-term condition for the survival of currently existing democratic societies. But what Arendt would have us see is that such a vision of a liberal world society does not exclude the danger of a civilized form of barbarism, in which thoroughly pacified beings find themselves stripped of the distinctively human capacity for action and the power to shape a shared world.

However, as I indicated above, there is a way of conceiving of liberal democracy such that one simply cannot deny that it contains at least *some* elements of the Arendtian idea of political freedom. In addition, I now want to note that, in stressing the "particularity" of political freedom, Arendt overlooked (and probably had to overlook) a tendency toward particularism which corresponds to the one inherent in the liberal-democratic framework's endorsement of the nation-state: a tendency towards particularism which already exists *within* the various nation-states. However, if both these positions are right, one would have to object that Arendt did not properly understand either the significance, or the potential, of the liberal-democratic framework. As a result, her simple opposition of representative and direct democracy – of liberal democracy and republican freedom – contains something not fully thought through, an unresolved problem. With this realization, we are in a position to see how the liberal democratic and Arendtian perspectives mutually challenge each other, and in a potentially fruitful fashion. For, on the one hand, Arendt's concept of political freedom clearly presents a challenge to contemporary theories of democracy; while on the other, the more sophisticated of these theories underline the limits of her thought and of its grounding oppositions.

The strength of the Arendtian challenge to contemporary political philosophy results from the nearly complete failure of liberal, social democratic, or even socialist political thought to offer categories through which the domain of public freedom (which is, after all, *essential* to liberal democracy) could be adequately conceptualized and discussed. The political theory of John Rawls is symptomatic of this failure. It seems obvious that when Rawls admits the interdependence of private and public autonomy (as he recently did in a debate with Habermas[13]), what he means by "public autonomy" is something different from what Arendt means by "public freedom." Rawls conceives of public autonomy essentially in terms of the *right* to vote and to stand for election; in terms of representative bodies, and democratic decision-making procedures, etc. The concepts he employs to sketch this "autonomy" are, as a result, insufficient for either reformulating or assimilating the Arendtian ideas of "direct" democracy, the joint action of citizens, and what I, following Habermas, would like to call a *communicative* public freedom.

Conversely, what is lacking among the theoreticians of communitarianism, who certainly stand closer to Arendt's republican ideas than does Rawls, is Arendt's radicalism, which immunizes her against all regressive dreams of community and the values which are supposed to create it, be they national, religious, or simply ethnic in nature. It was the potential of the new, of what had never yet been, that interested her in the freedom of the republics: the *opening up* of a shared world, not the return to one past. In this regard, her thinking was truly that of a revolutionary.

The challenge posed to Arendt by the more sophisticated theories of democracy consists in showing that her opposition of representative and direct democracy, liberal democracy and republican freedom, is deeply problematic, if not simply naive. Viewed from this perspective, Arendt's deconstruction of modern political thought seems itself to be in need of a deconstruction, especially if it is to engage contemporary political philosophy in a constructive manner.

The decisive objection to Arendt concerns her tendency to reify or "concretize" the opposition between representative democracy and republican freedom. This tendency reveals itself in an ambiguity found in her strenuous attempts to establish the autonomy of the political. Earlier I pointed out that Arendt considered this autonomy to be based, in the first instance, upon the irreducibility of the primary categories she draws on to elucidate the idea of public freedom: namely, joint action, plurality, power, etc. These aspects of public freedom cannot be *reduced* to moral, social, or legal categories. But, at the same time, Arendt also understands the autonomy of the political in the sense of its being a separate sphere with, as it were, *contents* of its own. This corresponds to her attempt to make a clear-cut distinction between *political* problems or questions and those pertaining to the spheres of morality, social welfare, private life, the economy, or the protection of basic human rights. The insistence on the autonomy of the political in this second sense dramatically illustrates Arendt's tendency to reify or concretize otherwise useful distinctions. This disturbing tendency is also apparent in her inclination to take the idea of a council system literally, while stripping it of all the social, administrative, and economic responsibilities which it had always taken upon itself whenever one emerged during a time of revolution.

These "concretizing" tendencies within Arendt's idea of authentic politics are the great weakness of her political theory, as well as the reason why some of her recent interpreters are prone to give her conception a non- or even anti-political reading (Heidegger's late revenge). Now, the public sphere is certainly not autonomous in the sense that it can simply turn its back on the problem of securing and institutionalizing basic human rights, or on the problems of social justice and of the economy. For even if we grant that public freedom is something other than negative liberty, or the protection of the rights of individuals, or social justice, or an efficient administration, the political sphere would still (so to speak) be floating in air if it did not *transform* all these concerns into *political* matters, making them issues of common *public* concern.[14] In the case of individual rights and social justice, it is not simply a question of the necessary *preconditions* for political freedom in modern societies (as Arendt was ready, on occasion, to admit), but rather of the primary *objects* of political discourse, and thus of the kind of "common concerns" that ought to be dealt with (according to the Arendtian understanding) in the institutions of a free republic.

As soon as one concedes this, however, it becomes clear that individual freedom, social justice, and public freedom stand in a complex relation of interdependence to one another that requires political thought and discourse to constantly turn back and reflect on its own foundations and preconditions. Furthermore, if one takes into account the fact that, within the basic framework of liberal democracy, individual rights are already internally linked to the right to political participation, then it becomes clear that individual rights and social justice are not only essential elements of the "common concerns" dealt with by public institutions, but that they also *require* a sphere of public freedom if they are to be implemented in a democratically *legitimate* way at all. If this is correct, then Arendt's idea of public freedom can be made fruitful for politics and political theory only when it is no longer simply set in opposition to the liberal, democratic, or socialist traditions, but is (rather) inscribed *within* them, enabling a productive re-reading of their basic concepts and aims.

I want to clarify this criticism of Arendt with three points. The first addresses the interpretation and implementation of basic human rights; the second the problem of social justice; and the third the tendency toward particularism to be found in various actual public spaces of freedom (in Arendt's sense). With respect to each of these issues, Arendt tended to put forward what are, epistemologically speaking, rather naive simplifications. If these simplifications are done away with, then the appearance of any *conceptual* opposition between parliamentary or representative democracy and republican freedom should disappear as well.

(1) Concerning individual rights, Arendt was misled by the classical liberal theorists, who had (as Rawls still does) simply situated them *prior to* democratic discourse. Yet positioning them in this way is adequate only in a conceptual, and not in a political or institutional, sense. Speaking abstractly, basic individual rights are not "given" in the sense of being the axioms of a logical deduction; rather, they are "given" only in the sense of being principles for the making of just decisions, and they can exist only in a historically

concrete form, namely, as a system of institutions and interpretations. While they are *binding* on democratic discourse, they always have to be generated (first) in the midst of such discourse – that is, they have to be repeatedly interpreted and implemented anew. There can be no quasi-juridical body *above* or *beyond* democratic discourse to decide ultimately what the *proper* interpretation and practice of these basic rights ought to be. Hence, liberal society depends upon democratic institutions and a democratic public sphere *to the extent that* these secure and extend individual rights in a manner that satisfies the claims of democratic legitimacy.

That individual rights precede democratic discourse and yet can first assume their concrete legal form only *in* and *through* this discourse is what I would like to call the unavoidable practical circle of democratic discourse.[15] It is clear that historical experiences, as well as interpretations of basic human needs and conceptions of the good life (both of which change in the course of history) will all play a part in any particular polity's interpretation and implementation of basic rights. Such experiences, interpretations, and conceptions all stand in need of clarification within the discursive medium of a democratic public sphere if they are not to enter the legislative process in a dogmatic or arbitrary manner. If one reflects upon the sense in which individual rights can legitimately be said to be "already given," as well as upon the role which interpretation plays in their legal institutionalization and implementation, then the consequence can be drawn (from this unavoidable practical "circle") that the idea of equal individual rights already requires a sphere of public freedom in which citizens are able to make the *meaning* of their freedom and equality a matter of public concern and debate. Hence, "private" and "public" freedom, properly understood, *require one another*: each is the condition of possibility of the other, and helps to sustain it.

(2) Concerning the problem of social justice, a parallel point can be made about how Arendt distinguishes it from political freedom. In the course of clarifying the autonomy of the political, Arendt occasionally suggests that, if need be, the problem of social justice could also be solved in a rational way by a properly functioning welfare bureaucracy. If not simply a bit of snobbery, this is naive in the extreme. It would have been far more consistent had she acknowledged that social questions – and economic ones as well – *become political* the moment they are considered, within the bounds of the public sphere, to be of common concern. Not only is the question of the interpretation and the standards of social justice a disputed, hence potentially political, one (the answer to which is bound to a specific historical and economic situation); more than that, the eminently political question concerns the *forms* in which social justice is to be realized. For example, should

the losers in a competitive market economy be made into the passive clients of an anonymous welfare bureaucracy, or should they be enabled to lead self-determined lives by being assured of basic social rights (such as a guaranteed basic income), which would also enable them to participate in civic affairs? Today, it almost seems a banality to observe that the outlook for political freedom in the modern world depends (in the long run) upon how successfully capitalism can be domesticated in a democratic way, and upon whether a minimum of social justice can be achieved on an international scale. Unfortunately, in her more than justified criticism of the socialist tradition's "forgetfulness of politics," Arendt arrived at formulations which had the effect of throwing the baby out with the bath water. She overlooked the fact that the problems Marx confronted are still our – political – problems, which means that they concern political freedom's conditions of possibility in the modern world.

One could treat, in similar fashion, many of the other questions which Arendt excludes from the legitimate concerns of the political realm. If it is *common* concerns that are at issue in joint action and political debate (as Arendt asserts), then the questions of ecology, economics, and administration are also potentially political questions. The autonomy of the political cannot possibly consist in politics having migrated to a region beyond these spheres of life. It must consist, rather, in the fact that issues raised by these spheres can be considered in the terms of political discourse, and from viewpoints which represent not those of the businessman, the private consumer, the scientist, or the bureaucrat, but rather *citizens* deciding how they want to live together and preserve their shared world. Political discourse is "autonomous" in that it gives neither private interest nor the knowledge and methods of the expert the last word. This is what Arendt meant when she insisted that politics is a sphere of *common* concerns and (thus) a sphere of opinion, persuasion, and judgment. She simply drew the wrong conclusion when she said that those areas of social life whose modes of functioning are determined by private interest, strategic action, or scientific competence must necessarily lie outside the political domain. This conclusion typifies what I have called Arendt's tendency to "concretize" the autonomy of the political.

(3) Concerning, finally, the tendencies toward particularism in various actual spaces of public freedom: hardly any proof is required to show that these are all too present. Political institutions and voluntary associations, citizens' initiatives and local government assemblies – all are constantly tempted to push through what is, in one way or another, a merely particular interest at the expense of the general interest. That Arendt scarcely mentions this fact probably has a lot to do with her desire to push everything designated by the word "interest" out of the political sphere. This is yet another

example of her reified concept of politics. Where the conflict between interests has been banished by the tacit appeal to civic virtue, there is no need or urgency to strike a political balance between particular interests and the general interest. The "league and alliance among separate units" – that is, the "federal principle" which Arendt thinks is inherent in "the elementary conditions of action" – will also not generate serious problems for the construction of political institutions, and for similar (if specious) reasons. However, if, unlike Arendt, we take the conflict between interests seriously as a problem in need of political attention, it will no longer be possible to think of the polity as being constructed solely from the bottom up, from the "local councils" of neighborhood wards to the federal level. We will also have to conceive of it as being built from the top down as well. This means, at least in the European political tradition, beginning with the centralized institutions of the nation-state.

However one might imagine the nation-state's being replaced, entirely or in part, by other, international forms of political organization, the fact remains that its abolition would be premature unless other institutions were found to fulfill its central, coordinating role of asserting the general or public interest. In theory, fulfilling this role requires that the state (or its future functional equivalents) take the part of an independent umpire, neutral or perhaps even hostile, *over against* particular interests. Although the private interests of individuals certainly have a central place within the protective legal framework of the liberal state, matters are not so simple with regard to the particular interests which play a role in political institutions and associations. Here there arises a problem of political "construction" of a different sort. For in the latter case, at least when what is at issue is not the activity of interest groups, but rather joint action in the public sphere (as with many citizens' initiatives, for example), a "particular" interest might already be a common concern; or, as is often the case, it might *become* a general concern (or at least claim to be). In other words, within the public realm, a transformation of "merely particular" interests into a common or even a general interest often takes place, and largely by virtue of their being made public in character (and so the proper objects of discourse and debate). Hence the peculiar and dual nature of such spaces, which provide both the nucleus of a democratic public sphere and the arena for the crystallization of a particular group interest. In the first role, such spaces help create the necessary conditions for political freedom and a democratic public sphere on a large scale; while in the second they often stand in need of the counterweight provided by centralized political institutions, which help restrain the particularism they are capable of generating. The limited or local public spaces of which Arendt speaks are, therefore, *necessary* for the proper functioning of the rule of law and for the sake of democratic legitimacy; and yet, if necessary, the democratic state must also be responsive to them and their effects through "umpirage" and regulation.

This, it seems to me, is another manifestation of what I have called the unavoidable practical circle of democratic discourse. Here no general theoretical solutions are possible. Once can, however, say that the relation between "representative" and "direct" democracy is clearly far more complicated than the mutually exclusive one described by Arendt. Not only do "public spaces of freedom" appear to be a constitutive element of liberal democracy itself; it is also clear that the legal sphere of democratic government has, for its part, a constitutive role in the creation and linkage of such spaces. It must have such a role if the "league and alliance among separate units" (Arendt's "elementary republics") is to have any reality worth mentioning, and if a balance between the "common concerns" of the smaller units and those of the larger polity that contains them is to be ever attained or approximated. In this sense, the plurality of (local or "grassroots") public spaces of freedom depends upon central legislative, executive, and judicial institutions of the kind known in contemporary democratic states. Thus, the ideas of "direct" and of "representative" democracy are not really opposites at all, but rather signify two necessary dimensions or "principles" of modern democracy: each requires the other, yet each can pose a challenge to the other.

If, as I have suggested, the sphere of the political is linked to the spheres of the social, the economy, administration, and the law in ways quite different from what Arendt implies, then the question of how to draw the boundaries between what should and should not be included in the proper domain of each becomes a political question in its own right. Conversely, every set of political institutions finds its relative autonomy restrained by a surrounding environment comprised of more or less autonomous systems (the economy, administration, law). If one also takes into account the various relations of dependence between the different levels of the political system, as well as the intricate connections between the political system, the associations and institutions of civil society, and the public sphere (broadly construed), then it becomes clear that Arendt's opposition of "direct" and "representative" democracy (which she understood as denoting two alternative forms of government) does little to illuminate the conditions of complex industrial societies.

Arendt's distinction does, however, have continuing power when it is understood not as distinguishing between different forms of government, but as pointing to different options *within* modern democratic polities. Then it marks out a spectrum of possibilities within them. At one end of this spectrum we would find the centralized state, with formal-democratic parliamentary representation of a sovereign people, and also, perhaps, the manipulation of public opinion by mass media. At the other, we would find a democratic culture of self-determination which would be alive on the level of everyday life and practice, together with a corresponding culture of public debate. Thus re-framed, Arendt's conception of the political continues to provide a necessary challenge, one relevant to contemporary political philosophy and politics.

When one takes Arendt's idea of the council system to be the metaphor it is, and understands the polarity between representative and direct democracy to indicate a spectrum of possibilities *within* modern democratic polities, then Arendt appears to have had good reason for stressing the importance of practices of *direct* democracy in her notion of public freedom, as well as for insisting that such freedom can be established only in a (relatively) autonomous political sphere. As I have argued in this chapter, this emphasis introduces a standard of political freedom which cannot be derived from the principle of equal (liberal democratic) rights. Political freedom in this sense is dependent upon the initiative, the imagination, the experience and the courage of those involved, as well as upon the binding force of mutual promises and agreements.[16] It is "fragile" in the sense that it will be constantly threatened by the colonizing powers of centralized political institutions and bureaucracies.

By bringing the idea of public freedom to the fore, Arendt transforms the concept of democratic legitimacy as such. A participatory and performative aspect is added to it. For what "we" the people, the democratic sovereign, can initiate or rationally agree upon depends not least upon how this "we" has organized itself in civil society and the institutions of the political system. Only where public freedom is experienced as a daily reality can it become a common value, one that is capable of acquiring a binding force in the decision-making processes of the political system. This "value," Arendt would contend, is not just *any* value among all the values which may compete with one another in democratic decision-making processes. It is, rather, *the* "value" on whose realization (however partial) depends whether – and to what extent – democracy is a form of government in which the power really rests (as one says) with the people, or whether – in the words of Benjamin Rush, quoted by Arendt – "although power is derived from the people, they possess it only on the days of their elections. After this it is the property of their rulers."[17] Seen in this manner, the extent of public freedom is a more comprehensive measure of a political system's claim to democratic legitimacy than the securing of equal political *rights*, or the notion of a democratic consensus, or even the idea of forming political will through public discussion. Instead one might say that the traditional concepts of democratic legitimacy are not sufficient for the articulation of a robust idea of public freedom, the very thing which the revolutionary tradition and all modern democratic movements have, more or less implicitly, always aimed at.

I would like to reformulate this point in a slightly different way. Earlier, I reinterpreted Arendt's opposition of "direct" and "representative" democracy to indicate what are, in fact, two necessary dimensions for a properly functioning modern democracy; each requiring, and yet also possibly challenging, the other. If the diagnosis of latent conflict between these two dimensions is at all correct, then a proper balance between them cannot be struck by invoking a (Rawlsian) principle of equal basic rights or the (Habermasian) idea of a democratic consensus. The idea of equal basic rights does not suffice because it represents only a necessary condition of democracy, one which leaves open the question of which institutional forms would enable the optimal articulation and exercise of these basic rights. The idea of a democratic consensus does not suffice because it is too vague about the conditions under which such a consensus can emerge and be reproduced. It would provide an adequate standard only when, from the welter of all possible agreements or quasi-consensuses, we were able to designate one and only one outcome as "rational" (which, I think, could only be done in a tautologous way).

When one asks how the idea of everyone's participation in the democratic process, as free and equal citizens, is to be realized institutionally (and this is the question of the "right balance" just discussed), then all the categories which Arendt uses to describe the revolutionary *constitutio libertatis* become relevant. Baldly stated, these categories cannot be reduced to those of an ideal form of rational discourse. Of course, to put it in Hegelian terms, a democratic form of "ethical life," one anchored in institutions, could be called "rational" (*vernünftig*); but we can only say this once we clearly comprehend the problems of political construction engendered by the *desire* for *freedom* and for *self-determination*. It is the history of this desire – repeatedly breaking out and repeatedly suppressed in the modern age – which Arendt details in *On Revolution*. It is a desire which the representative democracies of our time have failed to fully satisfy. In this respect I believe she is right to emphasize the voluntative, performative, and contingent aspects attending the realization of this desire, aspects which can be grasped neither by means of legal categories nor in the framework of rational discourse. Arendt's emphasis on these crucial characteristics of the *constitutio libertatis* directs our attention to an idea of political freedom which cannot be sufficiently articulated either in terms of rights or in terms of rational discourse.

This idea of political freedom, it seems to me, is Arendt's profoundest insight and most productive contribution to modern democratic theory. In this regard, her attempt in *On Revolution* to set the categories of liberal democratic political discourse in motion is perhaps more relevant now than ever. Of course, no theory can do more than to set the basic categories of political practice in motion. The question of *how* public freedom is to be secured in modern democracies is one which does not admit of a *philosophical* answer. Arendt's idea of a council system is, as we have seen, only the semblance of such an answer, at most a metaphor suited for turning the theoretical imagination in a new direction. In any event, I believe that Arendt's political thought provides a productive stimulus only when its frontal opposition to the traditions of liberal and social democracy is dissolved. For then her thought can be pressed into the service of a critical re-reading of these very traditions.

Finally, we might say something similar about Arendt's otherwise astute polemic against Marx, a polemic predicated upon an ultimately unfruitful opposition to his attempt to find a solution to the modern problem of freedom by means of the critique of political economy. Today it seems clear that, without some sort of a democratic domestication of capitalism, self-determination will cease to be viable as a *political* project. However, it is possible that – after the collapse of "really existing socialism" – the critique of political economy will experience a renaissance, one which helps to open up new perspectives on the prospects for political freedom in the modern world. If so, we could do worse than to attempt to wed the insights of such a critique to those of Hannah Arendt.

NOTES

1 Arendt, *OR*, 2nd edn.; in this chapter, Arendt's own German version, *Über die Revolution* (Munich: Piper Verlag, 1963), has also been cited when necessary.
2 *Über die Revolution*, p. 362; see *OR*, p. 275.
3 *OR*, p. 281.
4 In this sense, Arendt speaks of a (human) right to have (civil) rights, that is, to have the status of a "legal citizen." This is her answer to the problem of refugees, stateless people, and minorities without rights in the age of nationalism and totalitarianism, especially National Socialism. See her article, "'The Rights of Man': What are They?" *Modern Review* 3/1 (Summer 1949).
5 *OR*, p. 267; my italics.
6 See her essay, "What is Authority?," in *BPF*, pp. 120ff.
7 Ibid., p. 118.
8 *OR*, p. 175.
9 Dana R. Villa, *Arendt and Heidegger: The Fate of the Political* (Princeton: Princeton University Press, 1996).
10 Compare, for instance, Seyla Benhabib, "Modelle des öffentlichen Raums:

Hannah Arendt, die liberale Tradition und Jürgen Habermas," *Soziale Welt* 42 (1991), or *The Reluctant Modernism of Hannah Arendt* (Thousand Oaks, CA: Sage Publications, 1996), chapter 6; and above all, Habermas himself, in *Between Facts and Norms: Contributions to a Discourse Theory of Law and Democracy*, trans. William Rehg (Cambridge, MA and London: The MIT Press, 1996), esp. pp. 147ff.

11 But see my essay, "Conditions of a Democratic Culture: Remarks on the Liberal-Communitarian Debate," in *Endgames: The Irreconcilable Nature of Modernity*, trans. David Midgley (Cambridge, MA and London: The MIT Press, 1996), pp. 58ff.

12 A democratic world society need not (and probably *should* not) be a world *state*. For an illuminating discussion of the problems involved in the idea of a "world-wide civil society" (Kant), which would not be a world *state*, see Jean Cohen, "Rights, Citizenship, and the Social: Dilemmas of Arendtian Republicanism," *Constellations* 3/2 (October 1996).

13 Jürgen Habermas, "Reconciliation Through the Public Use of Reason: Remarks on John Rawls' Political Liberalism," and John Rawls, "Reply to Habermas," *The Journal of Philosophy* 92/3 (March 1995).

14 See Richard Bernstein's incisive essay, "Rethinking the Social and the Political," in *Philosophical Profiles* (Cambridge, MA and London: The MIT Press, 1986), esp. pp. 248ff.

15 Concerning this point, see Wellmer, "Conditions of a Democratic Culture," pp. 45ff.

16 *OR*, p. 175.

17 Ibid., p. 236.

PART VI

Judgment, philosophy and thinking

12

MAURIZIO PASSERIN D'ENTRÈVES

Arendt's theory of judgment

One of the most enduring contributions of Arendt's political thought is to be found in her reflections on judgment which were to occupy the last years of her life. Together with the theory of action, her unfinished theory of judgment represents her central legacy to twentieth-century political thought. It is to the role and function of judgment in the world of human affairs that I would first like to turn my attention, with a view to exploring its place in the architectonic of Arendt's theory of politics.

Among the faculties with which human beings are endowed, judgment – which Arendt saw as "the ability to tell right from wrong, beautiful from ugly"[1] – occupies a central place while being at the same time one of the most difficult to conceptualize. The reason for this difficulty probably lies in the fact that judgment, especially moral and political judgment, is closely bound to the sphere of action and thus exhibits all the problems of mediating theory (or the inner reflection that accompanies judgment) and practice. Moreover, compared to the faculties of thinking and willing, it lacks clear criteria of operation as well as precise standards of assessment. Thinking can be assessed in terms of consistency, logic, soundness, and coherence; willing by its resoluteness or capacity to determine our actions. Judgment, on the other hand, although it may share some of these features, is never exhausted by them. In judgment we look not only for soundness or consistency, or for the ability to determine our choices in problematic situations, but also for discrimination, discernment, imagination, sympathy, detachment, impartiality, and integrity.

Judgment: two models

Arendt's theory of judgment was never developed as systematically or extensively as her theory of action. She intended to complete her study of the life of the mind by devoting the third volume to the faculty of judgment, but was not able to do so because of her untimely death in 1975. What she left was a number of reflections scattered in the first two volumes on *Thinking* and *Willing*,[2] a series of lectures on Kant's political philosophy delivered at the New School for Social Research in the Fall of 1970,[3] an essay entitled "Thinking and Moral Considerations" written at the time she was composing *The Life of the Mind*, [4] and two articles included in *Between Past and Future* where judgment and opinion are treated in relation to culture and taste ("The Crisis in Culture") and with respect to the question of truth ("Truth and Politics").[5] However, these writings do not present a unified theory of judgment but, rather, two distinct models, one based on the standpoint of the actor, the other on the standpoint of the spectator, which are somewhat at odds with each other. Arendt's writings on the theme of judgment can be seen to fall into two more or less distinct phases, an early one in which judgment is the faculty of political actors acting in the public realm, and a later one in which it is the privilege of non-participating spectators, primarily poets and historians, who seek to understand the meaning of the past and to reconcile us to what has happened.[6] In this later formulation Arendt is no longer concerned with judging as a feature of political life as such, as the faculty which is exercised by actors in order to decide how to act in the public realm, but with judgment as a component in the life of the mind, the faculty through which the privileged spectators can recover meaning from the past and thereby reconcile themselves to time and, retrospectively, to tragedy.[7]

In addition to presenting us with two models of judgment which stand in tension with each other, Arendt did not clarify the status of judgment with respect to two of its philosophical sources, Aristotle and Kant. The two conceptions seem to pull in opposite directions, the Aristotelian toward a concern with the particular, the Kantian toward a concern with universality and impartiality.

It would appear, therefore, not only that Arendt's theory of judgment incorporates two models, the actor's – judging in order to act – and the spectator's – judging in order to cull meaning from the past – but that the philosophical sources it draws upon are somewhat at odds with each other.

Judgment and the *vita contemplativa*

Arendt's concern with judgment as the faculty of retrospective assessment that allows meaning to be redeemed from the past originated in her attempt to come to terms with the twin political tragedies of the twentieth century, Nazism and Stalinism. Faced with the horrors of the extermination camps and what is now termed the Gulag, Arendt strove to understand these phenomena in their own terms, neither deducing them from precedents nor placing them in some overarching scheme of historical necessity. This need to come to terms with the traumatic events of our century, and to understand them in a manner that does not explain them away but faces them in all their starkness and unprecedentedness, is something to which Arendt returns again and again. Our inherited framework for judgment fails us "as soon as we try to apply it honestly to the central political experiences of our own time."[8] Even our ordinary common-sense judgment is rendered ineffective, since "we are living in a topsy-turvy world, a world where we cannot find our way by abiding by the rules of what once was common sense."[9]

The crisis in understanding is therefore coeval with a crisis in judgment, insofar as understanding for Arendt is "so closely related to and interrelated with judging that one must describe both as the subsumption of something particular under a universal rule."[10] Once these rules have lost their validity we are no longer able to understand and to judge the particulars, that is, we are no longer able to subsume them under our accepted categories of moral and political thought. Arendt, however, does not believe that the loss of these categories has brought to an end our capacity to judge; on the contrary, since human beings are distinguished by their capacity to begin anew, they are able to fashion new categories and to formulate new standards of judgment for the events that have come to pass and for those that may emerge in the future. Thus,

> In the light of these reflections, our endeavoring to understand something which has ruined our categories of thought and our standards of judgment appears less frightening. Even though we have lost yardsticks by which to measure, and rules under which to subsume the particular, a being whose essence is beginning may have enough of origin within himself to understand without preconceived categories and to judge without the set of customary rules which is morality.[11]

For Arendt, therefore, the enormity and unprecedentedness of totalitarianism have not destroyed, strictly speaking, our ability to judge; rather, they have destroyed our accepted standards of judgment and our conventional categories of interpretation and assessment, be they moral or political. And in this situation the only recourse is to appeal to the imagination, which allows us to view things in their proper perspective and to judge them without the benefit of a pre-given rule or universal. As Arendt puts it:

> Imagination alone enables us to see things in their proper perspective, to put that which is too close at a certain distance so that we can see and understand it without bias and prejudice, to bridge abysses of remoteness until we can see and understand everything that is too far away from us as though it were our own affair. This "distancing" of some things and bridging the abysses to others is part of the dialogue of understanding.[12]

The imagination therefore enables us to create the distance which is necessary for an impartial judgment, while at the same time allowing for the closeness that makes understanding possible. In this way it makes possible our reconciliation with reality, even with the tragic reality of the twentieth century.

Arendt's participation in the trial of Eichmann in the early sixties made her once more aware of the need to come to terms with a reality that initially defied human comprehension. How could such an ordinary, law-abiding, and all-too-human individual have committed such atrocities? The impact of the trial also forced her to raise another problem concerning judgment, namely, whether we are entitled to presuppose "an independent human faculty, unsupported by law and public opinion, that judges anew in full spontaneity every deed and intent whenever the occasion arises."[13]

Judgment and the winds of thought

Arendt returned to this issue in *The Life of the Mind*, a work which was meant to encompass the three faculties of thinking, willing, and judging. In the introduction to the first volume she declared that the immediate impulse to write it came from attending the Eichmann trial in Jerusalem,[14] while the second, equally important motive, was to provide an account of our mental activities that was missing from her previous work on the *vita activa*. It was Eichmann's absence of thinking, his "thoughtlessness," that struck her most, because it was responsible in her view for his inability to judge in those circumstances where judgment was most needed. "It was this absence of thinking," she wrote,

> that awakened my interest. Is evil-doing (the sins of omission, as well as the sins of commission) possible in default of not just "base motives" . . . but of any motives whatever, of any particular prompting of interest or volition? Is wickedness . . . *not* a necessary condition for evil doing? Might the problem of good and evil, our faculty for telling right from wrong, be connected with our faculty of thought?[15]

Arendt attempted a reply by connecting the activity of thinking to that of judging in a twofold manner. First, thinking – the silent dialogue of me and myself – dissolves our fixed habits of thought and the accepted rules of conduct, and thus prepares the way for the activity of judging particulars without the aid of pre-established universals. It is not that thinking provides judgment with new rules for subsuming the particular under the universal. Rather, it loosens the grip of the universal over the particular, thereby releasing judgment from ossified categories of thought and conventional standards of behavior. It is in times of historical crisis that thinking ceases to be a marginal affair, because by undermining all established criteria and values, it prepares the individual to judge for him or herself instead of being carried away by the actions and opinions of the majority.

The second way in which Arendt connected the activity of thinking with that of judging is by showing that thinking, by actualizing the dialogue of me and myself which is given in consciousness, produces conscience as a by-product. This conscience, unlike the voice of God or what later thinkers called *lumen naturale*, gives no positive prescriptions; it only tells us what *not* to do, what to avoid in our actions and dealings with others, as well as what to repent of. Arendt notes in this context that Socrates' dictum "It is better to suffer wrong than to do wrong," and his proposition that "It would be better for me that my lyre or a chorus I directed should be out of tune and loud with discord, and that multitudes of men should disagree with me, rather than that I, *being one*, should be out of harmony with myself and contradict me," derive their validity from the idea that there is a silent partner within ourselves to whom we render account of our actions.[16] What we fear most is the anticipation of the presence of this partner (i.e., our conscience) who awaits us at the end of the day. Thus,

> a person who does not know that silent intercourse (in which we examine what we say and what we do) will not mind contradicting himself, and this means he will never be either able or willing to account for what he says or does; nor will he mind committing any crime, since he can count on its being forgotten the next moment. Bad people . . . are *not* "full of regrets."[17]

She goes on to note that thinking, as the actualization of the difference given in consciousness, "is not a prerogative of the few but an ever-present faculty in everybody; by the same token, inability to think is not a failing of the many who lack brain power, but an ever-present possibility for everybody."[18] For those who do engage in thinking, however, conscience emerges as an inevitable by-product. As the side-effect of thinking, conscience has its counterpart in judgment as the by-product of the liberating activity of thought. If conscience represents the inner check by which we evaluate our actions, judgment represents the outer manifestation of our capacity to think critically. Both faculties relate to the question of right and wrong, but while conscience directs attention to the self, judgment directs attention to the world.[19] In this respect, judgment makes possible what Arendt calls "the manifestation of the wind of thought" in the sphere of appearance.

Judgment and Kant's aesthetics

The foregoing account has explored the way in which Arendt attempted to connect the activity of thinking to our capacity to judge. To be sure, this connection of thinking and judging seems to operate only in emergencies, in those exceptional moments where individuals, faced with the collapse of traditional standards, must come up with new ones and judge according to their own autonomous values. There is, however, a second, more elaborated view of judgment which does not restrict it to moments of crisis, but which identifies it with the capacity to think representatively, that is, from the standpoint of everyone else. Arendt called this capacity to think representatively an "enlarged mentality," adopting the same terms that Kant employed in his Third Critique to characterize aesthetic judgment. It is to this work that we must now turn our attention, since Arendt based her theory of political judgment on Kant's aesthetics rather than on his moral philosophy. At first sight this might seem a puzzling choice, since Kant himself based his moral and political philosophy on practical reason and not on our aesthetic faculties. Arendt, however, claimed that the *Critique of Judgment* contained Kant's unwritten political philosophy, and that the first part of it, the "Critique of Aesthetic Judgment," was the most fruitful basis on which to build a theory of political judgment, since it dealt with the world of appearances from the point of view of the judging spectator and took as its starting point the faculty of taste, understood as a faculty of concrete and embodied subjects.[20]

For Arendt the capacity to judge is a specifically political ability insofar as it enables individuals to orient themselves in the public realm and to judge the phenomena that are disclosed within it from a standpoint that is relatively detached and impartial. She credits Kant with having dislodged the prejudice that judgments of taste lie altogether outside the political realm, since they supposedly concern only aesthetic matters. She believes, in fact, that by linking taste to that wider manner of thinking which Kant called an "enlarged mentality" the way was opened to a revaluation of judgment as a specific political ability, namely, as the ability to think in the place of everybody else. It is only in Kant's *Critique of Judgment* that we find a conception of judgment as the ability to deal with particulars in their particularity, that is, without subsuming them under a pre-given universal, but actively searching the universal out of the particular.[21] Kant formulated this distinction as that between *determinant* and *reflective* judgments. For him judgment in general is the faculty of thinking the particular as contained under the universal. If the universal (the rule, principle, or law) is given, then the judgment which subsumes the particular under it is determinant. If, however, only the particular is given and the universal has to be found for it, then the judgment is reflective.[22] For Kant determinant judgments were cognitive, while reflective judgments were non-cognitive. Reflective judgment is seen as the capacity to ascend from the particular to the universal without the mediation of determinate concepts given in advance; it is reasoning about particulars in their relation to the universal rather than reasoning about universals in their relation to the particular. In the case of aesthetic judgment this means that I can understand and apply the universal predicate of beauty only through experiencing a particular object that exemplifies it. Thus, upon encountering a flower, a unique landscape, or a particular painting, I am able to say that it is an example of beauty, that it possesses "exemplary validity."

It is important to note in this context that this notion of examples – or of the exemplary validity that a particular may possess – strikes Arendt as the most fruitful solution to the problem of mediating the particular and the universal. "Examples," she says quoting Kant, "are the go-cart of judgments."[23] They permit us to discover the universal in and through the particular, insofar as they embody a universal meaning while retaining their particularity.

For Arendt this notion of exemplary validity is not restricted to aesthetic objects or to individuals who exemplified certain virtues. Rather, she wants to extend this notion to events in the past that carry a meaning beyond their sheer happening, that is to say, to events that could be seen as exemplary for those who came after. It is here that aesthetic judgment joins with the retrospective judgment of the historian. The American and French Revolutions, the Paris Commune, the Russian soviets, the German revolutionary councils of 1918–19, the Hungarian uprising of 1956, all these events possess the kind of exemplary validity that makes them of universal significance, while still retaining their own specificity and uniqueness. Thus, by attending to these events in their particularity the historian or judging spectator is able to illuminate their universal import and thereby preserve them as "examples" for posterity.

For Arendt it is the spectators who have the privilege of judging impartially and disinterestedly, and in doing so they exercise two crucial faculties, *imagination* and *common sense*. Imagination is the faculty of representing in one's mind that which has already appeared to one's senses. Through the imagination one can represent objects that are no longer present and thus establish the distance necessary for an impartial judgment. Once this distancing has occurred, one is in a position to reflect upon these representations from a number of different perspectives, and thereby to reach a judgment about the proper value of an object.

The other faculty that spectators have to appeal to is common sense or *sensus communis*, since without it they could not share their judgments or overcome their individual idiosyncrasies. Kant himself declared that "In matters of taste we must renounce ourselves in favour of others . . . In taste egoism is overcome."[24] By this he meant that for our judgments to be valid (i.e., publicly recognised and accepted) we must transcend our private or subjective conditions in favour of public and intersubjective ones, and we are able to do this by appealing to our community sense, our *sensus communis*.

The criterion for judgment, then, is *communicability*, and the standard for deciding whether our judgments are indeed communicable is to see whether they could fit with the *sensus communis* of others. The term *sensus communis* is used by Kant to indicate not merely the common sense we expect everybody to have, but a special sense that fits us into a human community. It is a specifically *community* sense because communication and speech depend upon it, and without communication we could neither constitute nor enter into a community. Arendt points out that the emphasis on the communicability of judgments of taste and the correlative notion of an enlarged mentality link up effortlessly with Kant's idea of a united mankind living in eternal peace. After quoting Kant's insistence that "a regard to universal communicability is a thing which everyone expects and requires from everyone else, just as if it were part of an original compact dictated by humanity itself,"[25] she goes on to argue that

> It is by virtue of this idea of mankind, present in every single man, that men are human, and they can be called civilized or humane to the extent that this idea becomes the principle not only of their judgments but of their actions. It is at this point that *actor* and *spectator* become united; the maxim of the actor and the maxim, the "standard," according to which the spectator judges the spectacle of the world, become one. The, as it were, categorical imperative for action could read as follows: Always act on the maxim through which this original compact can be actualized into a general law.[26]

Here it would appear that Arendt once again acknowledges the links between the standpoint of the actor and that of the spectator. Let us then look at the way in which judgment operates from the standpoint of the actor.

Judgment and the *vita activa*

Arendt presented a model of judgment in the essays "The Crisis in Culture" and "Truth and Politics" which could be characterized as far more "political" than the one presented so far. In these essays, in fact, she treated judgment as a faculty that enables political actors to decide what courses of action to undertake in the public realm, what kind of objectives are most appropriate or worth pursuing, as well as who to praise or blame for past actions or for the consequences of past decisions. In this model judgment is viewed as a specifically *political* ability, namely, as "the ability to see things not only from one's own point of view but from the perspective of all those who happen to be present," and as being "one of the fundamental abilities of man as a political being insofar as it enables him to orient himself in the public realm, in the common world."[27] In fact, Arendt claims that

> the Greeks called this ability [to judge] *phronesis*, or insight, and they considered it the principal virtue or excellence of the statesman in distinction from the wisdom of the philosopher. The difference between this judging insight and speculative thought lies in that the former has its roots in what we usually call common sense, which the latter constantly transcends. Common sense . . . discloses to us the nature of the world insofar as it is a common world; we owe to it the fact that our strictly private and "subjective" five senses and their sensory data can adjust themselves to a nonsubjective and "objective" world which we have in common and share with others. Judging is one, if not the most, important activity in which this sharing-the-world-with-others comes to pass.[28]

Moreover, in discussing the non-coercive character of judgment, the fact that it can only appeal to but never force the agreement of others, she claims that "this 'wooing' or persuading corresponds closely to what the Greeks called *peithein*, the convincing and persuading speech which they regarded as the typically political form of people talking with one another."[29] Several commentators have claimed that there is a contradiction in Arendt's employment of the Aristotelian notion of *phronesis* alongside Kant's idea of an "enlarged mentality," since they supposedly pull in opposite directions, the former toward a concern with the particular, the latter toward universality and impartiality.[30] I would argue, however, that this contradiction is more apparent than real, since Kant's theory of aesthetic judgment is a theory of *reflective* judgment, that is, of those judgments where the universal is not given but must be searched out of the particular. In this respect the theory of aesthetic judgment to which Arendt appeals does have close affinities with Aristotle's notion of *phronesis*. Both are concerned with the judgment of particulars *qua* particulars, not with their subsumption under universal rules. If a distinction is to be made, it has more to do with the mode of *asserting validity*: In Aristotle *phronesis* is the privilege of a few experienced individuals (the *phronimoi*) who, over time, have shown themselves to be wise in practical matters; the only criterion of validity is their experience and their past record of judicious actions. In the case of judgments of taste, on the other hand, individuals have to appeal to the judgments and opinions of others, and thus the validity of their judgments rests on the consent they can elicit from a community of differently situated subjects.

For Arendt the validity of political judgment depends on our ability to think "representatively," that is, from the standpoint of everyone else, so that we are able to look at the world from a number of different perspectives. And this ability, in turn, can only be acquired and tested in a public forum where individuals have the opportunity to exchange their opinions on particular matters and see whether they accord with the opinions of others. In this respect the process of opinion formation is never a solitary activity; rather, it requires a genuine encounter with different opinions so that a particular issue may be examined from every possible standpoint until, as she puts it, "it is flooded and made transparent by the full light of human comprehension."[31] Debate and discussion, and the capacity to enlarge one's perspective, are indeed crucial to the formation of opinions that can claim more than subjective validity; individuals may hold personal opinions on many subject matters, but they can form *representative* opinions only by enlarging their standpoint to incorporate those of others. As Arendt says:

> Political thought is representative. I form an opinion by considering a given issue from different viewpoints, by making present to my mind the standpoints of those who are absent; that is, I represent them. This process of representation does not blindly adopt the actual views of those who stand somewhere else, and hence look upon the world from a different perspective; this is a question neither of empathy . . . nor of counting noses and joining a majority, but of being and thinking in my own identity where actually I am not. The more people's standpoints I have present in my mind while I am pondering a given issue, and the better I can imagine how I would feel and think if I were in their place, the stronger will be my capacity for representative thinking and the more valid my final conclusions, my opinion.[32]

Opinions, in fact, are never self-evident. In matters of opinion, but not in matters of truth, "our thinking is truly discursive, running, as it were, from place to place, from one part of the world to another, through all kinds of conflicting views, until it finally ascends from these particularities to some impartial generality."[33] In this respect one is never alone while forming an opinion; as Arendt notes,

> even if I shun all company or am completely isolated while forming an opinion, I am not simply together only with myself in the solitude of philosophical thought; I remain in this world of universal interdependence, where I can make myself the representative of everybody else.[34]

Judgment and validity

The representative character of judgment and opinion has important implications for the question of validity. Arendt always stressed that the formation of valid opinions requires a public space where individuals can test and purify their views through a process of mutual debate and enlightenment. She was, however, quite opposed to the idea that opinions should be measured by the standard of truth, or that debate should be conducted according to strict scientific standards of validity. In her view, truth belongs to the realm of cognition, the realm of logic, mathematics and the strict sciences, and carries always an element of coercion, since it precludes debate and must be accepted by every individual in possession of her rational faculties. Set against the plurality of opinions, truth has a despotic character: it compels universal assent, leaves the mind little freedom of movement, eliminates the diversity of views and reduces the richness of human discourse. In this respect, truth is anti-political, since by eliminating debate and diversity it eliminates the very principles of political life. As Arendt writes,

> The trouble is that factual truth, like all other truth, peremptorily claims to be acknowledged and precludes debate, and debate constitutes the very essence of political life. *The modes of thought and communication that deal with truth, if seen from the political perspective, are necessarily domineering*; they don't take into account other people's opinions, and taking these into account is the hallmark of all strictly political thinking.[35]

For Arendt, a truth "whose validity needs no support from the side of opinion strikes at the very roots of all politics and all governments."[36] She cites the famous statement of Jefferson in the Declaration of Independence that says "We hold these truths to be self-evident, that all men are created equal, that they are endowed by their Creator with certain unalienable rights," and argues that by saying "*We hold* these truths to be self-evident" Jefferson acknowledged that these truths were not self-evident, that they stood in need of agreement and consent, and therefore that the statement "All men are created equal" was a matter of opinion and not of truth.[37]

Arendt also quotes the remark by Lessing – "Let each man say what he deems truth, and let truth itself be commended unto God" – and interprets it as saying "Let us thank God that we don't know *the* truth." For Arendt this expressed the insight that "for men living in company, the inexhaustible richness of human discourse is infinitely more significant and meaningful than any One Truth could ever be."[38] Lessing's greatness for Arendt consisted not merely in having reached

> a theoretical insight that there cannot be one single truth within the human world, but in his *gladness* that it does not exist and that, therefore, the unending discourse among men will never cease so long as there are men at all. *A single absolute truth*, could there have been one . . . *would have spelled the end of humanity*.[39]

Arendt's defense of opinion is motivated not just by her belief that truth leaves no room for debate or dissent, or for the acknowledgment of difference, but also by her conviction that our reasoning faculties can only flourish in a dialogic or communicative context. She cites Kant's remark that "the external power that deprives man of the freedom to communicate his thoughts publicly deprives him at the same time of his freedom to think," and underlines the fact that for Kant the only guarantee of the correctness of our thinking is that "'we think, as it were, in community with others to whom we communicate our thoughts as they communicate theirs to us.' Man's reason, being fallible, can function only if he can make 'public use' of it."[40] She also quotes Madison's statement that "the reason of man, like man himself, is timid and cautious when left alone, and acquires firmness and confidence in proportion to the number with which it is associated."[41] It follows, therefore, that

> the shift from rational truth to opinion implies a shift from man in the singular to men in the plural, and this means a shift from a domain where, Madison says, nothing counts except the "solid reasoning" of one mind to a realm where "strength of opinion" is determined by the individual's reliance upon "the number which he supposes to have entertained the same opinion" – a number, incidentally, that is not necessarily limited to one's contemporaries.[42]

The appeal to Lessing, Kant, and Madison is meant to vindicate the power and dignity of opinion against those thinkers, from Plato to Hobbes, who saw it as mere illusion, as a confused or inadequate grasp of the truth. For Arendt opinion is not a defective form of knowledge that should be transcended or left behind as soon as one is in possession of the truth. Rather, it is a distinct form of knowledge which arises out of the collective deliberation of citizens, and which requires the use of the imagination and the capacity to think "representatively." By deliberating in common and engaging in "representative thinking" citizens are in fact able to form opinions that can claim intersubjective validity. It is important to stress in this context that Arendt does not want to dismiss the philosophers' attempt to find universal or absolute standards of knowledge and cognition, but to check their desire to impose those standards upon the sphere of human affairs, since they would eliminate its plurality and essential relativity, i.e., the fact that it is composed of a plurality of individuals who view it from different perspectives which are all relative to each other.[43] The imposition of a single or absolute standard into the domain of *praxis* would do away with the need to persuade others of the relative merits of an opinion, to elicit their consent to a specific proposal, or to obtain their agreement with respect to a particular policy. Indeed, for Arendt the imposition of such a standard would mean that individuals would no longer be required to exercise their judgment, develop their imagination, or cultivate an "enlarged mentality," since they would no longer need to deliberate in common. Strict demonstration, rather than persuasive argumentation, would then become the only legitimate form of discourse.[44]

Now, we must be careful not to impute to Arendt the view that truth has no legitimate role to play in politics or in the sphere of human affairs. She does indeed assert that "All truths – not only the various kinds of rational truth but also factual truth – are opposed to opinion in their mode of asserting validity,"[45] since they all carry an element of compulsion. However, she is only preoccupied with the negative consequences of rational truth when applied to the sphere of politics and collective deliberation, while she defends the importance of factual truth for the preservation of an accurate account of the past and for the very existence of political communities. Factual truth, she writes, "is always related to other people: it concerns events and circumstances in which many are involved; it is established by witnesses and depends upon testimony . . . It is political by nature."[46] It follows, therefore, that

> facts and opinions, though they must be kept apart, are not antagonistic to each other; they belong to the same realm. Facts inform opinions, and opinions, inspired by different interests and passions, can differ widely and still be legitimate as long as they respect factual truth. Freedom of opinion is a farce unless factual information is guaranteed and the facts themselves are not in dispute. In other words, *factual truth informs political thought just as rational truth informs philosophical speculation.*[47]

The relationship between facts and opinions is thus one of mutual entailment: if opinions were not based on correct information and the free access to all relevant facts they could scarcely claim any validity. And if they were to be based on fantasy, self-deception, or deliberate falsehood, then no possibility of genuine debate and argumentation could be sustained. Both factual truth and the general habit of truth-telling are therefore basic to the formation of sound opinions and to the flourishing of political debate.[48] Moreover, if the record of the past were to be destroyed by organized lying, or be distorted by an attempt to rewrite history (as was the case of Stalinist historiography), political life would be deprived of one of its essential and stabilizing elements. In sum, both factual truth and the practice of truth-telling are essential to political life. The antagonism for Arendt is between *rational* truth and well-grounded opinion, since the former does not allow for debate and dissent, while the latter thrives on it. Arendt's defense of opinion must therefore be understood as a defense of *political deliberation*, and of the role that persuasion and dissuasion play in all matters affecting the political community. Against Plato and Hobbes, who denigrated the role of opinion in political matters, Arendt reasserts the value and importance of political discourse, of *deliberation* and *persuasion*, and thus of a politics that acknowledges difference and the plurality of opinions.[49]

NOTES

1 *LM*, vol. I, *Thinking*, p. 193.
2 *LM*, vol. I, pp. 5–6, 69–70, 76, 92–98, 111, 129–130, 140, 192–193, 207–209, 213–16; *LM*, vol. II, *Willing*, pp. 59–62, 217.
3 *LKPP*: these lectures have been edited and introduced by Ronald Beiner.
4 "Thinking and Moral Considerations: A Lecture" appeared in *Social Research* 38/3 (Autumn 1971), and was reprinted in *Social Research* 51/1 (Spring 1984); all citations will be from the reprinted version.
5 "The Crisis in Culture" and "Truth and Politics" are included in *BPF*, at pp. 197–226 and pp. 227–264, respectively.
6 Arendt also endows judgment with the capacity to reclaim human dignity against those theories that would posit a world-historical process whose only criterion is "success." In the Postscriptum to *Thinking* she claims that: "If judgment is our faculty for dealing with the past, the historian is the inquiring man who by relating it sits in judgment over it. If that is so, we may reclaim our human dignity, win it back, as it were, from the pseudo-divinity named History of the modern age, without denying history's importance but denying its right to being the ultimate judge" (*Thinking*, p. 216).
7 Cf. R. Bernstein, "Judging – the Actor and the Spectator," in *Philosophical Profiles* (Cambridge: Polity Press, 1986).
8 "Understanding and Politics," *Partisan Review* 20 (1953): 379.
9 Ibid., p. 383.
10 Ibid.
11 Ibid., p. 391.
12 Ibid., p. 392.
13 "Personal Responsibility under Dictatorship," *The Listener*, August 6, 1964, p. 187.
14 *LM*, vol. I, *Thinking*, p. 3.
15 Ibid., *Thinking*, pp. 4–5.
16 "Thinking and Moral Considerations," pp. 29–30, 35.
17 *LM*, *Thinking*, p. 191.
18 Ibid.
19 Cf. "Collective Responsibility," in James W. Bernauer, ed., *Amor Mundi: Explorations in the Faith and Thought of Hannah Arendt* (Dordrecht: Martinus Nijhoff Publishers, 1987), pp. 43–50.
20 See *BPF*, pp. 219–220.
21 Arendt stresses that this capacity to judge the particular *qua* particular is not to be found in Kant's moral philosophy. As she puts it: "For judgment of the particular – *This* is beautiful, *This* is ugly; *This* is right, *This* is wrong – has no place in Kant's moral philosophy. Judgment is not practical reason; practical reason 'reasons' and tells me what to do and what not to do; it lays down the law and is identical with the will, and the will utters commands; it speaks in imperatives. Judgment, on the contrary, arises from 'a merely contemplative pleasure or inactive delight'" (*LKPP*, p. 15).

22 Immanuel Kant, *Critique of Judgment*, trans. with analytical index by J. C. Meredith (Oxford: Clarendon Press, 1952), p. 18.
23 *LKPP*, p. 76; Immanuel Kant, *Critique of Pure Reason*, trans. Norman Kemp Smith (New York: St. Martin's Press, 1965), B 173.
24 *LKPP*, p. 67 (cited from Kant's "Reflexionen zur Anthropologie," no. 767, in *Gesammelte Schriften*, Prussian Academy edn., vol. XV, pp. 334–335).
25 *LKPP*, p. 74; Kant, *Critique of Judgment*, p. 155.
26 *LKPP*, p. 75 (emphasis added).
27 *BPF*, p. 221.
28 Ibid.
29 Ibid., p. 222.
30 See C. Lasch, "Introduction," *Salmagundi* 60 (Spring–Summer 1983); R. Bernstein, "Judging – the Actor and the Spectator," in *Philosophical Profiles* (Cambridge: Polity Press, 1986); for a rejoinder, see S. Benhabib, "Judgment and the Moral Foundations of Politics in Hannah Arendt's Thought," in *Situating the Self* (Cambridge: Polity Press, 1992).
31 *BPF*, p. 242.
32 Ibid., p. 241.
33 Ibid., p. 242.
34 Ibid.
35 Ibid., p. 241.
36 Ibid., p. 233.
37 Ibid., p. 247.
38 Ibid., pp. 233–234.
39 *MDT*, p. 27 (emphases added).
40 *BPF*, pp. 234–235. For recent discussions on the Kantian themes of publicity and the free use of reason in public, see Onora O'Neill, "The Public Use of Reason," *Political Theory* 14/4 (November 1986): 523–551; John Christian Laursen, "The Subversive Kant: The Vocabulary of Public and Publicity," *Political Theory* 14/4 (November 1986): 584–603; John Rawls, "The Idea of Public Reason," Lecture VI of *Political Liberalism* (New York: Columbia University Press, 1993).
41 *BPF*, p. 234.
42 Ibid., p. 235. On the role and importance of opinion in Madison, see E. Vollrath, "That All Governments Rest on Opinion," *Social Research* 43/1 (Spring 1976): 46–61.
43 Arendt reproaches Kant for having proposed an absolute standard for morality in the form of the categorical imperative. This standard for Arendt is inhuman, because it "is postulated as absolute and *in its absoluteness introduces into the interhuman realm* – which by its nature consists of relationships – *something that runs counter to its fundamental relativity*" (*MDT*, p. 27, emphases added).
44 It is important to note that for Arendt persuasion is the only truly *political* form of speech. It is that form of speech designed to "woo the consent of everyone else in the hope of coming to an agreement with him eventually" (*BPF*, p 222). Because of this it is very different from demonstration or logical proof, which rests on compelling arguments that require the assent of every rational being. For the distinction between persuasive argumentation and strict demonstration, see Chaim Perelman, *The Realm of Rhetoric* (Notre Dame: University of Notre Dame Press, 1982); Perelman and Olbrechts-Tyteca, *The New Rhetoric: A*

Treatise on Argumentation (Notre Dame: University of Notre Dame Press, 1969); Perelman, *The Idea of Justice and the Problem of Argument* (London: Routledge & Kegan Paul, 1963).

45 *BPF*, p. 239. The distinction between rational truth and factual truth is derived from Leibniz. In the *Monadology* he distinguished *truths of reasoning* from *truths of fact* and stated that the former "are necessary and their opposite is impossible," while the latter "are contingent and their opposite is possible." G. W. Leibniz, *Philosophical Writings*, ed. G. H. R. Parkinson (London: Dent, 1973), p. 184.

46 *BPF*, p. 238.

47 Ibid., (emphases added). Arendt is fully aware that facts are theory-laden and that historical inquiry is always framed by interpretive categories. Nevertheless, she believes that facts cannot be changed at will and that the historian must always respect the line separating the interpretation of facts from their manipulation or distortion. See her comments on this issue in *BPF*, pp. 238–239.

48 Indeed, they are the basic preconditions for the establishment of self-identity and of an adequate sense of reality. As Arendt observes: "The result of a consistent and total substitution of lies for factual truth is not that the lies will now be accepted as truth, and the truth be defamed as lies, but that the sense by which we take our bearings in the real world – and the category of truth vs. falsehood is among the mental means to this end – is being destroyed" (*BPF*, p. 257).

49 On the importance of deliberation for a theory of democratic legitimacy, see B. Manin, "On Legitimacy and Political Deliberation," *Political Theory* 15/3 (August 1987): 338–368, at pp. 351–359, and J. Cohen, "Deliberation and Democratic Legitimacy," in A. Hamlin and P. Pettit, eds., *The Good Polity* (Oxford: Blackwell, 1989), pp. 17–34. For the importance of persuasion and deliberation as ways to address the conflict arising out of the plurality of interests and opinions, see Hanna Pitkin and Sara Shumer, "On Participation," *Democracy* 2/4 (Fall 1982): 43–54, esp. pp. 47–48.

13

FREDERICK M. DOLAN

Arendt on philosophy and politics

Philosophy and politics: a central concern

Hannah Arendt disavowed the title of "philosopher," and is known above all as a political theorist. But the relationship between philosophy and politics animates her entire *oeuvre*. We find her addressing the topic in *The Human Condition* (1958), in *Between Past and Future* (a collection of essays written in the early 1960s), and in *Men in Dark Times* (another collection of essays, this one from the late sixties). It is treated in her *Lectures on Kant's Political Philosophy*, composed during the seventies, and also in the posthumous *Life of the Mind*, two of three projected volumes of which were complete when she died in 1975. Certainly, Arendt's thought cannot be understood without taking into account her deep suspicion of and equally deep commitment to philosophy in the context of political reflection. For all that, her writings on this abiding preoccupation do not gel into a systematically articulated theory or programmatic statement. Instead, they reflect Arendt's appreciation of what remained for her a "vital tension" – an enigma.

Plato's trauma

The relationship between philosophy and politics is commonly thought to be one of mutual opposition. While the task of the philosopher is to engage a rarefied circle of thinkers on abstract, conceptual problems of enduring significance, that of the politician is to engage the public at large on concrete issues of ephemeral interest. While philosophers rarely win the agreement of their colleagues – or even care to, the achievement of consensus, however fleeting, is an urgent concern of politicians. But if politics and philosophy are opposed, they are also related. There are times – during the French and American revolutions, the American Civil Rights movement, and the international protest against the American war in Vietnam, for example – when philosophical ideas inspire dramatic political action. Conversely, political concerns shape philosophical debates – from discussions of euthanasia and abortion to the very question of the relationship between philosophy and politics itself.

To Arendt, that relationship is neither self-evident nor easily understood. Her first examination of the subject appears in a lecture she delivered in 1954 at the University of Notre Dame, which invites careful scrutiny as her most extended single treatment of the theme. In the lecture, which was published only in 1990, she formulates her basic insights into the problem and elaborates a variety of approaches that, while they were never entirely satisfactory to her, she never definitively abandoned.

To understand Arendt's approach to the problem of philosophy and politics, it is necessary to bear in mind the course of her own intellectual development. Her philosophical awakening at the age of fourteen, when the young Königsberger first read Kant, and subsequent study in the 1920s with Martin Heidegger and Karl Jaspers, were inspired, as she put it, by a fierce "need to understand."[1] Later, as a refugee in Paris and New York, Arendt rejected academic life and her study of philosophy, throwing herself for some two decades into work on behalf of Jewish refugees. The motivation for this change, she explained in an interview in 1964, was political:

> [A]mong intellectuals *Gleichschaltung* (i.e., adjusting to Nazi policy) was the rule . . . And I never forgot that. I left Germany dominated by the idea – of course somewhat exaggerated: Never again! I shall never again get involved in any kind of intellectual business. I want nothing to do with that lot.[2]

The academic's professional investment in ideas, Arendt suspects, leaves him a prisoner, robbing him of understanding and paralyzing him, preventing him from acting on all-too-crude facts and providing a ready source of all-too-sophisticated rationalizations. Between philosophical ideas and political reality, Arendt sensed, lies an abyss.

Arendt could not maintain this stark rejection of philosophy indefinitely: her need to understand was too compelling. But as she noted in the Notre Dame lecture, Western political thought hinges on a seminal event:

> The gulf between philosophy and politics opened historically with the trial and condemnation of Socrates, which in the history of political thought plays the same role of a turning point that the trial of Jesus plays in the history of religion.[3]

The condemnation of Socrates, Arendt says, "made Plato despair of polis life and, at the same time, doubt certain fundamentals of Socrates' teachings."[4] This is one of Arendt's crucial insights: that the Western tradition of political philosophy is rooted in a *hostility* to politics, and specifically, as Arendt dramatically imagines it, in the bitter loss and grief of Socrates' followers after his execution at the hands of the Athenian *polis*. The ensuing trauma, to use a psychoanalytic term, was determinative in causing the divorce between philosophy, or thinking, and politics, which is doing or acting. It was at this point that Plato radically redefined Socrates' conception of the relationship between politics and philosophy. Henceforth, the pursuit of philosophical truth demanded a withdrawal from politics, and just political action demanded the subordination of the political to the philosophical. In this vision of Plato as the philosopher who would make politics safe for philosophy at the expense of democracy, it is difficult not to see a projection of Arendt's early disillusionment with academic life. Arendt's distress was the mirror image of Plato's: where Plato condemned politics on behalf of philosophy, Arendt condemned (Platonic) philosophy on behalf of politics.

The *locus classicus* of Plato's project for philosophy and politics is to be found in the middle sections of the *Republic*, in Books v, vi, and vii. The philosopher requires education, the quality of education is related to the quality of the state, and so, Plato gloomily concludes, a corrupt state is likely to smother the rarest philosophical souls. At best, such a state engenders critics, individuals who are in but not of their society. A state with critics is better than one without them, and critical thinking is preferable to the unexamined life, but both are inferior to the authentically philosophical life, which must eschew the falsehoods and half-truths that control public life, and turn away from the "becoming" that opposes the eternal, essential truths of "being":

> The organ of knowledge must be turned around from the world of becoming together with the entire soul . . . until the soul is able to endure the contemplation of essence and the brightest region of being, that is to say, that which we call the good.[5]

Thus transformed, the philosopher returns to the *polis* and reorders it in the light of his knowledge of, and desire for, the good: "when they have thus beheld the good itself they shall use it for a model for the right ordering of the state and the citizens and themselves."[6] Relying on his superior standards, the philosopher-ruler undertakes to mold the state in accordance with ideals that his fellow citizens are incapable of grasping. For them, the "noble" lie.

Ideally, the political regime is one that accords with philosophical insight. In a corrupt regime, however, the philosopher will avoid entanglement in politics and free himself from the opinions and passions of the *polis*. This Platonic vision, Arendt believes, is normative for Western political thought. Stripped of its Platonic imagery, it holds that serious political thought proceeds from first principles arrived at through a purified form of reasoning, which depends not on the opinions and passions of the society in which the philosopher happens to live, but on universal, transhistorical principles that transcend "mere" particulars. For Platonists, this is the only means for distinguishing between political philosophy and mere ideological discourse. In other words, the very idea of political *philosophy* necessitates an *apolitical* starting-point. The gulf between philosophy and politics could hardly be more starkly rendered: philosophy demands a principled withdrawal from public life, while politics means living according to ideas that are at best half-true and at worst false.

How should we understand Arendt's characterization of Plato's reaction to the death of Socrates? If, as she says, it occasioned a radical change in perspective, it distorted our understanding of acting and thinking by demonizing the one and glorifying the other. In reality, thinking is not as autonomous as the Platonic tradition would have it, nor acting as thoughtless. But for Plato's grief, Arendt's fable suggests, we might understand this. Is her attitude, then, predominantly nostalgic? Arendt is often accused of hankering after the lost Greek *polis*, but her critics are confusing nostalgia and mourning. The work of mourning, as Freud understands it, is to dissipate our attachment to a lost object. The inability to mourn, to find in the world of the living a worthy object of love, leads to melancholia, the denial of the loved object's disappearance. To mourn, on the other hand, is to face loss – to experience its true extent and meaning. Arendt's celebration of a *polis* impossible to recover except in the imagination is an exercise in mourning in the grand style, a successful overcoming of her despair for modern intellectual life. And in casting this episode as the symptom of a trauma, Arendt is suggesting that it should spur us to find our way towards a cure – a more supple understanding of thought and action. Her intent is not to live in the past, but, by working through the death of Socrates, to prepare the inheritors of Plato's trauma for a new way to love this world, in the present.

Socrates *contra* Plato

In trying to imagine a non-Platonic view of the relationship between philosophy and politics, Arendt reconstructs what she regards as "the fundamentals of Socrates' teachings" as they appear *outside* the framework of Plato's trauma.[7] Unlike the Socrates of the *Republic*, an embodiment of the man of thought, a Socrates who denounces democracy, celebrates pure reason and ridicules sophism, Arendt's Socrates bears a strong resemblance to the sophists.[8] Arendt observes that:

> If the quintessence of the Sophists' teaching consisted in the *dyo logoi*, the insistence that each matter can be talked about in two different ways, then Socrates was the greatest Sophist of them all. For he thought that there are, or

> should be, as many different *logoi* as there are men, and that all these *logoi* together form the human world, insofar as men live together in the manner of speech.[9]

So far from being a believer in absolute first principles, Arendt's Socrates resembles nothing so much as a liberal pluralist. For him, each member of the *polis* possesses his individual *doxa*, his opinion or viewpoint on the world, and any such *doxa* is to be regarded, not as a falsehood or a distortion of reality, but as a potential truth waiting to be unfolded:

> To Socrates, as to his fellow citizens, *doxa* was the formulation in speech of what *dokei moi*, that is, of what appears to me. This *doxa* had as its topic . . . the world as it opens itself to me. It was not, therefore, subjective fantasy and arbitrariness, but also not something absolute and valid for all. The assumption was that the world opens up differently to every man, according to his position in it . . .[10]

What separates Socrates from the sophists, in Arendt's view, is his conviction that *doxai* contain truths, whereas for the sophists (and here, ironically, they agree with Plato) they are nothing but *falsa infinita*, limitless falsehoods. Arendt's Socrates does not deny the possibility of knowledge. Rather, he asserts, *contra* Plato's belief in the possibility of an absolute knowledge that cannot be qualified by any further experience or reflection, that a first principle can never be guaranteed. For Socrates, all such foundations – including Platonic ideas, no matter how purged of social and historical distortions – are themselves subject to transformation. It is in his openness to *dialegesthai*, to "talk something through with somebody,"[11] that Socrates knows that he knows nothing.

Socrates is aware that anything we think we know might be wrong, and that we come to realize this when we expose our ideas to the scrutiny of others. The corollary of this position, however, is that in every opinion, some truth resides:

> Every man has his own *doxa*, his own opening to the world, and Socrates must therefore always begin with questions; he cannot know beforehand what kind of *dokei moi*, of it-appears-to-me, the other possesses. He must make sure of the other's position in the common world. Yet, just as nobody can know beforehand the other's *doxa*, so nobody can know by himself and without effort the inherent truth of his own opinion. Socrates wanted to bring out this truth which everyone potentially possesses.[12]

As Arendt goes on to say, the Platonic opposition between truth and opinion is "the most anti-Socratic conclusion that Plato drew from Socrates' trial."[13] Opinions are based on experience, which shapes and limits the perspective of its possessor. We come to understand the opinions of others when we grasp their point of view. In the realm of human affairs, reality (and so by extension, truth) is multiple.

Because he did not regard truth as inherently opposed to opinion, Socrates saw no need to make a rigorous distinction between philosophy and persuasion, the political art *par excellence*. "What Plato later called *dialegesthai*, Socrates himself called maieutic, the art of midwifery: he wanted to help others give birth to what they themselves thought anyhow, to find the truth in their *doxa*."[14] Socratic philosophy

> brings forth truth *not* by destroying *doxa* or opinion, but on the contrary reveals *doxa* in its own truthfulness. The role of the philosopher, then, is . . . not to tell philosophical truths but to make the citizens more truthful. The difference with Plato is decisive: Socrates did not want to educate the citizens so much as he wanted to improve their *doxai*, which constituted the political life in which he too took part.[15]

Doxa, in its sense not only of opinion but also of splendor and fame, is incompatible with privacy, whereas Socrates, Arendt stresses, moved in the marketplace, "in the very midst" of *doxai*.[16] Arendt's Socrates, unlike Plato's, does not turn away from the *polis*. He avoids public affairs, but does not retreat to private life.

Arendt thus chooses to emphasize Socrates' affinity with the sophists, with their concern for public opinion and their respect for dialogue and its use in the service of persuasion, controversy, and consensus. Her intent is not to play down Socrates' moral purpose, for rendering the citizens' opinions richer, sharper, and deeper helps them to become better. Her Socrates, too, is opposed to Plato's morality of individual fidelity to the natural order, as embodied in the just, philosophically grounded state – what Arendt characterizes as a "tyranny of truth, in which it is not what is temporally good, of which men can be persuaded, but eternal truth, of which men cannot be persuaded, that is to rule the city."[17] Socrates, by contrast, believes that "the role of the philosopher . . . is not to rule the city, but to be its 'gadfly,'" that is, to encourage citizens to think for themselves, not to be instruments of a larger natural or metaphysical order.[18] For Arendt's Socrates, morality and persuasion go together, because the individual, even when alone, is always "two-in-one" insofar as he is thoughtful: in "speaking with myself I live together with myself."[19] For Socrates,

> living together with others begins by living together with oneself. Socrates' teaching meant: only he who knows how to live with himself is fit to live with others. The self is the only person from whom I cannot depart, whom I cannot leave, with whom I am welded together.[20]

Just as one needs the opinions of others to develop the truth of one's own, one must form an opinion of oneself and one's actions that is neither slavishly dependent on the prevailing *doxa* (as the sophists are) nor radically estranged from it (as Plato is). Diverging radically from Plato, Socrates posits solitude – that is, the cultivation of the self, or individual personality – as "the necessary condition for the good functioning of the polis, a better guarantee than rules of behavior enforced by laws and fear of punishment."[21]

From truth versus opinion to justice versus friendship

So far, I have described how Arendt makes philosophy friendly to politics by replacing the Platonic opposition of truth to opinion by a Socratic idea of the truth *of* opinion. This also allows her to redefine the traditional orientation of political philosophy toward the problem of justice. Taking Aristotle as a stand-in for Socrates, she writes:

> Aristotle concludes that it is friendship not justice (as Plato maintained in the Republic, that great dialogue about justice) that appears to be the bond of communities. For Aristotle, friendship is higher than justice, because justice is no longer necessary between friends.[22]

Justice requires subordination to a universal principle that overrides any relationship between individuals. Talking things through in order to arrive at the truth of an opinion, on the other hand, yields no fixed result, involves give and take, and implies that friendship matters more than any particular assertion that friends might dispute. For friends, "[t]o have talked something through, to have talked about something, some citizen's doxa, [is] result enough."[23] Establishing friendship among Athens's citizens is an ontological imperative, since friendship "consists of . . . talking about something the friends have in common," which over the course of time constitutes a world its own.[24] As Aristotle says, "a community is not made out of equals, but on the contrary of people who are different and unequal," and who therefore rely on the exchange of opinion in friendship to "equalize" themselves.[25] Socrates too, on Arendt's account, "seems to have believed that the political function of the philosopher was to help establish this kind of common world, built on the understanding of friendship, in which no rulership is needed."[26]

For Arendt, Socrates' view of opinion and friendship is a far more compelling model of an authentically political philosophy than Plato's commitment to truth and justice. Plato's outlook, as I have noted, is by contrast essentially apolitical – notwithstanding his interest in politics, a subject he treats not only in the *Republic* but also in the *Statesman*, the *Apology*, *Protagoras*, *Laws*, and elsewhere, to say nothing of his voyage to Syracuse on behalf of his Republic. Whereas Socrates understands the relative, plural character of truth and can appreciate the true worth of the political, Plato, who sees truth as absolute and singular, regards with "indifference and contempt . . . the world of the city,"[27] and so considers not "how philosophy looks from the viewpoint of politics but how politics, the realm of human affairs, looks from the viewpoint of philosophy."[28] Just as Socrates' insight into the intimate relation between truth and opinion gives him insight into human affairs, so Platonic dogmatism in philosophy accords with Platonic authoritarianism in politics; it attempts to subordinate the political to the philosophical, to the disadvantage of each. A properly political view of the world for Arendt is pluralistic and relativistic:

> This kind of understanding – seeing the world (as we rather tritely say today) from the other fellow's point of view – is the political insight par excellence. If we wanted to define, traditionally, the one outstanding virtue of the statesman, we could say that it consists in understanding the greatest possible number and variety of realities – not of subjective viewpoints, which of course also exist but do not concern us here – as those realities open themselves up to the various opinions of citizens; and, at the same time, in being able to communicate between the citizens and their opinions so that the commonness of this world becomes apparent.[29]

The Platonic political philosopher is interested in his point of view only; the Socratic political philosopher tests and elaborates his perspective against others'. A Socratic philosophy of multiple perspectives, amenable to rich and surprising development, accords well with the politics of a diverse citizenry: it is democracy perfected.

Wonder at being versus the tyranny of truth

The essential medium of human affairs is speech, but the inner spring of philosophy, Arendt says, is akin to speechlessness. Referring to passages in Plato's *Seventh Letter* and the *Theaetatus*, Arendt asserts that "the beginning of philosophy is wonder."[30] She writes:

> *Thaumadzein*, the wonder at that which is as it is, is according to Plato a *pathos*, something which is endured and as such quite distinct from *doxadzein*, from forming an opinion about something. The wonder that man endures or which befalls him cannot be related in words because it is too general for words. Plato must first have encountered it in those frequently reported traumatic states in which Socrates would suddenly, as though seized by a rapture, fall into complete motionlessness, just staring without seeing or hearing anything.[31]

Although she attributes this rapture to Socrates, what Arendt evidently has in mind is Martin Heidegger's "being of beings." That phrase is meant to capture the significance of the peculiar fact that there is something rather than nothing – that this fact makes a difference, so to speak, so that what is is meaningful not only with respect to its properties, qualities, and behavior, but as sheer, stark being. What separates the philosopher from his fellow citizens is that he is struck by the fact that he is, when he might as well never have been, or that there is anything at all, when there might as well have been nothing. Faced with this "miracle of being," the philosopher's only response is silent, speechless wonder – a state that our language, which is best suited to describing the properties, qualities, and behavior of things, is not adequate to express.

Given this experience,

> [t]he philosopher . . . finds himself in a twofold conflict with the polis. Since his ultimate experience is one of speechlessness, he has put himself outside the political realm in which the highest faculty of man is, precisely, speech . . . The philosophical shock, moreover, strikes man in his singularity, that is, neither in his equality with all others nor in his distinctness from them. In this shock, man in the singular, as it were, is for one fleeting moment confronted with the whole of the universe, as he will be confronted again only at the moment of his death. He is to an extent alienated from the city of men, which can only look with suspicion on everything that concerns man in the singular.[32]

If speechless wonder is the center of authentic philosophical activity, as Arendt thinks it was for Socrates, Plato, and Aristotle, philosophy becomes above all a mode of questioning – a way of posing and discussing questions that are not amenable to ordinary investigation and resolution. "As soon as the speechless state of wonder translates itself into words," Arendt writes, "it will not begin with statements but will formulate in unending variations what we call the ultimate questions – What is being? Who is man? What meaning has life? What is death? etc. – all of which have in common that they cannot be answered scientifically."[33] The only adequate "answer" to such questions is to ponder them.

In this way, Arendt says, "man establishes himself as a question-asking being."[34] Stilled and silenced by wonder, speaking only to ask unanswerable questions, the philosopher will shrink from forming "opinions on matters about which man cannot hold opinions because the common and commonly accepted standards of common sense do not here apply" – unlike *hoi polloi*, who avoid the experience of wonder, which they refuse to endure, by acquiring opinions on matters about which opinion is inadequate.[35] When he does speak with others, the philosopher is likely to express his disagreement with public opinion. This was Socrates' way: he sought to engage his fellow citizens in dialogue despite the fact that his sense of wonder separated him from them. Plato, on the other hand, was determined to prolong wonder indefinitely – a self-defeating enterprise, Arendt argues, since it attempts "to develop into a way of life . . . what can only be a fleeting moment."[36] In his attempt to become, as it were, utterly singular, the Platonist, Arendt concludes, destroys the human plurality within himself.

Initially, Arendt stressed the conflict between the philosophical commitment to a singular truth and the multiplicity of opinions in political life. Now, she draws our attention to the medium of politics – speech – and its conflict with an experience that cannot be articulated, at least in declarative statements. The Platonic philosopher is not only disdainful of politics' disregard for truth, but unable to participate in politics owing to its affiliation with a mode of speech that will only raise questions that can be answered. Not only does the Platonic philosopher refuse the idea of a plurality of truths, but his insight into the limits of articulate understanding as such prevents him from embracing a form of life that insists that man is the measure of all things. The political gravamen of Plato's philosophy is to be found, Arendt suggests, in his image (found in Book VII of the *Republic*) of the cave dweller who surfaces to glimpse the sun and returns to his companions with superior knowledge, but too dazed to deal intelligently with the world underground:

> The returning philosopher is in danger because he has lost the common sense needed to orient him in a world common to all, and, moreover, because what he harbors in his thought contradicts the common sense of the world.[37]

As Plato puts it, such a person "cuts a sorry figure and appears most ridiculous, if, while still blinking through the gloom, and before he has become sufficiently accustomed to the surrounding darkness, he is compelled . . . to contend about the shadows of justice."[38] The philosopher is as much in danger from the world as a danger to the world. His conviction that wonder is the central experience of human existence prejudices his judgment. In neglecting to cultivate Socrates' remarkable gift for both solitary wonder and friendly, questioning engagement with his fellow citizens, Arendt finds that philosophers after Plato, when they attend to politics at all, evaluate it on the basis of universal ideas – the latter are a misguided way to articulate the properly speechless wonder at the being of being. This does a disservice both to politics and to philosophy: philosophy remains blithely detached from the vagaries of human reality, and politics is given over to the formation of mere public opinion as opposed to the discovery of the truth of *doxai*.

Freedom and the nature of the political

The example of Socrates suggests a powerful alternative to the Platonic understanding of the relationship between philosophy and politics. The question, for Arendt, is to discover a conception of truth and inquiry which does not lead to a hierarchical, tyrannical understanding of politics, but which remains distinctively philosophical, in the sense that it arises out of the necessarily rare experience of wonder. But that question involves another one: whether we can discover a concept of the political more faithful to the reality of political life than the distorted version bequeathed to us by the Platonic philosophical tradition. In making the paradoxical assertion that Socrates, who avoided participating in public affairs, not Plato, who was actively interested in them, is the truly political philosopher, Arendt is relying on her distinctive conception of the political. For her, the supreme value of politics is freedom, and freedom in Arendt's sense depends on plurality, spontaneity, and the open-ended, unpredictable character of interaction through speech and deed.

Just as Arendt looks to a non-Platonic Socrates for a different view of political philosophy, she turns to Periclean Athens for a non-philosophical idea of freedom. Then and there, she writes, "freedom was understood to be the free man's status, which enabled him to move, to get away from home, to go out into the world and meet other people in deed and word."[39] This freedom, the freedom to appear in public, implies certain conditions: a "private sphere" (i.e., a household) that secures the necessities of life; the company of other free citizens ("[t]o be free meant both not to be subject to the necessity of life or to the command of another and not to be in command oneself. It meant neither to rule nor to be ruled"[40]); and a "public sphere," set aside for political life, "a space of appearances where [individuals can] act . . . a kind of theater where freedom [can] appear."[41] Freedom of this kind, Arendt points out, is neither "an attribute of thought [nor] a quality of the will."[42] It is a form of action – or rather, interaction, for "what the actor is concerned with is doxa, fame – that is, the opinion of others."[43]

Politics, then, is the cultivation of freedom, and freedom is a mode of action that can take place when one appears before an authentic public. A political act is above all a performance, and, as in music or dance, as opposed to the creative arts, "the accomplishment lies in the performance itself and not in an end which outlasts the activity."[44] As a performance, a political act is intended to be distinctive, and so requires "for its full appearance the shining brightness we once called glory," that is, fame, which is a form of opinion.[45] It is therefore in the nature of an authentic political act to stand out against the humdrum background of the everyday routine:

> Every act, seen from the perspective not of the agent but of the process in whose framework it occurs and whose automatism it interrupts, is a "miracle" – that is, something which could not be expected. If it is true that action and beginning are essentially the same, it follows that a capacity for performing miracles must likewise be within the range of human capacities.[46]

Political performances, however, are radically uncertain.[47] The reason is that political action, for Arendt, is intimately tied to speech: "the actor, the doer of deeds, is possible only if he is at the same time the speaker of words."[48] The kind of speech appropriate to a world of opinion is persuasion, or rhetoric; that is "the specifically political form of speech . . . the truly political art."[49] A political performance is "rhetorical" in the sense that it deals in probabilities, estimates, and perspectives. Its meaning and importance, therefore, are always subject to revision, as when the hero of one age becomes the villain of another, and are always in danger of falling into oblivion, as when what is said and done turns out to have been of merely topical interest. It is the miraculous quality of the act, if anything, that saves it from oblivion, because, as something great and extraordinary and inexplicable, it will always be relevant, at least so long as a sense of wonder is present.

Socrates brings philosophy and politics together by investing the faculty of wonder in the realm of human affairs. An adequate response to this specifically "human" wonder is not only sheer speechlessness, nor the bare assertion of opinions, but a unique discourse in which individuated personalities meet as equals to question one another and themselves on how the miracle appears to them. This way of being together with others is a form of political life that is faithful to both philosophical wonder and the anarchic pluralism of an authentically political society. The Socratic political thinker is apolitical, because he approaches public opinion from a distance, as something to be interrogated, justified, and improved, not merely accepted as commonsensical. As befits one who is able to experience wonder, he takes nothing for granted. Still, because he possesses no *absolute* knowledge against which to measure the value of public opinion, he does not feel obligated to order or manage human affairs. Politics is not central to his life, but he cannot be entirely indifferent to it, since wonder is a fleeting experience, and he must dwell for the most part in the world of common sense. But he has no reason to look upon politics with the contempt and *ressentiment* nursed by the Platonic political philosopher, and since he has some reason to enjoy political life, he is not as subject to the tyrannical temptations indulged by Plato and his followers.

Conclusion: philosophy and politics in modernity

The traditional tensions between philosophy and politics are based on the opposition between wonder at being and common sense, which takes it for granted that there is something rather than nothing and proceeds to make assertions, form opinions, and organize things. From the point of view of common sense, one who is caught up in philosophical wonder is blind and dumb; from the point of view of philosophical wonder, the bustling, opinionated citizenry are even more so. Plato resolved this difficulty by recasting the state as an instrument that would guarantee the experience of wonder that he prized. Socrates' resolution of the problem is clearly more appealing to Arendt, because infinitely wiser: he accepted the fact that wonder at being is a transitory experience, and learned to express it in the more circumspect form of cultivating the little miracles that arise in the realm of human affairs.

The radically different context of the modern world undercuts the relevance of Socrates' example. With what Arendt calls "the collapse of the tradition," common sense evaporates, so that "we can no longer fall back on authentic and undisputable experiences common to all."[50] Unlike Socrates,

> [w]e live today in a world in which not even common sense makes sense any longer. The breakdown of common sense in the present world signals that philosophy and politics, their old conflict notwithstanding, have suffered the same fate.[51]

Indeed, the destruction of common sense is prefigured by Socrates himself, especially in those Platonic dialogues that are most "Socratic," which undermine all opinions without offering a truth to replace them:

> The search for the truth in *doxa* can lead to the catastrophic result that the *doxa* is altogether destroyed, or that what had appeared is revealed as an illusion . . . Socrates, all his protests not to possess any teachable truth notwithstanding, must somehow already have appeared like an expert in truth. The abyss between truth and opinion, which from then on was to divide the philosopher from all other men, had not yet opened, but was already indicated, or rather foreshadowed, in the figure of this one man who, wherever he went, tried to make everybody around him, and first of all himself, more truthful.[52]

As Oedipus and Hamlet know, and as Friedrich Nietzsche argues, limitless inquiry can prove corrosive when the *examined* life turns out not to be worth living.

When the tension between common sense and the wonder at being is destroyed, we enter the bleak realm of the "social," of programmed life and scripted, poll-tested politics. In this Kafkaesque world, the suspension of what was once common sense is itself common, and hence uncannily banal.

Socratic political philosophy loses its purchase under such circumstances, because without real political life, there is nothing for the Socratic thinker to question, no truth to be found in the *doxai*.

This, I believe, is the point of view from which Arendt conducts her political theorizing. In her later work, Arendt turns to Kant, among others, to explore ideas of spectatorship, imagination, judgment, and critical thought.[53] As these themes suggest, thinking, for Arendt, is a powerfully individuated enterprise. Unlike Socratic political philosophy, however, this properly *Arendtian* political philosophy is wholly appropriate to the modern context:

> To live in a political realm with neither authority nor the concomitant awareness that the source of authority transcends power and those who are in power, means to be confronted anew, without the religious trust in a sacred beginning and without the protection of traditional and therefore self-evident standards of behavior, by the elementary problems of human living-together.[54]

The weakening of entrenched notions of common sense offers a rare opportunity to rethink our attitudes toward philosophy and politics – although, as Arendt's verbal straining at the end of that passage suggests, we may no longer feel justified in using the traditional nomenclature.

Such rethinking, for better or worse, characterizes much of the twentieth century – in literature, poetry, music, painting, and science no less than philosophy and political theory and politics. Arendt's thought is a contribution – probably the most important any political theorist has made – to that bold reassessment of the Western tradition that we broadly call "modernism." Like that of so many of her fellow modernists, her work does not lead to a settled outlook. She never arrived at a finished view of the relationship between philosophy and politics, nor did she intend to. But her concern for the problem, a sense of its complexity and drama and stakes, suffuses her writing. For this reason, Arendt can only awkwardly be classed with mainstream political philosophers, who to the present day take the Platonic, apolitical perspective as the starting point for political reflection, or, alternatively, pursue a Socratism without wonder. Arendt is one of a select group of thinkers – Michel Foucault is another – who perceive that thinking and acting have become newly enigmatic in our time. Arendt's contribution is not to have set right the relationship between philosophy and politics, but to have shown what nourishing food for thought is to be had by reflecting on it.

NOTES

1 Hannah Arendt, "What Remains? The Language Remains," in *EU*, p. 6. Hereafter referred to as WR.

2 WR, p. 11.

3 Hannah Arendt, "Philosophy and Politics," *Social Research* 57 (1990): 73. Hereafter referred to as PP.
4 PP, p. 42.
5 Plato, *Republic* 518d. The translation here and following is adapted from Paul Shorey, in the Loeb Classical Library edition (Cambridge, MA and London: Harvard University Press, 1994).
6 Plato, *Republic* 540a.
7 PP, p. 72.
8 Ibid., p. 92.
9 Ibid., p. 85.
10 Ibid., p. 80.
11 Ibid.
12 Ibid., p. 81.
13 Ibid., p. 75.
14 Ibid., p. 81.
15 Ibid.
16 Ibid.
17 Ibid., p. 78.
18 Ibid., p. 81.
19 Ibid., p. 86.
20 Ibid., pp. 86–87.
21 Ibid., p. 89.
22 PP, p. 83. Arendt's reference is to the *Nichomachean Ethics*. She assumes, without explanation, that "great parts of Aristotle's political philosophy, especially those in which he is in explicit opposition to Plato, go back to Socrates" (PP, p. 82).
23 PP, p. 82.
24 Ibid.
25 Ibid., p. 83.
26 Ibid., p. 84.
27 Ibid., p. 91.
28 Ibid., p. 96.
29 Ibid., p. 84.
30 Ibid., p. 97. The passages are at the *Seventh Letter* 341d and the *Theaetetus* 155d.
31 Ibid., pp. 97–98.
32 Ibid., pp. 99–100.
33 Ibid., p. 98.
34 Ibid., p. 99.
35 Ibid.
36 Ibid., p. 101.
37 Ibid., p. 95.
38 Plato, *Republic* 518b.
39 Hannah Arendt, "What is Freedom?," in *BPF*, p. 148. Hereafter referred to as WF.
40 Arendt, *HC*, 32.
41 WF, p. 154.
42 Ibid., p. 148.
43 Arendt, *LKPP*, p. 55.

44 WF, p. 153.
45 *HC*, p. 180.
46 WF, p. 169.
47 See *HC*, p. 91.
48 Ibid., p. 179.
49 PP, pp. 74–75.
50 Hannah Arendt, "What is Authority?," *BPF*, p. 91. Hereafter referred to as WA.
51 PP, pp. 102–104.
52 Ibid., pp. 90–91.
53 See *LKPP* and Arendt, *LM*, vol. 1, *Thinking*.
54 WA, p. 141.

14

RICHARD J. BERNSTEIN

Arendt on thinking

In the Introduction to *The Life of the Mind*, Arendt tells us that her preoccupation with mental activities (thinking, willing, and judging) had two different origins. The immediate impulse came from her reflections on the Eichmann trial. The most unsettling trait of Adolf Eichmann, who seemed to be completely entrapped in his own clichés and stock phrases, was his inability to think. The phenomenon of the banality of evil led her to ask: "Might the problem of good and evil, our faculty of telling right from wrong, be connected with our faculty of thought?" "Could the activity of thinking as such, the habit of examining whatever happens to come to pass or to attract attention, regardless of results and specific content, could this activity be among the conditions that make men abstain from evil-doing or even actually 'condition' them against it?" (*LM*, vol. 1, p. 5). The second source was "certain doubts" that had been plaguing her since she had completed *The Human Condition*. She originally intended to call the book *The Vita Activa* because she focused her attention on three fundamental human activities: labor, work, and action. But she realized that the very term, *vita activa*, was coined by those who primarily valued the *vita comtemplativa*. Such a tradition held that "thinking aims at and ends in contemplation, and contemplation is not an activity but a passivity" (*LM*, vol. 1, p. 6). Thus contemplation was valued above the active life.

Now it is commonly believed that Arendt started thinking about thinking only late in her career. But the truth is that Arendt's concern with thinking always exerted a powerful influence on the character of her own passionate thinking. The more closely one examines her writings, the more striking it becomes that thinking is a pervasive theme in her entire corpus. I want to review some of the highlights of her thinking about thinking (or more accurately her thinking *through* thinking); then I intend to step back in order to see how the various threads of her reflections are woven together; and finally I want to explore a deep unresolved tension in her own thinking, an internal debate that she never quite resolved.

I

One of her earliest explicit discussions of thinking appears in a context that may initially seem remote from the topic, but is actually quite relevant. In her 1944 essay, *The Jew as Pariah: A Hidden Tradition*, Arendt seeks to recover a vital but hidden tradition in modern Jewish thought. This is the tradition of the pariah, which she sharply contrasts with another Jewish type, the parvenu. Appropriating an idea taken from Max Weber, who claimed that the Jews are not only an "oppressed people," but a "pariah people," Arendt analyzes the pariah as a "human type" which has "supreme importance for the evaluation of mankind in our day" (*JP*, p. 68).[1] The poets, writers, and artists who exemplify the Jewish pariah are not simply outcasts, a status thrust upon them by society. They take advantage of this status by asserting their independence and their freedom. She describes four exemplars of this tradition: Heine, Chaplin, Lazare, and Kafka. In her discussion of Kafka, Arendt remarks: "For Kafka only those things are real whose strength is not impaired but confirmed by thinking . . . thinking is the new weapon – the only one with which, in Kafka's opinion, the pariah is endowed at birth in his vital struggle against society" (*JP*, p. 83). Arendt does not elaborate on what she means by "thinking" here, but her perceptive comments take on a heightened significance, especially in light of her later development. This passage makes clear that Arendt never thought of thinking as the exclusive mental activity of philosophers or "professional thinkers." On the contrary, genuine thinking is exemplified by poets, writers, and artists. Furthermore, she makes it clear that thinking is a "weapon," indeed a primary weapon in the struggle against the oppressive bureaucratic forces of society ("a society of nobodies") in the fight for genuine freedom.

This early characterization of the pariah as an individual who uses her thinking as a *weapon* is the germ of Arendt's idea of the *Selbstdenker* – the independent thinker. In her speech, "On Humanity in Dark Times: Thoughts about Lessing," which she gave when she received the Lessing Prize in 1959, Arendt elaborates this idea of *Selbstdenken*. Thinking, she tells us, is "another mode of moving in the world of freedom." When human beings are deprived of public space in dark times "they retreat into the freedom of their thought" (*MDT*, p. 9). Such independent thinking is "a new kind of thinking that needs no pillars and props, no standards and traditions to move freely without crutches over unfamiliar terrain" (*MDT*, p. 10). Here we touch upon one of the deepest themes of Arendt's own thinking. For she was convinced that with the catastrophic outbreak of totalitarianism in the twentieth century, there had been a radical break with tradition. We can no longer rely on tradition, accepted categories and guideposts. We have to learn to think in *new* ways. She epitomized this type of thinking as *Denken ohne Geländer* – thinking without banisters. This is the type of thinking that Arendt herself practiced. And what Arendt says in her eloquent essay on Walter Benjamin also might have been said about Arendt. She speaks of Benjamin's "gift of thinking poetically":

> This thinking, fed by the present, works with the "thought fragments" it can wrest from the past and gather about itself. Like a pearl diver who descends to the bottom of the sea, not to excavate the bottom and bring it to light but to pry loose the rich and the strange, the pearls and the coral in the depths and to carry them to the surface, this thinking delves into the depths of the past – but not in order to resuscitate it the way it was and to contribute to the renewal of extinct ages. What guides this thinking is the conviction that although the living is subject to the ruin of the time, the process of decay is at the same time a process of crystallization, that in the depth of the sea, into which sinks and is dissolved what was once alive, some things suffer a "sea change" and survive in new crystallized forms and shapes that remain immune from the elements, as though they waited only for the pearl diver who one day will come down to them and bring them up into the world of the living – as "thought fragments," as something "rich and strange," and perhaps even as everlasting *Urphänomene*. (*MDT*, pp. 205–206)

One of Arendt's most poetic descriptions of thinking is to be found in her Preface to the collection of essays *Between Past and Future*: *Six Exercises in Political Thought*. To express what she means by thinking, she again turns to Kafka. Commenting on a parable of Kafka and an aphorism of René Char, "Notre héritage n'est précédé d'aucun testament," she links thinking together with remembrance and story-telling. Remembrance is one of the most important "modes of thought," and it requires story-telling in order to preserve those "small hidden islands of freedom." This activity of thinking settles down in the timeless "gap between past and future." In Kafka's parable, the past and the future are taken to be forces which the "he" who is situated in this gap must always fight. The thinking that takes place in this gap is not to be identified with "such mental processes as deducing, inducing, and drawing conclusions whose logical rules of non-contradiction and inner consistency can be learned once and for all and then need only to be applied" (*BPF*, p. 14). Arendt is fully aware that traditionally thinking has been associated with such mental processes, and she is not suggesting that these are irrelevant to thinking. But we miss what she takes to be distinctive about the new thinking that is now demanded if we simply identify it with the mental processes of ratiocination. The thinking that she describes and *practices* is a creative activity which requires remembrance, story-telling, and imagination. It also requires the virtues of both courage and independence.

Furthermore, "thought itself arises out of incidents of living experience and must remain bound to them as the only guideposts by which to take its bearings" (BPF, p. 14). Later, we shall see that although all genuine thinking requires a withdrawal from everyday life, and indeed demands solitude and quietness, one of the greatest dangers of thinking is the illusion that human beings can escape from the everyday world of appearances. This is a temptation – a temptation to denigrate *doxa* and escape from the contingency of changing appearances – that has long been inherent in the philosophical tradition. It is a danger that always confronts "professional thinkers." And this is one of the main reasons why Arendt never thought of herself as a "professional thinker," and was reluctant to identify herself as a philosopher rather than an independent thinker.

In 1954 (four years before the publication of *The Human Condition*), Arendt gave a series of lectures at the University of Notre Dame. Her final lecture, "Philosophy and Politics" (which was published only in 1990), is crucial for understanding the nuances of her thinking about thinking, especially the *political* function of thinking. In this lecture Arendt deals with a problem that haunted her throughout her life – the tension between philosophy and politics.[2] According to Arendt, the main tradition of political philosophy began with Plato and ended with Karl Marx. She argues that when philosophers have turned their attention to the messy confused world of politics in which there is always the competing pluralistic contest of opinions (*doxai*), their primary aim has not been to understand politics, but rather to impose the "absolute standards" of philosophy upon politics. There has been a profound hostility against politics by philosophers. They have sought to escape from the "lunacy" of politics. Or they have sought to rule the city by appealing to fixed, permanent, absolute standards of "reality and truth." This is a tradition that has its origins in Plato's despair when the Athenian *polis* condemned Socrates. But Arendt draws a sharp contrast between Socrates and Plato.[3] Arendt's Socrates (in this essay) is not someone who wants to escape or *rule* the polis. He "moved in the marketplace, in the very midst of these *doxai*, these opinions . . . he wanted to help others give birth to what they themselves thought anyhow, to find the truth in their *doxa*."[4]

> Socrates wanted to make the city more truthful by delivering each of its citizens of their truths. The method of doing this is *dialegesthai*, talking something through, but this dialectic brings forth truth *not* by destroying *doxa* or opinion, but on the contrary reveals *doxa* in its own truthfulness. The role of the philosopher, then, is not to rule the city but to be its "gadfly," not to tell philosophical truths but to make citizens more truthful. The difference with Plato is decisive: Socrates did not want to educate the citizens so much as he wanted to improve their *doxai*, which constituted the political life in which he

> took part. To Socrates, maieutic was a political activity, a give and take, fundamentally on a basis of strict equality, the fruits of which could not be measured by the result of arriving at this or that general truth. ("Philosophy and Politics," p. 81)

Socrates sought to provoke his fellow citizens into becoming *thinking* persons. This thinking manifests itself in speech (*logos*). "For Socrates the chief criterion for the man who speaks truthfully his own *doxa* was 'that he be in agreement with himself' – that he not contradict himself and not say contradictory things . . ." (p. 85). Thinking for Socrates requires a dialogue with oneself. But even in this internal dialogue in which I am a two-in-one, "I am not altogether separated from that plurality which is the world of men . . ." (p. 88). With Socrates there "is an awareness that man is a thinking and acting being in one – someone, namely, whose thoughts invariably and unavoidably accompany his acts – [this awareness] is what improves men and citizens. The underlying assumption of this teaching is thought and not action, because only in thought do I realize the dialogue of the two-in-one who I am" (p. 89).

Now whatever we may think of the "historical" accuracy of Arendt's portrait of Socrates, the political significance of this "ideal" Socrates is of the utmost importance.[5] It makes absolutely clear that *thinking* is essential for politics, that thinking is essential for testing one's *doxai* and making them more truthful. For Socrates, man is not yet the "rational animal" of the philosophers, but a *thinking being* whose thought is manifested in speech. Furthermore, Arendt also stresses that thinking is essential for the formation of conscience. She claims that the supreme imperative for Socrates is to try to live in such a manner so that he is not in contradiction with himself. When Socrates claimed that "it is much better to be in disagreement with the whole world than being one to be in disagreement with myself," he was not only anticipating a fundamental point of logic but also of ethics. "Ethics, no less than logic, has its origin in this statement, for conscience in its most general sense is also based on the fact that I can be in agreement or disagreement with myself, and that means I do not only appear to others but also to myself" (p. 87). A fundamental reason why Arendt stresses the linkage of thinking, internal dialogue, solitude, and conscience is because of her experience with totalitarianism. "The frequently observed fact that conscience itself no longer functioned under totalitarian conditions of political organization" is explicable when we realize that totalitarian regimes seek to eliminate the very possibility of the solitude required for independent thinking. "No man can keep his conscience intact who cannot actualize the dialogue with himself, that is, who lacks the solitude required for all forms of thinking" (p. 90). Now the reason why I have stressed Arendt's characterization of Socrates is because it makes eminently clear what she means by political thinking, the thinking directed to making *doxa* more truthful, and how important such thinking is for the citizens of the *polis*.

Before taking a step back in order to weave together the several strands in Arendt's thinking about thinking, I want to turn briefly to *The Human Condition*. As I indicated earlier, one of Arendt's motivations for turning her attention to thinking in *The Life of the Mind* was her unease about the neglect of the topic in *The Human Condition*. But we should not forget that the entire book is *framed* by her critical references to thinking. In her Prologue – in a passage that can be read as an ominous warning – she tells us: "If it should turn out to be true that knowledge (in the modern sense of know-how) and thought have parted company for good, then we would indeed become the helpless slaves, not so much of our machines as of our know-how, thoughtless creatures at the mercy of every gadget which is technically possible, no matter how murderous it is" (*HC*, p. 3). Arendt describes the very project of *The Human Condition* as an exercise of thinking:

> What I propose in the following is a reconsideration of the human condition from the vantage point of our newest experiences and our most recent fears. This, obviously, is a matter of thought, and thoughtlessness – the heedless restlessness or hopeless confusion or complacent repetition of "truths" which have become trivial and empty – seems to me among the outstanding characteristics of our time. What I propose, therefore, is very simple: *it is nothing more than to think what we are doing*. (*HC*, p. 5, emphasis added)

Thinking, Arendt tells us, is "the highest and perhaps the purest activity of which men are capable." She reiterates this point in the very final paragraph of the book:

> For if no other test but the experience of being active, no other measure but the extent of sheer activity were to be applied to the various activities within the *vita activa*, it might well be that thinking would surpass them all. Whoever has any experience in this matter will know how right Cato was when he said: *Numquam se plus agere nihil cum ageret, numquam minus solum esse quam cum solus esset* – "Never is he more active than when he does nothing, never is he less alone than when he is by himself." (*HC*, p. 325)

II

Arendt frequently claims that the endless process of thinking is "like Penelope's web; it undoes every morning what it has finished the night before" (*LM*, vol. 1, p. 88). Although this simile captures the restless, self-destructive character of thinking which produces no settled result or product, it is nevertheless misleading. Arendt's thinking about thinking is more like a a gossamer veil that is woven and rewoven again and again, sometimes using older threads and sometimes introducing new threads into the fabric. There is continuity as well as discontinuity and difference. Our task now is to try to explore how the several threads of her analyses are woven into this fabric called thinking. In turning to this task I want to begin with a *via negativa* – with examining what thinking is not. This will enable us to forestall some typical misunderstandings about Arendt, and will help clear the way for her phenomenological description of the invisible, timeless, and ageless activity of thinking.

Arendt begins the first volume of *The Life of the Mind, Thinking*, with a quotation from Heidegger.

> Thinking does not bring knowledge as do the sciences.
> Thinking does not produce usable practical wisdom.
> Thinking does not solve the riddles of the universe.
> Thinking does not endow us directly with the power to act.
>
> (*LM*, vol. 1, p. 1)

Arendt endorses each one of these claims, and gives them a novel interpretation. The most important point is to distinguish thinking from knowing. Knowing is primarily concerned with *truth*, thinking deals with *meaning*. The success of knowing is to yield a tangible product, knowledge. But thinking never yields such a result, and its "success" is measured by its capacity to destroy what it thinks and to rethink afresh. To clarify her meaning, Arendt appeals to Kant's distinction between *Verstand* (which she insists on translating as "intellect" rather than "understanding") and *Vernunft*. What we achieve in common sense, science, and even philosophy (as traditionally understood as a form of *episteme* or *scientia*) is *knowledge*. There is a deep *thirst* for such knowledge but there is also a *need* to think – to think *beyond* what we can know. The faculty of thinking which Kant called *Vernunft* (reason) is altogether different than knowing, which seeks the truth. Thinking is the faculty by which we ask unanswerable questions, but questions that we can not help asking. It is the faculty by which we seek to understand the *meaning* of whatever we encounter. And in the quest for meaning there is (and can be no) finality. The search for knowledge and truth, and the quest for meaning are by no means totally unrelated. On the contrary, although we must not identify or confuse thinking with knowing, genuine knowing would be *impossible* without thinking, and thinking itself presupposes knowing:

> By posing the unanswerable questions of meaning, men establish themselves as question-asking beings. Behind all the cognitive questions for which men find answers, there lurk the unanswerable ones that seem entirely idle and have always been denounced as such. It is more than likely that men, if they were ever to lose the appetite for meaning we call thinking and cease to ask unanswerable questions, would lose not only the ability to produce those thought-things that we call works of art but also the capacity to ask all the answerable questions upon which every civilization is founded. (*LM*, vol. 1, p. 62)

Furthermore, thinking "does not solve the riddles of the universe." Philosophy, conceived of as a discipline which yields a special kind of knowledge that transcends scientific knowledge, gets entangled in metaphysical fallacies. Thinking, freed from demands of knowing, begins in wonder and increases our sense of wonder. From Arendt's perspective, Kant was not nearly radical enough in liberating thinking from the expectations and demands of knowing. Arendt is closer to Heidegger (who so profoundly influenced her own thinking about thinking) in linking thinking and poetry. And Arendt also agrees with Heidegger that the great danger of our time is the oblivion of genuine thinking – the seductive but disastrous tendency to identify thinking with the insatiable quest for scientific knowledge.

Thinking by itself does not "produce usable practical wisdom" and "does not endow us directly with the power to act." This point is especially important for Arendt. The traditional approaches of the disciplines morals and ethics are totally inadequate for coming to grips with the new forms of evil witnessed in our century. Earlier I cited the question that Arendt poses when she witnessed Eichmann's "absence of thinking": "Might the problem of good and evil, our faculty of telling right from wrong, be connected with our faculty of thought?" She continues by declaring: "To be sure, not in the sense that thinking would ever be able to produce the good deed as its result, as though 'virtue could be taught' and learned – only habits and customs can be taught, and we know only too well the alarming speed with which they are unlearned and forgotten when new circumstances demand a change in manners and patterns of behavior" (*LM*, vol. 1, p. 5). Arendt has in mind one of the most bitter lessons of totalitarianism – the ease with which habits, customs, and mores could be transformed. "Almost overnight and with scarcely any resistance the traditional commandment, 'Thou shalt not kill' was transformed into a new imperative, 'Thou shalt kill for the sake of the Führer.'" "We . . . have witnessed the total collapse of all established moral standards in public and private life during the thirties and forties." "Without much notice all this collapsed almost overnight and then it was as though morality suddenly stood revealed. . . as a set of *mores*, customs and *manners* which could be exchanged for another set with hardly more trouble than it would take to change the table manners of an individual or a people."[6] It was Arendt's deep skepticism about mores, habits, and customs that led her to place so much emphasis on thinking. Even though thinking by itself is not sufficient for yielding practical wisdom, in times of crisis, thinking *may* liberate the faculty of judging by which we do discriminate what is right and wrong, good and evil. In an essay written shortly after the appearance of *Eichmann in Jerusalem*, Arendt makes this point emphatically:

> The presupposition for this kind of judging is not a highly developed intelligence or sophistication in moral matters, but merely the habit of living together explicitly with oneself, that is, of being engaged in that silent dialogue between me and myself which since Socrates and Plato we usually call thinking. This kind of thought, though at the root of all philosophical thinking, is not technical and does not concern theoretical problems.[7]

And Arendt concludes "Thinking and Moral Considerations" (an essay which we shall shortly discuss in detail), by declaring:

> Thinking deals with invisibles, with representations of things that are absent; judging always concerns particulars and things close at hand. But the two are interrelated in a way similar to the way consciousness and conscience are interconnected. If thinking, the two-in-one of the soundless dialogue, actualizes the difference within our identity as given in consciousness and thereby results in conscience as its by-product, then judging, the by-product of the liberating effect of thinking, realizes thinking, makes it manifest in the world of appearances, where I am never alone and always much too busy to be able to think. The manifestation of the wind of thought is no knowledge; it is the ability to tell right from wrong, beautiful from ugly. And this indeed may prevent catastrophes, at least for myself, in the rare moments when the chips are down.[8]

We must be careful not to misinterpret what Arendt is (and is not) saying here. She is not trying to specify necessary and sufficient conditions that can "prevent catastrophes." For there are none; there are no guarantees against evil. To believe that there are (or can be) is to slip into the illusion that there are firm banisters. Arendt even warns us – in a manner that today seems prophetic – that "totalitarian solutions may well survive the fall of totalitarian regimes in the form of the strong temptations which come up whenever it seems impossible to alleviate political, social or economic misery in a manner worthy of man" (*OT*, p. 459). But unless one "stops and think," unless one develops the capacity to "*think from the standpoint of somebody else*," then it becomes all too easy to succumb to evil. Like Socrates' *daimon*, thinking may not tell us what we ought to do, but it may prevent us from tolerating or becoming indifferent to evil deeds. It was the inability to think in this manner that Arendt claimed was the most distinctive character trait of

Eichmann. "He was genuinely incapable of uttering a single sentence that was not a cliché" – clichés that protected him from a sense of reality, and sense of what he was doing. "The longer one listened to him, the more obvious it became that his inability to speak was closely connected with an inability to *think*, namely, to think from the standpoint of somebody else. No communication was possible with him, not because he lied but because he was surrounded by the most reliable of all safeguards against words and the presence of others, and hence from reality as such" (*EJ*, p. 49). Eichmann confirms what Arendt emphatically states. In his own handwritten notes he declares: "From my childhood, obedience was something I could not get out of my system. When I entered the armed services at the age of twenty-seven, I found being obedient not a bit more difficult than it had been during my life to that point. It was unthinkable that I would not follow orders." He continues: "Now that I look back, I realize that a life predicated on being obedient and taking orders is a very comfortable life indeed. Living in such a way reduces to a minimum one's need to think."[9]

Earlier I indicated that Arendt's project, especially in *The Life of the Mind*, might be characterized as developing a phenomenology of thinking. But there is something extraordinarily paradoxical about such a project. She tells us that thinking requires a withdrawal from the world of appearances. Thinking deals with invisibles; thinking (as distinguished from thought-objects) has no history, no temporality of past and future. The thinking ego is ageless. Thinking, as pure activity, seems to have no "substance"; it completely disappears when it is not active. So how can there be a phenomenology of what, strictly speaking, is not a *phenomenon*? Yet, oxymoronically, Arendt insists that her primary concern is with the *experience* of thinking and not with the "objects of thought." She appears to ask impossible questions such as "Where are we when we think?" The key for unraveling this paradox (without losing a sense of wonder) lies in her understanding of the relation of thinking to language and metaphor. We have noted that Arendt's favored trope for characterizing the thinking activity is Penelope's weaving and unweaving. Although everyone has the capacity to think, we are not *pure* thinking beings. As human beings, living our lives in a world of appearances, we may occasionally withdraw from this world in order to think in solitude, but even when we do, we "have an *urge to speak* and thus make manifest what otherwise would not be a part of the appearing world at all" (*LM*, vol. 1, p. 98). But the question arises: if thinking deals with invisibles, how can we make thinking manifest? How do we carry over our invisible thought processes into a world of speech. It is here that metaphor plays a crucial role. Arendt, once again, draws upon Kant in order to indicate that metaphorical language is essential for the *expression* of thinking. "The metaphor achieves the 'carrying over' – *metapherein* – of a genuine and seemingly impossible *metabasis eis allo genos*, the transition from one existential state, that of thinking, to another, that of being an appearance among appearances, and this can only be done by *analogies*" (*LM*, vol. I, p. 103). It is metaphor that bridges the gap between invisible thinking and the visible world of appearances; it is metaphor that bridges the abyss between invisible thinking and its manifestation in speech. The real paradox is not the need to express thinking in metaphorical language, but the illusion of philosophers that they can (and should) escape from metaphors. Philosophers, from Parmenides to Hegel (and beyond), have stressed the purity of true conceptual thinking. And yet when philosophers have sought to *tell* what thinking is really like, they inevitably rely on metaphors. Arendt is making a very strong claim when she insists that there is not (and cannot be) the tangible expression of thinking without employing metaphors.[10] "All philosophical terms are metaphors, frozen analogies, as it were, whose true meaning discloses itself when we dissolve the term into the original context, which must have been vividly in the mind of the first philosopher to use it" (*LM*, vol. I, p. 104). This is why Arendt suggests "how right Heidegger was when he called poetry and thinking close neighbors" (*LM*, vol. I, p. 108).

> Analogies, metaphors, and emblems are the threads by which the mind holds on to the world even when, absentmindedly, it has lost direct contact with it, and they guarantee the unity of human experience. Moreover, in the thinking process itself they serve as models to give us our bearings lest we stagger blindly among experiences that our bodily senses with their relative certainty of knowledge cannot guide us through. (*LM*, vol. I, p. 109)

The very title of her posthumous study of thinking, "The *Life* of the Mind," is not a dead metaphor for Arendt. "The only possible metaphor one may conceive of for the life of the mind is the sensation of being alive. *Without the breath of life the human body is a corpse; without thinking the human mind is dead*" (*LM*, vol. I, p. 123).

III

Arendt once characterized Heidegger's writings in a manner that is just as applicable to her own essays and books. Each of Heidegger's writings "reads as though he were starting from the beginning and only from time to time taking over the language already coined by him – a language, however, in which the concepts are merely 'trail marks,' by which a new course of thought orients itself."[11] This is why Arendt's reflections on thinking are at once so thought-provoking and so perplexing. If we think of *theoria* in its modern rather than in its archaic sense (as the witnessing of a festival), then we do *not* find a systematic theory of thinking. Many of her reflections lose their vitality and freshness when we try to force them into a unified coherent theory. And this is not because she is always unraveling what she has woven, but rather because the veil that she weaves and reweaves has many loose threads. Arendt would certainly acknowledge that her own thinking raises questions that she does not answer. Like Socrates, whom she so admired, she deliberately sought to infect others with the perplexities that were central to her own thinking. Nevertheless there is a deep troubling tension that Arendt never resolves; one that goes to the very heart of her thinking about thinking and evil. In her own internal dialogue – her two-in-one – she never achieved the type of agreement with herself that Socrates demanded. This is dramatically illustrated in two extremely important articles that were published almost simultaneously in the fall of 1971: "Thinking and Moral Considerations," and "Martin Heidegger at Eighty." The 1970s were the time in Arendt's life when she became increasingly preoccupied with the question of the relationship between thinking and evil. ("Thinking and Moral Considerations" was slightly revised and integrated into *The Life of the Mind*. And many of the themes treated in "Heidegger at Eighty" also appear in *The Life of the Mind*.)

In "Thinking and Moral Considerations," Arendt initially raises the question of examining the relation of the activity of thinking and evil. She emphatically states that if there is an "inner connection between the ability or inability to think and the problem of evil" then the faculty of thinking "must be ascribed to everybody; it cannot be a privilege of the few" (p. 425). Once again she turns to Socrates as a model, an "ideal type" of a thinker who illustrates what she means.[12] This time she speaks of Socrates – her model – as someone "who did think without becoming a philosopher." The natural abode of Socrates was the marketplace where he could actively engage in dialogue with his fellow citizens. Socrates is the thinker who asks "questions to which he does *not* know the answers" (p. 429). Socrates does not teach a doctrine, he seeks to "unfreeze" thoughts. He is not only a gadfly and a midwife, but he is also likened to an "electric ray, [a fish that] paralyzes others through being paralyzed itself" (quoted on p. 431). In the *Meno*, Plato portrays Socrates as someone who says: "It isn't that, knowing the answers myself, I perplex other people. The truth is rather that I infect them also with the perplexity I feel myself" (p. 431). In short, Socrates "did not teach anything for the simple reason that he had nothing to teach." But he did have the capacity to infect others with the perplexity that he himself experienced. This is the only way in which genuine thinking can be communicated to others. Socrates, who knew that thinking deals with invisibles and is itself invisible, "lacking all the outside manifestation of other activities, seems to have used the metaphor of the wind for it: 'The winds themselves are invisible, yet what they do is manifest to us and we somehow feel their approach'" (p. 433). Arendt tells us that although there are no "dangerous thoughts," thinking itself is inherently a dangerous activity. It is dangerous because it dissolves all stable convictions and creeds. "Thinking is equally dangerous to all creeds and does not, by itself, yield any positive doctrine" (p. 435). Some of Socrates' interlocutors took this as a license to be cynical. "They had not been content with being taught how to think without being taught a doctrine, and they changed the non-results of the Socratic thinking examination into negative results: If we cannot define what piety is, let us be impious – which is pretty much the opposite of what Socrates had hoped to achieve by talking about piety" (pp. 434–435). But if this thinking, if this restless quest for meaning that dissolves and critically examines all accepted doctrines, creeds, and rules, does not by itself yield any positive doctrine, then how precisely is it related to evil? "It does not create values, it will not find out, once and for all, what 'the good' is, and it does not confirm but rather dissolves accepted rules of conduct" (p. 445). Nevertheless, the political and moral significance of such thinking manifests itself in those rare moments in history when "'Things fall apart; the centre cannot hold; / Mere anarchy is loosed upon the world,' when 'The best lack all conviction, while the worst / Are full of passionate intensity'" (p. 445). At such moments, thinking is no longer a marginal affair. At such moments, thinking may liberate the faculty of judging particulars. And, in a passage that I have already cited, she concludes her essay by declaring: "The manifestation of the wind of thought is no knowledge; it is the ability to tell right and wrong, beautiful from ugly. And this indeed may prevent catastrophes, at least for myself, in the rare moments when the chips are down" (p. 446).

Now let us contrast this characterization of thinking with her description of Heidegger as the thinker par excellence of the twentieth century.[13] In "Martin Heidegger at Eighty" Arendt seeks to elicit the sense of excitement due to the rumor that spread throughout Germany when Heidegger first started teaching:

> The rumor about Heidegger put it quite simply: Thinking has come to life again; the culture treasures of the past, believed to be dead, are being made to speak, in the course of which it turns out that they propose things altogether different from the familiar, worn-out trivialities they had been presumed to say. There exists a teacher; one can perhaps learn to think. (p. 295)

This is not the type of thinking of the citizen who seeks to improve his fellow citizens by bringing out the truth of their *doxai*. This is not the thinker whose natural abode is the marketplace. This is a thinker who spent his entire life as a university professor – who, unlike the thinking citizen, Socrates, was a "professional philosopher." And whatever internal dialogue characterized his own thinking, there is scarcely any evidence that Heidegger had a *genuine* Socratic dialogue with his fellow citizens. Furthermore, it can hardly be said that the thinking exhibited by Heidegger "must be ascribed to everybody." It certainly *cannot* be said of Heidegger that at the moment of crisis, when things fell apart, his thinking *liberated* his faculty of judgment. However we judge what Heidegger did and did not do in 1933 (and after), I do not believe that even his most sympathetic defenders would claim that his thinking liberated his judgment and resulted in "conscience as its by-product".[14] For he failed to exercise the type of judgment that Arendt describes – the judgment that enables us to discriminate good and evil and which can prevent catastrophes. On the contrary, Heidegger seems to fit better the description of someone who – when the chips were down – was all too ready to adopt a new creed, a new ideology. I am not primarily interested in passing judgment on Heidegger. This is a complex and treacherous issue. My primary concern is Arendt's concern: the question of the relation between thinking and evil. At the very least, the example of Heidegger should make us *stop and think* whether there really is any "intrinsic" connection between thinking and evil. We need to account for the differences between the thinking of Heidegger and Socrates. But Arendt, who excelled in drawing distinctions, never turned her attention to an *explicit* analysis of the differences that really make a difference. And yet, it is these differences that cry out for clarification and explanation. Indeed when Arendt seeks to account for Heidegger's so-called "error," her analysis becomes even more dubious. Arendt, rather lamely, suggests that Heidegger was guilty of that "*déformation professionale*" characteristic of so many philosophers who were attracted to tyrants. (Hitler, by Arendt's own account, was not just another tyrant!) But she tends to excuse Heidegger as someone who "once succumbed to the temptation to change his 'residence' and to get involved in the world of human affairs . . . [Heidegger] was still young enough to learn from the shock of the collision, which after ten short hectic months thirty-seven years ago drove him back to his residence, and to settle in his thinking what he had experienced."[15] But what is so unsatisfactory about this suggestion is that Arendt herself emphasizes that we can never cut ourselves off completely from the world of everyday human affairs. The attempt to do so is disastrous. There is no permanent abode or dwelling of "pure thinking" or "pure wondering." Ironically, it is Arendt who warns that this temptation to live in the "abode" of pure thinking is itself a supreme danger. The great achievement of Socrates is that he resisted this danger. But in Arendt's description of Heidegger, she comes close to suggesting that Heidegger's real "error" was to get involved in the world of human affairs instead of staying "at home" in his proper abode of thinking, the place where one takes up "wondering as one's permanent abode."[16] Arendt's most novel and striking thesis – that there is an intrinsic connection between our ability or inability to think and evil – depends on discriminating the thinking that may prevent catastrophes from the thinking that does not. And I do not think that Arendt ever gave a satisfactory answer to this question. Perhaps it is to Arendt's credit that she could so admire the thinking of a Socrates and the thinking of a Heidegger, and that she was aware of the dangers of *both* these types of thinking: the Socratic dialogic thinking that destroys the stability of all creeds; and the Heideggerian *Denken* that seeks to reside outside "the habitations of human affairs." Nevertheless, she was pulled in different directions. In her own back-and-forth two-in-one dialogue with herself, she never resolved this deep internal conflict; she never achieved that internal agreement with herself which Socrates took to be the condition for thinking. If there is an inherent restlessness in the thinking activity itself, if the quest for meaning is an endless task, then Arendt's legacy consists of making *us* acutely aware of those perplexities and aporias which she did not resolve. For such aporias demand honest confrontation in our attempt to understand the relation between thinking and evil.

NOTES

1 Arendt first introduced the concept of the pariah in *Rahel Varnhagen: The Life of a Jewess*. Although Arendt began her study of Rahel in the late 1920s when she was still living in Germany, and completed the manuscript in Paris in the 1930s, the book was not published until 1958. See the discussion of the distinction of the pariah and the parvenu in my *Hannah Arendt and The Jewish Question* (Cambridge, MA: MIT Press, 1996).

2 For a very illuminating discussion of the complexities and tensions in Arendt's reflections on philosophy and politics see Margaret Canovan, *Hannah Arendt: A Reinterpretation of her Political Thought* (Cambridge: Cambridge University Press, 1992), chapter 7, "Philosophy and Politics."

3 Canovan likens Arendt's story to "a kind of myth of a philosophical Fall – a story which she evidently found tempting, although not entirely convincing" (ibid., p. 258). But although Arendt did think that the split between thought and action, as well as the divide between philosophy and politics, came to prevail in the history of the West, she always held out the possibility for a reintegration of thinking and action, for a new kind of political thinking.

4 "Philosophy and Politics," *Social Research* 57/1 (Spring 1990): 81.

5 Arendt is perfectly aware that her portrait of Socrates, and her strong contrast between Socrates and Plato, is controversial. Her "Socrates" is an ideal type – one that she uses to stress the difference between political thinking and the type of political philosophy that is hostile to such thinking.

6 These quotations come from a series of unpublished lectures that Arendt gave in 1965, "Some Questions of Moral Philosophy." See my discussion in *Hannah Arendt and The Jewish Question*, pp. 146–147.
7 "Personal Responsibility under Dictatorship," *The Listener*, August 6, 1964.
8 "Thinking and Moral Considerations: A Lecture," *Social Research* 38/3 (Fall 1971): 417–446. This passage is repeated with slight stylistic changes (by Mary McCarthy) in *LM*, vol. 1, p. 193.
9 Roger Cohen, "Why? New Eichmann Notes Try to Explain," *New York Times*, August 12, 1999: A1, A3.
10 In this respect, Arendt shares a close affinity with Nietzsche and Derrida, both of whom show the intimate and inextricable relation between thinking and metaphor.
11 Hannah Arendt, "Martin Heidegger at Eighty," *New York Review of Books*, October 21, 1971: 50–54; reprint *Heidegger and Modern Philosophy*, ed. M. Murray (New Haven: Yale University Press, 1978). The article originally was published in the German periodical *Merkur* in 1969.
12 It would be worthwhile to compare the similarities and differences between her characterization of Socrates in "Thinking and Moral Considerations" (1971) and her earlier analysis in "Philosophy and Politics" (1954). There are some striking differences. The significant event in Arendt's life that helps to account for some of these differences was the trial of Adolf Eichmann and the strong reaction to the publication of *Eichmann in Jerusalem*.
13 We should not forget that this article was specifically written to honor Heidegger, who was not only Arendt's lover, but also her first philosophy teacher when she went to Marburg in 1924. Heidegger's eightieth birthday was not the occasion to develop a full-scale critical analysis of Heidegger. My primary focus is on what this article tells us about the meaning of *thinking* for Arendt.
14 "Thinking and Moral Considerations," p. 446.
15 "Martin Heidegger at Eighty," pp. 301, 303.
16 Ibid., p. 301.

SELECT BIBLIOGRAPHY

WORKS BY ARENDT

Books

Arendt, Hannah. *Der Liebesbegriff bei Augustin*. Berlin: Springer, 1929 (translated as *Love and St. Augustine*. Chicago: University of Chicago Press, 1996).

The Origins of Totalitarianism. New York: Harcourt, Brace & Co., 1951. Second enlarged edition: New York: World Publishing Co., Meridian Books, 1958. Third edition, with new prefaces: New York: Harcourt, Brace & World, 1966, 1968, 1973.

The Human Condition. Chicago: University of Chicago Press, 1958.

Rahel Varnhagen: The Life of a Jewish Woman. New York: Harcourt Brace Jovanovich, 1958. New edition, 1974. Critical edition edited by Liliane Weissberg, Baltimore: The Johns Hopkins University Press, 1997.

Between Past and Future: Six Exercises in Political Thought. New York: Viking Press, 1961. Revised edition, including two additional essays, 1968.

Eichmann in Jerusalem: A Report on the Banality of Evil. New York: Viking Press, 1963. Revised and enlarged edition, 1965.

On Revolution. New York: Viking Press, 1963. Revised second edition, 1965.

Men in Dark Times. New York: Harcourt, Brace & World, 1968.

On Violence. New York: Harcourt, Brace & World, 1970.

Crises of the Republic. New York: Harcourt Brace Jovanovich, 1972.

The Jew as Pariah. Edited and with an Introduction by Ron H. Feldman. New York: Grove Press, 1978.

The Life of the Mind. New York: Harcourt Brace Jovanovich, 1978. (Two volumes of an uncompleted work, published posthumously and edited by Mary McCarthy.)

Lectures on Kant's Political Philosophy. Edited by Ronald Beiner. Chicago: University of Chicago Press, 1982.

Essays in Understanding: 1930–1954. Edited by Jerome Kohn. New York: Harcourt Brace & Co., 1994.

Correspondence

In English

Hannah Arendt – Karl Jaspers: Correspondence, 1926–1969. Edited by Lotte Kohler and Hans Saner, translated by Robert and Rita Kimber. New York: Harcourt Brace Jovanovich, 1992.

Between Friends: The Correspondence of Hannah Arendt and Mary McCarthy, 1949–1975. Edited and with an Introduction by Carol Brightman. New York: Harcourt Brace & Company, 1995.

In German

Hannah Arendt/Kurt Blumenfeld, ". . . *in keinen Besitz verwurzelt": Die Korrespondenz*. Edited by Ingeborg Nordmann and Iris Pilling. Hamburg: Rotbuch Verlag, 1995.

Hannah Arendt/Heinrich Blücher, *Briefe, 1936–1968*. Edited by Lotte Kohler. Munich: Piper GmbH & Co., 1996.

Hannah Arendt/Martin Heidegger, *Briefe, 1925 bis 1975*. Edited by Ursula Ludz. Frankfurt: Vittorio Klostermann, 1998.

Selected essays (items of exceptional importance which are neither collected nor incorporated in the works listed above)

Arendt, Hannah. "Totalitarian Imperialism: Reflections on the Hungarian Revolution." *Journal of Politics* 20/1 (February, 1958): 5–43 (added to only the 1958 Meridian edition of *The Origins of Totalitarianism*).

"Reflections on Little Rock." *Dissent* 6/1 (Winter 1959): 45–56.

"Personal Responsibility Under Dictatorship." *The Listener*, August 6, 1964, pp. 185–187, 205.

Introduction to *Auschwitz* by Bernd Naumann. New York: Frederick A. Praeger, 1966.

"Martin Heidegger at 80." *New York Review of Books* 17/6 (October 21, 1971): 50–54.

"Thinking and Moral Considerations: A Lecture." *Social Research* 38/3 (Fall, 1971): 417–446.

"Philosophy and Politics." *Social Research* 57/1 (Spring 1990): 73–103.

"Some Questions of Moral Philosophy." *Social Research* 61/4 (Winter 1994): 739–764.

WORKS ABOUT HANNAH ARENDT

Biographical/contextual

Barnouw, Dagmar. *Visible Spaces: Hannah Arendt and the German-Jewish Experience*. Baltimore: The Johns Hopkins University Press, 1990.

Ettinger, Elzbieta. *Hannah Arendt/Martin Heidegger*. New Haven: Yale University Press, 1995. A short, breathless account of Arendt's personal relationship to Heidegger.

Young-Bruehl, Elisabeth. *Hannah Arendt: For Love of the World*. New Haven: Yale University Press, 1982. By far the best biographical source available.

Selected studies of Arendt's thought

Benhabib, Seyla. *The Reluctant Modernism of Hannah Arendt*. Thousand Oaks, CA: Sage Publications, 1996.

Bernstein, Richard. *Hannah Arendt and the Jewish Question*. Cambridge, MA: MIT Press, 1997.
Bradshaw, Leah. *Acting and Thinking: The Political Thought of Hannah Arendt*. Toronto: University of Toronto Press, 1989.
Brunkhorst, Hauke. *Hannah Arendt*. Munich: Beck, 1999.
Canovan, Margaret. *The Political Thought of Hannah Arendt*. London: J. M. Dent, 1974.
Hannah Arendt: A Reinterpretation of Her Political Thought. Cambridge: Cambridge University Press, 1992.
Courtine-Denamy, Sylvie. *Hannah Arendt*. Paris: Belfond, 1994.
d'Entrevès, Maurizio Passerin. *The Political Philosophy of Hannah Arendt*. New York: Routledge, 1994.
Disch, Lisa Jane. *Hannah Arendt and the Limits of Philosophy*. Ithaca: Cornell University Press, 1994.
Dossa, Shiraz. *The Public Realm and the Public Self: the Political Theory of Hannah Arendt*. Waterloo, Ontario: Wilfred Laurier University Press, 1988.
Enegrén, André. *La Pensée Politique de Hannah Arendt*. Paris: Presse Universitaire Française, 1984.
Gottsegen, Michael G. *The Political Thought of Hannah Arendt*. Albany: State University of New York Press, 1993.
Hansen, Phillip. *Hannah Arendt: Politics, History, and Citizenship*. Stanford: Stanford University Press, 1993.
Isaac, Jeffrey C. *Arendt, Camus, and Modern Rebellion*. New Haven: Yale University Press, 1992.
Kateb, George. *Hannah Arendt: Politics, Conscience, Evil*. Totowa, NJ: Rowman and Allenheld, 1984.
Kristeva, Julia. *Hannah Arendt*. Volume 1 of *Le génie féminin*. Paris: Fayard, 1999.
McGowan, John. *Hannah Arendt: An Introduction*. Minneapolis: University of Minnesota Press, 1998.
Parekh, Bhiku. *Hannah Arendt and the Search for a New Political Philosophy*. London: Macmillan, 1981.
Pitkin, Hanna Fenichel. *The Attack of the Blob: Hannah Arendt's Concept of the Social*. Chicago: University of Chicago Press, 1998.
Ring, Jennifer. *The Political Consequences of Thinking*. Albany: State University of New York Press, 1997.
Taminiaux, Jacques. *The Thracian Maid and the Professional Thinker: Arendt and Heidegger*. Translated and edited by Michel Gendre. Albany: State University of New York Press, 1997.
Villa, Dana. *Arendt and Heidegger: The Fate of the Political*. Princeton: Princeton University Press, 1996.
Politics, Philosophy, Terror: Essays on the Thought of Hannah Arendt. Princeton: Princeton University Press, 1999.
Whitfield, Stephen. *Into the Dark: Hannah Arendt and Totalitarianism*. Philadelphia: Temple University Press, 1980.

Collections of articles on Arendt

Abensour, Miguel, *et al*. *Ontologie et Politique: Actes du Colloque Hannah Arendt*. Paris: Editions Tierce, 1989.

Bernauer, James W., ed. *Amor Mundi: Explorations in the Faith and Thought of Hannah Arendt*. Dordrecht: Martinus Nijhoff, 1987.

Calhoun, Craig and McGowan, John, eds. *Hannah Arendt and the Meaning of Politics*. Minneapolis: University of Minnesota Press, 1997.

Hill, Melvyn A., ed. *Hannah Arendt: The Recovery of the Public World*. New York: St. Martin's Press, 1979.

Hinchman, Lewis P. and Hinchman, Sandra A., eds. *Hannah Arendt: Critical Essays*. Albany: State University of New York Press, 1994.

Honig, Bonnie, ed. *Feminist Interpretations of Hannah Arendt*. University Park, PA: The Pennsylvania State University Press, 1995.

Kaplan, Gisela T. and Kessler, Clive S., eds. *Hannah Arendt: Thinking, Judging, Freedom*. London: Unwin Hayman Ltd., 1989.

Kielmansegg, Peter G., Mewes, Horst, and Glaser-Schmidt, Elizabeth, eds. *Hannah Arendt and Leo Strauss: German Emigres and American Political Thought*. Cambridge: Cambridge University Press, 1995.

Kohn, Jerome and May, Larry, eds. *Hannah Arendt – Twenty Years Later*. Cambridge: MIT Press, 1996.

Reif, Adelbert, ed. *Hannah Arendt: Materialien zu ihrem Werk*. Vienna: Europa Verlag, 1979.

Special journal issues devoted to Arendt

Cahiers de Philosophie. 4 (1987): *Hannah Arendt: Confrontations*.

Cahiers de Grif. 33 (1986): *Hannah Arendt*.

Esprit 6: *Hannah Arendt*.

History & Memory. 8/2 (1996): *Hannah Arendt and Eichmann in Jerusalem*.

Praxis International. 9/1–2 (1989): *Symposium on Hannah Arendt's Political Thought*.

Revue Internationale de Philosophie. 53/2 (1999): *Hannah Arendt* (essays in English, French, and German).

Salmagundi. 60 (1983): *Politics and the Social Contract*.

Social Research. 44/1 (1977): *Hannah Arendt*.

Social Research. 57/1 (1990): *Philosophy and Politics II, Hannah Arendt*.

Selected Articles and Book Chapters

Bakan, Mildred. "Hannah Arendt's Concepts of Labor and Work," in Hill, ed., *Hannah Arendt and the Recovery of the Public World*.

Beiner, Ronald. "Interpretive Essay: Hannah Arendt on Judging," in Hannah Arendt, *Lectures on Kant's Political Philosophy*.

"Action, Natality, and Citizenship: Hannah Arendt's Concept of Freedom," in Zbignew Pelczynski and John Gray, eds., *Conceptions of Liberty in Political Philosophy* (London: Athlone Press, 1984).

"Hannah Arendt and Leo Strauss: the Uncommenced Dialogue," *Political Theory* 18/2, 1990.

Bell, Daniel. "The Alphabet of Justice: On *Eichmann in Jerusalem*," *Partisan Review* 30/3, 1963.

Benhabib, Seyla. "Judgment and the Moral Foundations of Politics in Hannah Arendt's Thought," *Political Theory* 16/1, 1988.

"Hannah Arendt and the Redemptive Power of Narrative," *Social Research* 57/1, 1990 (reprinted in Hinchman and Hinchman, eds., *Hannah Arendt: Critical Essays*).

"Models of Public Space: Hannah Arendt, the Liberal Tradition, and Jürgen Habermas," in *Habermas and the Public Sphere*, ed. Craig Calhoun (Cambridge, MA: MIT Press, 1992).

Bernstein, Richard. "Hannah Arendt: The Ambiguities of Theory and Practice," in *Political Theory and Praxis*, ed. Terrence Ball (Minneapolis: University of Minnesota Press, 1977).

"Judging – the Actor and the Spectator," in Bernstein, *Philosophical Profiles* (Philadelphia: University of Pennsylvania Press, 1986).

"Rethinking the Social and the Political," in Bernstein, *Philosophical Profiles* (Philadelphia: University of Pennsylvania Press, 1986).

"Did Hannah Arendt Change Her Mind?: From Radical Evil to the Banality of Evil," in *Hannah Arendt – Twenty Years Later*, ed. Kohn and May (Cambridge, MA: MIT Press, 1996).

Botstein, Leon. "The Jew as Pariah: Hannah Arendt's Political Philosophy," *Dialectical Anthropology* 8, 1983.

Canovan, Margaret. "The Contradictions of Hannah Arendt's Political Thought," *Political Theory* 6/1, 1978.

"Politics as Culture: Hannah Arendt and the Public Realm," *History of Political Thought* 6/3, 1985 (reprinted in Hinchman and Hinchman, eds., *Hannah Arendt: Critical Essays*).

"Socrates or Heidegger? Hannah Arendt's Reflections on Philosophy and Politics," *Social Research* 57/1, 1990.

"Hannah Arendt as Conservative Thinker," in Kohn and May, eds., *Hannah Arendt – Twenty Years Later* (Cambridge, MA: MIT Press, 1996).

Cohen, Jean, and Arato, Andrew. "The Normative Critique: Hannah Arendt" in *Political Theory and Civil Society* (Cambridge, MA: MIT Press, 1992).

Crick, Bernard. "On Rereading *The Origins of Totalitarianism*," *Social Research* 44/1, 1977 (reprinted in Hill, ed., *Hannah Arendt: The Recovery of the Public World*).

d'Entrèves, Maurizio Passerin. "Modernity and the Human Condition: Hannah Arendt's Conception of Modernity," *Thesis Eleven* 30, 1991.

"Hannah Arendt and the Idea of Citizenship," in Chantal Mouffe, ed., *Dimensions of Radical Democracy* (New York: Verso, 1992).

Dietz, Mary G.. "Hannah Arendt and Feminist Politics," in Hinchman and Hinchman, eds., *Hannah Arendt: Critical Essays.*

Dossa, Shiraz. "Human Status and Politics: Hannah Arendt on the Holocaust," *Canadian Journal of Political Science* 13/2, 1980.

"Hannah Arendt on Eichmann: The Public, the Private, and Evil," *Review of Politics* 46/2, 1984.

Dostal, Robert. "Judging Human Action: Hannah Arendt's Appropriation of Kant," *The Review of Metaphysics* 37/4, 1984.

Feldman, Ron. "The Jew as Pariah: The Case of Hannah Arendt," Introduction to Hannah Arendt, *The Jew as Pariah* (New York: Grove Press, 1978).

Fuss, Peter. "Hannah Arendt's Conception of Political Community," in Hill, ed., *Hannah Arendt: The Recovery of the Public World* (New York: St. Martin's Press, 1979).

Gunnell, John. "Hannah Arendt: The Decline of the Public Realm" in Gunnell, *Political Theory: Tradition and Interpretation* (Cambridge: Winthrop Publishers, 1979).

Habermas, Jürgen. "Hannah Arendt's Communications Concept of Power," *Social Research* 44/1, 1977 (reprinted in Hinchman and Hinchman, eds., *Hannah Arendt: Critical Essays*).

Heller, Agnes. "Hannah Arendt on the *Vita Contemplativa*," in Kaplan and Kessler, eds., *Hannah Arendt: Thinking, Judging, Freedom* (Boston: Allen & Unwin, 1989).

Honig, Bonnie. "Arendt, Identity, and Difference," *Political Theory* 16/1, 1988.

"Declarations of Independence: Arendt and Derrida on the Problem of Founding a Republic," *American Political Science Review* 85/1, 1991.

"Arendt's Accounts of Action and Authority," in Honig, *Political Theory and the Displacement of Politics* (Ithaca: Cornell University Press, 1993).

Jacobitti, Suzanne. "Hannah Arendt and the Will," *Political Theory* 16/1, 1988.

Jay, Martin, and Botstein, Leon. "Hannah Arendt: Opposing Views," *Partisan Review* 45/3, 1979 (Jay's essay reprinted in Jay, *Permanent Exiles,* New York: Columbia University Press, 1986).

Kateb, George. "Freedom and Worldliness in the Thought of Hannah Arendt," *Political Theory* 5/2, 1977.

"Hannah Arendt: Alienation and America," *Raritan* 3/1, 1983.

"Death and Politics: Hannah Arendt's Reflections on the American Constitution," *Social Research* 54/3, 1987.

"Arendt and Individualism," *Social Research* 61/4, 1994.

"The Judgment of Arendt," *Revue Internationale de Philosophie* 53/2, 1999.

Knauer, James. "Motive and Goal in Hannah Arendt's Concept of Political Action," *American Political Science Review* 74/3, 1980.

Kohn, Jerome. "Thinking/Acting," *Social Research* 57/1, 1990.

Lacqueur, Walter. "Rereading Hannah Arendt," *Encounter* 52/3, 1979.

Luban, David. "Explaining Dark Times: Hannah Arendt's Theory of Theory," *Social Research* 50/1, 1983.

Miller, James. "The Pathos of Novelty: Hannah Arendt's Image of Freedom in the Modern World," in Hill, ed., *Hannah Arendt: The Recovery of the Public World* (New York: St. Martin's Press, 1979).

Morgenthau, Hans. "Hannah Arendt on Totalitarianism and Democracy," *Social Research* 44/1, 1977.

Nisbet, Robert. "Hannah Arendt and the American Revolution," *Social Research* 44/1, 1977.

O'Sullivan, Noel. "Hannah Arendt: Hellenic Nostalgia and Industrial Society," in A. de Crespigny and K. Minogue, eds., *Contemporary Political Philosophers* (London: Methuen, 1976).

Parekh, Bhiku. "Hannah Arendt's Critique of Marx," in Hill, ed., *Hannah Arendt: The Recovery of the Public World* (New York: St. Martin's Press, 1979).

Pitkin, Hanna. "Justice: On Relating Public and Private," *Political Theory* 9/3, 1981 (reprinted in Hinchman and Hinchman, eds., *Hannah Arendt: Critical Essays*).

Reisman, David. "The Path to Total Terror," *Commentary* 11/4, 1951.
Ricoeur, Paul. "Action, Story, and History: On Rereading *The Human Condition*," *Salmagundi* 60, 1983.
Riley, Patrick. "Hannah Arendt on Kant, Truth, and Politics," *Political Studies* 35/3, 1987.
Ring, Jennifer. "On Needing Both Marx and Arendt," *Political Theory* 17/3, 1989.
Schwartz, Benjamin. "The Religion of Politics: Reflections on the Thought of Hannah Arendt," *Dissent* 17/2, 1970.
Scott, Joanna Vecchiarelli, and Stark, Judith Chelius. "Rediscovering Hannah Arendt," in Hannah Arendt, *Love and St. Augustine* (Chicago: University of Chicago Press, 1996).
Shklar, Judith. "Rethinking the Past," *Social Research* 44/1, 1983.
Taminiaux, Jacques. "Arendt, disciple de Heidegger?," *Etudes Phenomenologiques* 1/2, 1985.
Villa, Dana R. "The Banality of Philosophy," in Kohn and May, eds., *Hannah Arendt: Twenty Years Later* (Cambridge, MA: MIT Press, 1996).
"The Philosopher vs. the Citizen: Arendt, Strauss, and Socrates," *Political Theory* 26/2, 1998.
"Conscience, the Banality of Evil, and the Idea of a Representative Perpetrator" in Villa, *Politics, Philosophy, Terror: Essays on the Thought of Hannah Arendt* (Princeton: Princeton University Press, 1999).
Vollrath, Ernst. "Hannah Arendt and the Method of Political Thinking," *Social Research* 44/1, 1977.
Weissberg, Liliane. "Hannah Arendt, Rahel Varnhagen, and the Writing of (Auto)Biography," Introduction to Hannah Arendt, *Rahel Varnhagen: The Life of a Jewess*, first complete edition (Baltimore: The Johns Hopkins University Press, 1997).
Wellmer, Albrecht. "Hannah Arendt on Judgment: The Unwritten Doctrine of Reason," in Kohn and May, eds., *Hannah Arendt – Twenty Years Later* (Cambridge, MA: MIT Press, 1996).
Wolin, Sheldon. "Hannah Arendt and the Ordinance of Time," *Social Research* 44/1, 1977.
"Democracy and the Political," *Salmagundi* 60, 1983 (reprinted in Hinchman and Hinchman, eds., *Hannah Arendt: Critical Essays*).
Young-Bruehl, Elisabeth. "Hannah Arendt's Storytelling," *Social Research* 44/1, 1977.
"Reflections on Hannah Arendt's *The Life of the Mind*," *Political Theory* 10/2, 1982.

INDEX